W9-ABR-796

LITERATURE AND PSYCHOANALYSIS

LITERATURE AND PSYCHOANALYSIS

Edited by
EDITH KURZWEIL and
WILLIAM PHILLIPS

Columbia University Press
New York   1983

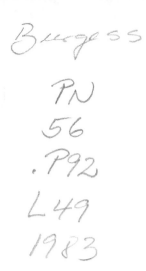

Burgess

PN
56
.P92
L49
1983

Library of Congress Cataloging in Publication Data
Main entry under title:

Literature and psychoanalysis.

Includes bibliographical references and index.
1. Psychoanalysis and literature—Addresses, essays,
lectures. I. Kurzweil, Edith. II. Phillips, William,
PN56.P92L49 1983 801'.92 82-23509
ISBN 0-231-05262-6
ISBN 0-231-05263-4 (pbk.)

Columbia University Press
New York Guildford, Surrey

Clothbound editions of Columbia University Press books are Smyth-
sewn and printed on permanent and durable acid-free paper.

CONTENTS

v

PREFACE

OUR AIM WAS to put together the best and the most representative essays, those that make a sophisticated use of psychoanalysis in the study of literature. Fortunately, we had many excellent essays on a broad range of topics and literary figures to choose from. Hence we are able to present the many different psychoanalytic and critical approaches at the highest levels of performance. Our own biases are evident in the balance of the selections but not to the exclusion of any legitimate points of view.

Notable contributions to the field have been made by analysts and literary critics, and we have tried to indicate this dual engagement by presenting examples from both professions, and by exemplifying how the same subject can be examined from different psychoanalytic perspectives. Some of the essays are theoretical, some are practical criticism of individual writers and works. We also thought it useful to divide the selections into several categories—while keeping in mind the changes in psychoanalytic criticism from Freud to Lacan.

It is hardly necessary to point out that the writing on the subject is so vast that it was possible to include only the landmarks along with a few recent pieces by analysts and critics who are not well known but whose work is of a high caliber. However, we wanted this book to reflect the range, the variety, and the collective insight of this wealth of material that has been proliferating since Freud first wrote on the subject. Hence this book should be of value to analysts, to critics, and to intellectually curious laymen as a handy compendium of writing on the relation of literature to psychoanalysis.

We would like to take this opportunity to thank the writers and the publishers of the contents of the volume for their gracious cooperation. We especially want to thank John Moore, editor-in-chief of Columbia University Press, for his encouragement. And we would like to acknowledge the assistance of Mary Barno and Jackie Doyle in going over the manuscript.

As part of the editorial division of labor, the general introduction was written by William Phillips, the introductions to the sections by Edith Kurzweil.

LITERATURE AND PSYCHOANALYSIS

General Introduction

THE COUPLING OF literature and psychoanalysis goes back to Freud himself. A new world of research and speculation began when he observed that the creative faculty draws on drives and fantasies buried in the unconscious, and that they provide the clue to understanding the imaginative mind as well as individual works. Freud also noted the parallels between literary composition and such common activities as children's play and daydreaming, and between literature and myths, which reveal the fantasies of entire communities and nations and even of the whole of early humanity.

Originally Freud thought that the force of such works as *Oedipus Rex* and *Hamlet* derived from the fact that their central themes touched on the psychic experience of modern man. He also believed that the unconscious of the writer was connected to that of the reader by the neuroses they shared. Later he placed more emphasis on literary talent and skill, though he felt that its secrets could not be explained by psychoanalysis. Freud's greatest contribution, however, was probably in the subtle application of his theories and discoveries to individual writers and artists, in the course of which he modified some of his earlier views.

Since then, Freud's original remarks have been expanded, developed, modified, and transformed, in an enormous mass of writing, turned out by psychoanalysts of various schools and by very different kinds of critics, coming from every conceivable position, and going in all directions. The diversity of themes and approaches has been so great that we can scarcely speak of a single subject—or a single question. What we have is a bewildering variety of subjects, methods, and assumptions. Countless books and essays have dealt with the creative process, the relation of literature to psychoanalytic theory, the links between writers' neuroses and their work, the neurotic elements of writers' lives, the connection between literature and health, and between literature and neurosis, the psychic content of specific works, the parallels between popular myths and unconscious motives. More recently, under the influence of the new theories of structuralism and deconstruction, there have been many attempts at a kind of psychoanalytic, free-wheeling reconstruction of the literary text. Also with the new idea of the reader as an accomplice of the author, some analysts and critics have tried to assimilate literary works to the psychic make-up of the ideal, or imaginary, reader.

The common denominator of all these studies is that there is no common denominator. And, unlike work in some more scientific disciplines, each new essay, while making a token bow to the seminal figure of Freud and to earlier writings in the field, actually ignores the findings of other analysts and critics. Rarely does a new study build on an old one. So great is the diversity that one suspects it might be due less to natural differences of opinion than to the fact that the subject itself, that is, the relation of psychoanalysis to literature, is one that makes for unbridled speculation and idiosyncratic approaches. Undoubtedly this laissez-faire state of thinking is encouraged by the fact that there are no accepted definitions of literature, or of the creative mind, or of the way psychic forces mesh with presumably more objective ideas and perceptions about the world.

One says "presumably," because we have learned both epistemologically and clinically that all views are colored by psychology and by personal history. In fact, one of the premises of modern philosophy, from Nietzsche through the later existentialists, has been that existence determines thinking. Clinically too, it has been found that there are no fixed, clearly defined connections between subjective and objective attitudes. And this is also true particularly in the area of literature, where the imagination plays games with observed reality. If indeed a good part of literature is a reconstruction, if not an invention, of actuality, then it is not always easy to find the dividing line between the so-called objective world and the subjective world of the writer.

The most striking thing about the writings on psychoanalysis and literature is that so many theories have been constructed on so few solid definitions and common assumptions. But perhaps some of the invisible logic of this seemingly disorganized field might be seen if we look back briefly at the stages in the literature on the subject. The early entries, by Freud and others, were attempts to relate the creative act to psychoanalytic theory, and to probe the life and work of famous artists whose known neuroses might lend themselves to generalizations about their psychic make-up, and its manifestation in their work. Thus Freud found that such spontaneous activities as daydreaming and play drew on hidden images much in the same way that writing or painting did. In later studies, such as those on Leonardo and Michelangelo, he drew parallels between artists' psychic lives and their careers. In neither case, however, was Freud able to show a connection between the artists' actual work and their neurotic dispositions, beyond their treatment of subject matter. The actual texture and quality of their work seemed to lie outside even Freud's analytic powers. The closest Freud came to dealing with all aspects of a work was in his brilliant essay on Dostoevsky, but here, too, only some components of Dostoevsky's fiction were illuminated. Psychoanalysis was not yet an instrument for dealing with the complex of meanings, ideas, and language that constitutes a work of fiction. Other figures, like Rank and Jung, without the perceptiveness of genius and Freud's uncanny sense of the appropriate, tackled the mysteries of creation and the secrets of individual works, usually focusing on special problems and themes. But the impression remained that the essence of art eluded—perhaps was bound to elude—the kind of analysis that psychology was able so far to bring to it. The fact remains that a psychoanalytic approach to literature is not necessarily literary criticism, though it may provide many useful insights.

A stream of essays by analysts and psychiatrists followed, mostly on individual writers. Among the better-known practitioners were C. G. Jung, Marie Bonaparte, Phyllis Greenacre, Erich Fromm, Henry Rosenzweig, Henry Murray, Selma Freiberg, Ernest Kris, Ernest Jones, Theodore Reik. They had an eye for the more neurotic writers, and they wrote what might be described as literary case studies, or, rather, case studies of literature, dealing with those creative figures who qualified as members of the neurotic but gifted tribe in our culture, from Swift to Kafka. These books and essays contained many remarkable insights into the lives and works of their subjects, and they added substantially to that store of information and perception that lies behind all good critical writing. But, again, something seemed to be missing. These studies were not based on any idea of literature, beyond the popular and conventional reduction of fiction and poetry to their manifest content. And most of

3

them emphasized such analytic themes as the Oedipus complex, anality, schizoid tendencies, latent or expressed homosexuality, guilt, etc., pointing out the roles they played in the works of the writers under discussion. What was lacking was a sense of the relation of these factors to the impact or the quality of the work as a whole, and the relation of psychic elements to those meanings and that mastery of the medium that makes a work of literature.

Consider, for example, one of the best exercises in psychoanalytic interpretation, Ernest Jones' very impressive essay on Hamlet. Taking his cue from Freud's observation that Hamlet's indecision was rooted in his Oedipal entanglements with his father and mother (the King and the Queen), Jones, with an irresistible psychological logic, ascribes every failure of Hamlet to act to his suppressed feelings of hate and love and his consequent paralyzing guilt. So far, so good. But to the question of the power of the play, rhetorical as well as thematic, Jones can only reply that Shakespeare, like Sophocles, engaged the deepest and most tortured conflicts in all men. Unfortunately this ignores the history and the special appeals of the medium. It fails to take into account Shakespeare's seductive and overpowering rhetoric, and his uncanny ability to lift a homely observation into a transcendent perception. Besides, only a few novels and plays have dealt with such basic ideas as the Oedipus complex. What do we do with all those fictions that make only marginal use of the main themes of psychoanalytic theory?

Another of the pioneers was Marie Bonaparte, whose massive study of Poe drew heavily on Freud's interpretation of dreams. Through detailed analyses of such stories as "The Black Cat," "Murders in the Rue Morgue," "The Purloined Letter," "The Gold Bug," "The Tell-Tale Heart," "The Fall of the House of Usher," Bonaparte indicated their similarity to the structure of dreams. Poe's fiction, according to Bonaparte, displayed the dream-like mechanisms of displacement, condensation, substitution, splitting of characters, and secondary elaboration. She argued that Poe's stories and poems are filled with infantile attachments, and with references to the basic symbolization of father, mother, and the genitalia. All of Poe's work, wrote Bonaparte, was charged with anxiety, and its power came from the resulting affects "which have reemerged from deep and hidden sources in the unconscious."

Also among the early contributions was Phyllis Greenacre's exhaustive work on Swift, which traced the neurotic components in his life and his writing. Greenacre's portrait of Swift is that of a witty, charming, tortured man with magnified oedipal problems, given to hypochondria, fear of death, masturbatory fantasies, homosexual inclinations, sexual fears, anal tendencies, and scatological fixations—the full load of neurotic possibilities. She makes a striking connection between the oversized and undersized people in Gulliver and Swift's own morbid concern with body parts and functions, following observations on this subject by Ferenczi. A central theme in Swift's life work, maintains Greenacre, was his distaste for women's bodies and his urge to neuter their femininity. The following passage, concisely summarizing Swift's psychic history, is typical of the psychoanalytic thinking of the time:

This study of Swift was stimulated by an interest in fetishism and the part played in its development by sensations of instability of body size. It is pertinent then to make some brief further references to these questions here. There is no indication that Swift was an overt fetishist, although he shares much in the structure of his personality with those who develop the manifest symptom. The anal fixation was intense and binding, and the genital response so impaired and limited at best, that he was predisposed to later weakness. A retreat from genital sexuality did actually occur in his early adult life, probably beginning with the unhappy relationship to Jane Waring, the first of the goddesses. After this he never again seemed willingly to consider marriage, while his expressed demands were that women who were closest to him should be as much like boys as possible. His genital demands were probably partly sublimated through his creative writings, but even these showed the stamp of his strong anal character. He did not need a fetish because he resigned from physical genitality. In a sense, his converting of the women of his choice into boys fulfilled a fetishistic need. Especially Stella was to be the faithful, dependable, unchanging bisexualized object, a cornerstone for his life. With her death he began to go to pieces.

Lemuel Gulliver went a step further than his creator in that he was a married man, who was however continually escaping from his marriage which was so predominantly disgusting to him, though his periodic sojourns at home sufficed sometimes for the depositing of a child with his wife. . . . The Travels appear as the acting out of Lemuel's masturbatory fantasies which, like the character of Swift, are closely interwoven with anal preoccupations and ambitions rather than with genital ones. (Phyllis Greenacre, *Jonathan Swift*. In *Art and Psychoanalysis*, ed. William Phillips [New York: Criterion, 1957], p. 133.)

Among those who added to the earlier thinking on literature and psychoanalysis, some of the more prominent were Theodore Reik, Fritz Wittels, and Franz Alexander. Reik's best-known study is of Offenbach's *The Tales of Hoffman*, which recounted the life of E. T. A. Hoffman and his three loves. Reik uncovers the sources of the three in Hoffman's unconscious. The seductress, says Reik, belonged to Hoffman's mature years; the doll was a reversal of Hoffman's own infantile dependencies as a child; and the third, the artist, is "the figure of death . . . the last image of woman as she appears to the old man."

Wittels wrote a suggestive analysis of the life and work of Heinrich von Kleist, the great German author who produced all his writing in only eight years, and committed suicide at the age of thirty-four. Wittels finds the core of Kleist's existence in his struggle against homosexuality, from which he could escape only through death. He fell in love with a sick and disfigured woman, who represented, according to Wittels, a denial of life and a door to death, and he acted out a double suicide pact with her. Kleist's plays and stories, argues Wittels, represented the masculine inversion in Kleist; hence they are full of torture, atrocities, and cruelty, approaching the horrors of the Nazi mind.

One of the more significant general statements about art was made by Franz Alexander in an essay on contemporary art. Alexander characterized the anti-rational and non-representative components of modern painting as a reaction against the orderly, optimistic views of an earlier epoch and a return to the unconscious mind. Though he saw this phenomenon as both a manifestation of disorder and an attempt to superimpose a sense of order, Alexander essentially disapproved of the new trends as reinforcements of the chaos of modern life. To be sure, one's perspective in these matters is decisive. Alexander's attitude is consistent with the rational and therapeutic side of analysis, as opposed to the more literary view of early modernist art as an exploitation of the medium and as a reaction against the commercial uses of representation.

Clearly one of the limitations of this early stage of psychoanalytic writing has been that it was done mostly by analysts, not by literary critics. The next stage—the chronology is impure—saw the entrance of professional critics into the enterprise. As might be expected, the level of literary sophistication rose perceptibly, as literary figures like Thomas Mann, W. H. Auden, Lionel Trilling, William Empson, Alfred Kazin, E. H. Gombrich, Meyer Schapiro, Geoffrey Hartman, William Barrett, began to address the subject. No longer was esthetic quality taken for granted, and formal questions as well as those broader ones involving literary tradition and social history were now being taken into consideration.

After all, writing about literature tends to be remote and scholastic when it is not infused with literary sensibility and a sense of the quality of the work one is talking about. With the entrance of professional critics into the psychoanalytic arena, there was less of the feeling that people from Mars were studying people from Venus. Thomas Mann was one of the earliest writers to relate literature to psychoanalysis formally rather than methodologically, but as belonging to the same ambiance. Mann not only concluded, he actually assumed that Freud was a leading exponent of the same mind that produced our novelists and poets. Auden, Trilling, Kazin, and other critics aware of the cultural meaning of Freud's daring speculations also took for granted that psychoanalysis and literature were part of a single imaginative enterprise. These modern critics addressed themselves to special literary and psychological problems more in the spirit of recent literary criticism, with its emphasis both on close reading and on the kind of analysis that derives from a historical sense.

Both Alfred Kazin and Erich Heller wrote about the psychic forces at play in modern literature. Heller focused on the special relation of the basic themes of modernism to psychoanalytic theory. Meyer Schapiro introduced another dimension by stressing the importance of scholarship, questioning some of Freud's facts in his famous essay on Leonardo, and indicating that many elements in Leonardo's painting attributed by Freud to the artist's psyche were actually accounted for in the history of the medium. E. H. Gombrich, in a remarkably original essay, was one of the first to connect psychoanalytic observations with the actual language of literature, by applying some of Freud's ideas about the linguistic aspects of wit to literary composition. Steven Marcus demonstrated further literary sophistication in his examination of the case history of Dora as a literary document—a work of fiction. He not only noted in Dora the kind of transformations and imaginative shifts one finds in novels and stories, but he posed the idea, for the first time, of countertransference as a literary as well as a psychological force.

Lionel Trilling and William Barrett raised one of the central questions concerning the sources of creative inspiration: the relation of neurosis to art. While this question frequently had been touched on before, it had never been resolved, and indeed often contradictory views had been entertained. On the one hand, art was associated with madness; on the other, with prophetic wisdom. When madness was dealt with specifically and clinically by psychoanalysis, art was connected with neurosis-psychosis, though more often by way of illustration than theoretically.

Of course, the question remained: if art drew its content as well as its strength from madness, how did it make its appeal to a varied, if not universal, audience? Was it a collective madness, as Laing and Szasz—in their different ways—appeared to believe, that united literature with its readers? Or was it something else, the catharsis of madness, that created the bond between writer and reader? In the eighteenth century, under the impetus of rationalism, the normal and healthy aspects of art were favored. Charles Lamb, for example, was the first to advance the view that art represented the victory of man's healthy faculties. For Lamb, the very act of creation was the assertion of one's rationality, which, almost by definition, was healthy. The nineteenth century began to probe abnormal psychology and the pendulum swung to the celebration of the neurotic artist. Freud, so far as we know, side-stepped the issue by emphasizing the common elements in the psyche of literature and the psyche of humanity, although he recognized the skill and esthetic power that separated the writer from the ordinary neurotic.

In the twentieth century, the debate was pursued by Trilling and Barrett, with Trilling leaning toward the healthy side of the equation, and Barrett toward the neurotic one. To be sure, neither side can be demonstrated either theoretically or clinically. It is largely a matter of persuasion, of an appeal to shared beliefs—in the end, perhaps, to common sense. But the issue is also fraught with semantic confusion, and with honorific arguments, often concealed by arbitrary definitions. Basically, when we speak of *neurosis* or *health* as the energy that produces art and shapes its content, we are employing vague, rhetorical concepts, neither of which are creators or organizers of the formal and intellectual elements of literature, not, at least, in an exact or concrete sense. However, the proponents of neurosis have this at least in their favor: most writers have been quite neurotic, if not mad, and neurosis is a force that takes possession of a person. Broadly defined, neurosis is the warp in a person's psyche stemming from some unresolved inner conflict. It is admittedly difficult to see how an unresolved conflict can produce that masterful combination of form and content that we think of as literature. Nevertheless, we have noted that neurotics, at least gifted ones, do seem to be propelled in certain significant directions in their thinking and their sensibility. It is not difficult to think of this propulsion—sometimes amounting to a compulsion—as the mainspring of literature. The idea of health in relation to literature is even vaguer and more hortatory than is that of neurosis. There is no accepted definition of a healthy mind, at least no definition that is ideological rather than clinical, nor is there a common idea of the kind of rational, healthy vision of man and society that can be counterposed to a neurotic vision. Unfortunately, there are no simple formulas in the area of thought of health and sickness, truth and neurotic distortion. Where do we put Nietzsche, Kafka, Dostoevsky, Beckett? It begins to appear that the entire argument has been couched in false terms and in oppositions that reflect ideological biases.

For those who view literature as an expression of the sunlit side of existence, of man's progress toward light and truth, the idea of writing drawing on man's "healthy" rather than his "sick" propensities will seem to be more attractive—and sounder. On the other hand, those who see literature, particularly modern literature, as a reflection of man's more morbid and perverse tendencies are likely to stress the neurotic components of the creative mind. Behind these stances, there is in addition the question haunting critical and esthetic inquiry of whether the aim of literature is to reveal some "truth," if not *the* "truth," about ourselves and the world we inhabit. This is of course a philosophical question, again one that cannot be empirically determined, and it has never been settled. For, as with so many other philosophical issues, the stand one takes depends on one's entire outlook. Plato, it will be recalled, regarded art as a source of false emotions and ideas, while Aristotle took the opposite position. Through the middle ages and up to the nineteenth century, mostly under the influence of Christian doctrine, art without uplift—form without content—was considered frivolous. It was only later in the nineteenth century, after Nietzsche had challenged the old idols of belief, that writers began to think of literature not as the expression of our moral and philosophical ideals, but as the mirror of the underside of life. Oscar Wilde described art as an elaborate lie—and not only to exercise his perverse wit. More recently, the modernist esthetic has tended to define art in adversary terms, understanding it not as the bearer of a common truth, but as the lens by means of which an alienated and subversive group reinterpreted "reality." The possible contradiction between this view of literature and the assumption that psychoanalysis deals with general psychic truths presents a further difficulty. How do these general "truths" pervade works that question the idea of general truth, that present biased, perhaps warped, versions of the human condition? Perhaps different orders of experience are involved, and what has been called the adversary strain does not necessarily come into conflict with deeper layers of human conduct. But yet another difficulty presents itself: are these problems more pertinent to literature than to the other arts, if only because they entail an old-fashioned idea of content not readily applicable to plastic art and music? The "content" of these other arts is in no way comparable to that of literature. It is not easily identifiable, perhaps non-existent in the sense that the term is commonly used.

Ironically, it would appear that as the approaches to psychoanalysis and literature became more sophisticated, they solved fewer old problems and raised more new ones. They also brought the thinking on the subject into distant reaches from which there seemed to be no return, and they introduced complexities of formulation and speculation that sometimes left one helplessly nostalgic for Freud's own simpler observations. This seems true of the latest stage, which might be characterized as the French appropriation of Freud and its application to the domain of literature. Two currents came together on the French scene. As latecomers to the recognition of Freud, the French were determined to outdo psychoanalysts in other countries in bringing Freud up to date. Parallel to this discovery and revision of Freud, structuralism and its offspring, deconstruction, were born, and soon took over much of French philosophy and criticism. These trends have dominated the French discussion of psychoanalysis and literature and have had considerable influence on American criticism, particularly in some academic circles.

It is difficult to pin down the meaning of this new ideological enterprise. For, in addition to the revision of Freud and the use of structuralism and deconstruction for literary criticism, the new approaches are steeped in the Saussurean school of linguistics, in Derrida's and Lacan's open-ended idea of all meanings, historical and textual, and in formalist theories of literature. Furthermore, certain Marxist attitudes have been absorbed into French criticism, such as an adversary position in relation to bourgeois culture and a belief in the necessity of its demystification, a view of history as relative and changing, and a generally radical stance on political and cultural questions. But if one were to try to distill the essence of these various strains, it is the notion that everything can be interpreted as a text. Meanings, events, ideas, theories, literary works— all are texts. In a sense, all life is a text. Thus, for example, Freud's and Marx's writings are texts to be reinterpreted so freely as to amount to revision. In this respect, the new French criticism and its American counterpart go beyond the ordinary textual analysis of the formalists. A new component has been added: the free exercise of the imagination on the part of the interpreter. And this depends on extending the old principle that readings of texts vary with new historical situations—extending it to the point where it is completely transformed, since in the past it was assumed that new readings could produce only small variations in a relatively fixed core of meanings. The premise behind what might be called a permanent revision of meanings is that each reader creates a new text out of the old one. Initially this seemed to sanction an interpretive free-for-all, particularly chaotic and meaningless since it ignored the competence of the reader-reinterpreter. The problem was soon resolved, however, by narrowing the idea of the reader to the ideally competent one, and by Stanley Fish's ingenious notion of the revamping of texts by a community of presumably informed readers. Fish's contribution did not really differ much from the view of literary history held by critics who are not structuralists or deconstructionists. As to the ideal readers, they turned out to be, for the most part, Derrida, Lacan, Barthes, Girard, Todorov, Genette, and their students.

These then are the ideological sources of a good deal of recent writing about psychoanalysis and literature. Lacan, of course, is central. His writings on literature reflect not only his revision of Freud in theory and in clinical practice, but also express his generally free-wheeling and cavalier attitude to Freud and Freudian analytic thinking. Lacan's much publicized piece on Poe's "Purloined Letter" utilizes his favorite concepts of phallic symbolism, the Other, the mirror image, and the linguistic structure of the unconscious. However it is a very narrow and one-sided reading of the story. Similarly, Lacan's discussion of Hamlet uses many of Freud's and Jones' observations, but it also focuses on the presumed phallic meaning of Hamlet's role in the play, and on the significance of word-play, another of Lacan's private notions. But most important in these and Lacan's other ventures into literary interpretation is what might be characterized as a free-associational form of thinking set up by the work under examination. Lacan spins ideological fantasies as he reinterprets and co-authors the text. As in actual analysis, anything goes. An ideological version of what the patient does in analysis is applied to the study of literature. What Lacan contributes as an analyst stems from his linguistic analysis of the unconscious of the leading characters.

Lacan's disciples in the analysis of literature are mainly critics, not analysts. And their method is more esoteric and even more idiosyncratic than his own. Many of them are to be found in seminars and publications associated with Yale and Johns Hopkins Universities, which have become intellectual centers in this country for structuralists and deconstructionists. Taking their cue from Lacan, they explore a text as though they were intellectual pioneers entering virgin territory. Even more than Lacan, their approach employs a combination of revisionist psychoanalytic theory and French linguistics. Hence their writing emphasizes the representation of signifiers and signified elements in literary works, and the language of texts. Needless to say, most analysts and non-academic critics, particularly in the United States and England, have not been persuaded by the Lacanian version of psychoanalytic criticism, and having been trained in Anglo-American traditions of criticism and psychoanalysis, they often find it incomprehensible.

But aside from the question of its validity, Lacanian criticism has brought the examination of psychoanalysis and literature full circle, to a point which is almost a reversal of the intentions of Freud and the early analysts. Freud, and those who followed his lead, assumed that the discoveries of psychoanalysis about human drives and motives threw some light on the lives of writers and the psychic mechanisms of their characters. They did not see psychoanalysis as an instrument for deconstructing, that is, for taking apart and recreating philosophical ideas, literary works, and historical events. To accomplish the latter, psychoanalysis itself had to be deconstructed, which meant it had not only to be textually revised, but had to be open to constant reinterpretation. Psychoanalysis, like a literary text, is now seen by the French and their American disciples as so much grist for the analysts' and the critics' creative mill.

With so many unforeseen and bewildering developments in psychoanalysis and in criticism, it would seem time to take stock and to reexamine the contributions that psychoanalysis can make to the understanding of literature. Obviously, the original aims have been sidetracked, when not completely transformed. It is doubtful that either literature or psychoanalysis has been advanced or illuminated in the process. What critics like Hartman, Doubrovsky, Girard, Genette, Todorov, and others coming out of the French school have produced are brilliant *tours de force*—captious, idiosyncratic, scattershot, with no effort at consistency or roundedness; and their connections with other writings on the subject are sporadic and highly personal. One is tempted to conclude that some very intelligent critics have become the exponents of a theory that gives free rein to all the creative and speculative impulses previously held in check by a sense of the limits of the subject. The theory that all of human culture is made up of texts, and that language is the common element in all these texts, diminishes the number of fixed—or relatively fixed—meanings, and vastly increases the possibilities of new meanings. Furthermore, the number of novel interpretations becomes endless if the reaction of the reader is legitimized as part of the text. Essentially, this has been accomplished by the elimination of history, thus making all texts contemporary—and eliminating traditional meanings.

In its more extreme forms, as in Lacan, we can see the danger of interpretation running wild. But the original difficulty, it would seem, comes from conceiving of criticism—and therefore psychoanalytic criticism—principally as interpretation. In fact, both the French and American approaches often appear to assume that criticism and psychoanalysis have similar functions, the former interpreting literature, the latter interpreting the psyche. The problem with such a parallel is that interpretation is only one of the functions of criticism, particularly when it leads to over-interpretation. And, generally, a certain amount of distortion is bound to result from the use of a single discipline or theory to analyze or interpret literature. We have seen the reductive and distorting effects of an exclusively social, or historical, or Marxist view of literature, and an attempt to fit literature into a psychoanalytic mold can be equally misleading.

In short, it should be clear that criticism is not a branch of psychoanalysis any more than psychoanalysis is a branch of criticism, and neither is a section of linguistics. It is not easy to define so complex and protean an activity as literary criticism, but if its nature is to be found in its history, then it has to be seen as combining many perspectives and aims—formal, historical, traditional, and textual. It tends to emphasize matters pertaining to craft and to literary tradition. But its main function is the exercise of taste and judgment. The best contemporary critics, such as Trilling, Empson, Howe, Kazin, Rahv, Heller, have taken advantage of the insights of analysis to add to the arsenal of criticism, instead of inventing a new linguistic-psychoanalytic method and terminology that often complicates simple questions and creates an aura of discovery around things that are known.

But whatever critical or analytic approach one takes to literature, there remain two major questions to be faced: a theoretical one concerning the relation of literature to neurosis, and the practical one of applying analytic knowledge to a given writer. If we take these questions out of the conceptual stratosphere of the new psycho-criticism, it may be possible to find some more mundane answers. If literature is taken to be the sum of its psychological components or as a variety of dream or fantasy, then we have no literary criteria for judging it, nor any way of distinguishing it from other kinds of dream or fantasy. If we attribute the power or significance of a work to the neurosis of the author, we have to assume that its meaning lies wholly in its psychological content, which, in turn, corresponds to the reader's. We would then have to read *The Possessed*, for example, as a story of the criminal mind, and we could not account for its stature as a political novel. Or, to take a different example, characterizing Rilke's spurts of activity between long fallow periods as signs of health would simply be to define the act of writing as a manifestation of health. One might just as well call it neurotic, since Rilke's process of composition was obsessive and dreamlike. Certainly writing often resembles compulsive acts and states of hallucination, and all we gain by calling it healthy rather than neurotic is the reassurance that we are not revelling in disease—a reassurance, incidentally, that Thomas Mann certainly did not require.

Ironically, a way out of the dilemma might be made possible by using the terms *neurosis* and *psychosis* more loosely. Viewed non-clinically, these disorders often involve a distortion of experience whereby certain human events are given an undue, even obsessive, emphasis. In those who are not writers, a distorted view of reality is simply part of illness and inability to adjust, and may be of no intellectual interest. In someone like Kafka, however, the paranoid picture of the world in both his life and his writing was coupled with a gift of a higher order and a mind capable of original and striking observation. The paranoia became plausible, if not "true." Similarly, D. H. Lawrence's sexual dreams would have had only a clinical interest without his literary powers.

To generalize further, much modern writing is centered in some obsessive theme or some biased image of human affairs, growing out of the fixations of the author. This seems true of even so carefully constructed a work as *The Waste Land*, whose meanings appear mainly cultural and religious. But Eliot's concern, in our culture and religion, as well as in our personal lives, is that we no longer know who we are, and the image of this failure is provided by the sexual ambiguity of Tiresias, the psychological core of the poem. The homosexual theme crops up constantly, often in an explicit way, but it is also expressed symbolically in the perversion of feelings and the spiritual impotence running through *The Waste Land*. One would have to know more about Eliot's private preoccupations to speculate further about the effect of his psychic make-up on his wasteland vision, but it is reasonable to assume that this vision reflects to some extent the more personal elements in his life.

What then does it mean to say that the work of writers like Swift, or Kafka, or Eliot contained some distortion of experience traceable in part to their own psychic history? From everything we know about writing, it would seem reasonable to assume that neurotic images of the world coincided with impressions which were not neurotic, and that they energized and organized each other.

Kafka is, of course, the classic example of this process, for his psychic disorders have been most visible and they have been integrated most clearly in all his writing. The merging in Kafka of neurotic and objective vision is perhaps clearer than in any other writer. It is probably for this reason that Kafka has been a favorite subject for psychological probing. His strange fictional world, in which dreams and realities, symbols and objects, fantasies and facts, are indistinguishable from each other, cannot be understood in the ordinary terms of fictional and literary criticism. Kafka might serve as an illustration of how psychoanalytic insights could enlarge the scope of a more traditional criticism. The paranoia, for example, which colored his social and sexual relations, became in his fiction a psychological focus for a world in which the characters are the victims of organized ignorance and authority. The living Kafka's search for psychological solutions merged in his writing with a search for religious and metaphysical solutions.

Kafka's novels and stories would seem to have many apparently distinct aspects: moral, religious, political, and psychological. Attempts have been made to read Kafka from each of these viewpoints—not only reducing Kafka's writing to one of its components but also reducing his stature as a writer. Other views of Kafka aside, the limitations of a psychological exegesis should be noted. There have been many such informed interpretations of Kafka's fiction (Fromm, Mitscherlich, and Hayman are included in this volume), and they have conscientiously probed the secrets of Kafka's inner life. By now we are familiar with his paranoia, his hypochondria, his insomnia, his awkward, inhibited relations with women, his inability until the end of his life to marry, his overpowering feelings of anxiety and guilt, his resentment and fear of his father. We also know of his compulsive, largely nocturnal writing habits and accompanying feverish and hallucinatory states. We can discern the representations, sometimes literal, often veiled, of these morbid, self-destructive elements in his fiction and his diaries. But unless we can see how these neurotic—or psychotic?—tendencies are merged with more objective attitudes and ideas, and made into a highly crafted whole, we are dealing with a disturbed patient, not a major writer. Some process, not yet known to psychology, fused the different parts of Kafka's unconscious and conscious mind into a unified vision. Even this more integrated approach is not enough, for Kafka's fiction would not have its uncanny, seductive, and unnerving effect if his sense of the world were not encased in a controlled, almost matter-of-fact prose, at once precise and full of nightmarish associations. Psychology cannot be separated from the history and use of the medium of fiction.

Kafka's paranoia and his feelings about arbitrary parental authority were translated in *The Trial* and other works into a sense of authority both suffocating and reassuring and at once political, religious, and metaphysical. So, too, his fear of women and his dependence on them, based to some extent on his family history, emerged in the soft, shadowy, ultimately unreliable accomplices of authority in his fiction. His story "The Burrow" is a fantastic projection into the underground existence of a burrow that affords an escape from the outside world but is full of its own dangers. Here, too, by means of a prose that creates a totally natural and exact description of the activities of the burrow, the world of the story takes on the menacing qualities of the human world where, for Kafka, the dangers one constantly faces were part of one's fate. The anxiety this evokes is given a biological cast when it is incorporated into the bodily sensations of the burrow. Perhaps most striking in Kafka is the conversion of personal guilt into the pervasive moral, psychological, and political guilt stemming not from specific transgression but rather from the accusatory power of all higher authorities. Again it must be emphasized that we are dealing here not only with a psychological but also a literary act, and if one might generalize further about the literary uses of psychology, one can see a suggestive link from Kafka to the subversive imagination of Dostoevsky. In *Notes from the Underground*, the self-lacerating "anti-hero" of the story says repeatedly that he feels like an insect, diminished and worthless. In *The Metamorphosis*, Gregor Samsa takes the logical and psychological next step. He becomes an insect.

Dostoevsky is another dramatic example of a major figure in whom conscious and unconscious components are both distinct and merged, and who requires, therefore, a combination of traditional criticism and psychoanalytic awareness. Elizabeth Dalton's essay in this volume is a strikingly original effort to locate Dostoevsky's psyche within the text itself, instead of the more customary correlations of an author's life with his work. But, in contrast to other new forms of criticism, she assumes a fairly stable and clear text, not one that is protean and infinitely variable. Her parallels between the fluctuating rhythms and the oceanic feelings of Dostoevsky's epilepsy and the wave-like moods and shifting action of *The Idiot* are particularly apt and illuminating.

In novels like *The Possessed* and *Crime and Punishment*, the blending of ideological motifs with morbid psychology is even more apparent. Both elements are essential not only in the workings of Dostoevsky's mind, but to the fictional power of the two books. Dostoevsky had strong convictions about the moral arrogance and intellectual emptiness of those personal or political ideas that led to the taking of lives. He viewed killing in the name of the revolution and murder in the name of some transcendent idea as parts of the same evil, rooted in atheism, divorce from the people, and the celebration of "Western" progressive ideas. A passionate Slavophile and a Christian, he believed that salvation could come only through confession and expiation of one's sins. Thus, criminality was identified with political hubris and Godlessness in the character of Raskolnikov, and in the revolutionists of *The Possessed*. The revolutionaries considered everything possible because they did not believe in God; Raskolnikov and Stavrogin could follow their evil impulses because of their criminal psychology. Raskolnikov had the dreams of a superman, Stavrogin the personality of one. Stavrogin was probably the most complete projection of Dostoevsky's dual nature, of his own destructive drives and of the elaborate structure he created to contain them; perhaps this is why Stavrogin is an unfinished character, one whom Dostoevsky could not develop fully without tearing himself apart. Without psychology, Dostoevsky would be another conservative, though one with prophetic vision; without ideology, Dostoevsky would be a novelist of the psychic underground; without literary genius he would be a writer of sensational stories.

The unique combination of neurotic experience with some apparently objective or plausible view of the world, such as we find in Kafka, or Proust, or Mann, seems to be characteristic of much modern literature. Indeed, it is this experience that we designate as the modern experience. Although this experience seems to be shared by a sufficient number of writers and readers to make up a tradition, it has at the same time certain affinities with neurotic experience. Themes such as loneliness, self-doubt, hypersensitivity, perversities of all kinds, estrangement from the community all have their counterparts among the common neuroses, and the two modes of experience, normal and abnormal, often have been joined in such a way that it becomes difficult to separate them.

What we have been describing is the literature of *modernism*. But it has been argued that the modernist movement is dead, and that we are in a post-modernist phase whose qualities and contours still have not been satisfactorily defined. The debate has not been resolved. However it is clear that most contemporary writing lacks the mythic force, the adversary posture, and the complicated sensibility associated with modernism. Fiction today is quieter, more modest, more naturalistic, less symbolic. It is sexually freer and more explicitly perverse, but in a way that would seem to reflect contemporary experience rather than private inclinations. A good deal of recent fiction is also concerned with social causes and liberating values. It is on the whole more open, and less layered; and its deeper psychological meanings are mostly on the surface, just as psychoanalysis itself is on the tips of all tongues. One wonders whether psychoanalytically oriented criticism will find contemporary fiction a fertile field to plow, and whether the highly theoretical and esoteric turn of the new psycho-criticism is not to some extent a reaction to a new fiction with fewer hidden psychological meanings, whether the complexities of criticism are compensating for the simpler experience of literature.

Perhaps these dilemmas will serve as a reminder that what Mann called "the psychology of the unconscious" cannot be equated with the history of consciousness, of which literature is a major part.

PART I

EARLY PSYCHOANALYTIC THEORY

THE FUNCTION OF THE WRITER, the meaning and value of his work, the essence of aesthetic experience, and much more have been questioned over the last twenty-five hundred years. No definitive answers have been found. Goethe remarked that he never wondered how his writing might benefit humanity; his attempt instead was to gain insight to enhance his own personality, and then to state simply what he found to be good and true. Freud, who frequently referred to Goethe, did not claim to know the sources of creative imagination. But he did believe that his discoveries about the functioning of the unconscious, which by now have permeated all of modern culture, would pave the way for new means of examining artistic works. Freud's genius lay not only in his pschyoanalytic theories but in his writing, although when he himself spoke of "writing," he thought of poetry or fiction.

When Freud addressed the importance of daydreaming for creative writers, he linked the imaginary activities of artists to those of children at play. Though deceptively simple, this connection not only revolutionized child-rearing practices, but opened up the most fruitful means of examining creative works in relation to their authors' lives and talents. Because both the artist and the child at play are serious about their worlds of fantasy, which they nevertheless distinguish clearly from reality, Freud proceeded to compare their activities and behavior. He found that both originate works of their own and rearrange the things of this world to please themselves. But when the writer taps his imagination, and transforms it with the help of technique, states Freud, he transcends his own person so that the product becomes "a source of pleasure for the hearers and spectators of the work." Such a writer, "a dreamer in broad daylight," is bound to project his emotions onto his central character, to turn his own ego into "the hero of every daydream and of every story." This is so, he continues, even when this character is peripheral or split into a number of different characters. Examining the work, then, can serve as the path to the artist's unconscious—an unconscious to be interpreted. Because the artist's unconscious is more "available," and possibly "richer" than everyone else's, Freud believed that its exploration would prove particularly fruitful to psychoanalysis, and to the analysis of (day)dreams with all their ambiguities. Freud's original conceptions, and his theoretical generalizations, were so broadly formulated, that they "invited" many psychoanalysts and literary critics to enlarge upon and to modify them. Thus Freudian analysts welcomed artists and writers as patients to broaden their own knowledge, and literary critics immersed themselves in psychoanalytic works.

Freud himself primarily continued to focus on the centrality of sexuality and of the Oedipus complex, and began by analyzing the Greek tragedy *Oedipus Rex*, to show how "a strong experience (usually belonging to childhood) . . . precedes a wish which finds its fulfillment in creative work." We continue to be moved by this tragedy, argues Freud, because something within us responds to Oedipus' conflict—our very early sexual impulses toward our mothers and feelings of hatred toward our fathers—and to the wishes he realized, and which we all have to repress. This theme, of course, which Freud went on to explore in *Hamlet*, and *Macbeth*, as well as in artists such as Leonardo da Vinci, Dostoevsky, and others, uses both the works and their creators to illustrate that "every genuine poetical creation must have proceeded from more than one motive, more than one impulse in the mind of the poet, and must admit of more than one interpretation." This celebration of openness encouraged others to interpret innumerable personality factors that might contribute to creativity: artists' childhood memories and traumas, relations to favorite and hated relatives, influences of teachers and nurses, congenital defects and attributes, narcissistic and other personality traits, hetero- and homosexuality, birth order and sibling rivalry, and others. Hamlet, for example, has been interpreted as evil or good, as lunatic or feminine, as murdering his love for Ophelia or being too close to his mother, as attacking mysticism or skepticism; he has been deemed very young or between twenty and thirty, mad and just pretending madness. Some analyses have centered on Hamlet's slow action—for situational reasons or psychological ones—attributing it to his sensibility, weakness, ineffectiveness, intellectualizations, scruples about revenge, or the shock of his mother's marriage. Whereas the narrower interpretations in this Hamlet industry try to force literature to conform with the Oedipus complex rather than use it heuristically for further exploration, the broader ones are extensive "free-associations" by the critics.

Ernest Jones' essay, "The Death of Hamlet's Father," begins by noting that versions of the story predated Shakespeare's play, and that he must have been familiar with a number of these. When translated into the language of symbolism, however, differences become apparent—differences that give us new insight into Shakespeare's personality. Claudius' attack on his brother, for instance, is interpreted as both a murderous aggression and homosexual assault, complementing Jones' previous contention that a readiness to interchange the sexes was a prominent theme in all of Shakespeare's plays, and that *Hamlet* was written as "a more or less successful abreaction on the intolerable emotions aroused by the painful . . . betrayal by both his beloved young noble and his mistress." His artistic response to these blows was privately to write the *Sonnets* and publicly to present *Hamlet*. Jones argues that this episode raises questions of active and passive homosexuality, questions illustrative of the Oedipus complex, where the attack of the younger brother on the older one replicates the father-son conflict; here the poisoning story represents the son castrating the father. It is because homosexuality, according to Freud, has its origin in narcissism, in mirror-love, that suicide can be so close to murder. Jones concludes that repressed hatred of Hamlet's father as well as the homosexual aspect of Hamlet's attitude made for the simultaneous presence of love and hate. Clearly the universality of the Oedipus complex encouraged similar associations and psychoanalytic explanations of literary works.

In an attempt to bring some order to the confusion, Carl Jung suggests that we separate psychological research about the formation of a work of art from the factors that make an individual artistically creative:

In the case of the work of art we have to deal with a product of complicated psychic activities—but a product that is apparently intentional and consciously shaped. In the case of the artist we must deal with the psychic apparatus itself. . . . Although these two undertakings are closely related and even interdependent, neither of them can yield the explanations that are sought by the other. (Carl Gustav Jung: *Psychology and Literature in the Creative Process*, edited by Brewster Ghiselin [New York: Mentor Books, 1963], p. 298.)

This separation of the artist from the work leads Jung to question the importance of the artist's experience to his work, and to postulate "a return to the state of *participation mystique*." But few who were close to Freud in the early days have left the "scientific" notions of psychoanalysis as far behind as Jung.

Otto Rank, while questioning sexuality as the central creative impulse, enlarges Freud's theoretical discussions. He maintains that the modern writer has reached a higher degree of consciousness than his earlier prototype; artists have become aware of their work and their mission as well as of their personality and its productiveness, and this, in turn, forms their personality and experience. For Rank the artist flees the life of actuality, a life that spells mortality and decay, by giving shape to his experience in the form of creative work and postulating the life impulse as the artist's road to immortality. Rank perceives a dynamic relationship among Impulse-Fear-Will as determinants of productivity. While the neurotic is unable to detach the creative process from his person, the productive artist is able to recreate himself, objectively, in an ideologically constructed ego. But much of Rank's discussion is aimed at others in Freud's circle, at Adler's notions of superiority/inferiority, and at outsiders such as Stekel or Lombroso. Rank also explores the value of the artist to the future life of his community, the collective elements of which are immortalized in the work and serve as binding ideologies. The artist thereby employs his personal will power, as well as social and artistic qualities, to give form or life to an ideology. On no account, insists Rank, can an artist's work be reconstructed or understood as a matter of individual psychology, because both personal development and the development of humanity are subject to inherent sexual dualism as well as to the conflicts and experiences which constitute the raw material of creation.

Henry Lowenfeld's case study of a woman artist is a typical example of how clinical data can supplement, or fill the gaps in, psychoanalytic theory. Agreeing with both Freud's and Rank's admonitions that the essential talent of the artist cannot be explained by psychoanalysis, he begins by recounting some of his patient's childhood experiences—the traumatic experiences that kept recurring in her dreams—and then proceeds to pinpoint the onset of her neurosis. The artist reacts more strongly to stimulation than the ordinary individual, he found, and therefore has more traumatic experiences which, themselves, are often provoked. Feelings of guilt, originally stemming from the Oedipus complex, are stronger than is "normal," but they are alleviated when the creative work is being appreciated, and feelings of narcissism as well are transferred to the work. Drawing on clinical reports, and theory by Freud, Sachs, Rank, and others, he reports that in "his" artist, as in all others, bisexuality is particularly strong. Lowenfeld quotes many instances where artists compare the pains of childbirth to "the struggle and pangs of labor in creating a work of art." This begetting alternately emphasizes masculine or feminine elements, "creation or surrender." The fantasies of Lowenfeld's patient expressed both conflict and tension, and her inherent frustration was only temporarily relieved when a work was completed. Essentially, Lowenfeld "proved" again that bisexuality was a significant factor in the life of this artist. This would suggest, he concludes, that only identification with both sexes could allow an artist to portray so faithfully both male and female characters. The artist, by reproducing unfulfilled experiences, and by identifying, is said to be in a process of alternate introjection and projection. It is a process full of charm, or even of magic, which helps the artist to overcome his conflicts through artistic sublimation.

We will end with Lowenfeld rather than extending our discussion to clinical studies of sublimation, such as the instances and importance of energy transformation, or the frequent presence of sexual stimulation during the creative act. These questions are concerned less with literature than with the sources of the writer's instinctual life and its relation to his work.

I.

Creative Writers and Daydreaming

Sigmund Freud

WE LAYMEN HAVE always been intensely curious to know—like the Cardinal who put a similar question to Ariosto [1]—from what sources that strange being, the creative writer, draws his material, and how he manages to make such an impression on us with it and to arouse in us emotions of which, perhaps, we had not even thought ourselves capable. Our interest is only heightened the more by the fact that, if we ask him, the writer himself gives us no explanation, or none that is satisfactory; and it is not at all weakened by our knowledge that not even the clearest insight into the determinants of his choice of material and into the nature of the art of creating imaginative form will ever help to make creative writers of *us*.

If we could at least discover in ourselves or in people like ourselves an activity which was in some way akin to creative writing! An examination of it would then give us a hope of obtaining the beginnings of an

Permission granted by Sigmund Freud Copyrights Ltd., the Institute of Psycho-Analysis, and the Hogarth Press Ltd., to quote from the *Standard Edition of the Complete Psychological Works of Sigmund Freud*, translated and edited by James Strachey (London: Hogarth Press, 1953–74). Also from *The Collected Papers of Sigmund Freud*, vol. 4, edited by Ernest Jones, M.D., authorized translation under the supervision of Joan Riviere. Published by Basic Books, Inc., by arrangement with the Hogarth Press Ltd., and the Institute of Psycho-Analysis, London. By permission of Basic Books, Inc., New York.

explanation of the creative work of writers. And, indeed, there is some prospect of this being possible. After all, creative writers themselves like to lessen the distance between their kind and the common run of humanity; they so often assure us that every man is a poet at heart and that the last poet will not perish till the last man does.

Should we not look for the first traces of imaginative activity as early as in childhood? The child's best-loved and most intense occupation is with his play or games. Might we not say that every child at play behaves like a creative writer, in that he creates a world of his own, or, rather, rearranges the things of his world in a new way which pleases him? It would be wrong to think he does not take that world seriously; on the contrary, he takes his play very seriously and he expends large amounts of emotion on it. The opposite of play is not what is serious but what is real. In spite of all the emotion with which he cathects his world of play, the child distinguishes it quite well from reality; and he likes to link his imagined objects and situations to the tangible and visible things of the real world. This linking is all that differentiates the child's "play" from "fantasying."

The creative writer does the same as the child at play. He creates a world of fantasy which he takes very seriously—that is, which he invests with large amounts of emotion—while separating it sharply from reality. Language has preserved this relationship between children's play and poetic creation. It gives [in German] the name of *Spiel* ["play"] to those forms of imaginative writing which require to be linked to tangible objects and which are capable of representation. It speaks of a *Lustspiel* or *Trauerspiel* ["comedy" or "tragedy": literally, "pleasure play" or "mourning play"] and describes those who carry out the representation as *Schauspieler* ["players": literally "show-players"]. The unreality of the writer's imaginative world, however, has very important consequences for the technique of his art; for many things which, if they were real, could give no enjoyment, can do so in the play of fantasy, and many excitements which, in themselves, are actually distressing, can become a source of pleasure for the hearers and spectators at the performance of a writer's work.

May we really attempt to compare the imaginative writer with the "dreamer in broad daylight" [*Der Träumer am hellichten Tag*], and his creations with daydreams? Here we must begin by making an initial distinction. We must separate writers who, like the ancient authors of epics and tragedies, take over their material ready-made from writers who seem to originate their own material. We will keep to the latter kind, and, for the purposes of our comparison, we will choose not the writers most highly esteemed by the critics, but the less pretentious authors of novels, romances, and short stories, who nevertheless have the widest and most eager circle of readers of both sexes. One feature above all cannot fail to strike us about the creations of these story-writers: each of them has a hero who is the center of interest, for whom the writer tries to win our sympathy by every possible means and whom he seems to place under the protection of a special Providence. If, at the end of one chapter of my story, I leave the hero unconscious and bleeding from severe wounds, I am sure to find him at the beginning of the next being carefully nursed and on the way to recovery; and if the first volume closes with the ship he is in going down in a storm at sea, I am certain, at the opening of the second volume, to read of his miraculous rescue—a rescue without which the story could not proceed. The feeling of security with which I follow the hero through his perilous adventures is the same as the feeling with which a hero in real life throws himself into the water to save a drowning man or exposes himself to the enemy's fire in order to storm a battery. It is the true heroic feeling, which one of our best writers has expressed in an inimitable phrase: "Nothing can happen to *me!*"[2] It seems to me, however, that through this revealing characteristic of invulnerability we can immediately recognize His Majesty the Ego, the hero alike of every daydream and of every story.[3]

Other typical features of these egocentric stories point to the same kinship. The fact that all the women in the novel invariably fall in love with the hero can hardly be looked on as a portrayal of reality, but it is easily understood as a necessary constituent of a daydream. The same is true of the fact that the other characters in the story are sharply divided into good and bad, in defiance of the variety of human characters that are to be observed in real life. The "good" ones are the helpers, while the "bad" ones are the enemies and rivals, of the ego which has become the hero of the story.

We are perfectly aware that very many imaginative writings are far removed from the model of the naïve daydream; and yet I cannot suppress the suspicion that even the most extreme deviations from that model could be linked with it through an uninterrupted series of transitional cases. It has struck me that in many of what are known as "psychological" novels only one person—once again the hero—is described from within. The author sits inside his mind, as it were, and looks at the other characters from outside. The psychological novel in general no doubt owes its special nature to the inclination of the modern writer to split up his ego, by self-observation, into many part-egos, and, in consequence, to personify the conflicting currents of his own mental life in several heroes. Certain novels, which might be described as "eccentric," seem to stand in quite special contrast to the type of the daydream. In these, the person who is introduced as the hero plays only a very small active part; he sees the actions and sufferings of other people pass before him like a spectator. Many of Zola's later works belong to this category. But I must point out that the psychological analysis of individuals who are not creative writers, and who diverge in some respects from the so-called norm, has shown us analogous variations of the daydream, in which the ego contents itself with the role of spectator.

If our comparison of the imaginative writer with the daydreamer, and of poetical creation with the daydream, is to be of any value, it must, above all, show itself in some way or other fruitful. Let us, for instance, try to apply to these authors' works the thesis we laid down earlier concerning the relation between fantasy and the three periods of time and the wish which runs through them; and, with its help, let us try to study the connections that exist between the life of the writer and his works. No one has known, as a rule, what expectations to frame in approaching this problem; and often the connection has been thought of in much too simple terms. In the light of the insight we have gained from fantasies, we ought to expect the following state of affairs. A strong experience in the present awakens in the creative writer a memory of an earlier experience (usually belonging to his childhood) from which there now proceeds a wish which finds its fulfillment in the creative work. The work itself exhibits elements of the recent provoking occasion as well as of the old memory.[4]

Do not be alarmed at the complexity of this formula. I suspect that in fact it will prove to be too exiguous a pattern. Nevertheless, it may contain a first approach to the true state of affairs; and, from some experiments I have made, I am inclined to think that this way of looking at creative writings may turn out not unfruitful. You will not forget that the stress it lays on childhood memories in the writer's life—a stress which may perhaps seem puzzling—is ultimately derived from the assumption that a piece of creative writing, like a daydream, is a continuation of, and a substitute for, what was once the play of childhood.

We must not neglect, however, to go back to the kind of imaginative works which we have to recognize, not as original creations, but as the refashioning of ready-made and familiar material. Even here, the writer keeps a certain amount of independence, which can express itself in the choice of material and in changes in it which are often quite extensive. In so far as the material is already at hand, however, it is derived from the popular treasure-house of myths, legends, and fairy tales. The study of constructions of folk-psychology such as these is far from being complete, but it is extremely probable that myths, for instance, are distorted vestiges of the wishful fantasies of whole nations, the *secular dreams* of youthful humanity.

Notes

1. Cardinal Ippolito D'Este was Ariosto's first patron, to whom he dedicated the *Orlando Furioso*. The poet's only reward was the question: "Where did you find so many stories, Lodovico?"

2. "Es kann dir nix g'schehen!" This phrase from Anzengruber, the Viennese dramatist, was a favorite one of Freud's. See "Thoughts for the Times on War and Death," *Collected Papers*, 4:288; *Standard Edition*, 14:296.

3. See Sigmund Freud, "On Narcissism: An Introduction," *Collected Papers*, 4:30; *Standard Edition*, 14:91.

4. A similar view had already been suggested by Freud in a letter to Fliess of July 7, 1898, on the subject of one of C. P. Meyer's short stories. Freud, *The Origins of Psycho-Analysis* (New York: Basic Books, 1954), Letter 92.

2.

The Interpretation of Dreams

Sigmund Freud

IF THE *Oedipus Rex* is capable of moving a modern reader or playgoer no less powerfully than it moved the contemporary Greeks, the only possible explanation is that the effect of the Greek tragedy does not depend upon the conflict between fate and human will, but upon the peculiar nature of the material by which this conflict is revealed. There must be a voice within us which is prepared to acknowledge the compelling power of fate in the *Oedipus*, while we are able to condemn the situations occurring in *Die Ahnfrau* or other tragedies of fate as arbitrary inventions. And there actually is a motive in the story of King Oedipus which explains the verdict of this inner voice. His fate moves us only because it might have been our own, because the oracle laid upon us before our birth the very curse which rested upon him. It may be that we were all destined to direct our first sexual impulses toward our mothers, and our first impulses of hatred and violence toward our fathers; our dreams convince us that we were. King Oedipus, who slew his father Laius and wedded his mother Jocasta, is nothing more or less than a wish-fulfillment—the fulfillment of the wish of our childhood. But we,

From *The Basic Writings of Sigmund Freud*, A. A. Brill, M.D., ed. and tr. (New York: Random House, Modern Library, 1938). Copyright renewed © 1965 Gioia B. Bernheim and Edmund R. Brill. Reprinted by permission.

more fortunate than he, in so far as we have not become psychoneurotics, have since our childhood succeeded in withdrawing our sexual impulses from our mothers, and in forgetting our jealousy of our fathers. We recoil from the person for whom this primitive wish of our childhood has been fulfilled with all the force of the repression which these wishes have undergone in our minds since childhood. As the poet brings the guilt of Oedipus to light by his investigation, he forces us to become aware of our own inner selves, in which the same impulses are still extant, even though they are suppressed. The antithesis with which the chorus departs—

> . . . Behold, this is Oedipus,
> Who unravelled the great riddle, and was first in power,
> Whose fortune all the townsmen praised and envied;
> See in what dread adversity he sank!

—this admonition touches us and our own pride, us who since the years of our childhood have grown so wise and so powerful in our own estimation. Like Oedipus, we live in ignorance of the desires that offend morality, the desires that nature has forced upon us, and after their unveiling we may well prefer to avert our gaze from the scenes of our childhood.[1]

In the very text of Sophocles' tragedy there is an unmistakable reference to the fact that the Oedipus legend had its source in dream-material of immemorial antiquity, the content of which was the painful disturbance of the child's relations to its parents caused by the first impulses of sexuality. Jocasta comforts Oedipus—who is not yet enlightened, but is troubled by the recollection of the oracle—by an allusion to a dream which is often dreamed, though it cannot, in her opinion, mean anything:

> For many a man hath seen himself in dreams
> His mother's mate, but he who gives no heed
> To suchlike matters bears the easier life.

The dream of having sexual intercourse with one's mother was as common then as it is today with many people, who tell it with indignation and astonishment. As may well be imagined, it is the key to the tragedy and the complement to the dream of the death of the father. The Oedipus fable is the reaction of fantasy to these two typical dreams, and just as such a dream, when occurring to an adult, is experienced with feelings of aversion, so the content of the fable must include terror and self-chastisement. The form which it subsequently assumed was the result of an uncomprehending secondary elaboration of the material, which sought to make it serve a theological intention.[2] The attempt to reconcile divine omnipotence with human responsibility must, of course, fail with this material as with any other.

Another of the great poetic tragedies, Shakespeare's *Hamlet*, is rooted in the same soil as *Oedipus Rex*. But the whole difference is the psychic life of the two widely separated periods of civilization, and the progress during the course of time, of repression in the emotional life of humanity, is manifested in the differing treatment of the same material. In *Oedipus Rex* the basic wish fantasy of the child is brought to life and realized as it is in dreams; in *Hamlet* it remains repressed, and we learn of its existence—as we discover the relevant facts in a neurosis—only through the inhibitory effects which proceed from it. In the more modern drama, the curious fact that it is possible to remain in complete uncertainty as to the character of the hero has proved to be quite consistent with the overpowering effect of the tragedy. The play is based upon Hamlet's hesitation in accomplishing the task of revenge assigned to him; the text does not give the cause or the motive of this hesitation, nor have the manifold attempts at interpretation succeeded in doing so. According to the still prevailing conception, a conception for which Goethe was first responsible, Hamlet represents the type of man whose active energy is paralyzed by excessive intellectual activity: "Sicklied o'er with the pale cast of thought." According to another conception, the poet has endeavored to portray a morbid, irresolute character, on the verge of neurasthenia. The plot of the drama, however, shows us that Hamlet is by no means intended to appear as a character wholly incapable of action. On two separate occasions we see him assert himself: once in a sudden outburst of rage, when he stabs the eavesdropper behind the arras, and on the other occasion when he deliberately, and even craftily, with the complete unscrupulousness of a prince of the Renaissance, sends the two courtiers to the death which was intended for himself. What is it, then, that inhibits him in accomplishing the task which his father's ghost has laid upon him? Here the explanation offers itself that it is the peculiar nature of this task. Hamlet is able to do anything but take vengeance upon the man who did away with his father and has taken his father's place with his mother—the man who shows him in realization the repressed desires of his own childhood. The loathing which should have driven him to revenge is thus replaced by self-reproach, by conscientious scruples, which tell him that he himself is no better than the murderer whom he is required to punish. I have here translated into consciousness what had to remain unconscious in the mind of the hero; if anyone wishes to call Hamlet a hysterical subject I cannot but admit that this is the deduction to be drawn from my interpretation. The sexual aversion which Hamlet expresses in conversation with Ophelia is perfectly consistent with this deduction—the same sexual aversion which during the next few years was increasingly to take possession of the poet's soul, until it found its supreme utterance in *Timon of Athens*. It can, of course, be only the poet's own psychology with which we are confronted in *Hamlet*; and in a work on Shakespeare by Georg Brandes (1896) I find the statement that the drama was composed immediately after the death of Shakespeare's father (1601)—that is to say, when he was still mourning his loss, and during a revival, as we may fairly assume, of his own childish feelings in respect of his father. It is known, too, that Shakespeare's son, who died in childhood, bore the name of Hamnet (identical with Hamlet). Just as *Hamlet* treats of the relation of the son to his parents, so *Macbeth*, which was written about the same period, is based upon the theme of childlessness. Just as all neurotic symptoms, like dreams themselves, are capable of hyper-interpretation, and even require such hyper-interpretation before they become perfectly intelligible, so every genuine poetical creation must have proceeded from more than one motive, more than one impulse in the mind of the poet, and must admit of more than one interpretation. I have here attempted to interpret only the deepest stratum of impulses in the mind of the creative poet.

Notes

1. None of the discoveries of psychoanalytical research has evoked such embittered contradiction, such furious opposition, and also such entertaining acrobatics of criticism, as this indication of the incestuous impulses of childhood which survive in the unconscious. An attempt has even been made recently, in defiance of all experience, to assign only a "symbolic" significance to incest. Ferenczi has given an ingenious reinterpretation of the Oedipus myth, based on a

passage in one of Schopenhauer's letters in *Imago*, vol. 1, 1912. The "Oedipus complex," which was first alluded to here in *The Interpretation of Dreams*, has through further study of the subject acquired an unexpected significance for the understanding of human history and the evolution of religion and morality. See *Totem and Taboo*.

2. See the dream-material of exhibitionism, *Basic Writings*, pp. 294–95.

3.

The Death of
Hamlet's Father

Ernest Jones

WHEN A POET takes an old theme from which to create a work of art it is always interesting, and often instructive, to note the respects in which he changes elements in the story. Much of what we glean of Shakespeare's personality is derived from such studies, the direct biographical details being so sparse. The difference in the accounts given in *Hamlet* of the way the King had died from that given in the original story is so striking that it would seem worthwhile to look closer at the matter.

The most obvious difference is that in the Saxo-Belleforest saga the murder is a public one, with Shakespeare a secret one. We do not know, however, who made this change, since an English play called *Hamlet*, thought to be written by Kyd, was extant some twelve years before Shakespeare wrote his; and he doubtless used it as well as the Belleforest version. That play no longer exists except in a much later and much distorted German version, but a Ghost probably appeared in it, and one can hardly imagine any other function for him than to disclose a secret murder. There is reason to suppose that Shakespeare may himself have had a hand in the Kyd play, but at all events he made the best possible use of the alteration.

From Ernest Jones, "The Death of Hamlet's Father," *International Journal of Psycho-Analysis* (1948), 29:174–76. Copyright 1948 by Ernest Jones. Reprinted by permission.

In the old saga Claudius (there called Feng) draws his sword on his brother the King (Horvendil)[1] at a banquet and slays him "with many wounds." He explains to the assembled nobles that he has done this to protect his sister-in-law (Geruth) from ill-treatment and imminent peril of her life at the hands of her husband—a pretext evidently a reflection of the infant's sadistic conception of coitus. Incidentally, in the Saxo saga (though not with Belleforest), there had here been no previous adultery with the Queen, so that Feng is the sole villain, and Amleth, unlike Hamlet, unhesitatingly kills him and reigns in his stead as soon as he can overcome the external obstacles. In *Hamlet*, as is well known, the plot is intensified by the previous incestuous adultery of the Queen, which convulses Hamlet at least as much as his father's murder and results in an animus against women that complicates his previously simple task.

In the *Hamlet* play, on the other hand, Claudius disclaims all responsibility for his brother's death and spreads a somewhat improbable story of his having been stung to death by a serpent while sleeping in an orchard. How he knew this we are not told, nor why the adder possessed this quite unwonted deadliness. There is much to be said about that "orchard," but we may assume that it symbolizes the woman in whose arms the King was murdered. The Ghost's version was quite different. According to him, Claudius had found him asleep and poured a juice of hebana into his ears, a still more improbable story from a medical point of view; he further tells us that the poison rapidly spread through his system resulting in "all his smooth body being barked about most lazarlike with vile and loathsome crust." Presumably its swift action prevented him from informing anyone of what had befallen him.

The source of this mysterious poison has been traced as follows.[2] Shakespeare seems to have taken the name, incidentally misspelling it, from the juice of "hebon," mentioned in a play of Marlowe's, who himself had added an initial letter to the "ebon" (ebony) of which the walls of the God of Sleep were composed (Ovid). Shakespeare apparently went on to confound this narcotic with henbane (hyoscyamus), which at that time was believed to cause mortification and turn the body black.[3] Two interesting beliefs connecting henbane with the ear are mentioned by Pliny: (1) that it is a remedy for earache, and (2) when poured into the ear it causes mental disorder.

The coarse Northern butchery is thus replaced by a surreptitious Italianate form of murder, a fact that has led to many inquiries, which do not concern us here, concerning Italian influence on Shakespeare. The identical method is employed in the Play Scene, where a nephew murders his uncle, who was resting after coitus, by dropping poison into his ear and immediately afterwards espouses the widow à la Richard III. Hamlet says he got the Gonzago story from an Italian play, but no such play has yet been traced. But there had been two instances of murder in an unhappy Gonzaga family. In 1538 a famous Duke of Urbino, who was married to a Gonzaga, died under somewhat suspicious circumstances. Poison was suspected, and his barber was believed to have poured a lotion into his ears on a number of occasions. So the story goes: whether poison thus administered is lethal to anyone with intact tympani is a matter we must leave to the toxicologists. At all events the Duke's son got the unfortunate barber torn in pieces by pincers and then quartered. In the course of this proceeding the barber asserted he had been put on to commit the foul deed by a Luigi Gonzaga,[4] a relative of the Duke's by marriage. For political and legal reasons, however, Luigi was never brought to trial.[5] Furthermore, in 1592 the Marchese Rudolf von Castiglione got eight bravos to murder his uncle the Marchese Alfonso Gonzaga, a relative of the Duke of Mantua. Rudolf had wished to marry his uncle's daughter and had been refused; he himself was murdered eight months later.

The names used make it evident that Shakespeare was familiar with the story of the earlier Gonzaga murder, as he possibly was with the later one too. The "poison in the ear" story must have appealed to him, since he not only used it in the Gonzago Play Scene—where it would be appropriate—but also in the account of Hamlet's father's death.

If we translate them into the language of symbolism the Ghost's story is not so dissimilar from that of Claudius. To the unconscious, "poison" signifies any bodily fluid charged with evil intent, while the serpent has played a well-known role ever since the Garden of Eden. The murderous assault had therefore both aggressive and erotic components, and we note that it was Shakespeare who introduced the latter (serpent). Furthermore, that the ear is an unconscious equivalent for anus is a matter for which I have adduced ample evidence elsewhere.[6] So we must call Claudius' attack on his brother both a murderous aggression and a homosexual assault.

Why did Shakespeare give this curious turn to a plain story of envious ambition? The theme of homosexuality itself does not surprise us in Shakespeare. In a more or less veiled form a pronounced feminity and a readiness to interchange the sexes are prominent characteristics of his plays, and doubtless of his personality also. I have argued that Shakespeare wrote *Hamlet* as a more or less successful abreaction of the intolerable emotions aroused by the painful situation he depicts in his Sonnets, his betrayal by both his beloved young noble and his mistress.[7] In life he apparently smothered his resentment and became reconciled to both betrayers. Artistically his response was privately to write the Sonnets (in the later publication of which he had no hand) and publicly to compose *Hamlet* not long afterwards, a play gory enough to satisfy all varieties of revenge.

The episode raises again the vexed question of the relation between active and passive homosexuality. Nonanalysts who write on this topic are apt to maintain that they represent two different inborn types, but this assertion gives one an unsatisfied feeling of improbability, and analytic investigation confirms these doubts by demonstrating numerous points of contact between the two attitudes. Certainly Claudius' assault was active enough; sexually it signified turning the victim into a female, i.e., castrating him. Hamlet himself, as Freud pointed out long ago,[8] was unconsciously identified with Claudius, which was the reason why he was unable to denounce and kill him. So the younger brother attacking the older is simply a replica of the son-father conflict, and the complicated poisoning story really represents the idea of the son castrating his father. But we must not forget that it is done in an erotic fashion. Now Hamlet's conscious attitude toward his father was a feminine one, as shown by his exaggerated adoration and his adjuring Gertrude to love such a perfect hero instead of his brother. In Freud's opinion homosexuality takes its origin in narcissism,[9] so that it is always a mirror-love; Hamlet's father would therefore be his own idea of himself. That is why, in such cases, as with Hamlet, suicide is so close to murder.

My analytic experience, simplified for the present purpose, impels me to the following reconstruction of homosexual development. Together with the narcissism a feminine attitude toward the father presents itself as an attempted solution of the intolerable murderous and castrating impulses aroused by jealousy. These may persist, but when the fear of the self-castration implied gains the upper hand, i.e., when the masculine impulse is strong, the original aggression reasserts itself—but this time under the erotic guise of active homosexuality.

According to Freud, Hamlet was inhibited ultimately by his repressed hatred of his father. We have to add to this the homosexual aspect of his attitude, so that Love and Hate, as so often, both play their part.

Notes

1. It was Shakespeare who changed his name to Hamlet, thus emphasizing the identification of son and father.

2. See Henry Bradley, *Modern Language Review* (1920), 15:85.

3. W. Thiselton-Dyer, *Shakespeare's England*, 1:509.

4. From whom Shakespeare perhaps got the name Lucianus for the murderer in the Play Scene.

5. See G. Bullough, "The Murder of Gonzago," *Modern Language Review* (1935), 30:433.

6. Ernest Jones, *Essays in Applied Psycho-Analysis* (London: Hogarth Press, 1923), pp. 341–46.

7. Ernest Jones, *Hamlet and Oedipus* (New York: Norton, 1949).

8. Sigmund Freud, *Die Traumdeutung* (*The Interpretation of Dreams*) (1901), p. 183.

9. *Collected Papers* 2:241.

4.

Life and Creation

Otto Rank

What would live in song immortally
Must in life first perish. . . .
   —Schiller

BEFORE WE TRACE the rise and significance of this "artist's art," if one may so call it, as it grows out of the primitive art ideologies, it is perhaps desirable to characterize more clearly its essential precondition: namely, the creative personality itself. In spite of all "unconsciousness" in artistic production (a point to which we shall return later), there can be no doubt that the modern individualist type of artist is characterized by a higher degree of consciousness than his earlier prototype: the consciousness not only of his creative work and his artist's mission, but also of his own personality and its productiveness. If, as it should seem, the instinctive will-to-art (Riegl), which creates abstract forms, has in this last stage of artistic development become a conscious will-to-art in the artist, yet the actual process which leads a man to become an artist is usually one of which the individual is not conscious. In other words, the act which we have described as the artist's self-appointment as such is in itself a spontaneous expression of the creative impulse, of which the first manifestation is simply the forming of the personality itself. Needless to say, this purely internal process does not suffice to make an artist, let alone a genius, for, as Lange-Eichbaum has said, only the community, one's contemporaries, or posterity can do that. Yet the self-labeling and self-training of an artist is the indispensable basis of all creative work, and without it general recognition could never arise. The artist's lifelong work on his own productive personality appears to run through definite phases, and his art develops in proportion to the success of these phases. In the case of great artists the process is reflected in the fact that they had either a principal or a favorite work, at which they labored all their lives. (Goethe's *Faust*, Rodin's *Porte d'enfer*, Michelangelo's Tomb of Julius, and so on), or a favorite theme, which they never relinquished and which came to be a distinct representation of themselves (as, for example, Rembrandt's self-portraits).

On the other hand, this process of the artist's self-forming and self-training is closely bound up with his life and his experiences. In studying this fundamental problem of the relation between living and creating in an artist, we are therefore again aware of the reciprocal influence of these two spheres. All the psychography and pathography (with its primary concern to explain the one through the other) must remain unsatisfactory as long as the creative impulse, which finds expression equally in experience and in productiveness, is not recognized as the basis of both. For, as I already showed in my essay on Schiller (written in 1905), creativeness lies equally at the root of artistic production and of life experience.[1] That is to say, lived experience can only be understood as the expression of volitional creative impulse, and in this the two spheres of artistic production and actual experience meet and overlap. Then, too, the creative impulse itself is manifested first and chiefly in the personality, which, being thus perpetually made over, produces artwork and experience in the same way. To draw the distinction quite drastically between this new standpoint and earlier ones, one might put it that the artist does not create from his own experience (as Goethe, for instance, so definitely appears to do), but almost in spite of it. For the creative impulse in the artist, springing from the tendency to immortalize himself, is so powerful that he is always seeking to protect himself against the transient experience, which eats up his ego. The artist takes refuge, with all *his own* experience only from the life of *actuality*, which for him spells mortality and decay, whereas the experience to which he has given shape imposes itself on him as a creation, which he in fact seeks to turn into a work. And although the whole artist psychology may seem to be centered on the "experience," this itself can be explained only through the creative impulse—which attempts to turn ephemeral life into personal immortality. In creation the artist tries to immortalize his mortal life. He desires to transform death into life, as it were, though actually he transforms life into death. For not only does the created work not go on living; it is, in a sense, dead; both as regards the material, which renders it almost inorganic, and also spiritually and psychologically, in that it no longer has any significance for its creator, once he has produced it. He therefore again takes refuge in life, and again forms experiences, which for their part represent only mortality—and it is precisely because they are mortal that he wishes to immortalize them in his work.

The first step toward understanding this mutual relation between life and work in the artist is to gain a clear idea of the psychological significance of the two phenomena. This is only possible, however, on the basis of a constructive psychology of personality, reaching beyond the psychoanalytical conception, which is a therapeutic ideology resting on the biological sex impulse. We have come to see that another factor must be reckoned with besides the original biological duality of impulse and inhibition in man; this is the psychological factor par excellence, the individual will, which manifests itself both negatively as a controlling element, and positively as the urge to create. This creator impulse is not, therefore, sexuality, as Freud assumed, but expresses the antisexual tendency in human beings, which we may describe as the deliberate control of the impulsive life. To put it more precisely, I see the creator impulse as the life impulse made to serve the individual will. When psychoanalysis speaks of a sublimated sexual impulse in creative art, meaning thereby the impulse diverted from its purely biological function and directed toward higher ends, the question as to what diverted and what directed is just being dismissed with an allusion to repression. But repression is a negative factor, which might divert, but never direct. And so the further question remains to be answered: what, originally led to such repression? As we know, the answer to this question was outward deprivation; but that again suggests a merely negative check, and I, for my part, am of the opinion that (at any rate from a certain definite point of individual development) positively willed control takes the place of negative inhibition, and that it is the masterful use of the sexual impulse in the service of this individual will which produces the sublimation.

But even more important for us than these psychological distinctions is the basic problem of why this inhibition occurs at all, and what the deliberate control of the vital impulse means to the individual. Here, again, in opposition to the Freudian conception of an external threat as the cause of the inhibition, I suggest that the internal threatening of the individual through the sexual impulse of the species is at the root of all conflict. Side by side with this self-imposed internal check, which is taken to be what prevents or lessens the development of fear, there stands the will as a positive factor. The various controls which it exercises enable the impulses to work themselves out partially without the individual's falling completely under their influence or having to check them completely by too drastic repression. Thus in the fully developed individual we have to reckon with the triad Impulse-Fear-Will, and it is the dynamic relationship among these factors that determines either the attitude at a given moment or—when equilibrium is established—the type. Unsatisfactory as it may be to express these dynamic processes in terms like "type," it remains the only method of carrying an intelligible idea of them—always assuming that the inevitable simplification in this is not lost sight of. If we compare the neurotic with the productive type, it is evident that the former suffers from an excessive check on his impulsive life, and, according to whether this neurotic checking of the instincts is effected through fear or through will, the picture presented is one of fear-neurosis or compulsion-neurosis. With the productive type the will dominates, and exercises a far-reaching control over (but not check upon) the instincts, which are pressed into service to bring about creatively a social relief of fear. Finally, the instincts appear relatively unchecked in the so-called psychopathic subject, in whom the will affirms the impulse instead of controlling it. In this type—to which the criminal belongs— we have, contrary to appearances, to do with *weak*-willed people, people who are subjected to their instinctive impulses; the neurotic, on the other hand, is generally regarded as the weak-willed type, but wrongly so, for his strong will is exercised upon himself and, indeed, in the main repressively so it does not show itself.

And here we reach the essential point of difference between the productive type who creates and the thwarted neurotic; what is more, it is also the point from which we get back to our individual artist type. Both are distinguished fundamentally from the average type, who accepts himself as he is, by their tendency to exercise their volition in reshaping themselves. There is, however, this difference: that the neurotic, in this voluntary remaking of his ego, does not get beyond the destructive preliminary work and is therefore unable to detach the whole creative process from his own person and transfer it to an ideological abstraction. The productive artist also begins (as a satisfactory psychological understanding of the "will-to-style" has obliged us to conclude) with that recreation of himself which results in an ideologically constructed ego; this ego is then in a position to shift the creative will power from his own person to ideological representations of that person and thus to render it objective. It must be admitted that this process is in a measure limited to within the individual himself, and that not only in its constructive, but also in its destructive, aspects. This explains why hardly any productive work[2] gets through without morbid crises of a "neurotic" nature; it also explains why the relation between productivity and illness has so far been unrecognized or misinterpreted, as, for instance, in Lombroso's theory of the insanity of genius. Today this theory appears to us as the precipitate left by the old endeavors to explain genius on rational psychological lines, which treated such features as depart from the normal as "pathological." However much in the Italian psychiatrist's theory is an exaggeration of the materialism of nineteenth-century science, yet undeniably it had a startling success, and this I attribute to the fact that genius itself, in its endeavor to differentiate itself from the average, has probably dramatized its pathological features also. But the psychologist should beware of deducing from this apparent factor any conclusions as to the production or total personality, without taking into account the feeling of guilt arising from the creative process itself; for this is capable of engendering a feeling of inferiority as a secondary result, even though the primary result may be a conviction of superiority. As I have said elsewhere, the fundamental problem is *individual difference*, which the ego is inclined to interpret as inferiority unless it can be proved by achievement to be superiority.

Even psychoanalysis in its turn did not succeed in surmounting Lombroso's materialist theory of insanity or supplementing his rational explanation by a spiritual one. All it did was to substitute neurosis for insanity (which was at bottom Lombroso's own meaning), thus tending either to identify the artist with the neurotic—this is particularly the case in Sadger's and Stekel's arguments—or to explain the artist on the basis of an inferiority feeling. (Alfred Adler and his school took the latter view.)[3] It is characteristic that during the last few years the psychiatrists (such as Lange-Eichbaum, Kretschmer, Plaut) who have contributed most toward clearing up the position of genius are precisely those who have managed to keep clear of the one-sidedness of these psychoanalytical schools. And if these researches have not made any important contribution to the understanding of the process of creating, psychoanalysis, even in its exaggerations, must at least be credited with having discovered that experience, in so far as it is the antithesis of production, embraces not only the relations of love and friendship, but also those morbid reactions of a psychic and bodily nature which are known as "neurotic." A real understanding of these neurotic illnesses could not, however, be satisfactorily obtained as long as we tried to account for them in the Freudian sense by thwarted sexuality. What was wanted in addition was a grasp of the general problem of fear and of the will psychology going therewith which should allow for the exercise of the will, both constructively and destructively, affecting the ego and the work equally. Only through the will-to-self-immortalization, which rises from the fear of life, can we understand the interdependence of production and suffering and the definite influence of this on positive experience. This does not preclude production being a creative development of a neurosis in objective form; and, on the other hand, a neurotic collapse may follow as a reaction after production, owing either to a sort of exhaustion or to a sense of guilt arising from the power of creative masterfulness as something arrogant.[4]

Reverting now from the production process to experience, it does not take long to perceive that experience is the expression of the impulse ego, production of the will ego. The external difficulties in an artist's experience appear, in this sense, but as manifestations of this internal dualism of impulse and will, and in the creative type it is the latter which eventually gains the upper hand. Instinct presses in the direction of experience and, in the limit, to consequent exhaustion—in fact, death— while will drives to creation and thus to immortalization. On the other hand, the productive type also pays toll to life by his work and to death by bodily and spiritual sufferings of a "neurotic" order; and conversely in many cases the product of a type that is at bottom neurotic may be his sole propitiatory offering to Life. It is with reason, therefore, that from the beginning two basic types of artist have been distinguished; these have been called at one time Dionysian and Apollonian, and at another Classical and Romantic.[5] In terms of our present dynamic treatment, the one approximates to the psychopathic-impulsive type, the other to the compulsion-neurotic volitional type. The one creates more from fullness of powers and sublimation, the other more from exhaustion and compensation. The work of the one is entire in every single expression, that of the other is partial even in its totality, for the one lives itself out, positively, in the work, while the other pays with the work—pays, not to society (for both do that), but to life itself, from which the one strives to win freedom by self-willed creation whereas for the other the thing created is the expression of life itself.

This duality within one and the same type is of outstanding significance in the psychology of the productive type and in the work it produces. For, while in the two classes of neurotics (frustrated by fear and by the will respectively) the form of the neurosis is of minor matter compared with the fact of breaking down the inhibition itself, by the curative process of dynamic equilibration, in the productive type the dynamism itself determines not only the kind but the form of his art. But this highly complicated problem is only mentioned here with a view to discussion later, and we will turn from the two artist types, which Müller-Freienfels, in his *Psychologie der Kunst* (2:100 ff.) characterizes as "expressive artists" and "formative artists," back to the problem of experience which is common to both. This problem, as was pointed out at the beginning of this chapter, only becomes intelligible through the conception of immortality. There appears to be a common impulse in all creative types to replace collective immortality—as it is represented biologically in sexual propagation—by the individual immortality of deliberate self-perpetuation. This is, however, a relatively late stage of development in the conception of immortality, after it has already become individualized—a stage preceded by attempts to create conceptions of collective immortality, of which the most important is religion. I have tried in another connection to show how, within religious development itself, the idea of the collective soul was gradually transformed into the idea of the individual god, whose heir the artist later became.[6] The initial conception of an individual god, subsequently to be humanized in the genius, had itself been helped on, and perhaps even only rendered possible, by art. But there was an early stage of artistic development, which was at the same time the climax of religious development, in which the individual artist played no part because creative power was still the prerogative of the god.

45

The individual artist, whose growth from the creative conception of a god has been sketched out, no longer uses the collective ideology of religion to perpetuate himself, but the personal religion of genius, which is the precondition of any productions by the individual artist type. And so we have *primitive art*, the expression of a collective ideology, perpetuated by abstraction which has found its *religious* expression in the idea of the soul; *Classical art*, based on a *social* art concept, perpetuated by *idealization*, which has found its purest expression in the conception of beauty; and, lastly, *modern art*, based on the concept of individual genius and perpetuated by *concretization*, which has found its clearest expression in the personality cult of the artistic individuality itself. Here, then, in contrast to the primitive stage, it is the artist and not art that matters, and naturally therefore the experience of the individual takes on the significance characteristic of the romantic artist type.[7] Here, obviously, not only do we see the tendency—in our view the basic tendency—of the artist type to put oneself and one's life into one's creative work; but we see also how, in the eyes of this type, the problem of the relation between experience and creation has become an artistic (aesthetic) one;[8] whereas it is really only a psychological one, which discloses, indeed, important points of contact with art (considered as an ideological conception), but differs from it in essence.

For the romantic dualism of life and production, which manifests itself as a mixture of both spheres, has, as a typical conflict within the modern individual, nothing to do with art, although obliged like art to express itself creatively. This romantic dualism of life and creation, which corresponds to our psychological dualism of impulse and will, is, in the last resort, the conflict between collective and individual immortality, in which we have all suffered so acutely since the decay of religion and the decline of art. The romantic type, flung hither and thither between the urge to perpetuate his own life by creating and compulsion to turn himself and life into a work of art, thus appears as the last representative of an art ideology which, like the religious collective ideology, is in process of dying out. This does not prevent this final attempt to rescue the semicollective "religion of genius" by taking it into modern individualism from bringing forth outstanding and permanently valuable works of art; perhaps, indeed (as Nietzsche himself, the ultra-Romantic, recognized), it requires that it should. On the other hand, it is just the appearance of this decadent type of artist which marks the beginning of a new development of personality, since the tendency to self-perpetuation is in the end transferred to the ego from which it originally sprang.

On this issue the romantic becomes identical, as a psychological type, with the neurotic—this is not a valuation, but merely a statement of fact—and for that matter the comparison may even be reversed, since the neurotic likewise has creative, or, at least, self-creative, forces at command. We can thus understand the experience problem of the individualist type of artist also only by studying the nature of neurosis, just as the therapy of the neurotic requires an understanding of the creative type.[9] Now, the neurotic represents the individual who aims at self-preservation by restricting his experience, thus showing his adherence to the naïve faith in immortality of the primitive, though without the collective soul ideology which supports that faith. The productivity of the individual, or of the thing created, replaces—for the artist as for the community—the originally religious ideology by a social value; that is, the work of art not only immortalizes the artist ideologically instead of personally, but also secures to the community a future life in the collective elements of the work. Even at this last stage of individual art creativity there function ideologies (whether given or chosen) of an esthetic, a social, or a psychological nature as collective justifications of the artist's art, in which the personal factor makes itself more and more felt and appreciated.

If the impulse to create productively is explicable only by the conception of immortality, the question of the experience problem of the neurotic has its source in failure of the impulse to perpetuate, which results in fear, but is also probably conditioned by it. There is (as I have shown) a double sort of fear: on the one hand the fear of life which aims at avoidance or postponement of death, and on the other the fear of death which underlies the desire for immortality. According to the compromise which men make between these two poles of fear, and the predominance of one or the other form, there will be various dynamic solutions of this conflict, which hardly permit of description by type labeling. For in practice, both in the neurotic and in the productive type—the freely producing and the thwarted—all the forces are brought into play, though with varying accentuation and periodical balancing of values. In general, a strong preponderance of the fear of life will lead rather to neurotic repression, and the fear of death to production—that is, perpetuation in the work produced. But the fear of life, from which we all

47

suffer, conditions the problem of experience in the productive type as in other people, just as the fear of death whips up the neurotic's constructive powers. The individual whose life is braked is led thereby to flee from experience, because he fears that he will become completely absorbed in it—which would mean death—and so is bound up with fear. Unlike the productive type, who strives to be deathless through his work, the neurotic does not seek immortality in any clearly defined sense, but in primitive fashion as a naïve saving or accumulation of actual life. But even the individualist artist type must sacrifice both life and experience to make art out of them. Thus we see that what the artist needs for true creative art in addition to his technique and a definite ideology is life in one form or another; and the two artist types differ essentially in the source from which they take this life that is so essential to production. The Classical type, who is possibly poorer within, but nearer to life, and himself more vital, takes it from without: that is, he creates immortal work from mortal life without necessarily having first transformed it into personal experience as is the case with the Romantic. For, to the Romantic, experience of his own appears to be an essential preliminary to productivity, although he does not use this experience for the enrichment of his own personality, but to economize the personal experiences, the burden of which he would fain escape. Thus the one artist type constantly makes use of life other than his own—in fact, nature—for the purpose of creating, while the other can create only by perpetually sacrificing his own life. This essential difference of attitude to the fundamental problem of life throws a psychological light on the contrast in styles of various periods in art. Whatever esthetic designation may be applied to this contrast, from the spiritual point of view the work of the Classicist, more or less naturalistic, artist is essentially *partial*, the work of the Romantic, produced from within, *total*.[10] This totality type spends itself perpetually in creative work without absorbing very much of life, while the partial type has continually to absorb life so that he may throw it off again in his work. It is an egoistical artist type of this order that Ibsen has described in so masterly a fashion. He needs, as it were, for each work that he builds, a sacrifice which is buried alive to ensure a permanent existence to the structure, but also to save the artist from having to give himself. The frequent occasions when a great work of art has been created in the reaction following upon the death of a close relation seem to me to realize those favorable cases for this type of artist in which he can dispense with the killing of the building's victim because that victim has died a natural death and has subsequently, to all appearances, had a monument piously erected to him.[11]

The mistake in all modern psychological biography lies in its attempt to "explain" the artist's work by his experience, whereas creation can be made understandable only through the inner dynamism and its central problems. Then, too, the real artist regards his work as more important than the whole of life and experience, which are but a means to production—almost, indeed, a byproduct of it. This refers, however, to the Classical type only, for to the Romantic type his personal ego and his experience are more important than, or as important as, his work; sometimes, indeed, production may be simply a means to life, just as to the other type experience is but a means to production. This is why Romantic art is far more subjective, far more closely bound up with experience, than Classical, which is more objective and linked to life. In no case, however, will the individual become an artist through any *one* experience, least of all through the experiences of childhood (which seem pretty universal). The becoming of the artist has a particular genesis, one of the manifestations of which may be some special experience. For the artistic impulse to create is a dynamic factor apart from the content of experience, a will problem which the artist solves in a particular way. That is, he is capable of forming the given art ideology—whether of the collective kind (style) or the personal (genius idea)—into the substance of his creative will. He employs, so to say, personal will power to give form or life to an ideology, which must have not only social qualities like other ideologies, but purely artistic ones, which will be more closely specified from the point of view of esthetics.

The subjective character of modern art, which is based on the ideology of a personal type of artist, imposes also a special outlook in the artist toward his own creative power and his work. The more production is an essential means to life (and not just a particular ideological expression of it), the more will the work itself be required to justify the personality—instead of expressing it—and the more will this subjective artist type need individuals to justify his production. From this point of view as well as others it is easy to see that experience, in its particular form of love experience, takes on a peculiar significance for the Romantic artist, whose art is based on the personality cult of the genius concept. The primitive artist type finds his justification in the work itself; the

49

Classical justifies the work by his life, but the Romantic must justify both life and experience by his work and, further, must have a witness of his life to justify his production. The fundamental problem of the Romantic artist is thus the self-justification of the individual raised above the crowd, while the Classical artist type expresses himself in his work—which receives a social justification by way of general recognition. But the Romantic needs, further, whether as contrast or as supplement to this social approval, a personal approbation of his own, because his feeling of the guilt of creation can no longer be allayed by a collective ideology any more than he can work effectively in the service of such an ideology. In this sense his artistic work is rather a forcible liberation from inward pressure than the voluntary expression of a fundamentally strong personality that is capable of paralyzing the subjective element to a great extent by making collective symbolism his own. The artist who approximates more nearly to the Classical type excels less, therefore, in the creating of new forms than in perfecting them. Further, he will make much more frequent use of old traditional material, full of a powerful collective resonance, as the content of his work, while the Romantic seeks new forms and contents in order to be able to express his personal self more completely.

Thus, as the artist type becomes more and more individualized, he appears on the one hand to need a more individual ideology—the genius concept—for his art, while on the other his work is more subjective and more personal, until finally he requires for the justification of his production an individual "public" also: a single person for whom ostensibly he creates. This goes so far in a certain type of artist, which we call the Romantic, that actual production is possible only with the aid of a concrete Muse through whom or for whom the work is produced. The "experience" which arises in this manner is not, like other sorts of experience, an external phenomenon set over against creative work, but is a part of it and even identical with it, always providing that the Muse—in practice, usually a real woman—is suited to this role or at least makes no objection to it, and so long as the artist can maintain such a relation on the ideological plane without confusing it with real life. It is this case, in which the conflict between life and creation reaches extreme intensity, that we so often see actualized in the modern type of artist. Here the woman is expected to be Muse and mistress at once, which means that she must justify equally the artistic ego, with its creativeness, and the real self, with its life; and this she seldom (and in any case only temporarily) succeeds in doing. We see the artist of this type working off on the woman his inward struggle between life and production or, psychologically speaking, between impulse and will. It is a tragic fate that he shares with the neurotic, who suffers from the same inner conflict. Another way out of the struggle is to divide its elements between two persons, of whom one belongs to the ideological creative sphere, and the other to the sphere of actual life. But this solution also presents difficulties of a psychological as well as a social order, because this type of artist has a fundamental craving for totality, in life as in work, and the inner conflict, though it may be temporarily eased by being objectivized in such an outward division of roles, is as a whole only intensified thereby.

The same applies to another solution of this ego conflict which the artist has in common with the neurotic, and one which shows more clearly even than the complicated love conflict that it is at bottom a question not of sexual but of creative problems. From the study of a certain class of neurotic we have found that in many cases of apparent homosexual conflicts it is less a sexual perversion than an ego problem that underlies them, a problem with which the individual can only deal by personifying a portion of his own ego in another individual. The same applies, it is true, to heterosexual love relations, from which the homosexual differs only in that the selfward part of this relation is stronger, or at any rate more distinct. If the poet values his Muse the more highly in proportion as it can be identified with his artistic personality and its ideology, then self-evidently he will find his truest ideal in an even greater degree in his own sex, which is in any case physically and intellectually closer to him. Paradoxical as it may sound, the apparently homosexual tendencies or actual relationships of certain artists fulfill the craving for a Muse which will stimulate and justify creative work in a higher degree than (for a man) a woman can do. It is only as the result of the artist's urge for completion, and his desire to find everything united in one person, that it is mostly a woman that is taken as, or made into, a Muse, although instances of homosexual relations between artists are by no means rare.

In the life of many an artist the relation to woman is a disturbing factor, one of the deepest sources of conflict, indeed, when it tends to force or beguile him into closer touch with life than is necessary or even advantageous to his production. To make a woman his Muse, or to name her as such, therefore, often amounts to transforming a hindrance into a helper—a compromise which is usually in the interest of productiveness, but renders no service to life. Here, again, everything naturally depends on the artist's dynamic type and his specific conflict over life and production. There are artists for whom even a feminine Muse represents nothing but a potential homosexual relation; for they see in her not so much the woman as a comrade of like outlook and like aims, who could equally well—and possibly better—be replaced by a male friendship. On the other hand, there is an artist type which is totally unable to produce at all without the biological complement of the other sex and indeed depends directly on the sexual life for its stimulus. For the type which is creative in and by means of sexual abstinence has its opposite in another type which, strange to say, is not only not exhausted by the sexual act but is definitely stimulated to create thereby. Schulte-Vaerting has described this type as the "sexual superman," but it seems to me rather that here too some hidden mechanism of fleeing from life is involved, which impels the artist from biological mortality to individual immortality in production after he has paid his tribute to sexuality.

This leads us to the profoundest source of the artistic impulse to create, which I can only satisfactorily explain to myself as the struggle of the individual against an inherent striving after totality, which forces him equally in the direction of a complete surrender to life and a complete giving of himself in production. He has to save himself from this totality by fleeing, now from the Scylla of life, now from the Charybdis of creation, and his escape is naturally accomplished only at the cost of continual conflict, both between these two spheres and within each of them separately. How this conflict and the triumph over it is manifested in creative working I seek to show elsewhere. For the moment we are dealing only with manifestations and attempted solutions within the sphere of life, irrespective of whether these are concerned with persons of the same or of the opposite sex. In every case the artist's relation to woman has more of an ideological than of a sexual significance, as Emil Lenk has demonstrated in a study on creative personalities (*Das Liebesleben des Genies*, 1926). Usually, however, he needs two women, or several, for the different parts of his conflict, and accordingly he falls into psychological dilemmas, even if he evades the social difficulties. He undoubtedly loves both these persons in different ways, but is usually not clear as to the part they play, even if—as would appear to be the rule—

he does not actually confuse them one with the other. Because the Muse means more to him artistically, he thinks he loves her the more. This is seldom the case in fact, and moreover it is psychologically impossible. For the other woman, whom, from purely human or other motives, he perhaps loves more, he often enough cannot set up as his Muse for this very reason: that she would thereby become in a sense defeminized and, as it were, made into an object (in the egocentric sense) of friendship. To the Muse for whom he creates (or thinks he creates), the artist seldom gives himself; he pays with his work, and this the truly womanly woman often refuses to accept. But if his relation takes a homosexual form, this giving is still more obviously a giving to himself; that is, the artistic form of giving through production instead of surrendering the personal ego.

True, from the standpoint of the ego, the homosexual relation is an idealizing of oneself in the person of another, but at the same time it is felt as a humiliation; and this is not so much the cause as the actual expression of internal conflicts. For, in the dynamism which leads him to create, the artist suffers from a struggle between his higher and his lower self which manifests itself equally in all the spheres and utterances of his life and also characterizes his attitude to woman. She can be for him at once the symbol of the highest and the lowest, of the mortal and the immortal soul, of life or of death. The same applies too, as we shall see, to the work itself or to creation, for which the artist is prepared to sacrifice everything, but which, in the hour of disappointment and dejection, he frequently damns and curses. There is in the artist that fundamental dualism from which we all suffer, intensified in him to a point which drives him with dynamic compulsion from creative work to life, and from life back to new and other creativity. According to the artist's personal structure and spiritual ideology, this conflict will take the form of a struggle between good and evil, beauty and truth, or, in a more neurotic way, between the higher and the lower self. It is a struggle which, as we shall presently see, determines the cultural genetic start and development of the creative instinct itself. In the personal conflicts of the individual artist the fundamental dualism which originally led to cultural development and artistic creation persists in all its old strength. It cannot, however, be reconstructed and understood as a matter of individual psychology from an analysis of the artist's personal past, because the modern individual not only comes into the world with human-

53

ity's fundamental dualism, but is also potentially charged with all the attempts to solve it, so that his personal development no longer provides any parallels with the development of the race.

Notes

1. *Das Inzest-Motiv in Dichtung und Sage* (chs. 3, 16). I found the same conception later in Simmel's *Goethe*.
2. This applies not only to most artists, but also, as Wilhelm Ostwald for one has convincingly proved, to the scientific creative type (*Grosse Männer*).
3. A characteristic instance of how, in avoiding the Scylla of Lombroso, one may fall victim to the Charybdis of analytical psychology is afforded by Victor Jonesco's book, *La Personnalité du génie artiste*, which I read only after the completion of my work. A praiseworthy exception is Bernard Grasset's original essay, *Psychologie de l'immortalité*.
4. How this feeling of guilt can hinder or, on the other hand, further productivity I have shown in my book *Wahrheit und Wirklichkeit* (1929) [*Truth and Reality: A Life History of the Human Will* (New York: Knopf, 1936)] in the section on the sense of guilt in creation.
5. E. von Sydow distinguished these polar opposites, from the standpoint of esthetic, as "eros-dominated" and "eros-dominating."
6. See *Seelenglaube und Psychologie* (1930) [*Psychology and the Soul* (New York: A. S. Barnes, 1961.)]
7. What interests us today in Byron, for instance, is his romantic life, and not his out-of-date poetry.
8. See W. Dilthey's book, *Erlebnis und Dichtung*. The artist personalities examined there in relation to this problem are, as is natural, chiefly romantic types (Lessing, Goethe, Novalis, Hölderlin).
9. This is a point of view which I endeavored to present in my last technical work: *Die Analyse des Analytikers und seine Rolle in der Gesamtsituation* (1931).
10. These types, evolved from a study of psychological dynamics (see my *Die Analyse des Analytikers*), are, as I have since discovered, accepted as the essential key concepts of all polar contrasts of style by P. Frankl in his *Entwicklungsphasen der neuren Baukunst*. True, Frankl's work is not limited merely to architecture, but more narrowly still to the contrast in style between Renaissance and Baroque. We shall presently see, however ("*Schönheit und Wahrheit*"), that this contrast between totality and partiality is a general spiritual distinction between the Classical-naturalistic and the primitive-abstract styles.
11. Shakespeare's *Hamlet* and Mozart's *Don Juan* are familiar examples of the reaction after a father's death, while Wagner's *Lohengrin* followed on the death of the composer's mother. These works are supreme examples of artists negotiating with the problem of the Beyond. To these instances may be added Ibsen's epilogue *When We Dead Awaken*; here the death is that of the artist himself.

5.

Psychic Trauma and Productive Experience in the Artist

Henry Lowenfeld, M.D.

THE FOLLOWING IS based on the analysis of a woman artist in the course of whose treatment some light was thrown on a process of artistic development that is characteristic of at least one type of artist.

A woman of thirty sought treatment for increasingly serious states of anxiety and various physical complaints and inhibitions in her work over a period of several years. She felt herself a failure, unable to complete anything she undertook. For years her leading symptom had been hypochondriacal ideas. She believed herself to be suffering from chronic, fatal diseases such as tuberculosis of the throat, arteriosclerosis, or tumor of the brain. Behind these hypochondriacal fears were partly concealed paranoid ideas.

She was a very vivacious, intelligent woman of fine appearance with a somewhat unfriendly facial expression. Her manner was partly insecure and shy, partly aggressive. She was preoccupied with her body and much of her time was spent in all sorts of activities revolving about her appearance and health. She was inclined to favor mannish, sport clothes.

She both drew and painted. In her early career she had drawn much

From *Psychoanalytic Quarterly* (1941), 10:116–30. Copyright 1941 *Psychoanalytic Quarterly*. Reprinted by permission.

from nude models, especially women; then for several years she painted pictures which grew out of dreamlike visions and had a fantastic, mysterious quality. At the age of about twenty-two, she gave up this type of work for commercial art. She was gifted and original, had a strong imagination, but was hindered in her work by a technical inadequacy resulting from her inability to devote herself to consistent study, a situation of which she was painfully conscious. Difficulties arising in her work created a feeling of complete insufficiency. Wrestling with these difficulties was sometimes fruitful of achievement which was sufficient to win her some degree of recognition. Despite a predominant feeling of inadequacy, she also had moods in which she felt distinctly talented and creative.

She had a brother, two and a half years older than she. She herself was a twin; the other child, a big handsome boy, died a few months after birth. She had been, she was told, a small and sickly child. She related that upon delivery she had been placed upon the floor and ignored because everyone was busy with the second, bigger child, a difficult delivery. The twin brother played an important part in her fantasy.

She described her father, a landowner who had died a few years before, as a coarse, brutal, and hot-tempered person; her mother as timid, anxious, constantly worrying and complaining. The older brother was favored by both parents. He was a bright, obedient child, while she was defiant, and was considered intolerably bad and disobedient by the whole family. She quarreled frequently with her father, who beat her when angered. On such occasions she would heap abuse on him with all the resources of her vocabulary and wish he were dead.

The period between her seventeenth and twenty-second years was artistically her most productive. A sexual experience with an older man was followed by several lesbian relationships in which she played the more passive role, and in which she felt comparatively content. During the same period she had several flirtations with men in which she remained indifferent until she met the man she married. She saw in him a powerful, athletic man. This attracted her and was, in her opinion, the decisive factor in her choice. But in the marriage relationship it developed that he took the more passive, devoted attitude toward her, while she played a more masculine active role, at times tormenting and sadistic. She could become sexually excited, but never completely satisfied.

From childhood and particularly frequently in recent years, she had dreams from which she awoke in terror or with feelings of horror. The dreams were mostly of scenes of war: revolution, bombardments, riots from which she was trying to flee though paralyzed with fear.

Her life consisted of an alternation between hunger for experiences and excitement—a "greed for impressions" as she called it—and escape and withdrawal. The short periods of hunger for experience and excitement quickly led to increased anxiety and to paranoid delusions in which she imagined herself being hurt, robbed, or persecuted by women. There were experiences in which it was impossible to determine what was delusion on her part and what reality, because she probably unconsciously provoked situations which made various women become her enemies. Hypochondriacal sensations of every type she interpreted as confirmation of her fears. She would get a feeling of being completely abandoned, unloved and incapable of loving. She would lose all contact with the world around her. This detached state likewise led to anxieties. Interest in her own body was her roundabout way of finding contact with the outer world once more. A new dress could banish her despair.

She had numerous recollections from early childhood of instances when her father, in a sort of rude tenderness, would place his whole weight upon her. She could not breathe and feared being crushed, suffocated. Her protests angered her father and this often led to violent scenes. On one such occasion (warding off her father with her knee drawn back) with the heel of her shoe she wounded her genitals sufficiently to cause bleeding. She was greatly frightened. Her mother, equally frightened, called a doctor. Toward her guilty father she felt revengeful satisfaction. This event was the basis of a sleeping ceremonial: to this day she sleeps with one hand on her genitals, one leg drawn back, as though in defense.

Another important experience of her childhood occurred in about her seventh year. After an address by her father in the legislature, a mob tried to force its way into her parents' house; stones were tossed against the windows, which were hastily shut. Her father was absent, and the family was in terror. Both of these traumatic experiences returned repeatedly in her dreams in combined form. From the same period she also has recollections of states of anxiety when on her father's return from one of his frequent trips she was sent from her parents' to her own adjoining bedroom. She would try to overhear what was taking place, and apparently experienced numerous primal scenes or fantasies in this way.

These experiences, recurrent in her anxiety dreams, were followed by two more experiences, decisive for the later onset of the neurosis. When she was about twenty-one, a well-known clairvoyant predicted that she would end her life in insanity or by suicide, and warned her not to masturbate so much. In order to understand fully the disastrous effect of this prophecy, one must know in detail the history of her infantile masturbation in which prohibitions and warnings of terrible sicknesses played an important part. It is sufficient here to point out that she had been in the habit, during almost intoxicated periods of artistic activity, of rubbing against the edge of her easel, thus providing herself with a sexual stimulus. Following the prophecy she gave up this type of activity, thus losing a safety valve for her tensions. From this point began the real development of her neurosis, at first evident in withdrawal and restraint, later in the occurrence of states of anxiety.

Following an unnecessary appendectomy and many other therapeutic failures she lost faith in doctors and now turned to spiritualism. While in a trance a medium received messages foretelling that the city in which the patient lived was to be destroyed by force from above. This prediction placed the patient in such a state of anxiety that she fled from home. The basis of her belief in this prophecy could be traced to her childhood. For years she had awaited the inevitable coming of disaster. By fearing it she sought to prevent it. Only if she thought of it constantly would it perhaps not occur. In her recollections from childhood her father appeared as an inexorable force, blocking every avenue of escape. This inescapable, inexorable force now appeared as the destructive danger from above. Or perhaps it was "a snake which climbs down the wall" into her bed; or the horror she felt at the sight of bloody fishes or small birds both in her dreams and in reality. This feeling of the inevitable was also a part of her delusion of sickness. We find here a feeling of guilt the consequences of which are inescapable.[1]

Vague occult ideas she sought to withhold from the analysis as her most intimate secrets. According to them, the human being lives several different lives, having to atone in each life for the guilt of the preceding one. She believed herself to have been one of the first feminists. Not having been able to reconcile herself to being a woman, she became a man. In her next incarnation she was to be born a boy but die young in atonement for her previous life. However she had to fulfill her fate as a woman. In another incarnation she was destined to die in childbirth. This conflict between masculine and feminine, mixed with feelings of guilt, found expression in her painting. She imagined that she did not create pictures herself, but made copies under the astral guidance of a man who transmitted them to her.

While this patient had rejected her father, she had sought by every means, particularly illness, to bind her mother more closely to her. She lived in constant fear that her mother would have another child. An aunt, living in the same house, she had seen pregnant several times. She loved her dearly and developed violent sadistic impulses against the pregnant body of her aunt who, in this condition, could no longer take her on her lap. Her childhood and later life were characterized by this strongly ambivalent attitude toward both parents.

The coincidence of artistic talent and neurotic disposition has long been observed. Artistically talented persons almost without exception are subject to neurotic conflicts. They suffer periods of neurotic inhibition in their work, periods of depression and hypochondria, fear of insanity, tendencies toward paranoid reactions, and, relatively frequently, schizophrenia. Freud has emphasized that the essential talent of the artist cannot be explained by psychoanalysis. In *Dostojewski und die Vatertötung* he speaks of Dostoevsky's "unanalyzable artistic talent." Artistic sublimation appears to be possible only with the concurrence of definite elements of talent. Nevertheless, one might ask what forces drive toward sublimation. In order to achieve a better understanding of the connection between artist and neurosis, one must investigate the nature of the artist's instincts and psychic structure. On this basis, the urge to artistic production as well as the danger of neurotic illness might be explained.

In the case here presented the striking element is the significance of traumata for the patient's life. Experiences which are little different from the experiences of other people take on a traumatic character and are fitted into the patient's traumatic pattern. Moreover, she provokes situations which for her become traumatic. Her early experiences with her father, it is true, must be regarded as typical psychic traumata—repeated stimuli of such character and intensity that the child is unable to cope with them. Although it must be assumed that every child has experiences which have traumatic effect upon the still weak ego, we seem to deal here with a degree of traumatic susceptibility exceeding the normal. Here one is reminded of the numerous statements of artists themselves concerning the nature of their experience. Out of the wealth of such familiar and often quoted autobiography, we quote from the famous dramatist, Hebbel: "I am often horrified at myself when I realize that my irritability, instead of decreasing, is constantly increasing, that every wave of emotion, arising even from a grain of sand thrown by chance into my soul breaks about my head." In Ricarda Huch's book on the romantic movement we find this alternation between oversensitivity and dullness and insensitivity presented in innumerable variations. The artist, she says, "is constantly occupied in reacting to the endless stimulations he receives, his heart, seat of irritability, tortures itself in this struggle, driving his blood violently through the organism to the point of powerless exhaustion, to be aroused by stimuli once more."[2]

If we very briefly summarize the comments about the artist to be found in analytic literature, we have the following: the essential material from which the artist constructs his work is derived from unconscious fantasies in which his unsatisfied wishes and longings find expression. The compelling experience stems from the Oedipus complex. The artist suffers, according to Sachs' formulation, more than others from a feeling of guilt from which, through the participation of others in his art, he achieves recognition and is able to free himself. The narcissism of the artist transfers itself to his work. In the literature of the past few years emphasis has been given to reparation of the destroyed object as a function of art.

In our case we find confirmation of these observations. As long as the patient's artistic work, relatively uninhibited, could serve as an outlet for her tensions, she was able to spare herself the formation of neurotic sysmtoms. In her work of this period, as in her dreams later on, she repeatedly portrayed the traumatic experiences of her childhood as well as traumata of her later life. The repetition compulsion demands that the injury be overcome again and again. But why does this not finally succeed? Why does this compulsion not cease, as in the genuine traumatic neuroses which after some time usually subside?

In genuine traumatic neurosis the stimulus defense is perpetrated by an external trauma. The intensity of the excitation is too great to be overcome at the instant of occurrence. The attempt to overcome it is continued afterwards, but the trauma itself remains a solitary experience. In our case—and this appears characteristic for artistic sensitivity—the trauma is re-experienced indefinitely. As long as the drive which led to the trauma is active, it remains unaltered and subject to the repetition compulsion. The danger feared is one of re-experiencing a former state of helplessness produced by an overwhelming excitation. A greater accessibility to the unconscious characteristic of the artist brings him to closer proximity to the strata of the psyche in which the primitive impulses rule.

The testimony of many artists bears witness to a particular irritability, a more than average impressionability conducive to psychic traumata, having its basis in the transformation of instincts and the "constitution" of the individual. We know more about the fate of the instincts than about constitution. The strong instinctual excitations, never completely discharged, give even trivial experiences a particularly impressive character. About the corresponding constitution little is known, but one is forced to assume its existence. One most important aspect of this constitution is the narcissism of the artist of whose significance the statements of artists themselves,[3] and the results of analytical studies, leave no doubt. The psychopathology of artists likewise points to narcissism: hypochondria, depressive and paranoid tendencies, frequent schizophrenias.

In *Dostojewski und die Vatertötung*, Freud states that a bisexual constitution is one of the conditions or furthering factors of the neurosis. "Such [a constitution] must definitely be assumed for Dostoevsky and manifests itself in potential form (latent homosexuality) in the significance for his life of friendships with men, in his remarkably tender attitude toward rivals in love and in his unusual understanding for situations which can only be regarded as repressed homosexuality, as many examples from his writings bear witness." Another part of the same paper says: "We may trace the fact of his extraordinary feeling of guilt as well as his masochistic way of living back to a particularly strong feminine component. That is the formula for Dostoevsky: a man of especially strong bisexual constitution."

This formula may well hold true for the artist in general. Above all, it throws light upon the coincidence of artist and neurosis. Heightened bisexuality, a complication in the resolution of the Oedipus phase, increases ambivalence and feelings of guilt, thus giving rise to conflicts which easily lead to neurosis.

The concept of bisexuality, emphasized by Freud for Dostoevsky, contains a truism which has been stated by most artists in moments of self-expression. In bodily structure, too, particularly in likenesses of young artists, we find a conspicuously large number of characteristics of the opposite sex. We are familiar with the relative frequence of overt homosexuality or strong homosexual tendencies in artists of both sexes. Sappho gave lesiban love its name. In Freud's Leonardo da Vinci, Sadger's Kleist, and in Hebbel and many others, the strong bisexual element is established. Kris writes in his paper on Franz Xavier Messerschmidt that in his self-portrait "the defense against seduction as a woman" plays the essential part. "What he creates—his own countenance—seems feminine to him." In Ricarda Huch's book on the German romantic movement, we find an abundance of such material.

In the case of the patient we have described, parturition fantasies were prominent in childhood and puberty. Later, pregnancy and childbirth filled her with horror and disgust. Her dream life was nevertheless filled with fear-wracked anal parturition fantasies which usually terminated in an incapacity to give birth and a return to her mother. Her variously determined physical symptoms proved in part to be distorted pregnancy fantasies. Beside the guilt feeling which ruled her life, the feeling of "inadequacy of her body" played a decisive part in the frustration of her desire for children. The feeling of inadequacy arose from comparison with the favored brother and with the beautiful deceased twin. The symbolic equation, child = penis, was also transferred to her artistic activity and was lost only temporarily when an artist birth act, after violent struggle, was successfully carried to completion.

We find such comparisons in the writings of numerous artists, in which the hardships as well as the pleasures of creation, in like manner, are repeatedly described as the pains and pleasures of giving birth, and in which their own works are spoken of as their children. Thus Thomas Mann writes that "all forming, creating, producing is pain, struggle and pangs of labor." Rank cites Alfred de Musset: "Creation confuses me and makes me shudder. Execution, always too slow for my desire, stirs my heart to terrible palpitation and weeping, holding back violent cries only with difficulty, I give birth to an idea." In another place: "It [the idea] oppresses and torments me, until it becomes realizable, and then the other pains, labor pains, set in, actual physical pains that I cannot define. Thus my life passes away, if I let myself be dominated by this giant of an artist who abides in me." Here we see the tension between the two elements distinctly expressed. The begetting in work emphasizes sometimes the masculine, sometimes the feminine element—creation or surrender. In the fantasies of my patient regarding her work, this split was clearly expressed by the fantasy that her drawings were delivered to her by a painter, a man; she merely copied them. In another life, she had been a man and the dead boy twin was a part of her for which she was constantly searching.

This conflict and tension can never be completely resolved in actual life; it represents, in a way, a condition of unavoidable, inherent frustration. This frustration is the source of the artist's fantasy, driving him again and again to forsake disillusioning reality and to create a world for himself in which he, in his imagination, can realize his desires. It forces him to sublimation. The play of the child too, to which Freud has linked the fantasy of the artist, develops from the circumstance that the child for biological reasons is still largely denied the realization of his desires and the mastering of reality. It is characteristic of the artist that gratification by fantasy alone does not satisfy him; he feels the urge to give form, to give birth to his work. The birth of the work leads temporarily to satisfaction and relief from tension.

The analogy to children's play is even closer, serving as it does the two purposes: one, the pleasurable gratification from fantasies in which unfulfilled wishes are realized; second, the mastering of painful experiences in repetitious acting-out. We find both elements in the artist's work. Frustration drives him to construct his own imaginary world of gratification, and in his art overcathexed experiences are constantly re-created as in play. In comparing the works belonging to different periods of an artist's life, we find a predominance now of one element and now of the other.

Returning briefly to the problem of susceptibility to trauma, one might speculate as to whether the traumatophilia of the artist cannot be linked to his heightened bisexuality. This bisexuality makes a unified, nonambivalent object relationship difficult in relation to both sexes, thus favoring narcissistic libido fixation which again increases the danger of trauma. In a very enlightening passage from Hebbel's diary, we find this concept implicitly stated. He writes that of the "two antitheses" only one is ever given to us.

The one having advanced into existence, however, yearns constantly towards the other, sunk back into the core. If it could really grasp it in spirit and identify itself with it; if the flower for example could really conceive the bird, then it would momentarily dissolve into it; flower would become bird, but now the bird would long to be the flower again; thus there would no longer be life but a constant birth and rebirth, a different kind of chaos. The artist has in part such a position to the universe; hence the eternal unrest in a poet, all eventualities come so close that they would embitter all reality for him, if the power which engenders them did not likewise liberate him from them, in that he, by giving them shape and form, himself assists them, in a way, to reality, thus breaking their magic spell; it requires, however, a great deal and far more than any human being who does not experience it himself, within himself, can surmise, not to lose equilibrium. And natures lacking genuine form-giving talent must of necessity be broken in spirit, whence, therefore, so much pain, and madness too.

A problem is touched upon here which is of basic significance for this discussion—the problem of identification. The significance of bisexuality in the life of the artist receives here its main support. For how could the artist succeed accurately in portraying so many characters of both sexes if he did not find them within the realm of his own experience? What, for instance, would bring the male artist to describe the life of a woman if he did not in so doing reproduce his own unfulfilled experience? In the striving to solve and overcome ambivalent attitudes, identification is always attempted. The artist projects his ego in polymorphous transformations into his work, that is, he projects his inner experiences into an imagined outer world. The *real* outer world, however, is also experienced by identification. We find then a process of alternate introjection and projection. No better description of this can be given than that found in a letter of Schiller:

All creatures born by our fantasy, in the last analysis, are nothing but ourselves. But what else is friendship or platonic love than a wanton exchange of existences? Or the contemplation of one's Self, in another glass? . . . The eternal, inner longing to flow into and become a part of one's fellow being, to swallow him up, to clutch him fast, is love.

Artistic expression is the sublimation of this eternal, inner longing. The quest for exactness of expression, the passion for the *mot juste* arises from this never fully satisfied urge; the struggle with the word is the struggle for identification in sublimated form. Flaubert, who would struggle for days for a single phrase, wrote: "If one possesses the picture or the feeling very exactly within one's self, then the word must follow."

How the urge to identification is experienced and the urge to creation arises from it is very sensitively described in a short story by Virginia Woolf. She describes a railroad journey. Opposite her sits a poor woman whose unhappy expression leaves her no peace. "Ah, but my poor, unfortunate woman, do play the game—do, for all our sakes, conceal it!" The game that all people should play is to conceal their feelings. The unfortunate woman had a twitch, a queer headshaking tic. The author attempts to keep herself from being influenced, tries to protect herself by reading the *Times*. In vain. Then they exchange a few words. And while the poor woman speaks, "she fidgeted as though the skin on her back were as a plucked fowl's in a poulterer's shop-window." Further on we read:

All she did was to take her glove and rub hard at a spot on the windowpane. She rubbed as if she would rub something out for ever—some stain, some indelible contamination. Indeed, the spot remained for all her rubbing, and back she sank with the shudder and the clutch of the arm I had come to expect. Something impelled me to take my glove and rub my window. There, too, was a little speck on the glass. For all my rubbing it remained. And then the spasm went through me; I crooked my arm and plucked at the middle of my back. My skin, too, felt like the damp chicken's skin in the poulterer's shop-window; one spot between the shoulders itched and irritated, felt clammy, felt raw. . . . But she had communicated, shared her secret, passed her poison.

Still seeking to protect herself, the author begins to fantasize about the life of the woman, filling the next twenty pages with her imaginings. She entitles the story, "An Unwritten Novel," by which she would seem to reveal that the resolution through identification has not been successful. Here we find pictured the urge to identification, as well as the threat to the ego from it, the threat of being overwhelmed by an exaggerated response to an external stimulus reaching traumatic proportions.

In this ready identification of the artist there remains an element of magic which is conspicuous in the imitativeness of children at play. The tendency quickly to identify is a basic feature of the world of magic. The artist, susceptible to magic to strong degree, is able to charm others so that they in turn feel themselves one with him.

It seems that surrender of the artist to the world is almost always automatically bound up with an attitude of defense and protection, so that the artist never seems to belong completely. It is only this defense attitude which allows him to express his experience in his work. It may very safely be asserted that artists who do not have this defensive attitude become incapable of living or creating. This is true of those artistic natures that succumb early to disease, seek narcotics, resort to drugs, and sooner or later destroy their personalities. In my patient, this defensive attitude was too rigid; she had no freedom of identification, the anxiety was too great, so that her artistic productivity was inhibited.

SUMMARY

Susceptibility to trauma, a strong tendency to identification, narcissism, and bisexuality in the artist are related phenomena.

The basis of the drive to artistic accomplishment lies in a heightened bisexuality. Closely related with this is a traumatophilia, compelling the artist to seek and then overcome the trauma in continual repetition. From the latent frustration develops the artist's fantasy. The urge to identification and expression in work appears as a sublimation of the bisexuality.

The frequency of neurosis in artists may be explained by their heightened bisexuality. They are spared neurosis to the degree that they succeed in overcoming their conflicts through artistic sublimation.

Notes

1. This recalls the *Ananke* of Greek fate dramas and oracular prophecies.
2. See Thomas Mann: "Es gibt einen Grad dieser Schmerzfähigkeit, der jedes Erleben zu einem Erleiden macht" ("There is a degree of this capacity to suffer which changes all experience to suffering") and Richard Wagner: "Ja immer im Widerstreit sein, nie zur vollsten Ruhe seines Innern zu gelangen, immer gehetzt, gelockt und abgestossen zu sein" ("Always to be torn with conflict, never to achieve complete tranquillity within oneself, always to be hunted, always attracted and repulsed").
3. Turgenev on Tolstoy: "His deepest, most terrible secret is that he can love no one but himself." Thomas Mann: "Liebe zu sich selbst ist immer der Anfang eines romanhaften Lebens" ("Love for one's self is always the beginning of living like a character in a novel"). Hebbel: "Lieben heisst, in dem andern sich selbst erobern" ("To love means to win one's self in the other person").

PART II

LITERARY APPROACHES AND THEORIES

Unlike the preceding essays, all written in the flush of Freud's early discoveries, and thus for the most part showing the relation between unconscious processes in artists and the creation of their works, the essays in the following section take this connection for granted. They stress that Freud did not invent the unconscious, but only its scientific study. They explore Freud's own changing ideas, such as his original notion of art as the result of neurosis, and later postulations of only a unique relationship between the two—a relationship deriving from, or exploited by, individual talent. Yet these authors all pay tribute to Freud's scientific discoveries, and to their relevance to literature.

Erich Heller opens his essay by arguing that the world had been ready for Freud long before he arrived, and that no one remains untouched by his thought: it is everywhere around us, part of the Zeitgeist. To prove his point, he outlines a scene from *Death in Venice* where Aschenbach's real will is revealed, when, after having decided to leave Venice, his suitcase is lost, thus impeding his departure. That Aschenbach "was almost convulsed with reckless delight, an unbelievable joy," is the manifestation of his unconscious desire to stay in Venice, of "fate."

Again, in *The Magic Mountain*, Hans Castorp waits seven years for the return of the Russian woman he had secretly fallen in love with, all the while using his minor illness as a pretext for remaining. Heller demonstrates that in both instances Mann developed characters as if tailored to "prove" Freud's theories, although he had not yet read Freud. Heller attributes this to the continuing fascination with Romanticism, and with the alliance between love, death, and sickness, as well as to the promises of the Enlightenment, of the rationality which made psychology possible—along with its many resulting frustrations.

Freud was naïve, argues Heller, when he thought he could get to the bottom of psychic phenomena, when he forgot that he was projecting the morality of his time onto the primeval murderers of their father, or when he assumed that these men possessed a conscience and the psychic disposition to believe in God. What individuals repress has itself to do with the historical epoch they live in. Thus psychoanalysis, though founded upon the awareness that people must choose and sacrifice, cannot set up a hierarchy of ethics and of traditions, which might guide the activities of the enlarged consciousness its process engenders. This very openness of psychoanalysis allows for the ensuing chaos. We can't know what is psychically most important; hence everything is given equal time.

But for the writer psychoanalysis has provided unbounded opportunities. The creation of works which Goethe would have praised for having *geprägte Form* is no longer possible; instead, we get "stream-of-consciousness" novels, and other experimental works bearing the imprint of Freudian consciousness—even when their authors disavow Freud. Since the nineteenth century, maintains Heller, psychology has dominated the novel; poetry is no longer, as Goethe described it, the hiding place of truth. Goethe's conscious praise of the unconscious was superseded by the Kleistian tension between mythology and psychology, only to be replaced by Nietzsche, who called himself the "first psychologist of Europe." This logical development preceded Freud and the Age of Analysis. It also makes Nietzsche and Freud "neighbors" in history: in their concern with psychology, in their insistence on the virtue of truth, and in their relentless determination to bare all illusion. But Freud's other "neighbor" is Kafka, who wanted "never again psychology." Heller's critique, it seems, is not of Freud but of some of the more flip applications of his ideas. He is not alone, of course, in his nostalgia for the writer as Flaubert perceived him—a god remaining above and beyond the creation he may manipulate at will.

William Barrett finds this view of the artist present in the young James Joyce, and completely abandoned by the time of *Ulysses*. As a philosopher, Barrett focuses on the writer's existence, tracing the search for truth from Hegel through Marx and Freud and to modern writers. Only *authentic* writers, he argues, are able to find this truth—with the help of their fantasy, at the precarious borderline between fantasy and insanity. Barrett uses Swift and Gulliver's travels into the country of the mad as an example. He finds that Swift's wish to be a horse was already indicated in *Gulliver*, though this did not detract from the work. For Barrett, the book's power derives from the fact that Swift was on the road to madness, and that the world of the work, in the end, is an adaptation to it. Scholars too often forget the desire for power which writers "seek to gratify through public fantasies." Following Alfred Adler, Barrett postulates an introverted disposition due to an excessive need for love, which a writer may gratify with power over the minds of his readers. This disposition is said to originate in the oedipal relation, in the ambivalence engendered by the indirectness of gratification and by the accompanying inordinate sense of guilt. It renders the writer's highly mental existence precarious; his world of impulses and motives is only an exaggeration of everyone else's. But the more gifted the writer, the more conscious he is of literary traditions and of the requirement of authenticity—and the greater the lure of producing a best seller, of giving up the lonely struggle against an ever more materialistic Zeitgeist. These external pressures exacerbate internal tensions, a fact Barrett holds responsible for the authentic writer's "slide over into the more tranquil and private self-indulgence of fantasy with a consequent weakening of the reality principle." The philosopher's fate, concludes Barrett, is somewhat easier, because he deals with concepts—and maybe with students—while the writer is alone, destined to create with the raw material of his own fantasies, often sleepless, and fighting "against death and the inexorable and dragging vista of time which is his being."

Lionel Trilling strongly argues against this theory in *Art and Neurosis*, and against the idea that the exercise of the imagination resembles insanity. He holds Freud responsible for some of these notions, part of the belief prevailing in his time that art springs from neurosis. Some of Freud's followers still look to his early ideas, although Freud himself later modified them. Myths about the poet as the *genus irritabile* who finds virtue in illness, genius in neurosis, or inspiration in his "wound," live on, maintains Trilling, because they serve to separate him from the philistines. True, psychoanalytic insights into family situations, and into temperament, have shown that the neurotic or psychotic perception of reality tends to be more intense than the normal one, and that such people may be closer to their unconscious than most others. Still, this does not locate the artist's power in his neurosis; it only acknowledges that it is the writer's job to exhibit his unconscious, that he is more aware of what happens to him, and that he is more articulate and truthful. Investigations of scientists and other intellectuals may unveil similar unconscious patterns, although these patterns tend to be less articulated. An artist's neurosis, concedes Trilling, may be the material on which he exercises his literary powers, but it says nothing of this power. In fact, as Freud found in the *Introductory Lectures*, neurotic activities are detrimental, involve suffering, sap an individual's energy, may lead to serious impoverishment or inability to function. Since to some extent we are all neurotic, neurosis can account for all mental functioning, and not only for that of genius. Nevertheless, Trilling acknowledges that the artist has a special relationship to his neurosis as an *activity*, as an activity of *conflict*—a conflict he exploits. "He is what he is by virtue of his successful objectification of his neurosis." His genius, however—of perception, realization, and representation—is an irreducible gift.

W. H. Auden makes a similar point after quoting a long passage about the artist from Freud's introductory lectures. But Auden goes on to argue that becoming an artist, also, is one of the five means available to the mentally awakened child of escaping the demands of an unhappy family situation. Such a child's fantasy must be combined with craftsmanship. Auden, of course, speaks from experience when he emphasizes the poet's preoccupation with symbols and technical problems rather than with words, and when he insists that "creation, like psychoanalysis, is a process of reliving in a new situation"—a situation determined by the artist's existence, his selective internalization of the world, and the artistic medium he chooses as a means of communication. Thus, Freudianism too is placed in its environment, and is shown to influence both the artist and the man in the street, even though the latter's "Freudian" literature is somewhat distorted. Auden summarizes sixteen essential Freudian points, from libido theory, sexuality, and morality as the element distinguishing men from animals, to the discussions in literature about the extent of this morality, its relation to immorality and to good and evil. He indicates how we now can recognize illness as both purposive and an attempt at cure; how change is caused by frustration, tension, and our sense of guilt; how our moral ideas depend upon the nature of our relations with our parents; and how psychology or art cannot tell people how to behave, but can stimulate their thinking. Essentially Auden stresses Freud's technical influence on literature, the manner in which he directed the writer's attention to the importance of dreams, of nervous tics, or of other peculiarities. Beyond this, Freud has shown the place and function of the serious writer in society, and the importance that art and intellect retain—even when compared to those impulses against which man is powerless.

E. H. Gombrich concentrates more clearly on Freud's own esthetics, on his influence on art criticism, and particularly on the importance of the use of wit for any artistic endeavor. These connections are as applicable to writers as they are to painters. Gombrich argues that, by explaining the "dreamlike" condensation of meaning in jokes, which have their roots in spontaneous thought combinations, Freud showed us how new structures of ideas can derive from unconscious mechanisms. While it is easiest to apply this model to creative writing (puns depend on language and on double meaning), Freud insisted that all artistic activity, though influenced by biological drives and childhood memories, depends upon a "degree of adjustment to reality that alone turns a dream into a work of art." Moving from discussions of expressionism to Pasternak's *Dr. Zhivago*, to objective contexts, and to "art born of art," Gombrich shows how only unconscious ideas attuned to reality can be communicated; and how, like Paul Klee, he perceives the artist as a builder of structures that are lifted up into a new order. It is an order deriving from temporally accepted conventions, however, and from the artist's penchant for playfulness, riddles, and fantasies—along with the desire to explore and master his medium. Too many simplistic applications of psychoanalysis rely on childhood recollections and traumatic experiences, concludes Gombrich, which Freud himself would have rejected. Freud repeatedly stressed the elements of mastery and seriousness in children's (and adults') play, and never claimed to exhaust all the answers, saying "we know so little." But, as Gombrich and the other critics in this section show, Freud, this "cultivated 'Victorian' of Central Europe," knew so much.

That the general level of cultivation has dropped is a recurring lament in today's psychoanalytic circles. Partly because the cultivated Victorians no longer exist, partly because psychoanalysts are required to have a medical rather than a humanistic education, and partly for cultural reasons having to do with types of patients and the stress on "science," the range of psychoanalytic interpretations has narrowed. And this is why literary critics keep going back to Freud himself, and why we selected contributions which do not rely primarily on case work.

6.

Observations on Psychoanalysis and Modern Literature

Erich Heller

IN THE HISTORY of thought it occurs again and again that a privileged mind turns a long-nurtured suspicion into a system and puts it to the good, or not so good, uses of teachers and learners. When this happens, we say that it has been in the air for a long time. This is so in the case of psychoanalysis, and whatever its future fate, its historical importance is beyond doubt. For it is impossible not to come into contact with it or to avoid the collision, even if one merely wanted to say to it that it has no business being there. A theory owes this kind of inescapability to its long maturation in the womb of Time. It is born and casts its spell upon a world that seems to have been prepared for quite a while to receive it. Pallas Athene, it is said, sprang from her father's head in full armor. But surely, before this birth took place Zeus must have spent many a day pondering Athenian thoughts and must have done so in the Athenian dialect; and our world had awaited Freud long before it heard his name.

This is why psychoanalysis appears to be more than merely one among many possible theories about the psyche; rather, it comes close to being the systematic consciousness that a certain epoch has of the

From *Psychiatry and the Humanities*, Joseph H. Smith, M.D., ed. (New Haven: Yale University Press, 1976), 1:35–50. Copyright © 1976 Yale University Press. Reprinted by permission.

nature and character of its soul. Therefore it would be an endless enterprise to speak of Freud's influence on modern literature; and literature, whatever else it may be, is also the esthetic form assumed by the self-awareness of an age. If a writer today speaks of fathers or sons, of mothers or dreams, of lovers or rivals, of accidents that determine destinies or destinies rooted in character, of the will to live or the longing for death—and what else is it that poets and writers talk about?—how can he remain untouched by Freudian thoughts even if he has never read a line by Freud? And the more he were to try to extinguish or "repress" this "influence," the more he would become its victim. Could a post-Freudian poet say what Goethe's Egmont says: "As if whipped on by invisible demons, the sun-born horses of Time rush along with the fragile chariot of our destiny, and nothing is left to us but intrepidly to hold fast to the reins and keep the wheels from pushing against a wall of rock or driving into an abyss" (*Egmont*, 2:2)—could a contemporary writer put such words into the mouth of his hero without suspecting that he has learned it from Freud?—that the invisible demons with their whip are really the unconscious, the id, and the rather helpless charioteer, the ego with its good intentions?

From Goethe, Novalis, the German arch-Romantic, and Kleist, the one and only naturally tragic poet of German literature (even if Goethe once cursed him as *Unnatur*—"Diese verdammte Unnatur," he said), and certainly from the literature we have uppermost in mind when speaking of the later nineteenth century—from Stendhal, Flaubert, and de Maupassant, from Tolstoy and Dostoevsky—there is a much shorter way to Freud than the maps of literary history usually show; and the subsequent literature is altogether domiciled in a country the cartographer of which is Freud. It may not be the most pertinent of questions to ask whether Hofmannsthal, Schnitzler, Broch, Musil, Kafka, Rilke, Hermann Hesse, or Thomas Mann have been "influenced" by Freud, or whether Joyce or Virginia Woolf, Hemingway or Faulkner have "learned" from him; for the question—to which the answer may be in some cases yes and more frequently no—is almost as irrelevant as it would be to ask whether the first builders of aircraft were inspired by Newton. Airplanes fly in Newtonian space, trusting, as it were, in the validity of the law of gravity. What, then, are the qualities of the sphere of the psyche traversed by modern literature?

Out of its multitudinous characteristics I wish to select two from the writings of Thomas Mann. The first bears upon the problem of man's responsibility for his decisions and actions—that is, the problem of morality itself. A masterpiece among novellas, *Death in Venice*, supplies our first example. We remember the episode (in the third section of the story) that is decisive in the development of the plot, when Gustav von Aschenbach for the last time tries to take the moral initiative in the encounter with his destiny. He wants to escape from the sickly oppression— from the Venetian air, heavy and sultry with the sirocco, where the deadly epidemic would soon luxuriate, but also from his growing passion for the beautiful boy Tadzio. He determines to leave and orders his luggage to be taken to the railway station on the hotel's early-morning motor boat, whereas he himself, believing that there is enough time for an unrushed breakfast and, without acknowledging this to himself, perhaps for a last silent encounter with Tadzio, chooses to take a later public steamship. But when he arrives at the station, his luggage has gone off on a wrong train. This accident makes his moral determination collapse. He decides to wait for his trunk in Venice, returns to his Lido hotel and to his erotic enchantment. He is ready now for the approaching disease and for death.

Fate and accident are ancient allies; yet only in the Freudian era could *this* accident have been woven in this manner into the texture of destiny. For as Thomas Mann tells the story, the accident is not, as any similar event in Greek tragedy would be, a weapon in the hands of a divine antagonist with whom the hero's will is interlocked in combat, and not a cunning maneuver of that friend or foe called Fate. It is rather the revelation of Aschenbach's true will that gives the lie to his declared intention to depart. If Aschenbach is clearly innocent of the mistake made in the dispatching of his luggage, he is innocent only after the canon of traditional moral judgments. According to the new dispensation he is responsible; and in his soul he knows this, or comes to know it, as he ecstatically welcomes that travel mishap as if it were the gift of freedom itself. "Aschenbach," we read, "found it hard to let his face assume the expression that the news of the mishap required, for he was almost convulsed with reckless delight, an unbelievable joy."

The basic idea of Thomas Mann's novel *The Magic Mountain* can be stated almost in one sentence: Hans Castorp, a seemingly "well-adjusted" young shipbuilding engineer from Hamburg, has planned a visit of three weeks in a Swiss sanatorium for tubercular diseases where his cousin is a patient, but remains there for seven years. Certainly, he becomes ill himself, but his physical symptoms are by no means serious. What then is the *real* reason for his tarrying? It is his hidden wish, a secret perhaps to himself, to await the return of Clavdia Chauchat. He has fallen in love with the Russian woman, and she, as she leaves, promises that she will return: and Hans Castorp waits seven years. His illness is merely a pretext for his waiting. Against all "humanistic" reasonableness and moral principles, his *true* will has asserted itself. And Thomas Mann began to read Freud only *after* he had written *The Magic Mountain*. Voilà, the Zeitgeist!

Both *Death in Venice* and *The Magic Mountain* would be unthinkable were it not for the Romantic fascination with the alliance between love and sickness and death; and this is almost as much as to say: unthinkable without depth psychology. These works are situated in a territory of the psyche the ethics of which are radically different from those of the Enlightenment (to name only one of the preceding epochs). It is strange that the strongest hostile response evoked by Freud's teaching was, at least to begin with, moral indignation. Freud, it was held, undermined morality and catastrophically narrowed the domain in which ethical laws could be applied unquestioningly. A profounder criticism would have been to show that, on the contrary, he extended a person's responsibility so immeasurably that it became in practice all but unworkable.

The rationalistic doctrine of morality, which until the Romantic period had dominated the moral philosophy of Western civilization, saw the moral person triumph or succumb in a *conscious* struggle with forces which, no matter whether they were called "nature" or "instinct" or "inclination," were the simple antagonists of the ethically wakeful human being. In Freud's doctrine, deeply indebted to the Romantic sensibility, the moral conflict becomes total warfare. It is waged even in places where once upon a time the warrior sought and found relaxation from the strains of morality: in sleep, in dreams, in fantasies, in innocently involuntary action. Let anyone say now: "I have only dreamt this," or "I did not intend to say this; it was a mere slip of the tongue," or "I was determined to do what I promised, but then I forgot": instantly he will be persuaded that he dreamt what he dreamt, said what he said, forgot what he forgot, because he was prompted by his deepest and truest will. While the moralist of the rational Enlightenment proved himself or failed in what he consciously *willed* or *did*, the Romantic and Freudian morality is once again concerned with the innermost character of a person, with his *being*. Once again; for there was a time, long ago, when a prophet struck fear and terror—albeit by speaking in a different idiom—into the minds of the Pharisees by putting the goodness of the hidden soul or the rebirth of the whole man ethically above righteous observance of the law by the publicly displayed good will. This was the essence of the moral revolution of Christianity.

As psychoanalysis, with all its variations and eclectic modifications, is a dominant part of the epoch's consciousness, it has a share in its calamity. This manifests itself—speaking, as would seem appropriate, in medical terms—in the vast superiority of presumed diagnostic insights over therapeutic possibilities. Has there ever been a doctor who has diagnosed as many pathological irritations as Freud? The psyche is to him an inexhaustible reservoir of abnormalities, precariously dammed in by the most delicate concept of health. All pleasures and all oppressions of the soul, all sins and all virtues, restlessness of the heart as well as the great constancy of love, fear of evil as well as faith in God—all these may in the twinkling of the diagnostic eye degenerate into signs of psychic imbalance. But what is the health of the soul? Compared to the resourcefulness and ingenuity of the diagnosis, the only answer that can be given within the limits of psychology is primitive, pedestrian, and simpleminded: the ability to control the controllable conditions of existence and the adjustment to the unalterable. But who has drawn the frontier between the controllable and the unalterable? Where exactly does it run? Is it fixed by God, this fabrication of the father-bound neurotic psyche? Or by nature who has created the boy after the image of Oedipus and then handed him over to the healing practices of psychological *ratio?* Or by society or the state? By *which* society and *which* state? By that Victorian society whose numerous pathological symptoms have called forth psychoanalysis? Or by the enlightened, generously liberal, thoroughly "demythologized" society that on both sides of the Atlantic sends swarms of patients into the consulting rooms of psychologists? Or by the tyrannical state that prohibits their activities?

The questions are endless and unanswerable. For it is true to say that if there were an answer, there would be no psychoanalysis. It would not have been invented had it not been for the disappearance from our beliefs of any certainty concerning the nature of human being. Thus we have become the incurable patients of our all but nihilistic skepticism, indulging a conception of the soul that stipulates more, many more, psychic possibilities than can be contained in one existence. Whichever possibilities we choose, we miss out on the others—and distractedly feel our loss without being able ethically to justify it. Inevitably foregoing uncounted possibilities, we experience this as the betrayal of a vaguely conceived "fullness of life." For our beliefs do not acknowledge any reason to sacrifice possibilities in order to gain our reality—a reality that for us has assumed the character of the arbitrary and the indefinable. Thus we are haunted by as many dead possibilities as there is room for in the wide region of frustrations. It is the accomplished hypochondria of unbelief.

Paradoxically enough, Freud himself, over long stretches of his enterprise, was securely at home in that rationalistic Enlightenment faith whose increasing instability was the historical occasion of his doctrine, just as the doctrine in its turn added to the disturbance. But because he himself was hardly affected by it, he had no ear for the question his own theory raised, and certainly did not have the *philosophical* genius to meet it. With astonishing naïveté he examined the "how" of psychic conditions, as if such labors could yield clear answers to the "what" of psychic phenomena, of their meaning and their possible relatedness to the possibly true nature of being. Thus he believed, for instance, that primeval murderers of their fathers created from the agony of their guilt a godfather to be worshipped—a theory which, of course, presupposes that those savage creatures in all their savagery possessed a conscience and the psychic disposition to believe in God. Yet Freud did not ask to what end human beings should have the ability to feel guilty or the capacity for religious beliefs, but took for granted that the conscience and the faith of his savages corresponded to nothing real in the world and fed on sheer illusions; and his readers, just as he himself did, looked upon certain *contents* of guilt and faith understandably as being antiquated, without paying attention to the *form* and quality of these psychic dispositions. But are those dispositions not exceedingly curious if they have no correlative whatever in the order of reality? Of course, Freud would rightly have said that this was not a psychological question, but a metaphysical or ontological one. True. But to doubt the very validity of such questions, quite apart from the inability to answer them, is the main psychological characteristic of the epoch that has produced psychoanalysis as its representative psychology.

One of its most important tenets is the theory of repression. From the beginning of his history man has suffered from the compulsion to "repress," and only because he "represses" has he a history, for historical epochs or cultures differ one from the other by the changing molds in which they cast some human possibilities at the expense of others. This is why the ancient Greeks were, despite Pythagoras and the Pythagoreans, not rich in great natural scientists, but in artistic accomplishments unsurpassed by any other age; or why we have the most self-assured and effective technology, but arts that are exceedingly tentative, uncertain, restless, and experimental; or why creations of nature have been, ever since the discovery of Nature, the great comfort and pleasure of the Romantic sensibility: because this tree or that range of mountains appears to be the sum total, without loss or sacrifice, of *all* its potentialities, and therefore never hurts our esthetic sense by insinuating to us that it might have done much better had it only chosen another career. For one of the things that set man apart from all other beings is that the sum of his potentialities by far exceeds the measure of their realizability in one human life or even in one historical epoch. Man has been given language (in the sense of all his means of expression) so that he can say what he has not chosen to be silent about. He is such an eloquent creature because he is unspeakably secretive. This is the natural-historical aspect of human transcendence, the psychological side of his "existential problem."

Human existence is choice, resignation, sacrifice—and, indeed, neurotic repression if a man has to make his inescapable choices and sacrifices under the dim enforcement of social norms he no longer believes in, instead of basing his decisions upon the belief in the greater virtue of what he has chosen, no matter whether he does so consciously or unconsciously, from lucid insight or from faithful, unreflective obedience. If he no longer feels that there is any compelling reason why he should forego this in order to achieve that, if his existence is not illuminated by any shimmer of its transcendence, then his rejected potentialities (or, for that matter, injuries sustained by the child in his religiously or ethically "agnostic" society) grow into neuroses in the darkness of the unconscious. And psychoanalysis shares with existential philosophy the tragic fate that, although it is, of course, founded upon the awareness of the universal human need to choose, to select, and to sacrifice, it is at the same time, like most other creations of the age, deprived of the means to transcend this distressing human condition.

From this follows the "scientific" intention of psychoanalysis to disregard any hierarchy that religion or metaphysics or ethics or tradition has set up concerning the activities of consciousness. It may well be true to say that this has been the first such attempt in the history of man's efforts to know himself. There is for psychoanalysis no preestablished order of the psyche: it is impossible to discern, at least initially, what is important to it and what is unimportant. It is a theory that lets itself in with chaos. If there is to be any order, it has to be created—somewhat in keeping with the aperçu of that arch-Romantic Novalis (in his celebrated fragment of 1799, "Christendom or Europe") that only anarchy will once again beget a true spiritual order: "Religion will rise from the chaos of destruction as the glorious founder of a new world." [1]

Psychoanalysis—like the sensibility of romanticism (as opposed to that of classicism)—is imbued with the suspicion that everything, every tatter of a dream, every scrap of memory, every seemingly arbitrary association our thinking makes between this and that, may be of hitherto unsuspected significance within the economy of the soul, just as Marcel (in the first volume of Proust's vast novel *À la recherche du temps perdu*) receives those sudden messages of a great and hidden truth, those unpredictable intimations of eternity, from a stone the surface of which reflected the sunlight, or from the clanging of a bell, or from the smell of fallen leaves—"a confused mass of different images, under which must have perished long ago the reality"—the absolute reality he was seeking. Nietzsche's great and truly dreadful experiment consisted in his assuming that the history of the Western mind was nothing but a conspiracy to conceal the truth; and where such concealment is looked upon as the rule, the suspicion is bound to arise that, vice versa, anything—literally anything—may unexpectedly "conduct" the mind toward a tremendous illumination. It is precisely this that distinguishes modern literature from, above all, the myth-bound poetry of ancient Greece. And what Hofmannsthal said, in his poem "Lebenslied," of the "heir" of this long process of disinheritance, is as true of psychoanalysis as it is of the artist of the psychoanalytical age:

Ihm bietet jede Stelle
Geheimnisvoll die Schwelle—

meaning that he who is without a home in an ordered world will entrust himself to any current of chance to take him anywhere, for anywhere may be the threshold of the mystery.

Proust's great novelistic oeuvre, the attempt to catch hold of a withdrawing world by means of an exquisitely woven net of memories; James Joyce's *Ulysses*, this monster work of genius that turns the experience of one day into a kind of lyrical-epical encyclopedia; Hermann Broch's time-consuming record of Virgil's dying; not to mention the many minor "stream of consciousness" novels—all these are the literary products of an epoch whose soul has been analyzed by Sigmund Freud. And whatever will remain of this literature will bear the imprint of a consciousness that Freud has helped to become conscious of itself— and thus, given the nature of consciousness, has helped to come into being. But can a consciousness that is so thoroughly conscious of itself ever achieve that *geprägte Form*, as Goethe called it in *Umworte-Orphisch*, the oneness of deliberate form and "naïve" spontaneity that has always been the hallmark of great art?

Speaking of Freud and modern literature, we cannot help concerning ourselves with the unusual, and in all probability critical, situation of literature in an age that is constantly in search of an acceptable theory of its soul. For the relationship of art to that self-understanding of the soul which culminates in Freud is by no means free of conflicts, and these tensions have been in the making ever since the truth about man has been sought not in myth or religion but in psychology. Psychology—the psychology, for instance, that dominates the novel of the nineteenth century—is the science of disillusionment. Its climate is, as some of the Romantics believed, unfavorable to poetry; and in a serious sense it is true to say that the history of the psychological novel is the progressive dissolution of what traditionally has been regarded as poetic. Novalis, who wrote that psychology is one of the "ghosts" that have "usurped the place in the sanctuary where the monuments of gods should be," knew what he did when he countered the Romantic enthusiasm for Goethe's *Wilhelm Meister*, indeed his own fascination with that novel, by calling it a "Candide aimed at poetry," a satire of the poetic mode.[2]

Goethe, in his turn, accused Kleist, this *Ur*-patient and *Ur*-practitioner of depth analysis, of aiming at the confusion of feelings. What he meant by this was very likely the war that Kleist's imagination, in love with the heroic and the mythic, fought with his analytical intelligence;

and this intelligence was at the same time in unrelenting pursuit of the psychological truth. It is a feud that reverberates throughout Kleist's dramatic verse and prose. Indeed, the source of the particular fascination wielded by his dramas and stories is the clash, and at times the unquiet marriage, between poetry and neurosis. Goethe was bound to abhor this poet as intensely as Kafka admired him. For Goethe believed—at least at times—that poetry prospered only when it was left to grow and mature in the unconscious. He said so to Schiller in a letter of April 6, 1801, and added that poetry presupposes in those who make it "a certain good-natured and even simple-minded love for the real which is the hiding-place of truth."

Unconscious, good-natured, simple-minded, trusting that the hidden truth may, after all, reveal itself to the naïve mind in the phenomenal world—if one were to define Kleist's genius, indeed the spirit of modern literature, by means of its perfect opposite, this would be its negative definition. Should it ever happen that a history of modern literature is written in honor of Sigmund Freud—by a literary historian who also possesses a thorough knowledge of psychoanalysis without having become intellectually enslaved by it—it might begin with Goethe's highly conscious praise of the unconscious; contemplate afterwards the Kleistean tension between mythology and psychology, which is at the same time so characteristic of a whole literary epoch; and then arrive at the writings of Nietzsche, that astonishing prompter of psychoanalysis, "the first psychologist of Europe," as, not very modestly, he called himself (and Freud himself all but acknowledged his claim)—Nietzsche, who at the same time never tired of pointing to the perils of the mind's psychological pursuit of itself, and believed he knew that there was a kind of knowledge that may become "a handsome instrument for perdition."[3] Such an essay in literary history might conclude with Kafka's dictum from "Reflections on Sin, Suffering, Hope, and the True Way": "Never again psychology!"

In honor of Sigmund Freud? Would it not, rather, be a polemical performance? No. For is the stance of the polemicist appropriate to the inevitable? Our imaginary historian of literature would show that there is a compelling logical development from German Romanticism, the fountainhead of so many currents in modern literature, to the works of Sigmund Freud. How is this?—the medical sobriety of the founder of psychoanalysis brought into the vicinity of a literary-philosophical movement that is reputed to have fostered every conceivable extravagance of the fancy? Still, the connection exists; and it is a mistaken belief, hardly more than a facile superstition, that the early German Romantics were bent simply on discrediting realistic wakefulness in order to rescue the dreamily poetic, or on fortifying the domain of the imagination against the encroachments of the real.

True, the poet in Novalis was sometimes outraged by the prosaic realism of Goethe's *Wilhelm Meister*. On these occasions he would say of it that it elevated "the economic nature of man" to the rank of his "only true nature" (and he might have said: the nature of man insofar as it is accessible to psychology); or that it was "a piece of poetic machinery to deal with recalcitrant material"; or that with this novel he made his final bid for quasi-bourgeois respectability: "The Pilgrim's Progress toward a knighthood." But in a different mood he called it a supreme masterpiece, "the novel *par excellence*," and its author "the true vicar of the poetic spirit on earth."[4] It is clear that even Novalis, the true poet in the first group of German Romantics, played his part in the strategy of Romantic irony, an attitude of mind that would surely be useless in any ferocious defense of the imagination against the attacks of rationality. No, Romantic irony is a play played around a center of great seriousness. Its ambition is to save the authentic life of the imagination from the wreckage of illusions. Just as lifeboat instruction is given on luxurious ocean liners, so Romantic irony aims at teaching the spirit of poetry how to keep afloat in the approaching floods of what Goethe named the Prosaic Age: the Age of Analysis.

Friedrich Schlegel, the Grand Intellectual Master of the early Romantics, demanded that poetry should be practiced like a science, while every science should become a new kind of poetry. This was Schlegel's outré manner of expressing what Schiller, in his celebrated essay "On Spontaneous and Reflective Poetry," hoped for: that at the highest point of consciousness man would acquire a new and higher "naïveté." Novalis said even more: "Those who uncritically believe in their health make the same mistake as those who uncritically regard themselves as sick: both are diseased"—because, one assumes, of their want of critical alertness; and still more, that certain kinds of physical sickness are best treated through treating the psyche, because the soul has the same influence upon the body that the body has upon the soul. If these sayings were offered as utterances of Freud's, the attribution would not meet with much incredulity. And the following *is* all but said by Freud, although it was said by Novalis too: "All that is involuntary must come under the control of the conscious will."[5] This means the same as "*Ego* shall be where *Id* was."

As one reads what Freud says of the relationship between "I" and "It," of the wounds which the struggles between the two inflict upon the soul, and how the soul may regain its lost integrity through the enhanced consciousness of itself, it is impossible not to relate this great psychological utopia to the vision of a future paradise with which Kleist ends his meditations "On the Marionette Theatre"—or rather, on the neurotic derangement, the false self-consciousness, of the inhibited psyche; and even though the Eden of original innocence and unselfconscious grace is shut for ever, we must, Kleist writes, "embark on the journey around the world in order to find out whether we may not be received through a back door." In the future *perfection of consciousness*, we may recover what we lost in the Fall; we shall have to "eat of the Tree of Knowledge again to fall back into the state of innocence."

Schiller, in that essay on "Spontaneous and Reflective Poetry," means something similar, if not the same, when he speaks of our gaining a new and purified spontaneity through the infinite increase of our reflective power. And what else is it that the philosopher of Romantic pessimism, Schopenhauer, has in mind when he, intimately knowing the terror of the *Id*, the dark impulses of the will, glorifies in his magnum opus, *The World as Will and Idea*, the freedom that the *Ego* may attain through the understanding of that *Id* and itself? And finally Freud and Nietzsche: even if the mountain tops of the prophet Zarathustra seem worlds apart from the consulting room of the analyst, they are nonetheless neighbors, and not only in the sequence of time. For one of Nietzsche's two divinities is Dionysus, the god of the intoxicated will to live—but the other is Apollo, the god who possesses the power of clear articulation and disciplined insight. Nietzsche, too, longed for the ultimate rule of Apollo—not *over* Dionysus but *together with him* in an utopian oneness of mind and will, intellect and impulse.

Yet Nietzsche and Freud are neighbors above all by virtue—virtue? well, sometimes it seems a necessity imposed by history—by virtue of the determination with which they pursued the truths of psychology, a psychological radicalism intolerant of any gods that were not more than the illusory comforters of sick souls. But if the unimaginable day ever comes when men, beyond sickness and illusion, live in the integrity of being, then the spirits of Freud and Nietzsche may give their assent to Kafka's resolve, unrealizable in his time: "Never again psychology!"

Notes

1. Novalis, *Fragmente*, edited by Ernst Kamnitzer (Dresden: Wolfgang Yess, 1929), p. 738.
2. *Ibid.*, pp. 381, 633.
3. Friedrich Nietzsche, *Gesammelte Werke* (Munich: Musarion, 1922), 6:48.
4. Novalis, *Fragmente*, pp. 632–33, 656, 652.
5. *Ibid.*, p. 383.

7.

Writers and Madness

William Barrett

EVERYTHING SWIFT WROTE, Leslie Stephen says with penetrating good
sense, is interesting because it is the man himself. (If this is true of many
other writers, there is on the other hand a special and compelling sense
in which it holds of Swift—another reason for my finding his case so
apposite.) Does it look as if I were only about to say, with Buffon, "the
style is the man"? But "style" does not say enough, and it is not enough
to remain happy with the judicious aphorism or with Stephen's judicious
critical observation. The modern critic cannot rest easy with this
eighteenth-century piece of astuteness, which long ago passed into the
stock of our critical assumptions; we begin to know too much and we
must dig mines beneath its truth.

But it is well to begin from such broad and obvious data of criticism
(instances of which we could multiply indefinitely) for we may now pass
on to the more complex and really monumental example provided us by
James Joyce. In his *Portrait of the Artist* Joyce develops a theory of literary creation, anchored on the metaphysics of St. Thomas but essentially
expressing the Flaubertian view of the writer as a god who remains above
and beyond his creation which he manipulates as he wills. But in *Finnegans Wake* the universal human symbol of the writer has now become the
infant Earwicker twin scrawling with his own excrement on the floor!
(Between the two, somewhere near the midpoint of this remarkable evo-

From *Partisan Review* (1947), 14:5–22. Copyright 1947 *Partisan Review*. Reprinted by permission.

lution, Stephen Dedalus declares, in the famous discussion of Shakespeare in *Ulysses*, that the writer, setting forth from his door for the encounter with experience, meets only himself on the doorstep.) If Joyce is the great case of a rigorous and logical development among modern writers, each step forward carrying the immense weight of his total commitment and concentration, we are not wrong then to find in this changing portrait of the artist a measure of how far he has matured as man and writer from the once youthful and arrogant aesthete. And if we will not learn from our own experience, do we not remain formalists toward literature only at the expense of neglecting Joyce's far deeper experience?

But in fact we already know there is no escape from ourselves. Existence is a dense plenum into which we are plunged, and every thought, wish, and fear is "overdetermined," coming to be under the infinite pressures within that plenum of all other thoughts, wishes, and fears. Fingerprints and footprints are our own, and Darwin has pointed out that our inner organs differ from person to person as much as our faces. The signature of ourselves is written over all our dreams like the criminal's fingerprints across his crime. The writer, no more than any other man, can hope to escape this inescapable density of particularity. But his difference is precisely that he does not merely submit but insists upon this as his fate. It is *his own* voice which he wishes to resound in the arena of the world. He knows that the work must be his, and to the degree that it is less than his, to the degree that he has not risked the maximum of his being in it, he has missed the main chance, his only chance. The scientist too may insist on the personal prerogative of discovery: he wants the new element, planet, or equation to bear his name; but if in this claim for prestige he responds to one of the deepest urges of the ego, it is only that this prestige itself may come to attend his person through the public world of other men; and it is not in the end his own being that is exhibited or his own voice that is heard in the learned report to the Academy.

So we have come quickly to the point, and may now let the categories of *authentic* and *unauthentic* out of the bag. I am not very happy about the terms, I wish we had better in English, but it should be clear from our instances so far that they are not really new notions, and that they do come forth now at the real pinch of the subject matter. If a certain amount of faddism has recently and regrettably become attached to their use, they have on the other hand also become obsessive for the modern mind—a recommendation which we, existing historically, cannot help finding a little persuasive. The Marxist will not fail to point out that a highly developed technology, which is not directed toward human ends but capable on the other hand of overrunning all areas of the social life, has plunged us into this civilization of the slick imitation, celluloid and cellophane, kitsch and chromium plating, in the morass of which we come inevitably to speak of "the real thing" and "the real right thing" with an almost religious fervor. And he will go on to explain then why the category of authenticity should play such a crucial role in modern existential thought. He would be right, of course, but he ought also to drop his bucket into the deeper waters of the well. One deeper fact is that modern man has lost the religious sanctions which had once surrounded his life at every moment with a recognizable test capable of telling him whether he was living "in the truth" or not; Hegel drew a map of the divided consciousness, and Freud explored it empirically beyond anything Hegel ever dreamed, showing us, among other things, that Venus is the goddess of lies; and so we come, as creatures of the divided and self-alienated consciousness, to wrestle with the problem of how we are to live truthfully. But if these categories have become historically inevitable, and we borrow their formulation from existentialist philosophers, we have on the other hand to insist that it is not these philosophers who can tell us, after all, how authenticity is to be achieved either in art or life. Freud, not Heidegger, holds the key. The mechanism by which any work of art becomes authentic—flooded in every nook and cranny with the personal being of the author—can only be revealed by the searchlight of psychoanalytic exploration.

How then is authenticity—this strange and central power of a fantasy to *convince* us—achieved? A first and principal point: it seems to involve a fairly complete, if temporary, identification with the objects of fantasy. The difference between Kafka and most of his imitators becomes a *crucial* instance here. When Kafka writes about a hero who has become an insect, about a mouse or an animal in a burrow, he is, during the course of the lucid hallucination which is his story, that insect, mouse, or animal; it is he himself who lives and moves through the passages and chambers of his burrow; while his imitators, even when they are fairly successful, strike us as simply using so much clever machinery borrowed from him and often more ingeniously baroque than his, but which lacks precisely that authenticity of identification. But this identification with the objects of fantasy is also in the direction of insanity; and perhaps this is just what the ancients knew: that the poet in inspiration ventures as close to that undrawn border as he can, for the closer he goes the more vitality he brings back with him. The game would seem to be to go as close as possible without crossing over.

Now imagine, for a moment, Swift in the modern pattern. After the downfall of the Harley ministry he retires to his wretched, dirty doghole and prison of Ireland, has a nervous breakdown, a crack-up, is patched together by several physicians and analysts, continues in circulation thereafter by drinking hard but spacing his liquor carefully, and dies at an earlier age of cirrhosis of the liver. Shall we call this: Living on the American Plan? It is the violence of the new world, after all, that has made a system of violent drinking. Now to be drunk and to go mad are both ways of overcoming the world. If in the interests of human economy we are left no choice but to prefer the American Pattern, would we not, however, feel a little cheated had Swift's actual history been different? Before the ravening gaze of his miserable species he flings down his madness as the gage of his commitment and passion, and it has now become an inseparable part of the greatness of the human figure that rises out of history toward us.

When Simon Dedalus Delany, amiable and easygoing, remarked of a mutual acquaintance that "He was a nice old gentleman," Swift retorted, "There is no such thing as a nice old gentleman; any man who had a body or mind worth a farthing would have burned them out long ago." Does not this become his own comment on his eventual madness? The man who retorted thus, it is clear, lived with his whole being flung continuously toward the future at the end of the long corridor of which was the placid if disordered chamber of madness. To have gone mad in a certain way might almost seem one mode of living authentically: one has perhaps looked at the world without illusion and with passion. Nothing permits us to separate this life from this writing: if the extraordinary images the biography provides us—the old man exclaiming, over and over again, "I am what I am," or sitting placidly for hours before his Bible open on Job's lament, "let the day perish wherein I was born,"— if these move us as symbols of a great human ruin, they are also the background against which we must read the last book of *Gulliver*. The game is to go as close as possible without crossing over: poor Gulliver the traveler has now slipped across the border into the country of the mad, but this journey itself was only a continuation of the Voyage among the Houyhnhnms. A moment comes and the desire to escape takes on a definite and terrible clothing, and the whole being is shaken by the convulsions of what we may call the totem urge—the wish to be an animal. Rat's foot, crow's skin, anything out of this human form! The Ainu dances and growls and is a bear, the Bororo Indians chatter and become parakeets; Swift wanted to be a horse, a beautiful and gentle animal— and probably nobler on the whole than most human beings. This is the madness already present in *Gulliver*.

We do not mean to deny all the other necessary qualities that are there: the once laughter-loving Dean, lover of *la bagatelle*, King of Triflers, the great eighteenth-century wit, the accomplished classicist. Precisely these things give Swift the great advantage over a writer like Céline, whose rage is, by comparison, choking and inarticulate—like a man spitting and snarling in our face and in the end only *about* himself, so that we are not always sure whether we are being moved by literature or by a mere document of some fearful human extremity. What for the moment I am calling "madness," the perhaps simpler thing the Greeks called "madness," must somehow flow freely along the paths where all men can admire. If it erupts like a dam bursting it only inundates and swamps the neighboring fields; conducted into more indirect and elaborate paths, it irrigates and flows almost hidden to the eye. The flow from the unconscious of writer to reader would seem, then, to be more effective precisely where the circuit is longer and less direct, and capable therefore of encompassing ampler territory in its sweep. Lucidity, logic, form, objective dramatization, traditional style, taste—all these are channels into which the writer must let his anguish flow. And the denser his literary situation, the more he is surrounded by a compact and articulate tradition, the more chances he can take in casting himself adrift. But whatever Swift's advantages in literary and moral milieu, we cannot forget that he himself lived to write his own epitaph and in this final summing-up had the last word on the once laughter-loving Dean. And it is just his *saeva indignatio*—the mad wrath which, as he said to Delany, did "eat his flesh and consume his spirits"—that establishes the deeper authenticity of *Gulliver* which separates it from any other production of eighteenth-century wit. He himself as Gulliver towers over his Lilliputian enemies, and flees from the disgusting humans into the quiet stables of the horses. How far his madness had already taken him, he could scarcely have guessed, for it had unconsciously carried him, an unquestioning Christian, for the moment outside Christianity: the rational and tranquil Houyhnhnms do not need a Messiah's blood and a historically revealed religion in order to be saved, while the Yahoos could not possibly be redeemed by any savior. Swift might not have gone mad after writing *Gulliver*, but much of the power of that book comes from the fact that he was already on the road.

Once a writer imposes his greatness on us he imposes his figure totally, and we then read every scrap and scribble against the whole, and we will not find it strange that Joyce should invoke even the scrawling of the Earwicker twin as part of the image of Everymanthewriter. The man who wrote the charming prattle of the *Journal to Stella* is the same who comes to howl at bay before the human race. In his life he made two bluestockings love him desperately (a significant choice this, that they should be bluestockings; but one, to his surprise, turned out, as sometime happens, a very passionate bluestocking); and one he loved all his life long. In the simple *Prayers for Stella*, sublimating, he gropes, touches, fondles her in God. What happened beyond this we do not know. But we need no very fanciful imagination to guess the frustration which produces that mingled disgust and fascination at the biology of the female body. He did more, however, than release this into a few scatological verses about milady at and on her toilet; he was able to project his frustration and rage into the helpless Irish face about him, the insouciant Saxon face, churchmen, bishops, Lord Mayors, quacks, and pedants; "the corruptions and villainies of men in power"; and through these into a total vision of the human condition.

Here at last we come close to the secret: if one characteristic of neurosis is always a displacement somewhere, then perhaps the test of a writer's achievement may be precisely the extent and richness of displacement he is able to effect. In the process of literary expression, the neurotic mass acquires energies which are directed toward reality and seek their satisfaction in reality. As the writer displaces the neurotic mass further afield he is led to incorporate larger and larger areas of experience into his vision. Everything begins to appear then *as if* the world he pictures were itself sufficient to generate this vision (which we may know, in fact, to have been rather the product of quite unconscious compulsions and conflicts); *as if* the ego, really master in its own house, were simply responding appropriately to the world as seen in the book. Thus the peculiar sense of conquest and liberation that follows literary creation cannot be analyzed solely as that fulfillment of wishes which normally occurs in daydreaming or fantasy. Why in that case would it be necessary to complete the literary work at all? And why should the liberation it gives be so much more powerful and durable? No; this conquest is also one for the ego itself, which now seems momentarily to have absorbed the unconscious into itself so that the neurotic disgust itself appears an appropriate response to reality. And if this is an illusion from the analyst's point of view, it may not always be an illusion from the moralist's point of view. The world as it appears in Swift's writings is, in the end, adequate to his madness.

Now Swift's (unlike Cowper's, to cite another literary madman) was a very strong ego, and the fact that he broke in old age only tells us how great were the visions, tensions, and repressions he had to face. We do not know enough to establish his "case," but we know enough to say that his madness probably did not have its source in the literary condition at all—however much incipient madness may have informed and made powerful his writings.

Do we build too much on his example then? Perhaps; but his figure, in its broad strong outlines (and the very simplicity of these outlines is to our advantage here), takes such a grip on the imagination that, pursuing this rather nocturnal meditation, I am loath to let him drop. He has taken us so far already that it seems worthwhile to journey a little way with him still into the darkness.

Certainly there is nothing, or very little, about Swift to make him a modern figure. He sits so solidly amid the prejudices and virtues of his age that we search in vain for any ideas in him that would seem to anticipate us. He was a man of parts rather than of ideas; and his very "rationality" is a kind of eighteenth-century prejudice, having little in common with what we struggle toward as our own, or even what the same century later in France was to discover so triumphantly as its own. He lived before modern political alternatives became very real or meaningful, and only his human hatred of the abuses of power might connect him remotely with some of our own attitudes. As a literary man, he is at the farthest distance from that neurotic specialist, the modern littérateur; he is not even a professional literary man in the sense of his contemporary, Pope, much less in the sense of the consecrated *rentier*, Flaubert. Thus we have no quarrel at all with certain professorial critics who point out that Swift was primarily interested in power and that he came by writing as an instrument of power or simply as a diversion. (What an unhappy conclusion, though, if we thought we had therefore to exclude him from something called "literature"!) And we might even go along a certain way with the generous hint of these critics that the frustration of his desires for power explains both his misanthropy and final insanity.

But does not logic teach us that an induction is strengthened more by a confirming instance further afield? and which at first glance might not seem to fall altogether under the class in question? And if Swift, who sits so solidly in his own age, leads us, when we but plunge deeply enough, into the world of the modern writer, should we not feel all the more assured that we have got at least a little below the surface? Already, beneath the solid outlines of his eighteenth-century figure, I begin to descry the shadows and depths of a *psychic type*, the writer—which has emerged, to be sure, spectacularly only in the two following centuries.

Now the trouble with the professors (and not only when they censure Swift for his craving for power) is that they have unconsciously created a figure of the writer in their own image: a well-bred person with well-tubbed and scrubbed motives, who approaches something specialized and disinterested that they call "literature" as if his function in the end were merely to provide them with books to teach. Perhaps the great writers themselves have unwittingly helped toward this deception? Has any one of them ever told us why he had to become a writer? They tell us instead: "To hold a mirror up to nature"; "To carry a mirror dawdling down a lane"; "To forge the uncreated conscience of my race"; etc., etc.—great blazons of triumph, formulae of their extraordinary achievement, before which we forget even to ask why they had to become writers. The great writer is the victorious suitor who has captured a beautiful bride in an incomparable marriage. There seems almost no point in asking him why he had to love and seek marriage: his reasons seem all too abundant, he has only to point to the incomparable attractions of his beloved. He has lost his private compulsions in the general—in the positive and admirable qualities, known to all men, of the thing achieved. (The Kierkegaardians, by the way, should remind themselves that life must be just such a conquest and appropriation of universals.) But life does not contain only such happy bridegrooms, otherwise we might never know all the enormities and paradoxes of love; and if there were only great geniuses among writers, perhaps we might never know this other truth: the compulsions and paradoxes on the dark side of their calling—which they, the great ones, could afford to forget in the daylight blaze of their triumph.

The mistake is not to have invoked the idea of power but, once invoked, not to have seen it through: we have but to pursue it far enough and we can find it present everywhere in Swift's writings, and indeed the central impulse of his prose itself (perhaps the best in English). What is that stripped and supple syntax but the design of greatest possible economy and force, by which he launches each sentence at its mark like a potent and well-aimed missile? (And each missile thuds against the bestial human face from which he would escape.) Swift's lack of interest in being a literary man as such may account, then, for some of his strongest qualities. The conception of literature as an instrument or a diversion or even a vanity may exist along with the power to produce the greatest literature: Pascal's conviction of the vanity of eloquence is one reason why he is a greater prose writer than Valéry, the aesthete, who mocks at this conviction. Here it seems almost as if from examining Swift's writings themselves we might arrive at Freud's perception: that the writer is more than commonly obsessed by a desire for power which he seeks to gratify through his public fantasies.

Because of an introverted disposition, he is unable to gratify this desire in the usual arenas of external action. Introversion is the brand of his calling: he is the divided man, his consciousness always present but a little absent, hovering over itself, ready to pounce and bring back some fragment to his notebooks. The introverted disposition suggests some excessive and compelling need to be loved; and we would suspect that here too it must result primally from some special strength or strain in the Oedipal relation. But whatever our speculation as to its source, the point of power remains clear; and if he seeks it by a detour, the writer's claims are nonetheless total: it is power of the most subtle kind that the writer wants, power over the mind and freedom of other human beings, his readers.

Such extraordinary claims of power, and particularly their indirectness of gratification, suggest immediately an ambivalent connection with that more than usually acute sense of guilt with which writers as a class seem to be endowed. (That Swift suffered from extraordinary obsessions of guilt toward the end of his life, we know by accounts of several sources;

93

but most of his life, since he accepted Christianity without question, these guilt feelings were tapped and drained off into religion; hence it is that in his writing we usually encounter the aggressive and outgoing parts of his personality.) Georges Blin, in "The Gash" (*Partisan Review*, Spring 1946), has presented very eloquently some of the sadistic motives that operate in the artist. We should expect—in accordance with the usual ambivalence—a masochistic pattern to be equally operative, and perhaps even more to the fore because of the essential indirectness of the artist's drives toward power and sadism. What else explains the writer's extraordinary eagerness for the painful humility of his yoke as he crouches over his desk stubbornly weaving and reweaving his own being hundreds of times? "Thought, study, sacrifice, and mortification"—how he trembles with joy to put on these hair shirts of his solitude and calling! These punishments he inflicts upon himself over his desk will help to make clear then why writing should satisfy the claims of guilt upon him; why he should search so passionately for redemption upon the written page, and why as the paragraph takes shape beneath his pen he can feel for moments that his step has become a little less heavy on the face of the earth. But we should also know this ambivalence of power and guilt from phenomenological scrutiny. We never live in a purely private world, our consciousness is penetrated at every point by the consciousness of others, and what is it but one step from seeking redemption in one's own eyes to seeking it in the eyes of others? The movement by which we stoop to lift ourselves out of the pit of self-contempt is one and unbroken with that thrust which would carry us above the shoulders of our fellow-men.

And is not this ambivalent urge to power-guilt but the sign of that excessive need to be loved which has driven the writer into a profession where he must speak with *his own* voice, offer to the public gaze of the world so much of his own existence? Love to be conquered by force, or taken as a gift of tenderness and pity for his confession.

But both the satisfaction (of power) and relief (from guilt), though they glow brightly, glow, alas, only for moments, and we live again in the shadow of ourselves. Nothing in the world (we are told) is a substitute for anything else, and if there is a point beyond which the writer can never satisfy these urges in literature itself, then this inability can no longer be regarded as peculiar to Swift, a deficiency of his "case," but an essential and mortifying aspect of the literary condition everywhere. So we come back to our point: Swift is certainly not a modern literary man, but we only had to go deep enough, and we have arrived at a world of impulses and motives that we recognize as our own.

The more gifted the writer the more likely he is to be critically conscious of his literary tradition—the more conscious, that is, of the reality principle as it operates in the literary sphere—and the harder it becomes for him to fall into one of the easy publicist styles of his day. Recently I read about a young writer who had written a best seller in four weeks and made $400,000 out of it—$100,000 a week, almost as good pay as a movie star. If books could be written from the top of one's mind merely (even books of this kind), it is naïve to think a major writer would not do it: after four weeks of absence he returns to support himself for many years in the prosecution of his own unremunerative and serious tasks. But it seems impossible to write a best seller in complete parody, one has to believe in one's material even there, and it is impossible to fake unless one is a fake. Joyce has written in *Ulysses* a superb parody of the sentimental romance for schoolgirls, but it is quite obvious from that chapter that Joyce could not have turned out a novel in this genre for money: his irony and self-consciousness would have got in the way, and the book would not have attracted its readers but in the end only Joyce's readers. The writer writes what he can, and if he decides to sell out it is by corrupting and cheapening his own level, or perhaps slipping down a step below it; but writing is not so uncommitted an intellectual effort that he can drop down facilely to a very much lower level and operate with enough skill there to convince that kind of reader. Joyce did not write *Finnegans Wake* out of a free decision taken in the void, but because his experience of life and Western culture was what it was, and he had to write that book if he was to write anything.

It is perhaps not a very pleasant thought, but it seems inescapable, that even the commonest best seller is the product of the personal being of the author and demands its own kind of authenticity. Life also imprisons us in its rewards; and we may draw some satisfaction from the thought that these gay reapers of prestige and money, if they are to keep on terms with their audience, can have in the end only lives adequate to their books: *On écrit le livre qu'on mérite*. Our satisfaction might be greater if we were not on the other hand also painfully acquainted with the opposite phenomenon: the gifted people who find it difficult to produce precisely because they are too intelligent and sensitive to tailor their writing to the reigning market. The very awareness of standards inhibits them from writing, and, not being geniuses, they are unable to break through and produce anything adequate to those standards. The literary future in America, and perhaps the West generally, seems to be leading to this final and lamentable split: on the one hand, an enormous body of run-of-the-mill writing (machine-made, as it were), becoming ever more slick as it becomes more technically adequate through abundant competition and appropriation of the tricks of previous serious writing, and in the end generating its own types of pseudo authenticity, like Steinbeck or Marquand; on the other hand, an occasional genius breaking through this wall here and there, at ever more costly price in personal conflict, anguish, and difficulty. Modern poetry already provides us its own and extreme version of this exacerbating split; think of the extremity of personal difficulty required to produce the authentic poetry of our time: the depth of anguish which secreted the few poems of Eliot; and Yeats, we remember, had to struggle through a long life of political unrest, personal heartbreak, see the friends and poets of his youth die off or kill themselves, before he came into his own and could produce poems capable of convincing us that this poetry was not merely a kind of "solemn game."

Some of the more internal difficulties that beset the pursuit of literature are being very much discussed in France by writers like Maurice Blanchot and Brice Parain. Blanchot finishes one essay, in which he has explored certain aspects of anxiety, silence, and expression, with the devastating remark, "It is enough that literature should continue to seem possible," though the reader by the time he has waded through Blanchot's rarefactions to that point may very well have lost the conviction that even the possibility remained. These French researches are of a quite special character, continuing the tradition of Mallarmé—or, rather, attempting to see the esthetic problems of Mallarmé from the human anguish of Pascal. (As the burdens of civilization become heavier and we see existence itself with fewer illusions, we have come perhaps to share Pascal's attitude toward poetry: a vanity, a "solemn game"; at any rate, we seem to demand more of the modern writer before we take him very seriously.) These difficulties are extreme and we need not share them in that form: after the rigors to which Mallarmé submitted poetry in his search for a *langage authentique*, no wonder silence should appear as the only and haunting possibility of speech. After Mallarmé, poetry had to swing back toward the language of what he calls *universal reportage*, and Eliot's poetry has shown us that this language, suitably charged and concentrated, can be the vehicle of very great poetry. Blanchot's difficulties persist but in another form (especially in a commercial culture). Not silence but garrulousness ("unauthenic chatter," as Heidegger would say) may be the threat confronting the writer; but always and everywhere the difficulty of securing authenticity.

The difficulties we face in America—a society which turns, as Van Wyck Brooks says, its most gifted men into crackpots—are obviously of a much more external and violent kind than in France. External pressures abet the internal tensions, which become unendurable, and at long last comes that slide over into the more tranquil and private self-indulgence of fantasy with a consequent weakening of the reality principle. One (a critic) develops a private language; another spins out elaborate literary theories without content or relevance; a third has maintained his literary alertness and eye for relevance through a sheer aggressiveness which has cost him his ability to maintain personal relations—and which appears therefore in his work as a mutilation too. Scott Fitzgerald's confidante in "The Crack-up" (perhaps his most mature piece of writing, at that) gives him the extraordinary advice: "Listen. Suppose this wasn't a crack in you—suppose it was in the Grand Canyon. . . . By God, if I ever cracked, I'd try to make the whole world crack with me." And she was right and profound, but Fitzgerald was tied by too many strings to the values of American life to see her truth. His crack-up was the dawning of a truth upon him which he could not completely grasp or recognize intellectually. Swift in that position would have seen that the crack is in the Grand Canyon, in the whole world, in the total human face about him. If he is powerful enough—now against greater odds—to make, the world crack in his work, the writer has at the least the gratification of revenge, and the ego that deeper conquest (described above) where its anguish now seems no more than an appropriate response to a world portrayed (and with some fidelity) as cracked. But, alas, these energies which seek reality and are capable of transforming the neurotic mass into the writer's special and unique vision of the world can also be blocked by the external difficulties in the literary situation. And when that happens we open the door, as Freud says, to the psychoses—at any rate, to the breakdown and crack-up.

Abi viator et imitare si poteris.
(Go, traveler, and imitate him if you can.)
    —Swift's epitaph, written by himself

And so I am brought back into the center of my theme. If I appeared to have abandoned the theme of neurosis for the difficulties, external and internal, that confront the modern writer, it was only because these difficulties as part of his alienation are the aggravating causes and public face of his madness.

Buy why (in the end) should it be the writer's fate—more than of any other intellectual profession—to confront his crack in the face of the world? Because his subject is the very world of experience as such, and it is this world, this total world, which he must somehow salvage. The scientist has his appointed place in the community of researchers, he confronts carefully delimited fragments of experience, the data from which he proceeds are publicly recognizable, and his whole being is to be, as it were, an incarnate outward public mind. But the writer is alone—potentially twenty-four hours a day, the luminal pill and the writing pad beside his bed for whatever welcome or unwelcome presence comes that night. On the other hand, it might seem that the philosopher, since he confronts in his own way the totality of experience, might also show some fatal tendency toward aberration. But the philosopher deals with concepts and out of these he may construct some kind of "meaning" for the world: when speculative systems were still believed, he had only to be agile enough to design one of these towering arks of salvation, and what if it leaked a little, he was a professor and he had something to do the rest of his professorial life plugging its gaps; now when the pretense to speculative theories is no longer even taken seriously the philosopher can construct an equally elaborate theory showing that the question itself has no meaning, and so philosophy continues to be possible. Whatever the impasse of insoluble antinomies at which his thought finally arrives, he can continue to arrange these in neat parallel columns, chip away at their edges, and perpetually recast their statement as if preparing bit by bit for a solution which in fact never arrives; and so continues in business, he has something to say, he "gets published"; and after the initial shocks and disturbance mankind has shown itself capable of settling down peacefully into positivism, and few people are more intellectually adjusted than the positivists. But it is not at the level of concepts that the appalling face of the world is seen, and it is another kind of "meaning" that the writer must construct. Out of the ravages of his experience, his desperate loneliness, he must put forth those works which look back into his gaze with conviction and authenticity and wear about them the gleams of interest—cathectic charges, in the technical term—which have fled from the vast bare blank face of the world as seen in the extreme situations of *his* truth: in sleeplessness, the nervous darkness, against death and against the inexorable and dragging vista of time which is his being.

Notes

The reader should compare, for a somewhat different view of the matter, Lionel Trilling's "Art and Neurosis" [included in this book]. By indicating my disagreements with Mr. Trilling's admirable essay, perhaps I may sum up, in more scientific terms, the psychoanalytic view which lies at the base (perhaps a little hidden) of my own discussion.

Mr. Trilling's main point, perhaps, is that neurosis by itself will not make anyone a great writer; a proposition with which I am in complete agreement. I would also agree with him that there are many neurotics among businessmen and scientists (though I doubt the scientists could match the incidence among literary men). But granting such widespread latent neuroticism (the wives of businessmen could tell us a lot, if they chose), the point would be that with the writer it is not latent but consciously exploited. My difference with Mr. Trilling is that I do not consider the question as primarily statistical: whether a certain group known as scientists contains as many neurotics as another group called writers. My main point, rather, is one about the *literary process* itself: that this process does, in a certain way, imitate the neurotic process and does exploit neurotic material.

Here it is pertinent to indicate my principal disagreement with Freud, who analyzes the effect of a literary work in terms of the pleasure obtained from fantasies and daydreams. This may do justice to our childish delight in romances—or to the level at which we read *Gulliver's Travels* in childhood. But it hardly does justice to the power which the fiction of Kafka, Joyce, or Proust has over us in our adult years. I hold instead that it is the writer's *identification* with his fantasy, rather than the aspect of fantasy itself, which has power over us, convinces us. (The phenomenon of identification, by the way, is very sparingly discussed by Freud, probably because the psychic transaction involved in it is still quite obscure.) And in this identification with fantasy the writer imitates, *up to a certain point*, one of the deepest and commonest phenomena of pathology.

Since Freud speaks of the cathexis (i.e., charge of psychic energy) which the child has toward the objects of play, he should have seen that the cathexis of the writer toward the objects of fantasy is more significant than the aspect of fantasy itself. We cited Kafka as a crucial case; equally crucial would be the case of Joyce, who rarely moves us through the elaborateness, surprise, or ingenuity of his fantasies, but *by the powerful charge he is able to lay on the most banal episode*.

The second element in my analytic view is, admittedly, more speculative, and concerns the *psychic type* which now seems to emerge with the modern writer. If we demand of the writer a deeper authenticity—identification with fantasy— then I think we must expect that more and more only a certain psychic type will be at once capable of this, and also driven to embrace it as his own painful profession. We have suggested (speculatively) that the individual who is driven to exhibit such large slices of his psyche to the world is compelled by an excessive need for the winning of love. Whether or not this hypothesis be verified by literary and biographical evidence, it should not surprise us, at any rate, that the modern writer (capable of satisfying our severe demands) has become, by and large, a neurotic type.

The third element of my view, however, attempts to separate the neurosis of the writer from that of other men. The writer's neurosis, through displacement and appropriation, attempts to square itself with reality—but only in the work. Here I reach some agreement with Mr. Trilling—but not completely or fundamentally. When he speaks of the writer's ability to "shape" the neurotic material, he seems to suggest that this latter may be some kind of clay external to the writer, and that there is some portion of the mind which remains completely outside the neurosis. This notion of control seems also to imply that the writer attains, through the work, health and wholeness in his life too. This strikes me as quite unguarded from an analytic point of view. The great counterexample that comes immediately to mind is one from painting: the case of Van Gogh (recently discussed by Meyer Schapiro), who, a few days after painting "Crows in the Wheatfield" and writing to his brother that the country was "healthful and strengthening," committed suicide! The triumph of the ego, in short, is in the work and not the life. It is, as I have said, an "as if" triumph. Swift did not heal himself by writing *Gulliver's Travels*.

The source of the catharsis, by the way, that Van Gogh obtained from that particular painting has to be analyzed in terms of this essay: the momentary triumph of the ego is that it has now appropriated elements from reality corresponding to its own torments, and depicted a scene to which these torments seem an adequate response, and so has the illusion that its own reality principle has been restored and safeguarded.

8.

Art and Neurosis

Lionel Trilling

THE QUESTION OF the mental health of the artist has engaged the attention of our culture since the beginning of the Romantic Movement. Before that time it was commonly said that the poet was "mad," but this was only a manner of speaking, a way of saying that the mind of the poet worked in different fashion from the mind of the philosopher; it had no real reference to the mental hygiene of the man who was the poet. But in the early nineteenth century, with the development of a more elaborate psychology and a stricter and more literal view of mental and emotional normality, the statement was more strictly and literally intended. So much so, indeed, that Charles Lamb, who knew something about madness at close quarters and a great deal about art, undertook to refute in his brilliant essay, "On the Sanity of True Genius," the idea that the exercise of the imagination was a kind of insanity. And some eighty years later, the idea having yet further entrenched itself, Bernard Shaw felt called upon to argue the sanity of art, but his cogency was of no more avail than Lamb's. In recent years the connection between art and mental illness has been formulated not only by those who are openly or covertly hostile to art, but also and more significantly by those who are most intensely partisan to it. The latter willingly and even eagerly accept the idea that the artist is mentally ill and go on to make his illness a condition of his power to tell the truth.

From Lionel Trilling, *The Liberal Imagination, Essays on Literature and Society* (New York: Viking, 1950; repr. Scribner's, 1976). Copyright 1945, 1947, 1950 Lionel Trilling. Reprinted by permission.

This conception of artistic genius is indeed one of the characteristic notions of our culture. I should like to bring it into question. To do so is to bring also into question certain early ideas of Freud's and certain conclusions which literary laymen have drawn from the whole tendency of the Freudian psychology. From the very start it was recognized that psychoanalysis was likely to have important things to say about art and artists. Freud himself thought so, yet when he first addressed himself to the subject he said many clumsy and misleading things. I have elsewhere and at length tried to separate the useful from the useless and even dangerous statements about art that Freud has made. To put it briefly here, Freud had some illuminating and even beautiful insights into certain particular works of art which made complex use of the element of myth. Then, without specifically undertaking to do so, his *Beyond the Pleasure Principle* offers a brilliant and comprehensive explanation of our interest in tragedy. And what is of course most important of all—it is a point to which I shall return—Freud, by the whole tendency of his psychology, establishes the *naturalness* of artistic thought. Indeed, it is possible to say of Freud that he ultimately did more for our understanding of art than any other writer since Aristotle; and this being so, it can only be surprising that in his early work he should have made the error of treating the artist as a neurotic who escapes from reality by means of "substitute gratifications."

As Freud went forward he insisted less on this simple formulation. Certainly it did not have its original force with him when, at his seventieth birthday celebration, he disclaimed the right to be called the discoverer of the unconscious, saying that whatever he may have done for the systematic understanding of the unconscious, the credit for its discovery properly belonged to the literary masters. And psychoanalysis has inherited from him a tenderness for art which is real although sometimes clumsy, and nowadays most psychoanalysts of any personal sensitivity are embarrassed by occasions which seem to lead them to reduce art to a formula of mental illness. Nevertheless Freud's early belief in the essential neuroticism of the artist found an all too fertile ground— found, we might say, the very ground from which it first sprang, for, when he spoke of the artist as a neurotic, Freud was adopting one of the popular beliefs of his age. Most readers will see this belief as the expression of the industrial rationalization and the bourgeois philistinism of the nineteenth century. In this they are partly right. The nineteenth century established the basic virtue of "getting up at eight, shaving close at a quarter-past, breakfasting at nine, going to the City at ten, coming home at half-past five, and dining at seven." The Messrs. Podsnap who instituted this scheduled morality inevitably decreed that the arts must celebrate it and nothing else. "Nothing else to be permitted to these . . . vagrants the Arts, on pain of excommunication. Nothing else To Be—anywhere!" We observe that the virtuous day ends with dinner—bed and sleep are naturally not part of the Reality that Is, and nothing must be set forth which will, as Mr. Podsnap put it, bring a Blush to the Cheek of a Young Person.

The excommunication of the arts, when it was found necessary, took the form of pronouncing the artist mentally degenerate, a device which eventually found its theorist in Max Nordau. In the history of the arts this is new. The poet was always known to belong to a touchy tribe—*genus irritabile* was a tag anyone would know—and ever since Plato the process of the inspired imagination, as we have said, was thought to be a special one of some interest, which the similitude of madness made somewhat intelligible. But this is not quite to say that the poet was the victim of actual mental aberration. The eighteenth century did not find the poet to be less than other men, and certainly the Renaissance did not. If he was a professional, there might be condescension to his social status, but in a time which deplored all professionalism whatever, this was simply a way of asserting the high value of poetry, which ought not to be compromised by trade. And a certain good nature marked even the snubbing of the professional. At any rate, no one was likely to identify the poet with the weakling. Indeed, the Renaissance ideal held poetry to be, like arms or music, one of the signs of manly competence.

The change from this view of things cannot be blamed wholly on the bourgeois or philistine public. Some of the "blame" must rest with the poets themselves. The Romantic poets were as proud of their art as the vaunting poets of the sixteenth century, but one of them talked with an angel in a tree and insisted that Hell was better than Heaven and sexuality holier than chastity; another told the world that he wanted to lie down like a tired child and weep away this life of care; another asked so foolish a question as "Why did I laugh tonight?"; and yet another explained that he had written one of his best poems in a drugged sleep. The public took them all at their word—they were not as other men. Zola, in the interests of science, submitted himself to examination by fifteen psychiatrists and agreed with their conclusion that his genius had its source in the neurotic elements of his temperament. Baudelaire, Rimbaud, Verlaine found virtue and strength in their physical and mental illness and pain. W. H. Auden addresses his "wound" in the cherishing language of a lover, thanking it for the gift of insight it has bestowed. "Knowing you," he says, "has made me understand." And Edmund Wilson in his striking phrase, "the wound and the bow," has formulated for our time the idea of the characteristic sickness of the artist, which he represents by the figure of Philoctetes, the Greek warrior who was forced to live in isolation because of the disgusting odor of a suppurating wound and who yet had to be sought out by his countrymen because they had need of the magically unerring bow he possessed.

The myth of the sick artist, we may suppose, has established itself because it is of advantage to the various groups who have one or another relation with art. To the artist himself the myth gives some of the ancient powers and privileges of the idiot and the fool, half-prophetic creatures, or of the mutilated priest. That the artist's neurosis may be but a mask is suggested by Thomas Mann's pleasure in representing his untried youth as "sick" but his successful maturity as senatorially robust. By means of his belief in his own sickness, the artist may the more easily fulfill his chosen, and assigned, function of putting himself into connection with the forces of spirituality and morality; the artist sees as insane the "normal" and "healthy" ways of established society, while aberration and illness appear as spiritual and moral health if only because they controvert the ways of respectable society.

Then too, the myth has its advantage for the philistine—a double advantage. On the one hand, the belief in the artist's neuroticism allows the philistine to shut his ears to what the artist says. But on the other hand it allows him to listen. For we must not make the common mistake—the contemporary philistine does want to listen, at the same time that he wants to shut his ears. By supposing that the artist has an interesting but not always reliable relation to reality, he is able to contain (in the military sense) what the artist tells him. If he did not want to listen at all, he would say "insane"; with "neurotic," which hedges, he listens when he chooses.

And in addition to its advantage to the artist and to the philistine, we must take into account the usefulness of the myth to a third group, the group of "sensitive" people, who, although not artists, are not philistines either. These people form a group by virtue of their passive impatience with philistinism, and also by virtue of their awareness of their own emotional pain and uncertainty. To these people the myth of the sick artist is the institutional sanction of their situation; they seek to approximate or acquire the character of the artist, sometimes by planning to work or even attempting to work as the artist does, always by making a connection between their own powers of mind and their consciousness of "difference" and neurotic illness.

The early attempts of psychoanalysis to deal with art went on the assumption that, because the artist was neurotic, the content of his work was also neurotic, which is to say that it did not stand in a correct relation to reality. But nowadays, as I have said, psychoanalysis is not likely to be so simple in its transactions with art. A good example of the psychoanalytical development in this respect is Dr. Saul Rosenzweig's well-known essay, "The Ghost of Henry James." This is an admirable piece of work, marked by accuracy in the reporting of the literary fact and by respect for the value of the literary object. Although Dr. Rosenzweig explores the element of neurosis in James' life and work, he nowhere suggests that this element in any way lessens James' value as an artist or moralist. In effect he says that neurosis is a way of dealing with reality which, in real life, is uncomfortable and uneconomical, but that this judgment of neurosis in life cannot mechanically be transferred to works of art upon which neurosis has had its influence. He nowhere implies that a work of art in whose genesis a neurotic element may be found is for that reason irrelevant or in any way diminished in value. Indeed, the manner of his treatment suggests, what is of course the case, that every neurosis deals with a real emotional situation of the most intensely meaningful kind.

Yet as Dr. Rosenzweig brings his essay to its close, he makes use of the current assumption about the causal connection between the psychic illness of the artist and his power. His investigation of James, he says, "reveals the aptness of the Philoctetes pattern." He accepts the idea of "the sacrificial roots of literary power" and speaks of "the unhappy sources of James' genius." "The broader application of the inherent pattern," he says, "is familiar to readers of Edmund Wilson's recent volume *The Wound and the Bow*. . . . Reviewing the experience and work of several well-known literary masters, Wilson discloses the sacrificial roots of their power on the model of the Greek legend. In the case of Henry James, the present account . . . provides a similar insight into the unhappy sources of his genius."

This comes as a surprise. Nothing in Dr. Rosenzweig's theory requires it. For his theory asserts no more than that Henry James, predisposed by temperament and family situation to certain mental and emotional qualities, was in his youth injured in a way which he believed to be sexual; that he unconsciously invited the injury in the wish to identify himself with his father, who himself had been similarly injured—"castrated": a leg had been amputated—and under strikingly similar circumstances; this resulted for the younger Henry James in a certain pattern of life and in a preoccupation in his work with certain themes which more or less obscurely symbolize his sexual situation. For this I think Dr. Rosenzweig makes a sound case. Yet I submit that this is not the same thing as disclosing the roots of James' power or discovering the sources of his genius. The essay which gives Edmund Wilson's book its title and cohering principle does not explicitly say that the roots of power are sacrificial and that the source of genius is unhappy. Where it is explicit, it states only that "genius and disease, like strength and mutilation, may be inextricably bound up together," which of course, on its face, says no more than that personality is integral and not made up of detachable parts; and from this there is no doubt to be drawn the important practical and moral implication that we cannot judge or dismiss a man's genius and strength because of our awareness of his disease or mutilation. The Philoctetes legend in itself does not suggest anything beyond this. It does not suggest that the wound is the price of the bow, or that without the wound the bow may not be possessed or drawn. Yet Dr. Rosenzweig has accurately summarized the force and, I think, the intention of Mr. Wilson's whole book; its several studies do seem to say that effectiveness in the arts does depend on sickness.

An examination of this prevalent idea might well begin with the observation of how pervasive and deeply rooted is the notion that power may be gained by suffering. Even at relatively high stages of culture the mind seems to take easily to the primitive belief that pain and sacrifice are connected with strength. Primitive beliefs must be treated with respectful alertness to their possible truth and also with the suspicion of their being magical and irrational, and it is worth noting on both sides of the question, and in the light of what we have said about the ambiguous relation of the neurosis to reality, that the whole economy of the neurosis is based exactly on this idea of the *quid pro quo* of sacrificial pain: the neurotic person unconsciously subscribes to a system whereby he gives up some pleasure or power, or inflicts pain on himself in order to secure some other power or some other pleasure.

In the ingrained popular conception of the relation between suffering and power there are actually two distinct although related ideas. One is that there exists in the individual a fund of power which has outlets through various organs or faculties, and that if its outlet through one organ or faculty be prevented, it will flow to increase the force or sensitivity of another. Thus it is popularly believed that the sense of touch is intensified in the blind not so much by the will of the blind person to adapt himself to the necessities of his situation as, rather, by a sort of mechanical redistribution of power. And this idea would seem to explain, if not the origin of the ancient mutilation of priests, then at least a common understanding of their sexual sacrifice.

The other idea is that a person may be taught by, or proved by, the endurance of pain. There will easily come to mind the ritual suffering that is inflicted at the tribal initiation of youths into full manhood or at the admission of the apprentice into the company of journeyman adepts. This idea in sophisticated form found its way into high religion at least as early as Aeschylus, who held that man achieves knowledge of God through suffering, and it was from the beginning an important element of Christian thought. In the nineteenth century the Christianized notion of the didactic suffering of the artist went along with the idea of his mental degeneration and even served as a sort of countermyth of it. Its doctrine was that the artist, a man of strength and health, experienced and suffered, and thus learned both the facts of life and his artistic craft. "I am the man, I suffered, I was there," ran his boast, and he derived his authority from the knowledge gained through suffering.

There can be no doubt that both these ideas represent a measure of truth about mental and emotional power. The idea of didactic suffering expresses a valuation of experience and of steadfastness. The idea of natural compensation for the sacrifice of some faculty also says something that can be rationally defended: one cannot be and do everything and the whole-hearted absorption in any enterprise, art for example, means that we must give up other possibilities, even parts of ourselves. And there is even a certain validity to the belief that the individual has a fund of undifferentiated energy which presses the harder upon what outlets are available to it when it has been deprived of the normal number.

Then, in further defense of the belief that artistic power is connected with neurosis, we can say that there is no doubt that what we call mental illness may be the source of psychic knowledge. Some neurotic people, because they are more apprehensive than normal people, are able to see more of certain parts of reality and to see them with more intensity. And many neurotic or psychotic patients are in certain respects in closer touch with the actualities of the unconscious than are normal people. Further, the expression of a neurotic or psychotic conception of reality is likely to be more intense than a normal one.

Yet when we have said all this, it is still wrong, I believe, to find the root of the artist's power and the source of his genius in neurosis. To the idea that literary power and genius spring from pain and neurotic sacrifice there are two major objections. The first has to do with the assumed uniqueness of the artist as a subject of psychoanalytical explanation. The second has to do with the true meaning of power and genius.

One reason why writers are considered to be more available than other people to psychoanalytical explanation is that they tell us what is going on inside them. Even when they do not make an actual diagnosis of their malaises or describe "symptoms," we must bear it in mind that it is their profession to deal with fantasy in some form or other. It is in the nature of the writer's job that he exhibit his unconscious. He may disguise it in various ways, but disguise is not concealment. Indeed, it may be said that the more a writer takes pains with his work to remove it from the personal and subjective, the more—and not the less—he will express his true unconscious, although not what passes with most for the unconscious.

Further, the writer is likely to be a great hand at personal letters, diaries, and autobiographies: indeed, almost the only good autobiographies are those of writers. The writer is more aware of what happens to him or goes on in him and often finds it necessary or useful to be articulate about his inner states, and prides himself on telling the truth. Thus, only a man as devoted to the truth of the emotions as Henry James was would have informed the world, despite his characteristic reticence, of an accident so intimate as his. We must not of course suppose that a writer's statements about his intimate life are equivalent to true statements about his unconscious, which, by definition, he doesn't consciously know; but they may be useful clues to the nature of an entity about which we can make statements of more or less cogency, although never statements of certainty; or they at least give us what is surely related to a knowledge of his unconscious—that is, an insight into his personality.[1]

But while the validity of dealing with the writer's intellectual life in psychoanalytical terms is taken for granted, the psychoanalytical explanation of the intellectual life of scientists is generally speaking not countenanced. The old myth of the mad scientist, with the exception of an occasional mad psychiatrist, no longer exists. The social position of science requires that it should cease, which leads us to remark that those partisans of art who insist on explaining artistic genius by means of psychic imbalance are in effect capitulating to the dominant mores which hold that the members of the respectable professions are, however dull they may be, free from neurosis. Scientists, to continue with them as the best example of the respectable professions, do not usually give us the clues to their personalities which writers habitually give. But no one who has ever lived observantly among scientists will claim that they are without an unconscious or even that they are free from neurosis. How often, indeed, it is apparent that the devotion to science, if it cannot be called a neurotic manifestation, at least can be understood as going very cozily with neurotic elements in the temperament, such as, for example, a marked compulsiveness. Of scientists as a group we can say that they are less concerned with the manifestations of personality, their own or others', than are writers as a group. But this relative indifference is scarcely a sign of normality—indeed, if we choose to regard it with the same sort of eye with which the characteristics of writers are regarded, we might say the indifference to matters of personality is in itself a suspicious evasion.

It is the basic assumption of psychoanalysis that the acts of *every* person are influenced by the forces of the unconscious. Scientists, bankers, lawyers, or surgeons, by reason of the traditions of their professions, practice concealment and conformity; but it is difficult to believe that an investigation according to psychoanalytical principles would fail to show that the strains and imbalances of their psyches are not of the same frequency as those of writers, and of similar kind. I do not mean that everybody has the same troubles and identical psyches, but only that there is no special category for writers.[2]

If this is so, and if we still want to relate the writer's power to his neurosis, we must be willing to relate all intellectual power to neurosis. We must find the roots of Newton's power in his emotional extravagances, and the roots of Darwin's power in his sorely neurotic temperament, and the roots of Pascal's mathematical genius in the impulses which drove him to extreme religious masochism—I choose but the classic examples. If we make the neurosis-power equivalence at all, we must make it in every field of endeavor. Logician, economist, botanist, physicist, theologian—no profession may be so respectable or so remote or so rational as to be exempt from the psychological interpretation.[3]

Further, not only power but also failure or limitation must be accounted for by the theory of neurosis, and not merely failure or limitation in life but even failure or limitation in art. Thus it is often said that the warp of Dostoevsky's mind accounts for the brilliance of his psychological insights. But it is never said that the same warp of Dostoevsky's mind also accounted for his deficiency in insight. Freud, who greatly admired Dostoevsky, although he did not like him, observed that "his insight was entirely restricted to the workings of the abnormal psyche. Consider his astounding helplessness before the phenomenon of love; he really only understands either crude, instinctive desire or masochistic submission or love from pity."[4] This, we must note, is not merely Freud's comment on the extent of the province which Dostoevsky chose for his own, but on his failure to understand what, given the province of his choice, he might be expected to understand.

And since neurosis can account not only for intellectual success and for failure or limitation but also for mediocrity, we have most of society involved in neurosis. To this I have no objection—I think most of society is indeed involved in neurosis. But with neurosis accounting for so much, it cannot be made exclusively to account for one man's literary power.

We have now to consider what is meant by genius when its source is identified as the sacrifice and pain of neurosis.

In the case of Henry James, the reference to the neurosis of his personal life does indeed tell us something about the latent intention of his work and thus about the reason for some large part of its interest for us. But if genius and its source are what we are dealing with, we must observe that the reference to neurosis tells us nothing about James' passion, energy, and devotion, nothing about his architectonic skill, nothing about the other themes that were important to him which are not connected with his unconscious concern with castration. We cannot, that is, make the writer's inner life exactly equivalent to his power of expressing it. Let us grant for the sake of argument that the literary genius, as distinguished from other men, is the victim of a "mutilation" and that his fantasies are neurotic.[5] It does not then follow as the inevitable next step that his ability to express these fantasies and to impress us with them is neurotic, for that ability is what we mean by his genius. Anyone might be injured as Henry James was, and even respond within himself to the injury as James is said to have done, and yet not have his literary power.

The reference to the artist's neurosis tells us something about the material on which the artist exercises his powers, and even something about his reasons for bringing his powers into play, but it does not tell us anything about the source of his power, it makes no causal connection between them and the neurosis. And if we look into the matter, we see that there is in fact no causal connection between them. For, still granting that the poet is uniquely neurotic, what is surely not neurotic, what indeed suggests nothing but health, is his power of using his neuroticism. He shapes his fantasies, he gives them social form and reference. Charles Lamb's way of putting this cannot be improved. Lamb is denying that genius is allied to insanity; for "insanity" the modern reader may substitute "neurosis." "The ground of the mistake," he says,

is, that men, finding in the raptures of the higher poetry a condition of exaltation, to which they have no parallel in their own experience, besides the spurious resemblance of it in dreams and fevers, impute a state of dreaminess and fever to the poet. But the true poet dreams being awake. He is not possessed by his subject but has dominion over it. . . . Where he seems most to recede from humanity, he will be found the truest to it. From beyond the scope of nature if he summon possible existences, he subjugates them to the law of her consistency. He is beautifully loyal to that sovereign directress, when he appears most to betray and desert her. . . . Herein the great and the little wits are differenced; that if the latter wander ever so little from nature or natural existence, they lose themselves and their readers. . . . They do not create, which implies shaping and consistency. Their imaginations are not active—for to be active is to call something into act and form—but passive as men in sick dreams.

The activity of the artist, we must remember, may be approximated by many who are themselves not artists. Thus, the expressions of many schizophrenic people have the intense appearance of creativity and an inescapable interest and significance. But they are not works of art, and although Van Gogh may have been schizophrenic he was in addition an artist. Again, as I have already suggested, it is not uncommon in our society for certain kinds of neurotic people to imitate the artist in his life and even in his ideals and ambitions. They follow the artist in everything except successful performance. It was, I think, Otto Rank who called such people half-artists and confirmed the diagnosis of their neuroticism at the same time that he differentiated them from true artists.

Nothing is so characteristic of the artist as his power of shaping his work, of subjugating his raw material, however aberrant it be from what we call normality, to the consistency of nature. It would be possible to deny that whatever disease or mutilation the artist may suffer is an element of his production which has its effect on every part of it, but disease and mutilation are available to us all—life provides them with prodigal generosity. What marks the artist is his power to shape the material of pain we all have.

At this point, with our recognition of life's abundant provision of pain, we are at the very heart of our matter, which is the meaning we may assign to neurosis and the relation we are to suppose it to have with normality. Here Freud himself can be of help, although it must be admitted that what he tells us may at first seem somewhat contradictory and confusing.

Freud's study of Leonardo da Vinci is an attempt to understand why Leonardo was unable to pursue his artistic enterprises, feeling compelled instead to advance his scientific investigations. The cause of this Freud traces back to certain childhood experiences not different in kind from the experiences which Dr. Rosenzweig adduces to account for certain elements in the work of Henry James. And when he has completed his study Freud makes this caveat:

Let us expressly emphasize that we have never considered Leonardo as a neurotic. . . . We no longer believe that health and disease, normal and nervous, are sharply distinguished from each other. We know today that neurotic symptoms are substitutive formations for certain repressive acts which must result in the course of our development from the child to the cultural man, that we all produce such substitutive formations, and that only the amount, intensity, and distribution of these substitutive formations justify the practical conception of illness.

The statement becomes the more striking when we remember that in the course of his study Freud has had occasion to observe that Leonardo was both homosexual and sexually inactive. I am not sure that the statement that Leonardo was not a neurotic is one that Freud would have made at every point in the later development of psychoanalysis, yet it is in conformity with his continuing notion of the genesis of culture. And the *practical*, the quantitative or economic, conception of illness he insists on in a passage in the *Introductory Lectures*. "The neurotic symptoms," he says,

are activities which are detrimental, or at least useless, to life as a whole; the person concerned frequently complains of them as obnoxious to him or they involve suffering and distress for him. The principal injury they inflict lies in the expense of energy they entail, and, besides this, in the energy needed to combat them. Where the symptoms are extensively developed, these two kinds of effort may exact such a price that the person suffers a very serious impoverishment in available mental energy which consequently disables him for all the important tasks of life. This result depends principally upon the amount of energy taken up in this way; therefore you will see that "illness" is essentially a practical conception. But if you look at the matter from a theoretical point of view and ignore this question of degree, you can very well see that we are all ill, i.e., neurotic; for the conditions required for symptom-formation are demonstrable also in normal persons.

We are all ill: the statement is grandiose, and its implications—the implications, that is, of understanding the totality of human nature in the terms of disease—are vast. These implications have never been properly met (although I believe that a few theologians have responded to them), but this is not the place to attempt to meet them. I have brought forward Freud's statement of the essential sickness of the psyche only because it stands as the refutation of what is implied by the literary use of the theory of neurosis to account for genius. For if we are ill, and if, as I have said, neurosis can account for everything, for failure and mediocrity—"a very serious impoverishment of available mental energy"— as well as for genius, it cannot uniquely account for genius.

This, however, is not to say that there is no connection between neurosis and genius, which would be tantamount, as we see, to saying that there is no connection between human nature and genius. But the connection lies wholly in a particular and special relation which the artist has to neurosis.

In order to understand what this particular and special connection is we must have clearly in mind what neurosis is. The current literary conception of neurosis as a *wound* is quite misleading. It inevitably suggests passivity, whereas, if we follow Freud, we must understand a neurosis to be an *activity*, an activity with a purpose, and a particular kind of activity, a *conflict*. This is not to say that there are no abnormal mental states which are not conflicts. There are; the struggle between elements of the unconscious may never be instituted in the first place, or it may be called off. As Freud says in a passage which follows close upon the one I last quoted, "If regressions do not call forth a prohibition on the part of the ego, no neurosis results; the libido succeeds in obtaining a real, although not a normal, satisfaction. But if the ego . . . is not in agreement with these regressions, conflict ensues." And in his essay on Dostoevsky Freud says that "there are no neurotic complete masochists," by which he means that the ego which gives way completely to masochism (or to any other pathological excess) has passed beyond neurosis; the conflict has ceased, but at the cost of the defeat of the ego, and now some other name than that of neurosis must be given to the condition of the person who thus takes himself beyond the pain of the neurotic conflict. To understand this is to become aware of the curious complacency with which literary men regard mental disease. The psyche of the neurotic is not equally complacent; it regards with the greatest fear the chaotic and destructive forces it contains, and it struggles fiercely to keep them at bay.[6]

We come then to a remarkable paradox: we are all ill, but we are ill in the service of health, or ill in the service of life, or, at the very least, ill in the service of life-in-culture. The form of the mind's dynamics is that of the neurosis, which is to be understood as the ego's struggle against being overcome by the forces with which it coexists, and the strategy of this conflict requires that the ego shall incur pain and make sacrifices of itself, at the same time seeing to it that its pain and sacrifice be as small as they may.

But this is characteristic of all minds: no mind is exempt except those which refuse the conflict or withdraw from it; and we ask wherein the mind of the artist is unique. If he is not unique in neurosis, is he then unique in the significance and intensity of his neurosis? I do not believe that we shall go more than a little way toward a definition of artistic genius by answering this question affirmatively. A neurotic conflict cannot ever be either meaningless or merely personal; it must be understood as exemplifying cultural forces of great moment, and this is true of any neurotic conflict at all. To be sure, some neuroses may be more interesting than others, perhaps because they are fiercer or more inclusive; and no doubt the writer who makes a claim upon our interest is a man who by reason of the energy and significance of the forces in struggle within him provides us with the largest representation of the culture in which we, with him, are involved; his neurosis may thus be thought of as having a connection of concomitance with his literary powers. As Freud says in the Dostoevsky essay, "the neurosis . . . comes into being all the more readily the richer the complexity which has to be controlled by his ego." Yet even the rich complexity which his ego is doomed to control is not the definition of the artist's genius, for we can by no means say that the artist is preeminent in the rich complexity of elements in conflict within him. The slightest acquaintance with the clinical literature of psychoanalysis will suggest that a rich complexity of struggling elements is no uncommon possession. And that same literature will also make it abundantly clear that the devices of art—the most extreme devices of poetry, for example—are not particular to the mind of the artist but are characteristic of mind itself.

But the artist is indeed unique in one respect, in the respect of his relation to his neurosis. He is what he is by virtue of his successful objectification of his neurosis, by his shaping it and making it available to others in a way which has its effect upon their own egos in struggle. His genius, that is, may be defined in terms of his faculties of perception, representation, and realization, and in these terms alone. It can no more be defined in terms of neurosis than can his power of walking and talking, or his sexuality. The use to which he puts his power, or the manner and style of his power, may be discussed with reference to his particular neurosis, and so may such matters as the untimely diminution or cessation of its exercise. But its essence is irreducible. It is, as we say, a gift.

We are all ill: but even a universal sickness implies an idea of health. Of the artist we must say that whatever elements of neurosis he has in common with his fellow mortals, the one part of him that is healthy, by any conceivable definition of health, is that which gives him the power to conceive, to plan, to work, and to bring his work to a conclusion. And if we are all ill, we are ill by a universal accident, not by a universal necessity, by a fault in the economy of our powers, not by the nature of the powers themselves. The Philoctetes myth, when it is used to imply a causal connection between the fantasy of castration and artistic power, tells us no more about the source of artistic power than we learn about the source of sexuality when the fantasy of castration is adduced, for the fear of castration may explain why a man is moved to extravagant exploits of sexuality, but we do not say that his sexual power itself derives from his fear of castration; and further the same fantasy may also explain impotence or homosexuality. The Philoctetes story, which has so established itself among us as explaining the source of the artist's power, is not really an explanatory myth at all; it is a moral myth having reference to our proper behavior in the circumstances of the universal accident. In its juxtaposition of the wound and the bow, it tells us that we must be aware that weakness does not preclude strength nor strength weakness. It is therefore not irrelevant to the artist, but when we use it we will do well to keep in mind the other myths of the arts, recalling what Pan and Dionysus suggest of the relation of art to physiology and superabundance, remembering that to Apollo were attributed the bow and the lyre, two strengths together, and that he was given the lyre by its inventor, the baby Hermes—that miraculous infant who, the day he was born, left his cradle to do mischief: and the first thing he met with was a tortoise, which he greeted politely before scooping it from its shell, and, thought and deed being one with him, he contrived the instrument to which he sang "the glorious tale of his own begetting." These were gods, and very early ones, but their myths tell us something about the nature and source of art even in our grim, late human present.

Notes

1. I am by no means in agreement with the statements of Dr. Edmund Bergler about "the" psychology of the writer, but I think that Dr. Bergler has done good service in warning us against taking at their face value a writer's statements about himself, the more especially when they are "frank." Thus, to take Dr. Bergler's notable example, it is usual for biographers to accept Stendhal's statements about his open sexual feelings for his mother when he was a little boy, feelings which went with an intense hatred of his father. But Dr. Bergler believes that Stendhal unconsciously used his consciousness of his love of his mother and his hatred of his father to mask an unconscious love of his father, which frightened him. See "Psychoanalysis of Writers and of Literary Productivity," *Psychoanalysis and the Social Sciences* (1947), 1:247–96.

2. Dr. Bergler believes that there is a particular neurosis of writers, based on an oral masochism which makes them the enemy of the respectable world, courting poverty and persecution. But a later development of Dr. Bergler's theory of oral masochism makes it *the* basic neurosis, not only of writers but of everyone who is neurotic.

3. In his interesting essay, "Writers and Madness" [included in this book], William Barrett has taken issue with this point and has insisted that a clear distinction is to be made between the relation that exists between the scientist and his work and the relation that exists between the artist and his work. The difference, as I understand it, is in the claims of the ego. The artist's ego makes a claim upon the world which is personal in a way that the scientist's is not, for the scientist, although he does indeed want prestige and thus "responds to one of the deepest urges of his ego, it is only that his prestige may come to attend his person through the public world of other men; and it is not in the end his own being that is exhibited or his own voice that is heard in the learned report to the Academy." Actually, however, as is suggested by the sense which mathematicians have of the *style* of mathematical thought, the creation of the abstract thinker is as deeply involved as the artist's—see *An Essay on the Psychology of Invention in the Mathematical Field* by Jacques Hadamard (Princeton, N.J.: Princeton University Press, 1945)—and he quite as much as the artist seeks to impose *himself*, to *express* himself. I am of course not maintaining that the processes of scientific thought are the same as those of artistic thought, or even that the scientist's creation is involved with his total personality *in the same way* that the artist's is—I am maintaining only that the scientist's creation is as *deeply* implicated with his total personality as is the artist's.

This point of view seems to be supported by Freud's monograph on Leonardo. One of the problems that Freud sets himself is to discover why an artist of the highest endowment should have devoted himself more and more to scientific investigation, with the result that he was unable to complete his artistic enterprises. The particular reasons for this that Freud assigns need not be gone into here; all that I wish to suggest is that Freud understands these reasons to be the working out of an inner conflict, the attempt to deal with the difficulties that have their roots in the most primitive situations. Leonardo's scientific investigations were as necessary and "compelled" and they constituted as much of a claim on the whole personality as anything the artist undertakes; and so far from being carried out for the sake of public prestige, they were largely private and personal, and were thought by the public of his time to be something very like insanity.

4. From a letter quoted in Theodor Reik's *From Thirty Years With Freud*, translated by Richard Winston (New York: Farrar and Rinehart, 1940), p. 175.

5. I am using the word *fantasy*, unless modified, in a neutral sense. A fantasy, in this sense, may be distinguished from the representation of something that actually exists, but it is not opposed to "reality" and not an "escape" from reality. Thus the idea of a rational society, or the image of a good house to be built, as well as the story of something that could never really happen, is a fantasy. There may be neurotic or non-neurotic fantasies.

6. In the article to which I refer in note 3, William Barrett says that he prefers the old-fashioned term "madness" to "neurosis." But it is not quite for him to choose—the words do not differ in fashion but in meaning. Most literary people, when they speak of mental illness, refer to neurosis. Perhaps one reason for this is that the neurosis is the most benign of the mental ills. Another reason is surely that psychoanalytical literature deals chiefly with the neurosis, and its symptomatology and therapy have become familiar; psychoanalysis has far less to say about psychosis, for which it can offer far less therapeutic hope. Further, the neurosis is easily put into a causal connection with the social maladjustments of our time. Other forms of mental illness of a more severe and degenerative kind are not so widely recognized by the literary person and are often assimilated to neurosis with a resulting confusion. In the present essay I deal only with the conception of neurosis, but this should not be taken to imply that I believe that other pathological mental conditions, including actual madness, do not have relevance to the general matter of the discussion.

9.

Psychology and Art Today

W. H. Auden

Neither in my youth nor later was I able to detect in myself any particular fondness for the position or work of a doctor. I was, rather, spurred on by a sort of itch for knowledge which concerned human relationships far more than the data of natural science.
—Freud

Mutual forgiveness of each vice
Such are the gates of paradise.
—Blake

To TRACE, in the manner of the textual critic, the influence of Freud upon modern art, as one might trace the influence of Plutarch upon Shakespeare, would not only demand an erudition which few, if any, possess, but would be of very doubtful utility. Certain writers, notably Thomas Mann and D. H. Lawrence, have actually written about Freud, certain critics, Robert Graves in *Poetic Unreason* and Herbert Read in *Form in Modern Poetry*, for example, have made use of Freudian terminology, surrealism has adopted a technique resembling the procedure in the analyst's consulting-room;[1] but the importance of Freud to art is greater than his language, technique, or the truth of theoretical details. He is the most typical but not the only representative of a certain attitude to life and living relationships, and to define that attitude and its importance to creative art must be the purpose of this essay.

THE ARTIST IN HISTORY

Of the earliest artists, the palæolithic rock-drawers, we can of course know nothing for certain, but it is generally agreed that their aim was a practical one, to gain power over objects by representing them; and it has been suggested that they were probably bachelors, i.e., those who, isolated from the social group, had leisure to objectify the fantasies of their group, and were tolerated for their power to do so. Be that as it may, the popular idea of the artist as socially ill adapted has been a constant one, and not unjustified. Homer may have been blind, Milton certainly was, Beethoven deaf, Villon a crook, Dante very difficult, Pope deformed, Swift impotent, Proust asthmatic, Van Gogh mental, and so on. Yet parallel with this has gone a belief in their social value. From the chiefs who kept a bard, down to the Shell-Mex exhibition, patronage, however undiscriminating, has never been wanting as a sign that art provides society with something for which it is worth paying. On both these beliefs, in the artist as neurotic, and in the social value of art, psychology has thrown a good deal of light.

THE ARTIST AS NEUROTIC

There is a famous passage in Freud's introductory lectures which has infuriated artists, not altogether unjustly:

Before you leave today I should like to direct your attention for a moment to a side of fantasy-life of very general interest. There is, in fact, a path from fantasy back again to reality, and that is—art. The artist has also an introverted disposition and has not far to go to become neurotic. He is one who is urged on by instinctive needs which are too clamorous; he longs to attain to honour, power, riches, fame, and the love of women; but he lacks the means of achieving these gratifications. So, like any other with an unsatisfied longing, he turns away from reality and transfers all his interest, and all his Libido, too, on to the creation of his wishes in life. There must be many factors in combination to prevent this becoming the whole outcome of his development; it is well known how often artists in particular suffer from partial inhibition of their capacities through neurosis. Probably their constitution is endowed with a powerful capacity for sublimation and with a certain flexibility in the repressions determining the conflict. But the way back to reality is found by the artist thus: He is not the only one who has a life of fantasy; the intermediate world of fantasy is sanctioned by general human consent, and every hungry soul looks to it for comfort and consolation. But to those who are not artists the gratification that can be drawn from the springs of fantasy is very limited; their inexorable repressions prevent the enjoyment of all but the meager daydreams which can become conscious. A true artist has more at his disposal. First of all he understands how to elaborate his daydreams, so that they lose that personal note which grates upon strange ears and become enjoyable to others; he knows too how to modify them sufficiently so that their origin in prohibited sources is not easily detected. Further, he possesses the mysterious ability to mold his particular material until it expresses the idea of his fantasy faithfully; and then he knows how to attach to this reflection of his fantasy-life so strong a stream of pleasure that, for a time at least, the repressions are outbalanced and dispelled by it. When he can do all this, he opens out to others the way back to the comfort and consolation of their own unconscious sources of pleasure, and so reaps their gratitude and admiration; then he has won—through his fantasy—what before he could only win in fantasy: honor, power, and the love of women.

Misleading though this may be, it draws attention to two facts: first, that no artist, however "pure," is disinterested: he expects certain rewards from his activity, however much his opinion of their nature may change as he develops; and he starts from the same point as the neurotic and the daydreamer, from emotional frustration in early childhood.

The artist like every other kind of "highbrow" is self-conscious, i.e., he is all of the time what everyone is some of the time, a man who is active rather than passive to his experience. A man struggling for life in the water, a schoolboy evading an imposition, or a cook getting her mistress out of the house is in the widest sense a highbrow. We only think when we are prevented from feeling or acting as we should like. Perfect satisfaction would be complete unconsciousness. Most people, however, fit into society too neatly for the stimulus to arise except in a crisis such as falling in love or losing their money.[2] The possible family situations which may produce the artist or intellectual are of course innumerable, but those in which one of the parents, usually the mother, seeks a conscious spiritual, in a sense, adult relationship with the child, are probably the commonest, e.g.,

1. When the parents are not physically in love with each other. There are several varieties of this: the complete fiasco; the brother-sister relationship on a basis of common mental interests; the invalid-nurse relationship when one parent is a child to be maternally cared for; and the unpassionate relation of old parents.
2. The only child. This alone is most likely to produce early life confidence which, on meeting disappointment, turns like the unwanted child, to illness and antisocial behavior to secure attention.
3. The youngest child. Not only are the parents old but the whole family field is one of mental stimulation.[3]

Early mental stimulation can interfere with physical development and intensify the conflict. It is a true intuition that makes the caricaturist provide the highbrow with a pair of spectacles. Myopia, deafness, delayed puberty, asthma—breathing is the first independent act of the child—are some of the attempts of the mentally awakened child to resist the demands of life.

To a situation of danger and difficulty there are five solutions: To sham dead: the idiot. To retire into a life of fantasy: the schizophrene. To panic, i.e., to wreak one's grudge upon society: the criminal. To excite pity, to become ill: the invalid. To understand the mechanism of the trap: the scientist and the artist.

ART AND FANTASY

In the passage of Freud quoted above, no distinction was drawn between art and fantasy, between—as Mr. Roger Fry once pointed out—*Madame Bovary* and a *Daily Mirror* serial about earls and housemaids. The distinction is one which may perhaps be best illustrated by the difference between two kinds of dream. "A child has in the afternoon passed the window of a sweetshop, and would have liked to buy some chocolate it saw there, but its parents have refused the gift—so the child dreams of chocolate"—here is a simple wish fulfilment dream of the *Daily Mirror* kind, and all art, as the juvenile work of artists, starts from this level. But it does not remain there. For the following dream and its analysis I am indebted to Dr. Maurice Nicoll's *Dream Psychology:*

A young man who had begun to take morphia, but was not an addict, had the following dream:

"I was hanging by a rope a short way down a precipice. Above me on the top of the cliff was a small boy who held the rope. I was not alarmed because I knew I had only to tell the boy to pull and I would get to the top safely." The patient could give no associations.

The dream shows that the morphinist has gone a certain way from the top of the cliff—the position of normal safety—down the side of the precipice, but he is still in contact with that which remains on the top. That which remains on the top is now relatively small, but is not inanimate like a fort, but alive: it is a force operating from the level of normal safety. This force is holding the dreamer back from the gulf, but that is all. It is for the dreamer himself to say the word if he wants to be pulled up (i.e., the morphinist is *deliberately* a morphinist).

When the common phrase is used that a man's will is weakening as he goes along some path of self-indulgence, it implies that something is strengthening. What is strengthening is the attractive power of vice. But in the dream, the attractive power of morphia is represented by the force of gravitation, and the force of gravitation is constant.

But there are certain variable elements in the dream. The position of the figure over the cliff can vary and with it the length of the rope. The size of the figure at the top of the cliff might also vary without in any way violating the spirit of the dream. If then, we examine the length of the rope and the size of the figure on the cliff top in the light of relatively variable factors, the explanation of the *smallness* of the figure on the cliff top may be found to lie in the length of the rope, as if the rope drew itself out of the figure, and so caused it to shrink.

Now the figure at the top of the cliff is on firm ground and may there symbolize the forces of some habit and custom that exist in the morphinist and from which he has departed over the edge of the cliff, but which still hold him back from disaster although they are now shrunken. The attractive power of the morphia is not increasing, but *the interest the morphinist takes in morphia* is increasing.

A picture of the balance of interest in the morphinist is thus given, and the dream shows that the part of interest situated in the cliff top is now being drawn increasingly over the precipice.

In this dream, we have something which resembles art much more closely. Not only has the censor transformed the latent content of the dream into symbols but the dream itself is no longer a simple wish fulfillment, it has become constructive, and, if you like, moral. "A picture of the balance of interest"—that is a good description of a work of art. To use a phrase of Blake's, "It's like a lawyer serving a writ."

CRAFTSMANSHIP

There have always been two views of the poetic process, as an inspiration and as a craft, of the poet as the Possessed and as the Maker, e.g.,

All good poets, epic as well as lyric, compose their beautiful poems not by art, but because they are inspired and possessed.—*Socrates*

That talk of inspiration is sheer nonsense: there is no such thing; it is a matter of craftsmanship.—*William Morris*

And corresponding to this, two theories of imagination:

Natural objects always weaken, deaden, and obliterate imagination in me.—*Blake*

Time and education beget experience: experience begets memory; memory begets judgment and fancy. . . . . Imagination is nothing else but sense decaying or weakened by the absence of the object.—*Hobbes*

The public, fond of marvels and envious of success without trouble, has favored the first (see any film of artists at work); but the poets themselves, painfully aware of the labor involved, on the whole have inclined toward the second. Psychoanalysis, naturally enough, first turned its attention to those works where the workings of the unconscious were easiest to follow—Romantic literature like *Peer Gynt*, "queer" plays like *Hamlet*, or fairy tales like *Alice in Wonderland*. I should doubt if Pope's name occurs in any textbook. The poet is inclined to retort that a great deal of literature is not of this kind, that even in a short lyric, let alone a sustained work, the material immediately "given" to consciousness, the automatic element, is very small, that, in his own experience, what he is most aware of are technical problems, the management of consonants and vowels, the counterpointing of scenes, or how to get the husband off the stage before the lover's arrival, and that psychology concentrating on the symbols, ignores words; in his treatment of symbols and facts he fails to explain why of two works dealing with the same unconscious material, one is esthetically good and the other bad; indeed that few psychoanalysts in their published work show any signs of knowing that esthetic standards exist.

Psychoanalysis, he would agree, has increased the artist's interest in dreams, mnemonic fragments, child art and graffiti, etc., but that the interest is a *conscious* one. Even the most surrealistic writing or Mr. James Joyce's latest prose shows every sign of being non-automatic and extremely carefully worked over.

THE CONSCIOUS ELEMENT

Creation, like psychoanalysis, is a process of re-living in a new situation. There are three chief elements:

1. The artist himself, a certain person at a certain time with his own limited conflicts, fantasies, and interests.
2. The data from the outer world which his senses bring him, and which, under the influence of his instincts, he selects, stores, enlarges upon, and by which he sets value and significance.
3. The artistic medium, the new situation, which because it is not a personal, but a racial property (and psychological research into the universality of certain symbols confirms this), makes communication possible, and art more than an autobiographical record. Just as modern physics teaches that every physical object is the center of a field of force which radiating outwards occupies all space and time, so psychology states that every word through fainter and fainter associations is ultimately a sign for the universe. The associations are always greater than those of an individual. A medium complicates and distorts the creative impulse behind it. It is, in fact, largely the medium, and thorough familiarity with the medium, with its unexpected results, that enables the artist to develop from elementary uncontrolled fantasy, to deliberate fantasy directed towards understanding.

WHAT WOULD BE A FREUDIAN LITERATURE

Freudianism can not be considered apart from other features of the contemporary environment, apart from modern physics with its conception of transformable energy, modern technics, and modern politics. The chart given here makes no attempt to be complete, or accurate; it ignores the perpetual overlap of one historical period with another, and highly important transition periods, like the Renaissance. It is only meant to be

	1st Period	*2d Period*	*3d Period*
First Cause:	God immanent and transcendent.	Official: God transcendent. The universal mechanic. Opposition: God immanent. Pantheism. Romantic.	Energy appearing in many measurable forms, fundamental nature unknown.
World View:	The visible world as symbol of the eternal.	Official: The material world as a mechanism. Opposition: The spiritual world as a private concern.	The interdependence of observed and observer.
The End of Life:	The City of God.	Official: Power over material. Opposition: Personal salvation.	The good life on earth.
Means of Realization:	Faith and work. The rule of the Church.	Official: Works without moral values. Opposition: Faith.	Self-understanding.
Personal Driving Forces:	Love of God. Submission of private will to will of God.	Official: Conscious will. Rationalized. Mechanized. Opposition: Emotion. Irrational.	The unconscious directed by reason.
The Sign of Success:	The mystical union.	Wealth and power.	Joy.
The Worst Sinner:	The heretic.	The idle poor (Opposition view—the respectable bourgeois).	The deliberate irrationalist.
Scientific Method:	Reasoning without experiment.	Experiment and reason: the experimenter considered impartial. Pure truth. Specialization.	Experiment directed by conscious human needs.
Sources of Power:	Animal. Wind. Water.	Water. Steam.	Electricity.

(Continued)	1st Period	2d Period	3d Period
Technical Materials:	Wood. Stone.	Iron. Steel.	Light alloys.
Way of Living:	Agricultural and trading. Small towns. Balance of town and country.	Valley towns. Industrialism. Balance of town and country upset.	Dispersed units connected by electrical wires. Restored balance of town and country.
Economic System:	Regional units. Production for use. Usury discouraged.	Laissez-faire Capitalism. Scramble for markets.	Planned socialism.
Political System:	Feudal hierarchy.	National democracy. Power in hands of capitalists.	International Democracy. Government by an Order.

suggestive, dividing the Christian era into three periods, the first ending with the fifteenth century, the second with the nineteenth, and the third just beginning; including what would seem the typical characteristics of such periods.

MISCONCEPTIONS

Freud belongs to the third of these phases, which in the sphere of psychology may be said to have begun with Nietzsche (though the whole of Freud's teaching may be found in *The Marriage of Heaven and Hell*). Such psychology is historically derived from the Romantic reaction, in particular from Rousseau, and this connection has obscured in the minds of the general public, and others, its essential nature. To the man in the street, "Freudian" literature would embody the following beliefs:

Sexual pleasure is the only real satisfaction. All other activities are an inadequate and remote substitute.

All reasoning is rationalization.

All men are equal before instincts. It is my parents' fault in the way they brought me up if I am not a Napoleon or a Shakespeare.

The good life is to do as you like.

The cure for all ills is *a*) indiscriminate sexual intercourse; *b*) autobiography.

THE IMPLICATIONS OF FREUD

I do not intend to take writers one by one and examine the influence of Freud upon them. I wish merely to show what the essence of Freud's teaching is, that the reader may judge for himself. I shall enumerate the chief points as briefly as possible:

1. The driving force in all forms of life is instinctive; a libido which of itself is undifferentiated and unmoral, the "seed of every virtue and of every act which deserves punishment."

2. Its first forms of creative activity are in the ordinary sense of the word physical. It binds cells together and separates them. The first bond observable between individuals is a sexual bond.

3. With the growth in importance of the central nervous system with central rather than peripheral control, the number of modes of satisfaction to which the libido can adapt itself becomes universally increased.

4. Man differs from the rest of the organic world in that his development is unfinished.

5. The introduction of self-consciousness was a complete break in development, and all that we recognize as evil or sin is its consequence. Freud differs both from Rousseau who denied the Fall, attributing evil to purely local conditions ("Rousseau thought all men good by nature. He found them evil and made no friend"), and also from the theological doctrine which makes the Fall the result of a deliberate choice, man being therefore morally responsible.

6. The result of this Fall was a divided consciousness in place of the single animal consciousness, consisting of at least three parts: a conscious mind governed by ideas and ideals; the impersonal unconscious from which all its power of the living creature is derived but to which it was largely denied access; and a personal unconscious, all that morality or society demanded should be forgotten and unexpressed.[4]

7. The nineteenth-century doctrine of evolutionary progress, of man working out the beast and letting the ape and tiger die, is largely false. Man's phylogenetic ancestors were meek and sociable, and cruelty, violence, war, all the so-called primitive instincts, do not appear until civilization has reached a high level. A golden age, comparatively speaking (and anthropological research tends to confirm this), is a historical fact.

8. What we call evil was once good, but has been outgrown, and re-

fused development by the conscious mind with its moral ideas. This is the point in Freud which D. H. Lawrence seized and to which he devoted his life:

> Man is immoral because he has got a mind
> And can't get used to the fact.

The danger of Lawrence's writing is the ease with which his teaching about the unconscious, by which he means the impersonal unconscious, may be read as meaning, "let your personal unconscious have its fling," i.e., the *acte gratuit* of André Gide. In personal relations this itself may have a liberating effect for the individual. "If the fool would persist in his folly he would become wise." But folly is folly all the same and a piece of advice like "Anger is just. Justice is never just," which in private life is a plea for emotional honesty, is rotten political advice, where it means "beat up those who disagree with you." Also Lawrence's concentration on the fact that if you want to know what a man is, you must look at his sexual life, is apt to lead many to believe that pursuit of a sexual goal is the only necessary activity.

9. Not only what we recognize as sin or crime, but all illness, is purposive. It is an attempt at cure.

10. All change, either progressive or regressive, is caused by frustration or tension. Had sexual satisfaction been completely adequate human development could never have occurred. Illness and intellectual activity are both reactions to the same thing, but not of equal value.

11. The nature of our moral ideas depends on the nature of our relations with our parents.

12. At the root of all disease and sin is a sense of guilt.

13. Cure consists in taking away the guilt feeling, in the forgiveness of sins, by confession, the re-living of the experience, and by absolution, understanding its significance.

14. The task of psychology, or art for that matter, is not to tell people how to behave, but by drawing their attention to what the impersonal unconscious is trying to tell them, and by increasing their knowledge of good and evil, to render them better able to choose, to become increasingly morally responsible for their destiny.

15. For this reason psychology is opposed to all generalizations; force people to hold a generalization and there will come a time when a situation will arise to which it does not apply. Either they will force the generalization, the situation, the repression, when it will haunt them, or they will embrace its opposite. The value of advice de-

pends entirely upon the context. You cannot tell people what to do, you can only tell them parables; and that is what art really is, particular stories of particular people and experiences, from which each according to his immediate and peculiar needs may draw his own conclusions.

16. Both Marx and Freud start from the failures of civilization, one from the poor, one from the ill. Both see human behavior determined, not consciously, but by instinctive needs, hunger and love. Both desire a world where rational choice and self-determination are possible. The difference between them is the inevitable difference between the man who studies crowds in the street, and the man who sees the patient, or at most the family, in the consulting room. Marx sees the direction of the relations between outer and inner world from without inwards, Freud vice versa. Both are therefore suspicious of each other. The socialist accuses the psychologist of caving in to the status quo, trying to adapt the neurotic to the system, thus depriving him of a potential revolutionary: the psychologist retorts that the socialist is trying to lift himself by his own boot tags, that he fails to understand himself, or the fact that lust for money is only one form of the lust for power; and so that after he has won his power by revolution he will recreate the same conditions. Both are right. As long as civilization remains as it is, the number of patients the psychologist can cure are very few, and as soon as socialism attains power, it must learn to direct its own interior energy and will need the psychologist.

CONCLUSION

Freud has had certain obvious technical influences on literature, particularly in its treatment of space and time, and the use of words in associational rather than logical sequence. He has directed the attention of the writer to material such as dreams and nervous tics hitherto disregarded; to relations as hitherto unconsidered as the relations between people playing tennis; he has revised hero-worship.

He has been misappropriated by irrationalists eager to escape their conscience. But with these we have not, in this essay, been concerned. We have tried to show what light Freud has thrown on the genesis of the artist and his place and function in society, and what demands he would make upon the serious writer. There must always be two kinds of art, escape-art, for man needs escape as he needs food and deep sleep, and parable-art, that art which shall teach man to unlearn hatred and learn love, which can enable Freud to say with greater conviction:

We may insist as often as we please that the human intellect is powerless when compared with the impulses of man, and we may be right in what we say. All the same there is something peculiar about this weakness. The voice of the intellect is soft and low, but it is persistent and continues until it has secured a hearing. After what may be countless repetitions, it does get a hearing. This is one of the few facts which may help to make us rather more hopeful about the future of mankind.

Notes

1. But not the first. The Elizabethans used madness, not as a subject for clinical description but as opportunity for a particular kind of associational writing (e.g., *Lear* or *The Duchess of Malfi*). Something of the kind occurs even earlier in the nonsense passages in the mummer's play.

2. For example, the sale of popular textbooks on economics since 1929.

3. The success of the youngest son in folk tales is instructive. He is generally his mother's favorite as physically weaker and less assertive than his brothers. If he is often called stupid, his stupidity is physical. He is clumsy and lazy rather than dull. (Clumsiness being due to the interference of fancies with sense data.) He succeeds partly out of good nature and partly because confronted with a problem he overcomes it by understanding rather than with force.

4. The difference between the two unconscious minds is expressed symbolically in dreams, e.g., motor cars and manufactured things express the personal unconscious, horses, etc., the impersonal.

10.

Freud's Aesthetics

E. H. Gombrich

IF CONFIRMATION WERE NEEDED for the conservative and traditional character of Freud's approach to art it would be found in the utterances on modern movements which are contained in his post-war letters. The uncompromising hostility that is expressed here must indeed have surprised those who saw in Freud the champion of all contemporary trends. In June 1920, Oscar Pfister had sent Freud his pamphlet on "The Psychological and Biological Background of Expressionist Patinings." In his introduction Pfister states that the movement of Expressionism had by now outgrown the stage in which it caused horrified spinsters to shriek. True, he continues, there still exist philistines who think that they have done enough if they affix the labels of ghastly, barbaric, bungling, perverse, or pathological to this new movement. The author wants to remind the reader that Expressionism is a movement that embraces all the arts and includes masters who cannot be accused of incompetence. Pfister proposes to approach the problem through psychoanalysis. The bulk of his pamphlet concerns the work of an Expressionist artist whom Pfister had in analysis. We are given the associations of the artist to his own drawings, which are treated like dreams. Asked for his associations to the angular cheek he drew, for instance, the artist said:

The cheek of my father, a beautiful strong bone. . . . Now I must think of something nonsensical. The angular rhythm of the cheek reminds me of the square chair on which my father used to sit.

From *Encounter* (1966), 26(1):30–39. Copyright © 1966 *Encounter*. Reprinted by permission.

The right-hand eye produced the association of the greatest fright of his life when a hare pursued by a dog had crossed the artist's path at night.

What Pfister concludes from these and other transcripts is that the Expressionist artist is an autistic, introvert type, imprisoned in his own repressions. Much as he respects the high seriousness of the movement he still concludes with the hope that a new idealism would create a new kind of art that would combine a profound sense of reality with genuine idealism.

Freud's response shows his usual combination of uncompromising honesty and good breeding:

I took up your pamphlet about Expressionism with no less eager curiosity than aversion and I read it in one go. In the end I liked it very much, not so much the purely analytic parts which can never get over the difficulties of interpretation for non-analysts, but what you connect with it and make of it. Often I said to myself: "What a good and charitable person free from all injustice Pfister is, how little you can compare yourself to him and how nice it is that you must come to agree with everything at which he arrives in his own way." For I must tell you that in private life I have no patience at all with lunatics. I only see the harm they can do and as far as these "artists" are concerned, I am in fact one of those philistines and stick-in-the-muds whom you pillory in your introduction. But after all, you yourself then say clearly and exhaustively why these people have no claim to the title of artist.

(21 June 1920)

Two years later Freud's position had hardened even more. Karl Abraham had sent him a drawing made by an Expressionist artist and this time Freud's response goes to the limit of politeness:

Dear Friend, I received the drawing which allegedly represents your head. It is ghastly. I know what an excellent person you are, I am all the more deeply shocked that such a slight flaw in your character as is your tolerance or sympathy for modern "art" should have been punished so cruelly. I hear from Lampl that the artist maintained that he saw you in this way. People such as he should be the last to be allowed access to analytic circles for they are the all-too-unwelcome illustrations of Adler's theory that it is precisely people with severe inborn defects of vision who become painters and draughtsmen. Let me forget this portrait in wishing you the very best for 1923.

(26 December 1922)

It took almost sixteen years and the powerful advocacy of an admired friend, Stefan Zweig, to persuade Freud to receive such a modern artist. He agreed to see Salvador Dali in the second month after his move to

London. The few lines he wrote on July 20th, 1938, after this visit contain the most revealing utterance by Freud on his attitude to art:

> I can really thank you for the introduction which yesterday's visitor brought me. For up to then I was inclined to consider the Surrealists who appeared to have chosen me as their patron saint, pure lunatics or let us say 95 per cent, as with "pure" alcohol. The young Spaniard with his patently sincere and fanatic eyes and his undeniable technical mastery has suggested to me a different appreciation. It would indeed be very interesting to explore the origins of such a painting analytically. Yet, as a critic, one might still be entitled to say that the concept of art resisted an extension beyond the point where the quantitative proportion between unconscious material and preconscious elaboration is not kept within a certain limit. In any case, however, these are serious psychological problems.

For all its brevity this letter throws a flood of light on Freud's ideas about art and on his reasons for rejecting both Expressionism and Surrealism as non-art. It confirms the brilliant analysis of Freud's theory of art which we owe to Ernst Kris. It was Kris who, in his *Psycho-Analytic Explorations in Art* (New York 1952, London 1953), pointed to Freud's book on *The Wit* (or to use Mr. James Strachey's superior translation, *The Joke*) as germinal model for any account of artistic creation along Freudian lines. It is indeed to this model that Freud alludes in the letter when he speaks of keeping the quantitative proportions between unconscious material and preconscious elaboration within certain limits.

For let us remember Freud's formula for the joke: "A preconscious idea is exposed for a moment to the workings of the unconscious." What the joke owes to the unconscious in this formula is not so much its content as its form, the dream-like condensation of meaning characteristic of what Freud calls the primary process. It is a process in which the impressions and experiences of our waking life are mixed and churned in unpredictable permutations and combinations. In the dream no less than in insanity the dynamism of this vortex overwhelms our waking thought, the reality principle of the ego. In the joke the ego merely makes use of this mechanism in order to invest an idea with a peculiar charm. A thought which it would perhaps be rude or indecorous to utter plain is dipped as it were into the magic spring of the primary process, as one can dip a flower or a twig into the calcine waters of Karlsbad where they emerge transformed into something rich and strange. In this new guise the idea is not only acceptable but even welcome.

What Freud had most in mind in constructing this model were puns. Take the famous answer to the question: "Is life worth living?"—"It depends on the liver."[1] It is easy to see what Freud calls the preconscious ideas which rise to the surface in this answer—ideas, that is, which are not unconscious in the sense of being totally repressed and therefore inaccessible to us but available to our conscious mind; in this case the joy in lots of alcohol which the liver should tolerate and the even more forbidden joy in the aggressive thought that there are lives not worth living. Respectability has imposed a taboo on both these ideas and to express them too boldly might cause embarrassment. But in the churning vortex of the primary process the two meanings of "liver" came accidentally into contact and fused. A new structure is created and in this form the ideas cause pleasure and laughter. But this laughter is caused among sane grownups only because they can appreciate the delicate balance between preconscious thought and unconscious elaboration. If the idea were smothered in a welter of punning the result would be more like gibberish than like a joke; if the pun were poor the idea would not be good enough to compensate for this lack of structure.

Clearly to Freud there was no artistic value in the primary process as such. It is a mechanism that belongs to every mind, the feeblest as well as the most developed. If he dismissed Expressionists and Surrealists as lunatics it was because he suspected these movements of confusing these mechanisms with art. Dali's "undeniable technical mastery" had convinced him that he had been a little rash in this conviction. He was not persuaded, however, that this mastery had been put to the use of investing a preconscious, that is, a communicable idea, with a structure derived from unconscious mechanisms.

One may argue about the complete applicability of Freud's model of the joke to other forms of artistic creation, but this model certainly has two supreme virtues which must recommend it to the historian and critic of art. It explains the relevance both of the medium and its mastery: two vital elements which are sometimes neglected in less circumspect application of psychoanalytic ideas to art.

That puns depend on the medium of a particular language scarcely needs demonstration. Without the accidental homophone the pun about the liver could not have seen the light of day. It is true that an ambitious genius has tried to translate this particular answer into French not without some measure of success: "La vie vaut-elle la peine?—Question de foie." But inspired as is this translation, it still lacks the *double entendre* that it also depends on whose life it is.

Puns are not made: they are discovered in the language, and what the primary process does in Freud's account is really to facilitate this discovery by its rapid shuttling of associations. Take the famous rhyme by Hilaire Belloc:

> When I am dead I hope it may be said
> His sins were scarlet but his books were read.

There can be few writers who never had this slightly shocking thought that fame is more important to them than a good reputation. But it is the accident of the medium that permits its condensation into a joke. It is the mastery of the writer, moreover, that gives the joke such a concise and memorable form.

Freud's book on wit gives at least one clue to this mastery which we neglect at our peril: the discussion of the role of the child's pleasure in playing with language which, to Freud, is a functional pleasure connected with the acquisition of mastery. Surely it is convincing to think that such accidents of sound and meaning as make up the perfect pun are discovered by those who cultivate the childhood pleasure of experimenting and playing with words and nonsense syllables. It is in this play that the ego gains control and mastery of the primary process and learns to select and reject the formations that emerge from the welter of the unconscious.

Seen in this light there is indeed a kinship between the poet and the punster. Both make their discovery in and through language. If great masters found satisfaction for many centuries in the device of the rhyme it was obviously not only because they were fond of jingling sounds. The search for the rhyme gives a purpose and satisfaction to the search for the poet's language. Poets' drafts often bear witness to this intention. Where Keats in the "Ode to a Nightingale" had first written "grief" he changed the word to "sorrow" to rhyme with "to-morrow." He surely would not have done so had the slight change of nuance not satisfied him, had he not tested it against his own feelings and found it answering his mood. But the possible rhymes in the English language remain a reality to which his poetry had to adjust.

It is the denial of such realities which Freud dismissed as "lunatic."

Far from looking in the world of art only for its unconscious content of biological drives and childhood memories he insisted on that degree of adjustment to reality that alone turns a dream into a work of art.

If this interpretation is correct it may permit us to formulate the vulgar misinterpretation of Freud's ideas in almost diagrammatic form. Expressionism and its derivatives in criticism appear to take the word *expression* almost literally. They believe that an unconscious thought troubles the artist's inside and is therefore expelled outward by means of art to trouble the minds of the public as well. Form, on this reading, is little more than a wrapping for the unconscious contents which the consumer in his turn unwraps and discards. Freud's view clearly allows us to look at the matter from the other angle. It is often the wrapping that determines the content. Only those unconscious ideas that can be adjusted to the reality of formal structures become communicable and their value to others rests at least as much in the formal structure as in the idea. The code generates the message.

One of the most famous messages in the English language is Nelson's signal before the battle of Trafalgar. We know that Nelson approached his Signal Officer and said:

"Mr. Paso, I wish to say to the Fleet, ENGLAND CONFIDES THAT EVERY MAN WILL DO HIS DUTY" and he added, "you must be quick. . . ." Paso replied, "If your Lordship will permit me to substitute the word *expects* for CONFIDES, the signal will soon be completed, because the word EXPECTS is in the vocabulary, and CONFIDES must be spelt."[2]

We owe the immortal formulation *England expects*, etc., to the character of the flag-code. We may owe some of the world's great masterpieces to similar accidents discovered in the potentialities of medium and style.

If we choose to call the Expressionist idea of art centrifugal, we might label this influence of the language on the message centripetal. It is this centripetal element that is so often neglected in popular accounts of artistic creation, despite the fact that artists have always stressed its supreme importance.

There is perhaps no more beautiful introspective account of poetic creation than the moving pages in Pasternak's *Dr. Zhivago* in which Yuri sits down, during a crisis in his life, to write poetry:

After two or three stanzas and several images by which he was himself astonished, his work took possession of him and he experienced the approach of what
is called inspiration. At such moments the correlation of the forces controlling
the artist is, as it were, stood on its head. The ascendancy is no longer with the
artist or the state of mind which he is trying to expess, but with language, his
instrument of expression. Language, the home and dwelling of beauty and meaning, itself begins to think and speak for man and turns wholly into music, not in
the sense of outward, audible sounds but by virtue of the power and momentum
of its inward flow. Then, like the current of a mighty river polishing stones and
turning wheels by its very movement, the flow of speech creates in passing, by
the force of its own laws, rhyme and rhythm and countless other forms and
formations, still more important and until now undiscovered, unconsidered and
unnamed.

At such moments Yuri felt that the main part of his work was not being
done by him but by something which was above him and controlling him: the
thought and poetry of the world as it was at that moment and as it would be in
the future. He was controlled by the next step it was to take in the order of its
historical development; and he felt himself to be only the pretext and the pivot
setting it in motion.

This feeling relieved him for a time of self-reproach, of dissatisfaction with
himself, of the sense of his own nothingness.[3]

The passage does more than merely confirm the role of language and of
mastery, the way the relation of content and form is "stood on its head,"
as Pasternak puts it. It throws an additional light on the psychological
relevance of this process, the way, as we read, in which the forces of
language relieve the artist of his "self-reproach." It is the medium, not
he, that is active and that expresses these thoughts. There is something
objective in his discoveries that rids the work of art of the taint of subjectivity and exhibitionism. Even the idea of historical forces whose instrument the artist becomes at such a moment can be stripped of its
Hegelian and "historicist" guise and placed in this objective context. For,
surely, it is true that it is not only the medium and its potentialities but
also the historical situation which the artist finds in the stylistic developments of his art which suggest, and sometimes even dictate, the solutions of which he makes use.

There is an element in all art—and certainly in all Western art—
which might for brevity's sake be called the "cat's cradle" element. Art,
as Malraux has stressed, is born of art. The young artist takes over the
game from his predecessors and as he does so he introduces variations.
In Western communities, at least, art has thus become a social game

played among artists and the pattern that emerges with each move owes at least as much to the moves that have gone before as it owes to the ingenious variations introduced by the present player.

In the introductory chapter to his *Psycho-analytic Explorations in Art*, Ernst Kris drew attention to this aspect: the development of art within a given problem-situation to which the artist adjusts and contributes. But the historian may be forgiven if he feels that in this problem of the interaction between medium, tradition, and personality a lot still remains to be done. If I may be permitted to quote a casual and private remark in this context, Ernest Jones himself expressed his perplexity to the writer as to what artists meant when they continually talked about "the problem"—the problem, that is, with which their paintings confronted them. But to those who play the game of cat's cradle these are real problems which are at least as much part of reality as are the problems of science or of daily life. They are dictated by the situation and not by the artist's mood or childhood experience. Once he is engrossed in this task of creating intricate and meaningful structures nothing else can matter to the artist. The problem has taken command.

There is a famous lecture by Paul Klee, *On Modern Art*, which contains as telling an introspective account of the modern painter's experience of the game as Pasternak's moving description of the poet's experience. Klee describes the many elements, line, color, shape, out of which the artist creates his order. Their importance, as he puts it, is decisive also in the negative sense since it is they which decide "whether a certain content may remain inexpressible despite the most favorable psychological disposition." Klee sees the artist as a builder of structures who lifts the element up into a new order:

While the artist is still entirely absorbed in his effort to group these formal elements so neatly and logically that each is necessary in its place and none impairs the others, there will be some layman who has been looking over his shoulder ready with the devastating remark: "This does not yet look like a real man at all." If the painter has enough self control he will think "real man" is neither here nor there, I must go on with my building. . . . This new building stone, he will tell himself, may be a shade too heavy and pulls the whole caboodle too much to the left; I shall have to put quite a telling counterpoise on the right to restore the balance.—And thus he alternates, adding something on either side till the pointer of the scales is centered. He will only be too glad if he finds that he did not have to upset the combination of a few suitable elements which had begun so well, at least no more than to introduce those contradictions and contrasts which, after all, are inseparable from any configuration that is alive.

Sooner or later, however, an association may occur to him even without the intervention of a layman and nothing prevents him from accepting it if it presents itself under a very fitting name. This assent to a representation may occasionally suggest in its turn one or the other addition that has a necessary connection with the formulated reference. If the artist is lucky these representational supplementations can still be fitted to a passage which faintly seems to ask for them from a formal point of view and they look as if they had always belonged there.[4]

The psychoanalyst who is confronted with such an account may at first be tempted to doubt it. If he submits entirely to what I have called the centrifugal theory of artistic expression he will take it for granted that the artist always knew unconsciously what object would emerge and that the whole elaborate pretense at building a formal structure first is nothing but a rationalization hiding the real process from the artist and his audience. But this is not the interpretation suggested by Freud's "centripetal" theory of wit. In this theory, it will be remembered, the aspect of play, the infantile pleasure in trying out combinations and permutations, is given due weight.

There must be (and there are) procedures in science and engineering where some medium or model is used for trying out structures through analogies and where techniques of systematic variation and permutation are used to discover fresh possibilities. The potentialities of these media—the way the analogue is and can be wired, as it were—its past history and results—all these form part of reality. To say that the experimenter knew somewhere, or somehow, beforehand which combination would prove useful for his purpose would surely be unrealistic. Wherever their disposition may stem from—and Freud never claimed to know the full answer—the painter will be inclined thus to play with forms, the musician with tones. Both of them may be no more able to predict these possibilities than anyone can predict what happens when we shake a kaleidoscope; but having shaken it we can admire and remember some of the results; we can even elaborate them when they strike us as meaningful while we discard and forget others. Hence the benefit even the greatest genius derives from the conventions of his time and from their mastery. Even a Mozart, when writing a light-hearted *divertimento*, may not have known or thought precisely what was going to happen to the simple theme he chose. But he knew that by putting it through the paces of certain modulations and developments something delightful was bound to emerge. Naturally his genius and his training made him select a theme suitable for this exercise, and even allowed him to foresee and reject out of the corner of his eye certain alternatives which would result in less interesting developments. But even a Mozart was indebted to the marvelous instrument of, say, the sonata or rondo form which his predecessors had handed to him and of which he had experienced the potentialities in continuous practice. The artist who thus experiments and plays—who looks for discoveries in language if he is a writer or a poet, in visual shapes if he is a painter—will no doubt select in that preconscious process of which Freud speaks the structures that will greet him as meaningful in terms of his mind and conflicts. But it is his art that informs his mind, not his mind that breaks through in his art. Just as the temptations of a pun may sometimes bring out an aggressive thought that would otherwise have remained unexpressed, so the structural possibilities of the cat's cradle or the shake of the kaleidoscope may sometimes bring out a mood or an experience that would have remained dormant in the artist but for this vital suggestion.

It is this aspect that needs stressing if we are to gain the full benefit of Freud's Theory of Wit. No psychoanalyst will be inclined to doubt the power of circumstance in "bringing out" a person's dormant or suppressed characteristic. When we say that "the emergency brought out the best in him" or that "army life brought out the worst in him" we mean precisely that these traits of the personality which would otherwise have been minimized by the conventions of everyday life were maximized by certain opportunities. Granted that it may be futile to ask whether it was the situation in literature that "brought out" the romantic in Byron or whether it was Byron's temperament and disposition that bent the tool of literature further in this direction, no serious analysis of an artist's life and art should ever neglect the centripetal force of traditions and trends. Even Byron's art is not all "self-expression." Nor, if it is not, need it therefore be an empty pose. The alternative between genuine expression and mere convention which both artists and critics have sometimes framed in Freudian terms finds no support in Freud's theory of art.

At least one artist challenged Freud to spell out his views of this problem, and the precious record of this exchange is also published in the correspondence. It was Yvette Guilbert, the great *diseuse*, who in 1931 sought Freud's opinion about the actor's psychology. Clearly, she seems to have implied, the idea of self-expression must break down here since what makes a great actor is the capacity to identify with any number of different characters.[5] From Yvette Guilbert's autobiography, *La Chanson de Ma Vie*, it is obvious why this problem concerned her so much. She had gained her success with *chansons* of most dubious morality, representing on the stage prostitutes and criminals. She had been hurt and worried by the vulgar identification of the actress with the characters she portrayed, and she had naturally stressed the distance that separates the two.

Freud did not want to allow her this easy way out:

> I should like to understand more about this and would certainly tell you all I know. Since I don't understand much of it I would ask you to be satisfied with the following hints. I would think that what you assumed to be the psychological mechanism of your art has been very frequently asserted, perhaps universally so. Yet this idea of the surrender of one's own person and its replacement by an imagined one has never satisfied me very much. It says so little, it naturally does not tell how it is done and, most of all, it does not tell us why something which allegedly all artists desire succeeds so much better in one case than in another. I would rather believe that something of the opposite mechanism must also come into play. Not that the actor's own person is eliminated but rather that elements of it—for instance, undeveloped dispositions and suppressed wishes—are used for the representation of intended characters and thus are allowed expression which gives the character concerned its truth to life. This may be less simple than that transparency of the ego you imagine. Naturally I would be eager to know whether you can sense anything of that other aspect. In any case this would be no more than one contribution towards the solution of the beautiful secret of why we shudder when we hear your "Voularde" or assent with all our senses when you ask "Dites-moi si je suis belle." But so little is known.
>
> (8 March 1931)

The actress was not satisfied, and in his next letter Freud enjoys what he calls "the interesting experience" of having to defend his theory against Yvette Guilbert and her husband, Max Schiller:

> Really I have no intention of giving in to you, beyond confessing that we know so little. Look, for example, Charlie Chaplin was in Vienna. . . . He is undoubtedly a great artist though admittedly he always acts one and the same character, the weakly poor helpless and awkward youth for whom however things turn out well in the end. Do you believe that he had to forget his own ego

playing this role? On the contrary he always acts himself as he was in his sad youth. He cannot get away from these experiences and still derives compensation today for the hardships and humiliations of those times. His is, as it were, a particularly simple and transparent case.

The idea that an artist's achievements are conditioned internally by child-hood impressions, destiny, suppressions and disappointments has yielded much enlightenment to us and that is why we set great store by it. I once ventured to approach one of the very greatest, an artist of whom unfortunately all too little is known, Leonardo da Vinci. I was able at least to make it probable that his St. Anne, which you can visit every day in the Louvre, would not be intelligible without the peculiar childhood story of Leonardo. Nor, possibly, would other works.

Now you will say that Madame Yvette has more than a single role, she embodies with equal mastery all possible characters; saints and sinners, co-quettes, the virtuous, criminals and *ingenues*. That is true and it proves an un-usually rich and adaptable psychic life. But I would not despair of tracing back her whole repertory to the experiences and conflicts of her early years. It would be tempting to continue here but something keeps me back. I know that unso-licited analyses cause annoyance and I would not like to do anything to disturb the cordial sympathy of our relationship. (26 March 1931)

How sad it seems for us now that this fascinating exchange was terminated in a polite disagreement to disagree. For if Yvette Guilbert had followed the hint and gone back to Freud's paper on Leonardo she would not only have found there the idea which Freud considered "prob-able," that the St. Anne reflected Leonardo's childhood story; she would also have found a much better documented account of Leonardo's in-triguing playfulness, his enjoyment of riddles and fantasies. Moreover, she could have reminded Freud of his own eloquent description in the opening pages of his study of Leonardo's many sketches "each of which varies every one of the motifs that occur in his paintings in the most manifold manner . . . displaying a wealth of possibilities between which he often wavers." Putting these two observations side by side she might have shown how many of the features of Leonardo's Louvre picture were pre-figured in earlier drawings of the Virgin and Child in which the interaction of mother and son is studied in ever fresh permutations. Thus, taking her cue from this "historical romance" she might have described to Freud what she was to describe in her memoirs—her own fascination with her medium and her ceaseless desire to explore and master all the potentialities of this instrument. It is not enough, we read there, for an actress or *diseuse* to articulate clearly:

In addition she must be able to set any word aflame or extinguish it, to bathe it in light or plunge it in darkness, to throw it in relief or to soften it, to caress it or grasp it harshly, to advance or withdraw it, to envelope [sic] it or expose it naked, to extend or shorten it. Anything that brings a text to life or kills it, anything that makes for vigour, colour, style, that imparts elegance or vulgarity, all this science was the constant object of my endeavours.

The story is told (and it is an authentic story) of a young singer who approached Yvette Guilbert for lessons. She declined, but she gave the aspiring artist one piece of advice: to practice any simple statement such as "Prenez place, Madame" in some twenty different nuances from haughtiness to humility and pity. The way in which this phrase is said could reveal a whole situation.

Clearly in playing this game the great actress would not have to rely on situations she experienced in her childhood. What may be connected with her history and disposition is not the mastery itself but the will to obtain mastery, the interest in what can be done with language, the enjoyment of the game. True, if we may venture to reconstruct a dialogue that never took place, once this mastery was achieved certain combinations and configurations of tone and language might indeed have evoked a particular response in the artist, an echo from her own past—it is here that what Freud calls "undeveloped dispositions and suppressed wishes" might have found an outlet inducing the actress to work on these with special zest and to embody these opportunities in her repertory. If that happened Freud might therefore have succeeded in making good his claim that he could trace these numbers in her programme back to their origins in an early personality trait—while Yvette Guilbert would still have remained right in claiming that the actor's art is rooted in the mastery of countless expressive elements.

It is this mastery alone which can arouse and liberate the dormant memories that come to life in the performance. Are we straining the meaning of Freud's words too much if we find this compromise implied in Freud's own remarks in the earlier of these two letters? He merely reminds the actress, after all, that besides her skill in impersonation "*something* of the opposite mechanism must *also* come into play" (my italics). There is nothing here that contradicts his observations in the letter about Dali that "the concept of art resists an extension beyond the point where the quantitative proportion between unconscious material and preconscious elaboration is not kept within certain limits."

The interpreter of the utterances of an admired master must especially guard against the danger of "Talmudism": the temptation to read into the text whatever he desires to propound. There are many questions that remain open in Freud's theory of art, but it seems to me that there is nothing in his published writings and letters that conflicts with his outlook and his taste, which are so firmly based on conservative standards. Unlike some of his less cautious followers, moreover, Freud never claimed to be in possession of the answer. He always stressed that "we know so little." It remains true.

Notes

1. I take this example from a lecture by Leonard Forster in *Translation*, Studies in Communication No. 2 (London, 1958).

2. E. B. Sargeant, *An Account of Lord Nelson's Signal* (London, 1908).

3. The translation in the English edition was by Max Hayward and Manya Harari (London: Collins and Harvill, 1959).

4. Paul Klee, *On Modern Art*, translated by Paul Findlay (London: Faber, 1966).

5. The actress could here rely on the authority of Diderot's famous dialogue on acting, *Paradoxe sur le Comédien*.

PART III

LITERARY APPLICATIONS

BECAUSE TALENTED WRITERS have been of particular interest to literary critics, their works have provoked a wealth of psychoanalytic interpretations. Genius has been subjected to so many examinations of influences, motivations, biographical commentaries, etc., that we now accept the fact that every writer who has been certified as a classic also deserves his own separate field of expertise. Psychoanalytic contributions which deal with the importance of trivia, insofar as repressed trivia is the meat of analysis, make up much of this literature, and speculation about the minor detail which could conceivably be linked to genius has become the legitimate task of critical activity. Consequently, every essay in the following section refers to the larger literary discussion as well as to specific writers, as the psychoanalyst Stanley A. Leavy comments on John Keats and the critics, Cushing Strout on Henry James, Jan Ellen Goldstein on the Woolfs, Elizabeth Dalton on Dostoevsky, Gail Simon Reed on Voltaire, and Steven Marcus on Freud as a unique type of writer.

We think of the clinical content of Freud's case histories, states Marcus, but forget that they are also major pieces of literature. Freud's presentations resemble the construction of a novel, or even a mystery story, as he unveils and interweaves story, symptoms, dreams, events, and analysis. Like a fiction writer, Freud uses, for instance, his Prefatory Remarks to the Dora case as a framing device, rehearsing motives, reasons, intentions, and events, as he divulges just enough of Dora's and the case's secrets to maintain the reader's interest. Yet Freud repeatedly disavows literary intentions, continues Marcus, itself a characteristic of modern literature and a technique to "soften up" the reader with his unique expository and narrative authority. Contrasting Freud's reports on the incoherence of his patients' stories with the case histories, Marcus finds an implicit contrast between mental illness and mental health—

with the latter as characteristic of the patient who appropriates her own history. The palimpsest-like quality of the prose, the copresence of various sequences and references, and the updating of history of both dreams and reality reveal Freud's writing and method as representative of the fully developed nineteenth-century novel, as well as of the beginning of the twentieth-century modernist one. Having placed Freud in his literary milieu, Marcus subjects the writing and its author to a psychoanalytic examination—a bit of *lèse-majesté*. Thus he focuses, for instance, on the dialogue about the "hidden connections" by both Freud and Dora, and finds that Freud is only half-aware of his own central place in Dora's first dream or treatment; by transforming transferences into writing and literature, he is using them defensively, and by the end of Dora's case history Freud has become the central character. Marcus concludes that Freud, who blamed Dora for the abrupt termination of her analysis, rather than his own inability to deal with her negative transference and his own negative countertransference, used the writing of this case history to deal with and neutralize the "cluster of unanalyzed impulses and ambivalences" in himself, just as any other creative writer would. In this way, he invented a new form of literature—a literature available for further analysis by literary critics.

Elizabeth Dalton begins her discussion of Dostoevsky's epilepsy with Freud's argument that this sickness was "the central expression of the author's neurosis, and thus fundamental to his life and character." Dalton bolsters this premise, noting that Dostoevsky's novels have several epileptics, and showing how Myshkin at once epitomizes the "equivocal relationship between the most debased and the most exalted aspects of human experience," and provides the framework for the style. Linking the writing of this novel to specific events in Dostoevsky's life, and to the course of his epilepsy, Dalton sees the novel as exploring the meaning of the illness—in imagery, and in the states of wild emotion and uncontrolled behavior which alternate with loss of control and physical and mental collapse. Breaks in narrative in *The Idiot* are connected to the pattern of Dostoevsky's own epilepsy which, despite its organic basis, assumed psychological meaning. Dalton explores this meaning, beginning with Freud's analysis that belief in the murder of Dostoevsky's father had led to a "negative" resolution of his Oedipus complex, so that the epileptic seizures acted as self-punishment of unconscious guilt. But she focuses on the writing, and specifically on Myshkin's fits, as these are described, associated to, and as they contribute to the narrative, and to the feelings and tensions of the novel. Myshkin's fits, argues Dalton, are overdetermined, given that he only passively experiences passion, lust, hatred, and aggression. At the same time, epilepsy sets Myshkin apart from others—not only insofar as he is weak and idiotic, but as he is capable of mystical experiences, and of a "sense of ecstatic merging." By comparing changes in the minds of mystics to what happens in manic-depressive illness, Dalton shows how "the brilliant, unlimited, harmonious vision that comes to Myshkin during the epileptic aura is a regression to the timeless world of the primitive ego . . . [and that] the fit is also the revenge of the superego which can be deposed only temporarily for the release of sexual and aggressive energy." From a sensitive and informed Freudian perspective, Dalton then concludes that epileptic seizures are always full of meanings, but that in *The Idiot* this illness, also, reveals tragedy and danger.

Like Dalton, Gail Reed uses a Freudian view when she explores the emotional aspects of Voltaire's fiction, and particularly of *Candide*, but her focus is the collective experience between the text and its readers. Guided by clinical psychoanalytic knowledge, Reed relates the reading of *Candide* to the text's representations of wish and frustration. Individuals bring "defensive and characterological responses" to literary works which relate to their responses alone, but there is also a "collective experience involving frustration." Assuming a broad definition of countertransference, Reed postulates a hypothetical reader, and a hypothetical collective reading experience. She summarizes the wide-ranging debate by critics over whether Voltaire "solves the problem of evil," arguing that the debate is evidence of the dialectic between desire and punishment, of expectation and betrayal. Frustration of the characters' sense of fulfillment, and their subsequent yearning for protection, are shown to parallel the readers' sense of expectation and relief. The changing shape of the characters, of the disguises and the oscillations, all allegedly conspire to make Candide incapable of judgment, and of irony. This "infantile openness" involves the reader—a reader whose subjective participation in Candide's desires is facilitated by "internal focus," by the frustration of chapter breaks, and by fictional ambiguities. As "fictional reality redefines language," the reader too becomes somewhat disoriented, although the distancing effect of the narration, according to Reed, counterbalances the instability of Candide's world. Because Voltaire's stylized descriptions depend on the reader's initial surprise for comic effect, and allow for release, the structure of the text engages the readers' constantly changing affect, which Reed finds to be "an essential and complex element in the aesthetic experience of *Candide*." This emphasis on textual structure, of course, is influenced by current French criticism, and by its American derivations.

Keats' poetry too, argues Stanley A. Leavy, contains psychological themes—the relations between his imagination and his dreams appear in both poems and letters. Leavy finds that Keats, though not a systematic psychologist, had a highly developed understanding of the workings of the human mind, and "exceptional access to the workings of his own." Instead of trying to uncover the unconscious intentions of Keats' ideas, Leavy sets out to determine how "the poet's experience as *he* understood it" may enrich psychoanalysis. Aware that emotion is aroused by ceaseless striving for truth, which can only be approximated, and that knowledge is not just the impression of the objective world on the mind and its objects, Keats described "this unitive process as he witnessed it in his own mind." Leavy applies Keats' own concept of *Negative Capability*, that is, the ability of an individual to be uncertain, to show how this "is the rule with Keats [where] the sanity of the projective thinking is guaranteed by the humor of the statement." Keats' letters to Baily, to Woodhouse, and to others, and his comments on Shakespeare, reveal the poet's marvelously unimpeded mind, the result of "certain peculiarities in his 'identity' " (a term Keats himself used). Through the poetry Leavy shows how mind merges with objects, how "the 'conception' of poetry is a bisexual process," and how "passivity" is a "withholding of judgment." He argues that the characteristic ambiguity of poetry is particularly open to psychoanalytic interpretation—a text similar to a "dream-text"—and that such analysis is fruitful because the poet, though uninhibited, nevertheless is subject to censorship and to various unconscious defensive purposes. Seeking experience, however, the poet creates works full of intricate condensations, allusions, and illusions, making exhaustive analysis, as in all true art, futile. But true art is itself a refashioning of the world which is absorbed into the "psyche," concludes Leavy, so that the poem becomes the poet's way of internalizing his experience.

The James family has received much more attention than either Blake or Keats. The presence of a number of certified geniuses, and the influence they had on each other, is particularly fertile territory for psychoanalytic criticism. As Cushing Strout points out in his essay, both William and Henry were interested in psychological matters, and each reported on a nightmare. Although Henry James never explicitly connected his dream about the Louvre and his fiction, Strout finds that this dream served as inspiration for "The Jolly Corner." This is so, he argues, even though a number of facts and ideas are reversed. Whether dream or story came first, Strout shows that ideas and themes overlap, that "the story is like the dream," and, further, that it involves Henry's rivalry with his older brother William. It is difficult to psychoanalyze without the "patient's" input, he maintains, but suggests that the story, too, must be understood as a drama of irony, within its larger context, and "as a historical document in the life of the subject." Ambiguities and ambivalences are manifestations of conflict, concludes Strout, so that writing the story alone could not free its author from the wishes reflected in his dream—whatever the date of the dream may have been.

Dates, once more, are important to the genesis of ideas among the Bloomsbury writers. How timing and events related to the proliferation of Freud's thought there, and how this thought was—privately—defended against, is the subject of Jan Ellen Goldstein's essay. Goldstein argues that the similarity between "Moorism" and Freudianism (both looked inward) first made for the group's interest in psychoanalysis, and later for its help in bringing Freud's ideas to England. Yet although Virginia Woolf consulted many doctors about her various breakdowns, she shunned the psychoanalysts, remaining "satisfied" with the fashionable diagnosis of "neurasthenia" and its concomitant rest cure; this satisfaction seemed to be contradicted, however, in her account in *Mrs. Dalloway*. Though "toying with the applicability of a Freudian conception of mental breakdown," she always rejected its potential use for herself. Most likely this was because of the importance art was accorded in the Bloomsbury intellectual scheme, conjectures Goldstein, which could not accommodate the artist as a "clever neurotic." Goldstein examines Woolf's feelings on the subject as expressed in her writing, letters, and diaries, finding that, insofar as she considered unconscious thought as artistically fruitful, she was bound to remain a "nonparticipant observer of the Freudian revolution."

All of the Bloomsbury intellectuals engaged in theoretical debates on the issues. James Strachey, though somewhat peripheral, was Freud's official translator. And Leonard Woolf even presents himself as a Freudian in his autobiography—implicitly and explicitly. Goldstein indicates, however, that Leonard Woolf's Freudianism was rare, and not always approving—diluting or even distorting its psychoanalytic bite, and "domesticating the unconscious." Yet the fact that Leonard Woolf came around to rethinking his own views is only another indication of the centrality of psychoanalysis to criticism, something all twentieth-century writers have dealt with, however ambivalent they have felt.

II.

Freud and Dora: Story, History, Case History

Steven Marcus

I

IT IS GENERALLY AGREED that Freud's case histories are unique. To-day, more than half a century after they were written, they are still widely read. Even more, they are still widely used for instruction and training in psychoanalytic institutes. One of the inferences that such a vigorous condition of survival prompts is that these writings have not yet been superseded. Like other masterpieces of literature or the arts, these works seem to possess certain transhistorical qualities—although it may by no means be easy to specify what those qualities are. The implacable "march of science" has not—or has not yet—consigned them to "mere" history. Their singular and mysterious complexity, density, and richness have thus far prevented such a transformation and demotion.

This state of affairs has received less attention than it merits. Freud's case histories—and his works in general—are unique as pieces or kinds of writing, and it may be useful to examine one of Freud's case histories from the point of view of literary criticism, to analyze it as a piece of writing, and to determine whether this method of proceeding may yield

From "Freud and Dora: Story, History, Case History," *Partisan Review* (1974), 41(1):12–23, 89–108. Copyright © 1974 *Partisan Review*. Reprinted by permission.

results that other means have not. My assumption—and conclusion—is that Freud is a great writer and that one of his major case histories is a great work of literature—that is to say, it is both an outstanding creative and imaginative performance and an intellectual and cognitive achievement of the highest order. And yet this triumphant greatness is in part connected with the circumstance that it is about a kind of failure, and that part of the failure remains in fact unacknowledged and unconscious.

"Fragment of an Analysis of a Case of Hysteria," better known as the case of Dora, is Freud's first great case history—oddly enough he was to write only four others. It may be helpful for the reader if at the outset I refresh his memory by briefly reviewing some of the external facts of the case. In the autumn of 1900, Dora, an eighteen-year-old young woman, began treatment with Freud. She did so reluctantly and against her will, and, Freud writes, "it was only her father's authority which induced her to come to me at all." Neither Dora nor her father were strangers to Freud. He had made separate acquaintance with both of them in the past, during certain episodes of illness that characterized their lives if not the life of the family as a whole. (Freud knew other members of the family as well.)

As for Dora herself, her afflictions, both mental and physical, had begun in early childhood and had persisted and flourished with variations and fluctuating intensities until she was presented to Freud for therapy. Among the symptoms from which she suffered were to be found dyspnea, migraine, and periodic attacks of nervous coughing often accompanied by complete loss of voice during part of the episode. Dora had in fact first been brought by her father to Freud two years earlier, when she was sixteen and suffering from a cough and hoarseness; he had then "proposed giving her psychological treatment," but this suggestion was not adopted since "the attack in question, like the others, passed off spontaneously." In the course of his treatment of Dora, Freud also learned of further hysterical—or hysterically connected—productions on her part, such as a feverish attack that mimicked appendicitis, a periodic limp, and a vaginal catarrh or discharge. Moreover, during the two-year interval between Dora's first visit and the occasion on which her father brought her to Freud a second time, and "handed her over to me for psychotherapeutic treatment . . . Dora had grown unmistakably neurotic." Dora was now "in the first bloom of youth—a girl of intelligent and engaging looks." Her character had, however, undergone an alteration. She had become chronically depressed, and was generally dissatisfied with both herself and her family. She had become unfriendly toward the father whom she had hitherto loved, idealized, and identified with. She was "on very bad terms" with her mother, for whom she felt a good deal of scorn. "She tried to avoid social intercourse, and employed herself—so far as she was allowed to by the fatigue and lack of concentration of which she complained—with attending lectures for women and with carrying on more or less serious studies." Two further events precipitated the crisis which led to her being delivered to Freud. Her parents found a written note in which she declared her intention to commit suicide because "as she said, she could no longer endure her life." Following this there occurred one day "a slight passage of words" between Dora and her father, which ended with Dora suddenly losing consciousness—the attack, Freud believed, was "accompanied by convulsions and delirious states," although it was lost to amnesia and never came up in the analysis.

Having outlined this array of afflictions, Freud dryly remarks that such a case "does not upon the whole seem worth recording. It is merely a case of *'petite hystérie'* with the commonest of all somatic and mental symptoms. . . . More interesting cases of hysteria have no doubt been published."

This disavowal of anything sensational to come is of course a bit of shrewd disingenuousness on Freud's part, for what follows at once is his assertion that he is going to elucidate the meaning, origin, and function of every one of these symptoms by means of the events and experiences of Dora's life. He is going in other words to discover the "psychological determinants" that will account for Dora's illnesses; among these determinants he lists three principal conditions: "a psychical trauma, a conflict of affects, and . . . a disturbance in the sphere of sexuality." And so Freud begins the treatment by asking Dora to talk about her experiences. What emerges is the substance of the case history, a substance which takes all of Freud's immense analytic, expository, and narrative talents to bring into order. I will again very roughly and briefly summarize some of this material.

Sometime after 1888, when the family had moved to B—— the health resort where the father's tuberculosis had sent them—an intimate and enduring friendship sprang up between them and a couple named K. Dora's father was deeply unhappy in his marriage and apparently made no bones about it. The K.'s too were unhappily married, as it later turned out. Frau K. took to nursing Dora's father during these years of his illness. She also befriended Dora, and they behaved toward one another in the most familiar way and talked together about the most intimate subjects. Herr K., her husband, also made himself a close friend of Dora's—going regularly for walks with her and giving her presents. Dora in her turn befriended the K.'s two small children, "and had been almost a mother to them." What begins to be slowly if unmistakably disclosed is that Dora's father and Frau K. had established a sexual liaison and that this relation had by the time of Dora's entering into treatment endured for many years. At the same time Dora's father and Frau K. had tacitly connived at turning Dora over to Herr K., just as years later her father "handed her over to me [Freud] for psychotherapeutic treatment." In some sense everyone was conspiring to conceal what was going on; and in some yet further sense everyone was conspiring to deny that anything was going on at all. What we have here, on one of its sides, is a classical Victorian domestic drama that is at the same time a sexual and emotional can of worms.

Matters were brought to a crisis by two events that occurred to Dora at two different periods of her adolescence. When she was fourteen, Herr K. contrived one day to be alone with her in his place of business; in a state of sexual excitement, he "suddenly clasped the girl to him and pressed a kiss on her lips." Dora responded with a "violent feeling of disgust," and hurried away. This experience, like those referred to in the foregoing paragraph, was never discussed with or mentioned to anyone, and relations continued as before. The second scene took place two years later in the summer when Dora was sixteen (it was just after she had seen Freud for the first time). She and Herr K. were taking a walk by a lake in the Alps. In Dora's words, as they come filtered to us through Freud, Herr K. "had the audacity to make her a proposal." Apparently he had begun to declare his love for this girl whom he had known so well for so long. "No sooner had she grasped Herr K.'s intention than, without letting him finish what he had to say, she had given him a slap in the face and hurried away." The episode as a whole leads Freud quite plausibly to ask: "If Dora loved Herr K., what was the reason for her refusing him in the scene by the lake? Or at any rate, why did her refusal take such a brutal form, as though she were embittered against him? And how could a girl who was in love feel insulted by a proposal which was made in a manner neither tactless nor offensive?" It may occur to us to wonder whether in the extended context of this case that slap in the face was a "brutal form" of refusal; but as for the other questions posed by Freud they are without question rhetorical in character.

On this second occasion Dora did not remain silent. Her father was preparing to depart from the Alpine lake, and she declared her determination to leave at once with him. Two weeks later she told the story of the scene by the lake to her mother, who relayed it—as Dora had clearly intended—to her father. In due course Herr K. was "called to account" on this score, but he "denied in the most emphatic terms having on his side made any advances" and suggested that she "had merely fancied the whole scene she had described." Dora's father "believed" the story concocted by Herr—and Frau—K., and it is from this moment, more than two years before she came to Freud for treatment, that the change in Dora's character can be dated. Her love for the K.'s turned into hatred, and she became obsessed with the idea of getting her father to break off relations with them. She saw through the rationalizations and denials of her father and Frau K., and had "no doubt that what bound her father to this young and beautiful woman was a common love-affair." Nothing that could help to confirm this view had escaped her perception, which in this connection was pitilessly sharp." Indeed, "the sharp-sighted Dora" was an excellent detective when it came to uncovering her father's clandestine sexual activities, and her withering criticisms of her father's character—that he was "insincere . . . had a strain of baseness in his character . . . only thought of his own enjoyment . . . had a gift for seeing things in the light which suited him best"—were in general concurred in by Freud. Freud also agreed with Dora that there was something in her embittered if exaggerated contention that "she had been handed over to Herr K. as the price of his tolerating the relations between her father and his wife." Nevertheless, the cause of her greatest embitterment seems to have been her father's "readiness to consider the scene by the lake as a product of her imagination." And although Freud was in his customary way skeptical about such impassioned protestations and repudiations—and surmised that something in the way of an opposite series of thoughts or self-reproaches lay behind them—he was forced to come to "the conclusion that Dora's story must correspond to the facts in every respect." If we try to put ourselves in the place of this girl between her sixteenth

STEVEN MARCUS

and eighteenth years, we can at once recognize that her situation was a desperate one. The three adults to whom she was closest, whom she loved the most in the world, were apparently conspiring—separately, in tandem, or in concert—to deny her the reality of her experience. They were conspiring to deny Dora her reality and reality itself. This betrayal touched upon matters that might easily unhinge the mind of a young person; for the three adults were not betraying Dora's love and trust alone; they were betraying the structure of the actual world. And indeed when Dora's father handed her over to Freud with the parting injunction "Please try and bring her to reason," there were no two ways of taking what he meant. Naturally he had no idea of the mind and character of the physician to whom he had dealt this leading remark.

II

Dora began treatment with Freud some time in October 1900. Freud wrote to Fliess that "the case has opened smoothly to my collection of picklocks," but the analysis was not proceeding well. The material produced was very rich, but Dora was there more or less against her will. Moreover, she was more than usually amnesic about events in her remote past and about her inner and mental life. The analysis found its focus and climax in two dreams. The first of these was the production by Dora of a dream that in the past she had dreamed recurrently. Among the many messages concealed by it, Freud made out one that he conveyed to his patient: " 'You have decided to give up the treatment,' " he told her, adding, " 'to which, after all, it is only your father who makes you come.' " It was a self-fulfilling interpretation. A few weeks after the first dream, the second dream occurred. Freud spent two hours elucidating it, and at the beginning of the third, which took place on December 31, 1900, Dora informed him that she was there for the last time. Freud pressed on during this hour and presented Dora with a series of stunning and outrageously intelligent interpretations. The analysis ended as follows: "Dora had listened to me without any of her usual contradictions. She seemed to be moved; she said good-bye to me very warmly, with the heartiest wishes for the New Year, and came no more." Dora's father subsequently called on Freud two or three times to reassure him that Dora was returning, but Freud knew better than to take him at his word.

Fifteen months later, in April 1902, Dora returned for a single visit; what she had to tell Freud on that occasion was of some interest, but he knew that she was done with him, as indeed she was.

Dora was actuated by many impulses in breaking off the treatment; prominent among these partial motives was revenge—upon men in general and at that moment Freud in particular, who was standing for those other men in her life who had betrayed and injured her. He writes rather ruefully of Dora's "breaking off so unexpectedly, just when my hopes of a successful termination of the treatment were at their highest, and her thus bringing those hopes to nothing—this was an unmistakable act of vengeance on her part." And although Dora's "purpose of self-injury" was also served by this action, Freud goes on clearly to imply that he felt hurt and wounded by her behavior. Yet it could not have been so unexpected as all that, since as early as the first dream, Freud both understood and had communicated this understanding to Dora that she had already decided to give up the treatment. What is suggested by this logical hiatus is that although Dora had done with Freud, Freud had not done with Dora. And this supposition is supported by what immediately followed. As soon as Dora left him, Freud began writing up her case history—a proceeding that, as far as I have been able to ascertain, was not in point of immediacy a usual response for him. He interrupted the composition of the *Psychopathology of Everyday Life* on which he was then engaged and wrote what is substantially the case of Dora during the first three weeks of January 1901. On January 25, he wrote to Fliess that he had finished the work the day before and added, with that terrifying self-confidence of judgment that he frequently revealed, "Anyhow, it is the most subtle thing I have yet written and will produce an even more ✓ horrifying effect than usual." The title he had at first given the new work—"Dreams and Hysteria"—suggests the magnitude of ambition that ✓ was at play in him. At the same time, however, Freud's settling of his account with Dora took on the proportions of a heroic inner and intellectual enterprise.

Yet that account was still by no means settled, as the obscure subsequent history of this work dramatically demonstrates. In the first letter of January 25, 1901, Freud had written to Fliess that the paper had already been accepted by Ziehen, joint editor of the *Monatsschrift für Psychiatrie und Neurologie*. On the fifteenth of February, in another letter to Fliess, he remarks that he is now finishing up *The Psychopathology of*

Everyday Life, and that when he has done so, he will correct it and the case history. About two months later, in March 1901, according to Ernest Jones, Freud showed "his notes of the case" to his close friend, Oscar Rie. The reception Rie gave to them was such, reports Freud, that "I thereupon determined to make no further effort to break down my state of isolation." On May 8, 1901, Freud wrote to Fliess that he had not yet "made up his mind" to send off the work. One month later, he made up his mind and sent if off, announcing to Fliess that "it will meet the gaze of an astonished public in the autumn." But nothing of the sort was to occur, and what happened next was, according to Jones, "entirely mysterious" and remains so. Freud either sent it off to Ziehen, the editor who had already accepted it, and then having sent it asked for it back. Or he sent it off to another magazine altogether, the *Journal für Psychologie und Neurologie,* whose editor, one Brodmann, refused to publish it. The upshot was that Freud returned the manuscript to a drawer for four more years. And when he did at last send it into print, it was in the journal that had accepted it in the first place.

III

If we turn now to the Prefatory Remarks it may be illuminating to regard them as a kind of novelistic framing action, as in these few opening pages Freud rehearses his motives, reasons, and intentions and begins at the same time to work his insidious devices upon the reader. First, exactly like a novelist, he remarks that what he is about to let us in on is positively scandalous, for "the complete elucidation of a case of hysteria is bound to involve the revelation of intimacies and the betrayal of . . . secrets." Second, again like a writer of fiction, he has deliberately chosen persons, places, and circumstances that will remain obscure; the scene is laid not in metropolitan Vienna but "in a remote provincial town." He has from the beginning kept the circumstance that Dora was his patient such a close secret that only one other physician—"in whose discretion I have complete confidence"—knows about it. He has "postponed publication" of this essay for "four whole years," also in the cause of discretion, and in the same cause has "allowed no name to stand which could put a non-medical reader on the scent." Finally he has buried the case even deeper by publishing it "in a purely scientific and technical

periodical" in order to secure yet another "guarantee against unauthorized readers." He has in short made his own mystery within a mystery,
and one of the effects of such obscure preliminary goings-on is to create
a kind of Nabokovian frame—what we have here is a history framed by
an explanation which is itself slightly out of focus.

Third, he roundly declares, this case history is science and not literature: "I am aware that—in this city, at least—there are many physicians who (revolting though it may seem) choose to read a case history
of this kind not as a contribution to the psychopathology of neuroses,
but as a *roman à clef* designed for their private delectation." This may
indeed be true; but it is equally true that nothing is more literary—and
more modern—than the disavowal of all literary intentions. And when
Freud does this again later on toward the end of "The Clinical Picture,"
the situation becomes even less credible.

Freud then goes on to describe other difficulties, constraints, and
problematical circumstances attaching to the situation in which he finds
himself. Among them is the problem of "how to record for publication"
even such a short case—the long ones are as yet altogether impossible.
Moreover, since the material that critically illuminated this case was
grouped about two dreams, their analysis formed a secure point of departure for the writing. (Freud is of course at home with dreams, being
the unchallenged master in the reading of them.) Yet this tactical solution pushes the *entire problematic* back only another step further, since
Freud at once goes on to his additional presupposition, that only those
who are already familiar with "the interpretation of dreams"—that is,
The Interpretation of Dreams (1900), whose readership in 1901 must have
amounted to a little platoon indeed—are likely to be satisfied at all with
the present account. Any other reader "will find only bewilderment in
these pages." As much as it is like anything else, this is like Borges—as
well as Nabokov. This off-putting and disconcerting quality, it should be
without saying, is characteristically modern; the writer succumbs to no
impulse to make it easy for the reader; on the contrary, he is by preference rather forbidding and does not extend a cordial welcome. The reader
has been, as it were, "softened up" by his first encounter with this unique
expository and narrative authority; he is thoroughly off balance and is as
a consequence ready to be "educated," by Freud. By the same token,
however, if he has followed these opening few pages carefully, he is
certainly no longer as prepared as he was to assert the primacy and prior-

ity of his own critical sense of things. He is precisely where Freud—and any writer—wants him to be.

Freud proceeds to specify what it is that is wrong with the stories his patients tell him. The difficulties are in the first instance formal shortcomings of *narrative:* the connections, "even the ostensible ones—are for the most part incoherent," obscured and unclear; "and the sequence of different events is uncertain." In short these narratives are disorganized, and the patients are unable to tell a coherent story of their lives. What is more, he states, "the patients' inability to give an ordered history of their life in so far as it coincides with the history of their illness is not merely characteristic of the neurosis. It also possesses great theoretical significance." What we are led at this juncture to conclude is that Freud is implying that a coherent story is in some manner connected with mental health (at the very least with the absence of hysteria), and this in turn implies assumptions of the broadest and deepest kind about both the nature of coherence and the form and structure of human life. On this reading, human life is, ideally, a connected and coherent story, with all the details in explanatory place, and with everything (or as close to everything as is practically possible) accounted for, in its proper causal or other sequence. And inversely illness amounts at least in part to suffering from an incoherent story or an inadequate narrative account of oneself.

Freud then describes in technical detail the various types and orders of narrative insufficiency that he commonly finds; they range from disingenuousness, both conscious and unconscious, to amnesias and paramnesias of several kinds and various other means of severing connections and altering chronologies. In addition, he maintains, this discomposed memory applies with particular force and virulence to "the history of the illness" for which the patient has come for treatment. In the course of a successful treatment, this incoherence, incompleteness, and fragmentariness are progressively transmuted, as facts, events, and memories are brought forward into the forefront of the patient's mind. And he adds as a conclusion that these two aims "are coincident"—they are reached simultaneously and by the same path. Some of the consequences that can be derived from these extraordinary observations are as follows. The history of any patient's illness is itself only a substory (or a subplot), although it is at the same time a vital part of a larger structure. Furthermore, in the course of psychoanalytic treatment, nothing less than

"reality" itself is made, constructed, or reconstructed. A complete story—
"intelligible, consistent, and unbroken"—is the theoretical, created end
story. It is a story, or a fiction, not only because it has a narrative structure but also because the narrative account has been rendered in language, in conscious speech, and no longer exists in the deformed language of symptoms, the untranslated speech of the body. At the end—
at the successful end—one has come into possession of one's own story.
It is a final act of self-appropriation, the appropriation by oneself of one's
own history. This is in part so because one's own story is in so large a
measure a phenomenon of language, as psychoanalysis is in turn a demonstration of the degree to which language can go in the reading of all
experience. What we end with, then, is a fictional construction which is
at the same time satisfactory to us in the form of the truth, and as the
form of the truth.

No larger tribute has ever been paid to a culture in which the various narrative and fictional forms had exerted for centuries both moral
and philosophical authority and which had produced as one of its chief
climaxes the great bourgeois novels of the nineteenth century. Indeed we
must see Freud's writings—and method—as themselves part of this culmination, and at the same moment, along with the great modernist novels of the first half of the twentieth century, as the beginning of the end
of that tradition and its authority. . . .

The historical difficulties are compounded by several sequential net-
works that are mentioned at the outset and that figure discernibly
throughout the writing. First there is the virtual Proustian complexity of
Freud's interweaving of the various strands of time in the actual account;
or, to change the figure, his geological fusing of various time strata—
strata which are themselves at the same time fluid and shifting. We observe this most strikingly in the palimpsest-like quality of the writing
itself, which refers back to *Studies on Hysteria* of 1895; which records a
treatment that took place at the end of 1900 (although it mistakes the
date by a year); which then was written up in first form during the early
weeks of 1901; which was then exhumed in 1905, and was revised and
rewritten to an indeterminable extent before publication in that year; and
to which additional critical comments in the form of footnotes were finally appended in 1923. All of these are of course held together in vital
connection and interanimation by nothing else than Freud's consciousness. But we must take notice as well of the copresence of still further

163

different time sequences in Freud's presentation—this copresence being itself a historical or novelistic circumstance of some magnitude. There is first the connection established by the periodically varied rehearsal throughout the account of Freud's own theory and theoretical notions as they had developed up to that point; this practice provides a kind of running applied history of psychoanalytic theory as its development is refracted through the embroiled medium of this particular case. Then there are the different time strata of Dora's own history, which Freud handles with confident and loving exactitude. Indeed he is never more of a historical virtuoso than when he reveals himself to us as moving with compelling ease back and forth between the complex group of sequential histories and narrative accounts, with divergent sets of diction and at different levels of explanation, that constitute the extraordinary fabric of this work. He does this most conspicuously in his analytic dealings with Dora's dreams, for every dream, he reminds us, sets up a connection between two "factors," an "event during childhood" and an "event of the present day—and it endeavors to reshape the present on the model of the remote past." The existence or recreation of the past in the present is in fact "history" in more than one of its manifold senses.

Just as Marx regards the history-makers of the past as sleepwalkers, "who required recollections of past world history in order to drug themselves concerning their own content," so Freud similarly regards the conditions of dream-formation, of neurosis itself, and even of the cure of neurosis, namely the analytic experience of transference. They are all of them species of living past history in the present. If the last of these works out satisfactorily, then a case history is at the end transfigured. It becomes an inseparable part of an integral life history. Freud is of course the master historian of those transfigurations.

IV

At the very beginning, after he had listened to the father's account of "Dora's impossible behavior," Freud abstained from comment, for, he remarks, "I had resolved from the first to suspend my judgment of the true state of affairs till I had heard the other side as well." Such a suspension inevitably recalls an earlier revolutionary project. In describing the originating plan of *Lyrical Ballads*, Coleridge writes that it "was agreed that my endeavours should be directed to persons and characters super-natural, or at least romantic; yet so as to transfer from our inward nature a human interest and a semblance of truth sufficient to procure for these shadows of imagination that willing suspension of disbelief for the mo-ment, which constitutes poetic faith." We know very well that Freud had a more than ordinary capacity in this direction, and that one of the most dramatic moments in the prehistory of psychoanalysis had to do precisely with his taking on faith facts that turned out to be fantasies. Yet Freud is not only the reader suspending judgment and disbelief until he has heard the other side of the story; and he is not only the poet or writer who must induce a similar process in himself if he is to elicit it in his audience. He is also concomitantly a principal, an actor, a living character in the drama that he is unfolding in print before us. Moreover, that suspension of disbelief is in no sense incompatible with a large body of assumptions, many of them definite, a number of them positively alarming.

They have to do largely with sexuality and in particular with female sexuality. They are brought to a focus in the central scene of Dora's life (and case), a scene that Freud orchestrates with inimitable richness and to which he recurs thematically at a number of junctures with the tact and sense of form that one associates with a classical composer of music (or with Proust, Mann, or Joyce). Dora told this episode to Freud toward the beginning of their relation, after "the first difficulties of the treatment had been overcome." It is the scene between her and Herr K. that took place when she was fourteen years old—that is, four years before the present tense of the case—and acted Freud said as a "sexual trauma." The reader will recall that on this occasion Herr K. contrived to get Dora alone "at his place of business" in the town of B——, and then without warning or preparation "suddenly clasped the girl to him and pressed a kiss upon her lips." Freud then asserts that "this was *surely* just the situation to call up a *distinct* feeling of sexual excitement in a *girl* of *fourteen* who had *never before* been approached. But Dora had at that mo-ment a violent feeling of disgust, tore herself free from the man, and hurried past him to the staircase and from there to the street door" (all italics are mine). She avoided seeing the K.'s for a few days after this, but then relations returned to "normal"—if such a term survives with any permissible sense in the present context. She continued to meet Herr K., and neither of them ever mentioned "the little scene." Moreover, Freud adds, "according to her account Dora kept it a secret till her confession during the treatment," and he pretty clearly implies that he believes this.

This episode preceded by two years the scene at the lake that acted as the precipitating agent for the severe stage of Dora's illness; and it was this later episode and the entire structure that she and others had elaborated about it that she had first presented to Freud, who continues thus:

> In this scene—second in order of mention, but first in order of time—the behavior of this child of fourteen was already entirely and completely hysterical. I should without question consider a person hysterical in whom an occasion for sexual excitement elicited feelings that were preponderantly or exclusively unpleasurable; and I should do so whether or not the person were capable of producing somatic symptoms.

Also, in Dora's feelings of disgust an obscure psychical mechanism called the "reversal of affect" was brought into play; but so was another process, and here Freud introduces—casually and almost as a throwaway—one more of his grand theoretical-clinical formulations, namely the idea of the "displacement of sensation," or as it has more commonly come to be referred to, the "displacement upward." "Instead of the genital sensation which would certainly have been felt by a healthy girl in such circumstances, Dora was overcome by the unpleasurable feeling which is proper to the tract of mucous membrane at the entrance to the alimentary canal—that is by disgust." Although the disgust did not persist as a permanent symptom but remained behind residually and potentially in a general distaste for food and poor appetite, a second displacement upward was the resultant of this scene "in the shape of a sensory hallucination which occurred from time to time and even made its appearance while she was telling me her story. She declared that she could still feel upon the upper part of her body the pressure of Herr K.'s embrace." Taking into account certain other of Dora's "inexplicable"—and hitherto unmentioned—"peculiarities" (such as her phobic reluctance to walk past any man she saw engaged in animated conversation with a woman), Freud "formed in my own mind the following reconstruction of the scene. I believe that during the man's passionate embrace she felt not merely his kiss upon her lips but also his erect member against her body. The perception was revolting to her; it was dismissed from her memory, repressed, and replaced by the innocent sensation of pressure upon her thorax, which in turn derived an excessive intensity from its repressed

166

source." This repressed source was located in the erotogenic oral zone, which in Dora's case had undergone a developmental deformation from the period of infancy. And thus, Freud concludes, "the pressure of the erect member probably led to an analogous change in the corresponding female organ, the clitoris; and the excitation of this second erotogenic zone was referred by a process of displacement to the simultaneous pressure against the thorax and became fixed there."

The actual case of Dora was full of such literary and novelistic devices or conventions as thematic analogies, double plots, reversals, inversions, variations, betrayals, etc.—full of what the "sharp-sighted" Dora as well as the sharp-sighted Freud thought of as "hidden connections"—though it is important to add that Dora and her physician mean different things by the same phrase. And as the case proceeds Freud continues to confront Dora with such connections and tries to enlist her assistance in their construction. For example, one of the least pleasant characteristics in Dora's nature was her habitual reproachfulness—it was directed mostly toward her father but radiated out in all directions. Freud regarded this behavior in his own characteristic manner: "A string of reproaches against other people," he comments, "leads one to suspect the existence of a string of self-reproaches with the same content." Freud accordingly followed the procedure of turning back "each simple reproach on the speaker herself." When Dora reproached her father with malingering in order to keep himself in the company of Frau K., Freud felt "obliged to point out to the patient that her present ill-health was just as much actuated by motives and was just as tendentious as had been Frau K.'s illness, which she had understood so well." At such moments Dora begins to mirror the other characters in the case, as they in differing degrees all mirror one another as well.

Part of that sense, we have come to understand, is that the writer is or ought to be conscious of the part that he—in whatever guise, voice, or persona he chooses—invariably and unavoidably plays in the world he represents. Oddly enough, although there is none of his writings in which Freud is more vigorously active than he is here, it is precisely this activity that he subjects to the least self-conscious scrutiny, that he almost appears to fend off. For example, I will now take my head in my hands and suggest that his extraordinary analysis of Dora's first dream is inadequate on just this count. He is only dimly and marginally aware of his central place in it (he is clearly incorporated into the figure of Dora's father), comments on it only as an addition to Dora's own addendum to the dream, and does nothing to exploit it. Instead of analyzing his own part in what he has done and what he is writing, Freud continues to behave like an unreliable narrator, treating the material about which he is writing as if it were literature but excluding himself from both that treatment and that material. At one moment he refers to himself as someone "who has learnt to appreciate the delicacy of the fabric of structures such as dreams," intimating what I surmise he incontestably believed, that dreams are natural works of art. And when, in the analysis of the second dream, we find ourselves back at the scene at the lake again; when Dora recalls that the only plea to her of Herr K. that she could remember is "You know I get nothing out of my wife"; when these were precisely the same words used by Dora's father in describing to Freud his relation to Dora's mother; and when Freud speculates that Dora may even "have heard her father make the same complaint . . . just as I myself did from his own lips"—when a conjunction such as this occurs, then we know we are in a novel, probably by Proust. Time has recurred, the repressed has returned, plot, double plot, and counterplot have all intersected, and "reality" turns out to be something that for all practical purposes is indistinguishable from a systematic fictional creation.

Finally when at the very end Freud turns to deal—rudimentarily as it happens—with the decisive issue of the case, the transferences, everything is transformed into literature, into reading and writing. Transferences, he writes, "are new editions or facsimiles" of tendencies, fantasies, and relations in which "the person of the physician" replaces some earlier person. When the substitution is a simple one, the transferences may be said to be "merely new impressions or reprints": Freud is explicit about the metaphor he is using. Others "more ingeniously constructed . . . will no longer be new impressions, but revised editions." And he goes on, quite carried away by these figures, to institute a comparison between dealing with the transference and other analytic procedures. "It is easy to learn how to interpret dreams," he remarks, "to extract from the patient's associations his unconscious thoughts and memories, and to practise similar explanatory arts: for these the patient himself will always provide the text." The startling group of suppositions contained in this sentence should not distract us from noting the submerged ambiguity in it. The patient does not merely provide the text; he also *is* the text, the writing to be read, the language to be interpreted. With the transference, however, we move to a different degree of difficulty and onto a different level of explanation. It is only after the transference has been resolved, Freud concludes, "that a patient arrives at a sense of conviction of the validity of the connections which have been constructed during the analysis." I will refrain from entering the veritable series of Chinese boxes opened up by that last statement, and will content myself by proposing that in this passage as a whole Freud is using literature and writing not only creatively and heuristically—as he so often does—but defensively as well.

The writer or novelist is not the only partial role taken up unconsciously or semiconsciously by Freud in the course of this work. He also figures prominently in the text in his capacity as a nineteenth-century man of science and as a representative Victorian critic—employing the seriousness, energy, and commitment of the Victorian ethos to deliver itself from its own excesses. We have already seen him affirming the positive nature of female sexuality, "the genital sensation which would certainly have been felt by a healthy girl in such circumstances," but which Dora did not feel. He goes a good deal further than this. At a fairly early moment in the analysis he faces Dora with the fact that she has "an aim in view which she hoped to gain by her illness. That aim could be none other than to detach her father from Frau K." Her prayers and arguments had not worked; her suicide letter and fainting fits had done no better. Dora knew quite well how much her father loved her, and, Freud continues to address her:

I felt quite convinced that she would recover at once if only her father were to tell her that he had sacrificed Frau K. for the sake of her health. But, I added, I hoped he would not let himself be persuaded to do this, for then she would have learned what a powerful weapon she had in her hands, and she would certainly not fail on every future occasion to make use once more of her liability to ill-health. Yet if her father refused to give way to her, I was quite sure she would not let herself be deprived of her illness so easily.

This is pretty strong stuff, considering both the age and her age. I think, moreover, that we are justified in reading an overdetermination out of this utterance of Freud's and in suggesting that he had motives additional to strictly therapeutic ones in saying what he did.

How far he is willing to go begins to be visible as we observe him sliding almost imperceptibly from being the nineteenth-century man of

STEVEN MARCUS

science to being the remorseless "teller of truth," the character in a play by Ibsen who is not to be deterred from his "mission." In a historical sense the two roles are not adventitiously related, any more than it is adventitious that the "truth" that is told often has unforeseen and destructive consequences and that it can rebound upon the teller. But we see him most vividly at this implacable work in the two great dream interpretations, which are largely "phonographic" reproductions of dramatic discourse and dialogue. Very early on in the analysis of the first dream, Freud takes up the dream element of the "jewel-case" and makes the unavoidable symbolic interpretation of it.

As the case history advances it becomes increasingly clear to the careful reader that Freud and not Dora has become the central character in the action. Freud the narrator does in the writing what Freud the first psychoanalyst appears to have done in actuality. We begin to sense that it is his story that is being written and not hers that is being retold. Instead of letting Dora appropriate her own story, Freud became the appropriator of it. The case history belongs progressively less to her than it does to him. It may be that this was an inevitable development, that it is one of the typical outcomes of an analysis that fails, that Dora was under any circumstances unable to become the appropriator of her own history, the teller of her own story. Blame does not necessarily or automatically attach to Freud. Nevertheless, by the time he gets to the second dream he is able to write, "I shall present the material produced during the analysis of this dream in the somewhat haphazard order in which it recurs to my mind." He makes such a presentation for several reasons, most of which are legitimate. But one reason almost certainly is that by this juncture it is his *own* mind that chiefly matters to him, and it is *his* associations to her dream that are of principal importance.

At the same time, as the account progresses, Freud has never been more inspired, more creative, more inventive; as the reader sees Dora gradually slipping further and further away from Freud, the power and complexity of the writing reach dizzying proportions. At times they pass over into something else. Due allowance has always to be made for the absolutizing tendency of genius, especially when as in the case of Dora the genius is writing with license of a poet and the ambiguity of a seer. But Freud goes beyond this.

When Dora reports her second dream, Freud spends two hours of inspired insight in elucidating some of its meanings. "At the end of the second session," he writes, "I expressed my satisfaction at the results." The satisfaction in question is in large measure self-satisfaction, for Dora responded to Freud's expression of it with the following words uttered in "a depreciatory tone: 'Why, has anything so remarkable come out?' " That satisfaction was to be of short duration, for Dora opened the third session by telling Freud that this was the last time she would be there—it was December 31, 1900. Freud's remarks that "her breaking off so unexpectedly just when my hopes of a successful termination of the treatment were at their highest, and her thus bringing those hopes to nothing—this was an unmistakable act of vengeance on her part" are only partly warranted. There was, or should have been, nothing unexpected about Dora's decision to terminate; indeed Freud himself on the occasion of the first dream had already detected such a decision on Dora's part and had communicated this finding to her. Moreover, his "highest" hopes for a successful outcome of the treatment seem almost entirely without foundation. In such a context the hopes of success almost unavoidably become a matter of self-reference and point to the immense *intellectual* triumph that Freud was aware he was achieving with the material adduced by his patient. On the matter of "vengeance," however, Freud cannot be faulted; Dora was, among many other things, certainly getting her own back on Freud by refusing to allow him to bring her story to an end in the way he saw fit. And he in turn is quite candid about the injury he felt she had caused him. "No one who, like me," he writes, "conjures up the most evil of those half-tamed demons that inhabit the human breast, and seeks to wrestle with them, can expect to come through the struggle unscathed."

This admission of vulnerability, which Freud artfully manages to blend with the suggestion that he is a kind of modern combination of Jacob and Faust, is in keeping with the weirdness and wildness of the case as a whole and with this last hour. That hour recurs to the scene at the lake, two years before, and its aftermath. And Freud ends this final hour with the following final interpretation. He reminds Dora that she was in love with Herr K.; that she wanted him to divorce his wife; that even though she was quite young at the time she wanted " 'to wait for him, and you took it that he was only waiting till you were grown up enough to be his wife. I imagine that this was a perfectly serious plan for the future in your eyes.' " But Freud does not say this in order to contradict it or categorize it as a fantasy of the adolescent girl's unconscious imagination. On the contrary, he has very different ideas in view, for he goes on to tell her,

"You have not even got the right to assert that it was out of the question for Herr K. to have had any such intention; you have told me enough about him that points directly towards his having such an intention. Nor does his behavior at L____ contradict this view. After all, you did not let him finish his speech and do not know what he meant to say to you."

He has not done with her yet, for he then goes on to bring in the other relevant parties and offers her the following conclusion:

"Incidentally, the scheme would by no means have been so impracticable. Your father's relation with Frau K. . . . . made it certain that her consent to a divorce could be obtained; and you can get anything you like out of your father. Indeed, if your temptation at L____ had had a different upshot, this would have been *the only possible solution for all the parties concerned.*" (italics mine)

No one—at least no one in recent years—has accused Freud of being a swinger, but this is without question a swinging solution that is being offered. It is of course possible that he feels free to make such a proposal only because he knows that nothing in the way of action can come of it; but with him you never can tell—as I hope I have already demonstrated. One has only to imagine what in point of ego strength, balance, and self-acceptance would have been required of Dora alone in this arrangement of wife-and-daughter-swapping to recognize at once its extreme irresponsibility, to say the least. At the same time we must bear in mind that such a suggestion is not incongruent with the recently revealed circumstance that Freud analyzed his own daughter. Genius makes up its own rules as it goes along—and breaks them as well. This "only possible solution" was one of the endings that Freud wanted to write to Dora's story; he had others in mind besides, but none of them were to come about. Dora refused or was unable to let him do this; she refused to be a character in the story that Freud was composing for her, and wanted to finish it herself. As we now know, the ending she wrote was a very bad one indeed.

V

In this extraordinary work Freud and Dora often appear as unconscious, parodic refractions of each other. Both of them insist with im-

placable will upon the primacy of "reality," although the realities each
has in mind differ radically. Both of them use reality, "the truth," as a
weapon. Freud does so by forcing interpretations upon Dora before she
is ready for them or can accept them. And this aggressive truth bounds
back upon the teller, for Dora leaves him. Dora in turn uses her version
of reality—it is "outer" reality that she insists upon—aggressively as well.
She has used it from the outset against her father, and five months after
she left Freud she had the opportunity to use it against the K.'s. In May
of 1901 one of the K.'s children dies. Dora took the occasion to pay them
a visit of condolence—

She took her revenge on them. . . . To the wife she said: "I know you have an
affair with my father"; and the other did not deny it. From the husband she
drew an admission of the scene by the lake which he had disputed, and brought
the news of her vindication home to her father.

She told this to Freud fifteen months after she had departed, when she
returned one last time to visit him—to ask him, without sincerity, for
further help, and "to finish her story." She finished her story, and as for
the rest Freud remarks, "I do not know what kind of help she wanted
from me, but I promised to forgive her for having deprived me of the
satisfaction of affording her a far more radical cure for her troubles."

But the matter is not hopelessly obscure, as Freud himself has already confessed. What went wrong with the case, "its great defect, which
led to its being broken off prematurely," was something that had to do
with the transference; and Freud writes that "I did not succeed in mastering the transference in good time." He was in fact just beginning to
learn about this therapeutic phenomenon, and the present passage is the
first really important one about it to have been written. It is also in the
nature of things heavily occluded. On Dora's side the transference went
wrong in several senses. In the first place there was the failure on her
part to establish an adequate positive transference to Freud. She was not
free enough to respond to him erotically—in fantasy—or intellectually—
by accepting his interpretations: both or either of these being prerequisites for the mysterious "talking cure" to begin to work. And in the
second, halfway through the case a negative transference began to emerge,
quite clearly in the first dream. Freud writes that he "was deaf to this
first note of warning," and as a result this negative "transference took me
unawares, and, because of the unknown quantity in me which reminded

Dora of Herr K., she took her revenge on me as she wanted to take her revenge on him, and deserted me as she believed herself to have been deceived and deserted by him." This is, I believe, the first mention in print of the conception that is known as "acting out"—out of which, one may incidentally observe, considerable fortunes have been made.

We are, however, in a position to say something more than this. For there is a reciprocating process in the analyst known as the countertransference, and in the case of Dora this went wrong too. Although Freud describes Dora at the beginning of the account as being "in the first bloom of youth—a girl of intelligent and engaging looks," almost nothing attractive about her comes forth in the course of the writing. As it unwinds, and it becomes increasingly evident that Dora is not responding adequately to Freud, it also becomes clear that Freud is not responding favorably to this response, and that he doesn't in fact like Dora very much. He doesn't like her negative sexuality, her inability to surrender to her own erotic impulses. He doesn't like "her really remarkable achievements in the direction of intolerable behavior." He doesn't like her endless reproachfulness. Above all, he doesn't like her inability to surrender herself to him. For what Freud was as yet unprepared to face was not merely the transference, but the countertransference as well—in the case of Dora it was largely a negative countertransference—an unanalyzed part of himself. I should like to suggest that this cluster of unanalyzed impulses and ambivalences was in part responsible for Freud's writing of this great text immediately after Dora left him. It was his way—and one way—of dealing with, mastering, expressing, and neutralizing such material. Yet the neutralization was not complete; or we can put the matter in another way and state that Freud's creative honesty was such that it compelled him to write the case of Dora as he did, and that his writing has allowed us to make out in this remarkable fragment a still fuller picture. As I have said before, this fragment of Freud's is more complete and coherent than the fullest case studies of anyone else. Freud's case histories are a new form of literature—they are creative narratives that include their own analysis and interpretation. Nevertheless, like the living works of literature that they are, the material they contain is always richer than the original analysis and interpretation that accompany it; and this means that future generations will recur to these works and will find in them a language they are seeking and a story they need to be told.

12.

Myshkin's Epilepsy

Elizabeth Dalton

IN "DOSTOEVSKY AND PARRICIDE," Freud argues that Dostoevsky's epilepsy was the central expression of his neurosis, and thus fundamental to his life and character. If this is indeed the case, epilepsy must also have crucial significance for Dostoevsky's work. Throughout most of his adult life, he endured not only the violent and humilating *grand mal* seizures, which during some periods occurred several times a week, but also the agitated, irritable disorientation that preceded them and the hours and days of weakness and depression that followed. The extraordinary experiences associated with the fits and the state or condition of being an epileptic must certainly have shaped Dostoevsky's work and the conception of experience that informs it in some intimate and profound way.

There are several epileptics in the novels. In *The Brothers Karamazov*, the epileptic Smerdyakov is a parricide, the debased alter-ego of Ivan and indeed of all the brothers. In *The Possessed* it is suggested that Kirilov, the tormented and visionary young nihilist who commits suicide, is or might have become epileptic. And above all there is Myshkin, the hero of *The Idiot*. Myshkin is one of the most extraordinary creations in all of fiction. Dostoevsky intended him to be the representation of ideal and absolute moral beauty—"a positively beautiful man," a sort of Russian Christ who would point the way to the moral regeneration of Russia and even the world. And Myshkin is indeed an irresistibly attractive and

From "Myshkin's Epilepsy," *Partisan Review* (1978), 65(4)595–610; also in Dalton, *Unconscious Structure in "The Idiot"* (Princeton, N.J.: Princeton University Press, 1979).

lovable character—gentle, compassionate, charming—a radiant figure of Christian charity. Yet his charity is strangely flawed, and almost entirely destructive in its effects. Although Myshkin himself is chaste, and indeed apparently impotent, he is drawn compulsively to the brutal passion of Nastasya and Rogozhin. Every life he touches deeply is ruined, and at the end of the novel Myshkin himself sinks into idiocy and stupor.

At the heart of the enigma presented by Myshkin and the novel is epilepsy. It is a terrifying and degrading illness: the seizure is a sudden and total loss of control and even of consciousness. But at the same time, epilepsy is the sacred disease of shamans and prophets, who are said to experience ecstasies and visions during the "aura" preceding the fit: thus the seizure can also be seen as a representation of the violent descent of divine power. Much of the extraordinary psychological excitement and aesthetic tension of Dostoevsky's fiction comes from the juxtaposition of the darkest forces in the human soul with radiant images of great spiritual beauty. In *The Idiot* the epileptic seizure itself appears as the violently condensed expression of that intimate, equivocal relationship between the most debased and the most exalted aspects of human experience. The novel also reflects in a pervasive way what might be called the rhythm of epilepsy, the sudden fluctuations of energy and violent alterations of consciousness that characterize the disease. *The Idiot* suggests the importance of epilepsy not only for Dostoevsky's conception of experience, but also for his style, for his narrative and dramatic structure, and especially for that peculiar compulsion towards extreme mental states that gives to the novels their almost unbearable intensity.

The novel was written during a period of great turmoil in the author's life. Dostoevsky had gone to Europe with his pregnant wife under threat of arrest from his creditors; he left Russia, as he wrote his friend Maikov, "to save my health and even my life." Epileptic seizures were recurring once a week: "it was unbearable to be fully *conscious* of the disorder of my nerves and *brain*. I was going mad, that's the truth. I felt it; the disorder of my nerves sometimes drove me to moments of furious madness." He went to Dresden, to Hamburg, and then to Baden, where he suffered an intense recurrence of his gambling mania. Finally his wife managed to get him to Geneva, where, nearly destitute, he began work on *The Idiot*. We know from the notebooks that Dostoevsky had great difficulty in projecting the plot of the novel. And because of his commitment to his editor and his terrible financial plight, each section had to be submitted for publication before the next had been written or even sketched out. In these desperate circumstances, it would seem that Dostoevsky was forced back upon the spontaneous images and rhythms of his mental life to a greater extent than in any other work. It is perhaps because the novel reveals so openly the nature of that life that its author's feelings about it were peculiarly intense. Something about the novel evidently had quite special significance for him. "As for *The Idiot*," he wrote to Maikov, "I'm afraid, I'm so afraid—you can't imagine. A kind of unnatural fear such as I've never felt before." The progress of the novel was intimately linked in Dostoevsky's mind to the course of his epilepsy. As the story of the epileptic prince took shape, Dostoevsky's own condition worsened: "the disorder of my nerves has increased and my fits are more frequent and violent." He complained of being in "the most terrible depression . . . The day before yesterday I had a very serious attack [of epilepsy]. Nevertheless I wrote yesterday, in a state close to madness." The excitement that informs the climactic scenes with their fury and brilliance expressed itself in life in the epileptic seizures, and Dostoevsky reckoned the cost of the great scenes in fits: "I wrote this finale [Nastasya's birthday party] in a state of inspiration, and it cost me two fits in a row." Dostoevsky endowed all of his characters with parts of himself, but it is to Myshkin alone among his principal heroes that he gave the ambiguous gift of his illness. The novel is in an important sense an attempt to understand that illness; it is at some level Dostoevsky's exploration of the meaning of his epilepsy.

One has the sense in reading *The Idiot* that the action of the novel is balanced perilously, that just beyond or beneath its precarious coherence is a kind of maelstrom or abyss in which emotion might lose its connection with intelligible form and manifest itself in some unimaginably direct, "raw" state; here ordinary coherent speech and gesture might give way to frenzy or blankness. And indeed the novel does present us with the image of this extremity in the epileptic fit. In fact, the seizure is a sort of paradigm of the emotional progression of the book's great scenes. In most of these scenes there is a pattern of rising excitement focused upon one central figure whose consciousness becomes more and more strained or exalted, until a moment of unbearable tension, when there is a loss of control, followed by physical and mental collapse.

This is the pattern of the climactic episode at Nastasya's birthday party, when Nastasya throws the hundred thousand rubles into the fire and Ganya faints. It is also the pattern of Ippolit's confession, read in a state of growing delirium culminating in Ippolit's suicide attempt. This sequence appears most clearly in the two episodes that end with Myshkin's epileptic attacks. The last scene of the novel, in which the murderer Rogozhin leads Myshkin to the body of Nastasya, ends with a total loss of control: Rogozhin goes mad, and Myshkin collapses into idiocy and blankness. In lesser forms, the same phenomenon appears throughout the novel, in the constant tendency to uncontrolled behavior and wild emotion.

The novel also shows this "epileptic pattern" in its larger structure: the action seems to progress unevenly, in waves of tension that gather and burst in climactic scenes of spectacular emotional violence, leaving the narrative energy of the novel depleted and for a time directionless, until a new wave of tension begins to accumulate. This spasmodic rhythm produces serious structural flaws, gaps, and inconsistencies in the narrative sequence that threaten the integrity of the entire conception. The first and most obvious break of this kind occurs after Nastasya's birthday party, which ends Part I; the opening of Part II is almost like the beginning of a new novel. The next episode is Myshkin's long day in Petersburg, ending in the climactic scene on the staircase when Rogozhin tries to murder him and Myshkin falls in the seizure. Again, after this scene, there is a sort of break in the narrative, and then a new action begins. The narrative connection from one climactic scene to the next is rather tenuous.

Myshkin's epilepsy appears to be so much a condition of the soul that one almost forgets its connection with the body. Medically, epilepsy remains a complex and little understood disorder—a configuration of symptoms rather than a single clinical entity. The symptoms may come from a number of quite different sources, including a physiological alteration of the central nervous system such as a lesion or chemical imbalance, a psychological cause such as a traumatic incident or hysteria, or some combination of physical and psychological elements. The data on Dostoevsky's illness are hard to decipher. However, even if his epilepsy was based on an organic predisposition, as seems likely, the disease certainly assumed a psychological meaning for him in the context of his experience and personality.

Freud argues that Dostoevsky's epilepsy was probably "affective" and hysterical in character. The epileptic reaction, whatever its organic basis, was available for the expression of his neurosis; thus the psychological function of the seizure was to get rid, by somatic means, of masses of stimuli that could not be dealt with psychically. From information about Dostoevsky's life and personality, Freud concludes that in him the Oedipus complex took a particular turn that led to the "negative" resolution, in which the body abandons his identification and rivalry with a forbidding father and adopts instead a passive, "feminine" attitude in the attempt to be loved as a woman and to avoid rivalry and the threat of castration. Paradoxically, however, the woman's sexual role also seems to the boy to imply being castrated; thus the Oedipal hatred of the father is heightened by the fear of being made to play the "feminine" role in relation to him, intensifying parricidal wishes. The guilt associated with such wishes was strengthened disastrously by their fulfillment in reality: the death of the elder Dostoevsky, who was always thought to have been murdered by his serfs, could well have been construed as a kind of parricide. (New evidence described in Joseph Frank's recent biography suggests that the death may have been due to natural causes. However, what is psychologically significant is not what actually happened, but what Dostoevsky believed, and he believed that his father had been murdered.) Freud sees the epileptic attacks as self-punishment: in the seizure the son became temporarily dead, like the murdered father, for whose death he unconsciously held his own guilty desires responsible.

About Dostoevsky's attacks we can only speculate; we cannot claim to understand the mysterious illness of a man long dead. But about a character in literature we have all the relevant information, for his entire existence is contained in the words of the text. Myshkin has two epileptic seizures in *The Idiot*. The first and more spectacular takes place near the beginning of Part II. Myshkin has spent a long day wandering about Petersburg in a pre-epileptic state of increasing anxiety and disorientation. He goes to visit Rogozhin, the crudely powerful young merchant who is both his rival for Nastasya and his shadowy counterpart, a sort of negative double embodying all the violent and lustful impulses repressed in his own personality. The two men compare their different kinds of love for Nastasya. Myshkin loves her chastely, with compassion, while Rogozhin feels for her mingled lust and hatred. Nonetheless, each man offers to give her up for the other. During this strange conversation, Myshkin finds himself absently toying with a knife—the one with which Rogozhin will later murder Nastasya.

Throughout the day Myshkin is tormented by the feeling of a thought pressing for consciousness. His attention is frequently fixed in a peculiar way on bizarre and apparently unrelated impressions, such as the vision of a pair of "strange, glowing eyes"—evidently Rogozhin's—following him intermittently. At Rogozhin's house he notices a shop on the ground floor owned by the Skoptsy, a sect who practice self-castration. In Rogozhin's rooms his attention is captured by a picture—Holbein's painting of the bruised body of the dead Christ. This picture prompts Myshkin to tell a story that for him defines the essence of Russian religious feeling. The story is about two peasants who are preparing to go to bed in an inn, when one is suddenly seized with a desire for the other's silver watch. Praying "God, forgive me for Christ's sake!" he cuts his friend's throat.

After leaving Rogozhin, Myshkin returns to his hotel in a state of growing confusion. Just before the hotel gate, he thinks of Rogozhin's knife. At that moment the thunderstorm which has been building up all day breaks, there is a downpour, and the tension that has accumulated throughout this long hallucinatory sequence comes to a climax. Myshkin sees a man standing in the half-darkness under the arched gateway; he tries to overtake him, but the man vanishes.

The confusion and mounting panic of the day, the sensation of a frightful thought hovering at the back of consciousness, the peculiar attention to the eyes, the knife, and the painting of the dead Christ, all gather and burst here in a violent revelation of instinctual fury. In the conversation earlier in the day, Myshkin and Rogozhin have, as it were, verbally passed Nastasya back and forth between them. Myshkin, imagining what Rogozhin will do to her, has said, "I won't hinder you." However, at parting Rogozhin has said, "Take her then . . . I give in to you!" It is as if this strange transaction, in which each man has somehow given the other permission to do as he will with Nastasya, evokes in Myshkin a fantasy of intercourse in which the act takes the peculiar form dictated by certain repressed infantile wishes and fears. At the literal level, of course, the scene "really happens." But at the level of unconscious meaning, the sequence embodies a fantasy of parental intercourse in which the childish wishes to see and to participate are both gratified. The primal scene here takes the sadomasochistic form of a violent attack, in which Myshkin's identification is not with the sadistic father, but with the sadistically violated mother. The intense emotion and hallucinatory vividness are signals of an unusually direct and concentrated expression of the unconscious comparable to that in a dream.

The essentially visual aspect of the primal scene explains the recurring apparition throughout the day of the eyes of Rogozhin. Rogozhin's eyes represent at once the visual aspect of the child's sexual wishes and the threat of discovery as well as the punishment for those wishes, which is castration. When Myshkin looks round, the eyes meet his own, and the man moves towards him until they are almost touching. Myshkin tries to see the other man more clearly; and at this crucial moment, when the wish to see and the wish to touch are both about to be gratified, "Rogozhin's eyes flashed and a smile of fury contorted his face. His right hand was raised and something gleamed in it." The undefined fear that has pursued Myshkin all day suddenly materializes in this terrifying image. This knife that so fascinated him and that will later be used on Nastasya represents at once the instrument that penetrates, the sadistic penis itself, and the instrument of castration. And castration is the penalty for all the wishes expressed in this scene. It is the punishment for looking at forbidden things and for wishing to replace the father, to compete with him for the mother in an aggressive way: but it is also the price of the wish that emerges most clearly here, the wish to avoid the competition with the father and to submit to him in a passive "feminine" way. Being loved as a woman also seems possible only at the terrible price of loss of the penis.

All the events of the day that have attracted Myshkin's attention in a fixed way or evoked the sense of a repressed idea struggling to consciousness suggest the emergence of the feared homosexual wish and the penalty for submission: the significance of Rogozhin's eyes and his knife are clear; the Skoptsy, the tenants of Rogozhin's house, practice self-castration; the Holbein painting of Christ, his body so bruised and so thoroughly dead that, as Myshkin says, "that picture might make some people lose their faith," depicts the terrible fate of the Son who submits to the Father: "not my will, but thine, be done." Even the story of the peasant who slits his friend's throat and steals his watch as they prepare for bed together suggests the submerged homosexual wish and fear.

The wish and the fear are periously close to realization in the image of Rogozhin with his knife raised. At this point the excitement aroused by the desire to submit sexually to the father and by the terror of castration becomes unbearably intense and the ego is overwhelmed in the epileptic attack; the barriers of the ego are broken and it is flooded with instinctual excitement. The cry, the convulsive movements, and the loss of consciousness of the fit are at once a sort of exaggerated representation of and a substitute for the release of orgasm, the logical culmination of this symbolic coitus in which Myshkin is both spectator and participant. The scene ends with Myshkin falling downstairs and striking his head; the fit has saved him from Rogozhin's knife, but through a familiar equation by which the head stands for the penis, the feared injury to the genital is represented symbolically in the bloodied head. Moreover, the head is perhaps punished as the source of evil impulses, the representation of the mind in which the whole fantastic episode has originated.

One curious aspect of this sequence is the guilt that Myshkin feels throughout the day whenever he becomes momentarily aware of his fear of Rogozhin:

(Oh, how the prince was tortured by the hideousness, the "degradation" of this conviction, of "that base foreboding," and how he had reproached himself!) "Say of what if you dare," he kept telling himself continually with reproach and challenge. "Formulate all your thought, dare to express it clearly, precisely, without faltering! Oh, I am ignoble!" he repeated with indignation and a flush on his face. "With what eyes shall I look upon that man for the rest of my life! Oh, what a day! Oh, God, what a nightmare!"

Myshkin assumes that his suspicions of Rogozhin, his loss of confidence in him, are in some way responsible for Rogozhin's attack on him. In the deepest sense, this is true, for the attack is in fact a representation of Myshkin's thoughts and desires. The chaste and gentle prince has the same passions as other men, the same energies of lust and hatred. What distinguishes him from the violent souls around him is that Myshkin can only experience these forces passively; they must appear to overwhelm him from outside, through the agency of Rogozhin, who represents both the violation from outside that is the destiny of the meek soul, and the violence that it fears within itself and projects outwards onto the figure of the aggressor. The form in which instinctual forces are expressed in the scene of the attack, the absolutely primitive lust and aggression of Rogozhin, suggests the reason for the terror these forces inspire in Myshkin, and explains the unearthly purity of his personality: the expression of instinct is conceived of as leading to mutilation and even to death.

In *The Idiot*, then, the epileptic seizure is overdetermined in an extremely complex way; it is a sort of nodal point at which all the strands of sexual and aggressive feeling are tied into a single expression. It has a sexual meaning as a substitute for and a symolic representation of erotic contact with the father, which implies the terrifying corollary of castration. But the suffering or deathlike aspect of the attack also serves as a punishment for the parricidal wishes aroused by the fear of castration, here reinforced by the homosexual wish. As it is represented in the novel, the epileptic personality is one in which sexual and aggressive drives have assumed a particularly dangerous character, involving homosexual and parricidal wishes so threatening to the ego that they must be entirely repressed. The epileptic seizure, then, represents the periodic eruption of these energies in the form of a violent attack in which the ego does indeed lose all control.

But Myshkin's epilepsy has also another dimension, a powerfully positive aspect that makes it the fundamental enigma of his being, the point of transformation at which disease may become sanctity. This double quality of Myshkin's illness suggests that the dualism and the violent antinomies of Dostoevsky's whole conception of moral experience may originate in part in the radically opposed meanings of epilepsy. Epilepsy is what sets Myshkin apart from other men in every way: it is weakness, illness, idiocy. But if it is illness, it is the *morbus sacer*, the sacred disease of shamans and prophets who are torn by the rough hand of God, who see through this rent in the fabric of their beings into another world, a luminous reality free of the limitations and ambiguities of ordinary experience. This mystical aspect of Myshkin's epilepsy is concentrated in the aura, the momentary alteration of consciousness that precedes the fit, which is described in the following passage:

he always had one minute just before the epileptic fit . . . when suddenly in the midst of sadness, spiritual darkness and oppression, there seemed at moments a flash of light in his brain, and with extraordinary impetus all his vital forces suddenly began working at their highest tension. The sense of life, the consciousness of self, were multiplied ten times at these moments, which passed like a flash of lightning. His mind and his heart were flooded with extraordinary light; all his uneasiness, all his doubts, all his anxieties were relieved at once; they were all resolved into a kind of lofty calm, full of serene, harmonious joy and hope, full of understanding and the knowledge of the ultimate cause of things. But these moments, these flashes, were only the prelude of that final second . . . with which the fit began. That second was, of course, unendurable.

He wonders whether this is only a morbid effect of his illness.

And yet he came at last to an extremely paradoxical conclusion. "What if it is disease?" he decided at last. "What does it matter that it is an abnormal intensity, if the result, if the minute of sensation, remembered and analysed afterwards in health, turns out to be the acme of harmony and beauty, and gives a feeling, unknown and undivined till then, of completeness, of proportion, of reconciliation, and of ecstatic devotional merging in the highest synthesis of life?" . . . These moments were only an extraordinary quickening of self-consciousness—if the condition was to be expressed in one word—and at the same time of the direct sensation of existence in the most intense degree.

The features repeatedly stressed in this account of the aura are the flashes and floods of light, the heightened intensity and directness of the sensation of self and of existence, and above all the ecstatic sense of harmony in which qualities of reconciliation, synthesis, and merging are emphasized. In this "ecstatic devotional merging" Myshkin, like others who have had the mystical experience, feels a sudden resolution of doubts and conflicts and a sense of oneness with something outside himself, with the "highest synthesis of life." This sense of oneness with the universe seems to be the "oceanic feeling" described by Freud in *Civilization and Its Discontents,* where he explains it as a dissolution of the boundaries of the ego, a regression to the primordial state of the infant at the breast, who "does not as yet distinguish his ego from the external world as the source of the sensations flowing in upon him."

The "extraordinary quickening of self-consciousness" in the aura may seem inconsistent with the loss of the sense of an individualized self suggested by the oceanic feeling and by Myshkin's sense of ecstatic merging. However, the "self" in this passage seems to be not Myshkin's everyday self, which is often beset by doubt and guilt, but a quite different self free of any sense of limitation, open to "the direct sensation of existence in the most intense degree."

The change in the functions and relations of the different parts of the mind in mystical experience can be compared with what happens in manic-depressive illness. Although the mystic and the manic-depressive are different in obvious ways, there are interesting resemblances which suggest that the underlying pattern of sudden changes in the distribution of energy within the mind may be similar. In manic-depressive illness, the personality is dominated for long periods by a severe superego, which prohibits instinctual expression. At the onset of the manic phase, the dammed-up instinctual energy associated with repressed ideas and impulses erupts explosively, overthrowing the superego and producing a feeling of elation and fantasies of omnipotence.

The personality of the mystic, at least that typical of the great Catholic mystics of Europe, is also dominated by superego: the mystic lives under a severe regime of mortification of the flesh, fasting, and chastity. But this instinctual deprivation is apparently compensated by the joy of the mystical experience, for which denial of the senses is the preparation. The mystical vision is often preceded by a terrible period of intellectual and sexual temptation, doubts, and obscene visions, not unlike the ordeal of Myshkin's long day in Petersburg before the fit. After enduring this torment, the mystic is rewarded by the mystical revelation. This revelation may include the apparition of Christ, the saints, or the Virgin, often described in intensely sexual language. Or it may be a more generalized experience—an ineffable sense of beatitude or absorption into the radiance of the divine being such as Myshkin has during the epileptic aura. As in mania, there is an eruption of long-repressed instinctual energy and the superego is overthrown; the ego is free to experience the gratification of id impulses, although in a form disguised by and consonant with religious beliefs.

Thus the sense of merging, reconciliation, and synthesis in mystical experience refers not only to the feeling of oneness with the external world, but also to the annihilation of internal conflict as the repressive superego is overthrown and id energy rushes into the ego, producing the intensely heightened feeling of self-consciousness and of "the direct sensation of existence." The "extraordinary light" that floods the mind and heart of Myshkin appears to be an image of this surge of energy. The reality principle is deposed by the pleasure principle, which seeks immediate gratification. Thus the sense of time, a function of the ego associated with the delay of gratification, is suspended during the mystical experience, which is always described as somehow outside of time. Myshkin understands during the ecstatic moment the saying "there shall be no more time"; it is this moment, he says, "which was not long enough for the water to be spilt out of Mahomet's pitcher, though the epileptic prophet had time to gaze at all the habitations of Allah." Thus the brilliant, unlimited, harmonious vision that comes to Myshkin during the epileptic aura is a regression to the timeless world of the primitive ego, buried in the oldest layers of the mind and illuminated during the instant of the aura like a dark landscape in a flash of lightning.

The moment of the aura is virtually the only point in *The Idiot* at which instinctual impulses break through the barriers of repression with sufficient force to be felt as pleasurable and gratifying. At this point the sexual and aggressive feelings usually experienced by Myshkin in the disguised masochistic form of suffering rush into the ego with an effect of ecstatic and joyful release. But the ego cannot tolerate the force of these energies in their original form, nor can it allow the ideas attached to them—the wishes towards the father contained in the primal scene fantasy—to rise into conscious awareness. The moment of orgiastic release is followed by the total eclipse of the ego in the epileptic seizure. The fit is also the revenge of the superego, which can be deposed only temporarily; for the release of sexual and aggressive energy it exacts the talion penalty of symbolic castration and death. The instinctual drives are once more experienced under the negative sign of superego, in the form of asceticism and suffering.

The epileptic scenes are the points in the novel at which experience reaches its highest intensity; these episodes are in a sense the prototypes of the emotional experience of *The Idiot*. In the great scenes of climactic emotion or violent confrontation, the reader is led to participate in a kind of loss of control: the ego of the protagonist, under the assault of repressed impulses, gives way to energies and fantasies usually inaccessible to it and undergoes an enormous expansion of its capacity for perception and feeling. But this momentary expansion also exposes it to the possibility of annihilation through the savage force of id energies and the retaliation of superego. The result is the collapse of the ego in frenzy, loss of consciousness, or epileptic convulsions.

This characteristic mode of emotional response is what might be called the "epileptic pattern" in the novel. Its positive value is in one sense enormous: at its most acute, in the aura, it constitutes the claim for the "mystical" quality of Myshkin's insight and of his personality. These moments of heightened consciousness represent a breakthrough beyond the barriers of repression that define the normal conditions of the ego into a state in which the darker regions of personality are illuminated and the sense of existence is immeasurably intensified. In such states the conscious mind appears to be offered the possibility of penetrating a limitless reality. The condition of this final knowledge is, of course, annihilation. This is the ambiguity and the fundamental paradox of the moments of greatest intensity in the novel: the most piercing consciousness of the self comes at the point of the destruction of personality, at the moment when the ego is about to give way and the mind to return to a primitive and undifferentiated mode of response. The moment of highest meaning in Myshkin's experience—the brilliant awareness of the texture of existence itself in the epileptic aura—is also the very moment when existence is on the verge of collapse into meaningless emptiness. Myshkin himself knows this:

he often said to himself that all these gleams and flashes of the highest sensation of life and self-consciousness, and therefore also of the highest form of existence, were nothing but disease . . . and if so, it was not at all the highest form of being, but on the contrary must be reckoned the lowest.

And later: "Stupefaction, spiritual darkness, idiocy stood before him conspicuously as the consequence of these 'higher moments' "; but "for the infinite happiness he had felt in it, that second really might well be worth the whole of life."

No single meaning can be attributed to epileptic seizures in general. Myshkin's illness, however, manifests itself in a quite specific context, in which the seizure is densely inscribed with meaning. His convulsion occurs as he mounts an internal staircase around a column, tries not to see and yet does see a standing man in a niche, and is then attacked with a knife. These images evoke the wish for penetration, active and passive, and the fear of punishment. The penetration is at once physical, visual, and psychological: a body is entered, but at the same time something is seen, and the frontier of forbidden knowledge and desire is crossed.

In the compulsion towards such extreme and opposed mental states lies much of Dostoevsky's extraordinary power and tension. Each of the novels is a sort of spiritual experiment with the darkest forces of the psyche; in the outcome the protagonist hovers for a time between omnipotence and annihilation, then falls to annihilation. In *The Idiot* the connections between that conception of the spiritual life and the dangerous excitements of epilepsy are clear.

It is into the darkness that lies beyond the controls of the ego, the perilous region of unmodified instinct and savage retaliation, that we are invited by the great scenes of mounting tension and final frenzy and collapse. In *The Idiot* more than anywhere else in Dostoevsky we are taken beyond intellectual speculation about the description of these states into the actual experience itself. Again and again the novel leads us out onto this treacherous ground; beyond this precipice is the abyss of total abandonment in frenzy or stupor—the loss of the ego and all its complicated negotiations between the inner world of instinctual drives and the outer world of external reality. In the compulsion to lean out over that abyss the novel also risks its own existence as an aesthetic object. In their explosive force, the great scenes threaten to escape the control of the plot, to disrupt the continuity of the narrative and drive it into incoherence. This flirtation with loss of form is the analogue in the structure of the novel to the courting of loss of ego control in the protagonists, especially Myshkin. Thus the novel, in its terrible fidelity to psychological experience, almost loses itself in the gamble.

Almost, but not quite. Form and meaning are salvaged periously, although *The Idiot* does not always give its meanings their true names. Like all dark forces, they must sometimes be called holy, as the Furies were named Gracious Ones. The knowledge of those forces is in some way bound up with the profound ambiguities of epilepsy: in the representation of the epileptic seizure the most primitive energies of psychic life, its oldest and most forbidden meanings, are symbolically enacted, animating with their tremendous power a vision in which degradation and sanctity are inextricably mingled. In *The Idiot* the experience of epilepsy is not only illness and incapacity, but tragic and dangerous revelation.

13.

Candide: Radical Simplicity
and the Impact of Evil

Gail S. Reed

SEVERAL OF VOLTAIRE'S best known tales are similar in shape and plot, apparent variations on an inner theme. *Zadig* (1741), *Candide* (1759), and *L'Ingénu* (1767) all involve a naïve or idealistic protagonist wandering the world in search of a woman who had been denied him by fate and authority, grappling the while with the frustration imposed by arbitrary and powerful men and carried out through their often impersonal and cruel institutions. At the chronological center of the tales *Candide* has an emotional impact lacking in the others; it has been frequently asserted that it is the product of personal crisis and represents the author's confrontation with the existence of evil.[1] Philosophic and biographical implications aside, for these have been frequently discussed elsewhere, what formal factors, absent in the other tales, compel this impression of the impact of evil?

Like any other attempt to explore the emotional aspect of fiction, this one requires assumptions about a reader, that literary figure who of late has become more controversial than the literature he reads. Critics of several persuasions, while in agreement on the interdependence of reader and text, have been divided over whether the reader should be considered an objective or subjective entity.[2] Such differences threaten

This essay is published here for the first time.

to cloud the valuable perspective which the participatory model has opened for us and might best be resolved by recognizing a spectrum of response encompassing both individual differences and (not necessarily conscious) collective experience engendered by a literary text. It is the latter end of the spectrum which will concern me.

The assumption that readers not only react idiosyncratically to a text but also share in a collective experience seems justified on the grounds of their participation both in the human condition itself and in a particular culture where, *inter alia*, common educational practices, language, history, mythology, values, and ideals foster a more specific communality. Freud has pointed out the role of unconscious fantasy shared between the creative writer and his audience,[3] and Hans Sachs has described a community of daydreams.[4] More recently Beres and Arlow have suggested that a reservoir of shared experience as it is elaborated in fantasy forms the basis of empathy, that quality of feeling with another which lies at the root of esthetic participation.[5]

It is not, however, my intention to explore the emotional impact of *Candide* by searching for an unconscious fantasy. The search for latent content raises methodological questions outside the scope of this essay.[6] Rather, I shall follow a suggestion of Hutter,[7] and relate collective response to the structure of the text utilizing psychoanalytic knowledge of normal development as a guide. Accordingly, I shall make no attempt to discern what latent wish or accompanying fantasy might underlie the manifest content of *Candide*. It suffices that the representation of that wish, the hero's pursuit of a woman who combines maternal and sexual qualities, sets in motion a plot characterized by the interplay between the realization of a representation of desire and its frustration. Although the represented wish may conceivably furnish a symbolic structure for several individual wishes, the experience of wish and frustration, which characterizes a reading of *Candide*, is universal.

The problem of defining a collective experience on the basis of an emotional response which will in many be unconscious remains difficult. Not all readers react in the same conscious way to elements in a literary work. For example, the sequence of wish and frustration of wish present in *Candide* tends to evoke anger. The small child will have a tantrum when the frustration of a wish results in an increase of undischarged tension which is experienced as "unpleasure."[8] Some readers, however, may derive gratification from the frustration itself and be consciously immune to the anger it engenders. Others, to avoid experiencing the anger, may idealize the philosophical resolution at the end, concentrate entirely on historical issues, or see only the ironic overlay which minimizes the considerable sadism especially present in the first half of the work. These defensive and characterological responses do not necessarily contradict the assertion of a particular collective experience involving frustration; to the psychoanalytically informed they rather confirm the presence of something consciously unknown.

What is at work in reading is akin to what psychoanalysis calls countertransference in its broadest sense, the emotional responses of the analyst to the patient which, scrutinized, may provide him with valuable information about the patient or, unscrutinized, may interfere with his understanding of and response to the patient. Freud's original description of countertransference was narrower in scope, concerned with interference from the analyst's unconscious exclusively.[9] Gradually, however, definitions have broadened to include the patient's contribution. Several modern theoreticians even hold that in the severer pathologies countertransference reactions are induced, an effort on the part of the patient to recreate his early experiences, or to rid himself of his most fragmenting feelings.[10] The relative merits of these various theoretical developments need not concern us here. What is useful to remember is that certain aspects of countertransference phenomena are not unique to a treatment situation. Conscious response often represents a distortion of the underlying experience and these distorted reactions may occur in all experiences of everyday life, including reading. In fact, such reactions may well account for the strident passion with which rival groups of critics hold fast to contradictory interpretations when the more interesting question remains whether something in the text inspires this disagreement.

The emotional flexibility to explore rather than interpret and hold fast, however, requires the same vigilance to unconscious response as the clinician must exercise: scrutiny of feeling and fantasy, of intense reactions or their absence, of silence or over-talkativeness. Knowledge derived from clinical practice and observations of development shows that certain forms of presentation, certain sequences, certain types of material ought generally to evoke a particular response. Since there is no entirely objective standard by which to identify countertransference reactions, knowledge of hypothetical tendency must be supplemented by self-knowledge, intuition, and experience. We will need, then, to be satisfied with a rather subjective standard after all, a hypothetical reader whose reading experience represents a hypothetical collective experience.[11] If this uncertainty flies in the face of wishes for scientific rigor, it should be recalled that accepting uncertainty is a necessary corallary to accepting the unconscious.

One may, however, be reasonably certain of the intensity of Candide's emotional impact on the reader,[12] despite both the balance achieved as the second half progresses and the ever present element of ironic distance. To describe this impact in terms of manifest theme, one is drawn to the horrifying—because arbitrary—weight of "civilized" evil. Surely the critical debate over whether Voltaire "solves" the "problem of evil" reflects this impact.[13] Whatever the substance of critics' disagreements, it is much less significant than the fact that they conceive of Voltaire's success or failure in these terms, as though by solving the problem he could in some way protect them from the feeling of vulnerability his work awakens.

What factors in Candide could account for this impact of evil? One is the organization of the plot. Beneath the distancing and mitigating ironic tone which characterizes the narrator's presentation, the world of Candide is built upon a fundamental rhythm of expectation and betrayal. Candide is a dialectic of desire and punishment, of trust and the brutal deception of that trust. The hero, innocently desiring Cunégonde and faithfully believing his tutor, is cast out into a best of all possible worlds which proves a mutilating inferno. Despairing, cold, hungry, and penniless, he finds his flagging faith restored by two strangers who treat him to dinner—then brusquely trick him into military servitude where he is robbed of any modicum of individuality and freedom, and finally stripped of his skin in a beating. His fellow sufferer, the old woman, in her parallel journey through life, is deprived by murder of a princely husband at the moment when she joyously anticipates marriage, then ravished, enslaved, and made witness to the dismemberment of her mother and attendants. A eunuch she believes kind fortunately rescues her from the bloody pile of corpses onto which she has collapsed, then quickly sells her anew into slavery.

These betrayals, rhythmic norms rather than exceptions in Candide, frustrate fulfillment; within the fiction they break down the characters' integrity; without, they assault the reader's sense of security through continual frustration of his conventional expectations of the marvelous. The two travelers, so often brutalized and betrayed, withdraw into a state of numbness in which, separate from their bodies, they feel neither physical nor emotional pain; they merely endure. Candide wordlessly traverses a war-torn countryside, objective correlative to his burnt-out inner state; the old woman, less and less desired, becomes first concubine, then slave, then an object dispatched from city to city, until her body is reduced to its most concrete physicality and becomes food. In a final bitter irony, buttock replaces breast in a gruesome parody of the primordial experience of security.

One result of this catastrophic rhythm is the intensified search for warmth and safety. The main characters yearn for protection, for a magic circle of comfort, security, and satiety, as is attested to by their frequent hunger, their stubborn innocence and comic grandiosity, their idealization of Westphalia, and their constant and oft contradicted assertions that they are infallible, perfect, or deserving of the best. Characters and reader are temporarily granted that protection in Eldorado.

Another and parallel result is the release of destructive forces. Indeed the fictional reality of the tale does not permit retreat for long. Outside that magic circle of perfection resides the social world into which the characters are constantly propelled. And this evil outside world is a place where the social institution seeks out the individual to destroy him. Children are castrated to sing in operas, slaves dismembered for disobedience, the military takes brutal possession of Candide's body. In fact, the double row of soldiers poised to club him becomes a giant devouring maw. In this evil social world, rationalized sadism runs rampant. There are, of course, the overt acts of individuals who enslave, rob, rape, and disembowel, but the esthetically pleasing ritual of an auto-da-fé camouflages equally sadistic yet socially sanctioned wishes. When brutality is committed in the name of good, when justice condones robbery and charges a fee, when freedom involves a choice between death by clubbing or firing squad, then language becomes the agent of social deception and the social world beyond the magic circle a place of uncertain perception as well as of danger. Deceiving characters emerge from its midst conferring names on themselves, promising uniqueness and coveting riches, and then merge back into its anonymity. Thus the false Cunégonde is only "une friponne." [14] Candide also becomes part of the universe of shifting forms—separated from his name—stepping back from naïve candor into the socially conferred guise of mercenary. In rapid succession he offers his loyalty to the Spanish, then the Jesuits, avows his German birth and finds Cunégonde's brother, then disguises himself as Jesuit in order to flee, and is held prisoner and threatened with death by the Oreillons because accoutrements designate him as Jesuit. He escapes with his life only by slipping out of the clothing of his assumed identity. This social world, representing the individual's rage at frustration, destroys the self. In becoming part of its spreading insubstantiality, the individual momentarily ceases to exist.

One way in which the evil realm incorporates the self is by undermining the individual's perceptions and thus depriving him of his ability to anticipate, judge, and experience himself as a subjective continuity in time. Encountering Candide, the major characters emerge out of the treacherous social world in continuously changing shapes. The "femme tremblante, d'une taille majestueuse, brillante de pierreries, et couverte d'une voile" (VII,107) is Cunégonde, though the other veiled woman is a fraud. One of the women "qui étendaient des serviettes sur des ficelles pour les faire sécher" is also Cunégonde "rembrunie, les yeux éraillés, la gorge sèche, les joues ridées, les bras rouges & écaillés" (XXIX,217). The commander, "le bonnet à trois cornes en tête, la robe retroussée, l'épée au côté, l'esponton à la main," is the young Baron (XIV,136). He metamorphoses into friend, then into arrogant aristocrat, changes effected with a chameleon-like speed paralleled by Candide's confusion of names: " 'Mon révérend père, . . . mon ancien maître, mon ami, mon beau-frère' " (XV, 140–41). Pangloss reappears as an ineffective galley-slave, as a corpse dissected back to life, and most frighteningly as that phantom who throws himself on Candide:

un gueux tout couvert de pustules, les yeux morts, le bout du nez rongé, la bouche de travers, les dents noires, & parlant de la gorge, tourmenté d'une toux violante, & crachant une dent à chaque effort. (III,94)

The destructiveness represented by the instability of the social realm and of the self here intersect, for Pangloss' ghostly "disguise" is a mutilation which ordinarily belongs to nightmare. By making disguise a matter of body, the text turns the possible illusion of the ghost into the fictional reality of a disfigured tutor. As the physical body yields its integrity, the character becomes his disguise, becomes, that is, other.

Both the savageness of the fictional reality and the rhythm of the plot depend on the radical simplicity of the hero for their full effect. An

appropriate accompaniment to the cruel and unstable reality which sur-
rounds him, the characteristics united by the name of Candide designate
him incomplete. The oscillations of his spirits according to the fullness
of his stomach, his taking in of Pangloss' teachings because of the facili-
tating presence of the beautiful Cunégonde, his profound dependence on
her to give his life shape and direction, his belief that a high degree of
happiness consists in *being* her, all suggest that Voltaire has constructed
a developmentally primitive literary character. So much, in fact, is Candide's simplicity coupled with devices which suggest infantile experience, that it shocks us to discover in the last chapter that as he has
reached maturity he has acquired a beard.

Despite this growth—for much of the tale Candide is so lacking in
self-definition that he is "incapable of irony," as Coulet aptly notes [15]—he
is devoid of judgment. Thus, he is dependent on guides to judge for
him. Whether they prove trustworthy, like Cacambo, or treacherous,
like Venderdendur, is a hazard of his radical simplicity, for his lack of
differentiation manifests itself in uncritical, open-mouthed, passive receptivity.

It is this infantile openness, moreover, that involves the reader in
the fictional world and thus in its brutal betrayals. Nothing masks Candide's primitive yearning for Cunégonde, or for that best world promised
by Pangloss, and these wishes, emerging contrapuntally against the cruel
deceptions of the plot, tend to elicit the reader's empathic wishes for
food, warmth, and protection. Thus, when Candide's are abruptly frustrated, so too, our own.

The reader's subjective participation in Candide's desires is facilitated in a number of ways. Among the most important is the adroit use
of "internal focus," [16] Genette's term for the restriction of the reader's
field of vision to that of a given character. Of course, internal focus is
not the norm of *Candide* where the narration, like that of most tales, is
omniscient. Rather, internal focus represents a temporary shift of perspective away from narrative omniscience. Sometimes nearly impercep-
tible, such a shift may also involve the reader quite dramatically and
subjectively in fictional danger. Immediately after the safe arrival in Bue-
nos Aires where Cunégonde and Candide have fled together, new danger
supervenes.

Elle court sur le champ à *Candide*. "Fuyez," dit-elle, "ou dans une heure vous
allez être brûlé." Il n'y avait pas un moment à perdre; mais comment se séparer
de *Cunégonde*, & où se réfugier? (XIII, 133)

Objective description cedes to an internal focus upon Candide's experience of his predicament. At this point, the chapter ends, the danger unresolved and under-distanced.

The reader's vision is reduced to a restricted internal focus that limits his knowledge of the fictional world as severely as Candide's and renders him equally helpless. Thus the reader becomes temporarily one with a character of neither judgment nor knowledge, and the force of that sadistic reality through which the child-hero is deprived of wished-for security increases. The sense of helplessness is complemented by the frustration of the chapter break,[17] a device which, as a formal analogue to Candide's sense of being trapped, places the reader in the same position of powerlessness in relation to the narrator as the hero finds himself in vis-à-vis the causal events of the fiction.

Nor is this the only instance in which a formal analogue furnishes the reader with the fictionally appropriate response. Just as within the fiction the characters' perception of self is threatened by the menacing transformation of the body, so the reader's perception of the fictional world is undermined by the use of an ambiguous signifier. During the carnival in Venice Candide encounters six men who are addressed as kings. " 'Tout n'est qu'illusion & Calamité' " (XXIV, 190), he has earlier sighed, preparing to consider the six kings as part of the locally sanctioned disguise. Since Cacambo, so closely allied to Vice and his classical counterpart the slave who manages the comic plot, also appears incognito, the dinner seems designated as theater. What appears to be disguise, however, turns out to be calamity. The kings are exiled and impoverished sovereigns with neither status nor power who cling to meaningless social forms and designations. When one of them actually begs for money, the signifier, "King," becomes dissociated from its conventional connotation of money and power. Fictional reality redefines language.

In this way, the reader shares in attenuated fashion in an experience of disorganization. Fooled by the carnival and Cacambo, then disoriented by the redefinition of the signifier "King," the reader's hold on fictional reality becomes somewhat precarious. The question arises for him: what is real carnival if what appears to be carnival is reality? Although it is not answered, the implied answer is the unsettling one that there is no distinction: fictive illusion and fictive reality merge. Which events are then reliable, asks the reader, the hanging and murder of Candide's friends, either witnessed or committed by Candide, or their existence as galley slaves before his eyes? And if these slaves with disfigured faces are named Pangloss and the Baron, are they, like the kings, Pangloss and the Baron in name only?

What spares the reader too much disorientation is the distancing effect of the omniscient narration. The narrator, reliable, objective, in control, gives a counterbalancing stability to the unstable fictional world and authority to the events he describes. The breadth and scope of his vision creates a distance from fictional event which permits the reader the anticipation of danger, the illusion of safety, and the luxury to appreciate irony. With this broader perspective, the narrator exposes the naiveté of Candide and the self-importance of his companions, enabling us, *Dieu merci*, to find release in laughter.

Yet this relief is not so complete as we might suspect. It alleviates, but does not prevent, our subjective reaction to the dangers of the fictional world. In the presentation of the earthquake, for instance, disaster strikes mimetically:

A peine ont-ils mis le pied dans la ville en pleurant la mort de leur bienfaiteur, qu'ils sentent la terre trembler sous leurs pas; la mer s'élève en bouillonnant dans le port, & brise les vaisseaux qui sont à l'ancre. (V, 101)

The restrained description of upheaval in and of itself hardly moves. Rather, its placement in a sequence in which natural disaster and human cruelty follow each other precipitously surprises. When Plangloss and Candide set foot on shore after the death of Jacques and the shipwreck, reader and characters alike prepare for a respite. But safety is accorded only an introductory subordinate clause—in the main clause new disaster shocks.

Only after the reader is startled into subjectivity, does the narrative present the exaggerated and idiosyncratic reactions of the victims: the sailor looks for booty, Pangloss for a way of justifying his philosophic system, Candide for solace. Shock is countered by comedy. Yet these stylized descriptions are dependent on the reader's initial surprise for their comic effect. They afford him release secondarily because they allow him to escape his subjective involvement and to regard the beleaguered characters objectively.

Nor is the earthquake scene an exception. For the first half of the tale, over and over again, deftly and economically, the narrative moves the reader from safety to new danger: Candide and Cunégonde tell leisurely and objectively of the horrors of their lives in the comfort of a sea journey only to be separated the moment they come to port. Further, the narrative moves the reader from safe objectivity to the intimacy of the subjective not only by means of such formal devices as shifts of focus and manipulation of chapter divisions, but also by means of a play with convention which turns the events of the fiction into versions of chance as haphazard and out of control as the fictional world itself.[18]

The rhythm of trust and betrayal, safety and danger thus finds its counterpart in the oscillation of the reader between participation in the danger of the fictional world and a more comfortable sharing of the omniscient narrator's objectivity. Until Candide begins to grow in the second half of the tale, his radical simplicity, evoking as it does a universal infantile defenselessness, emerges as a crucial subjective focus from which objective narration must rescue us before the boundaries of comedy are transgressed.

Through the structure of the text, then, the reader of *Candide* is engaged in a cycle of wish, frustration, and reactive anger which facilitates a transient identification with an infantile hero, on the one hand, and lends the impact of anger to the arbitrary external authority which assails him, on the other. The plot itself and formal elements such as the ordering of the action, the handling of narrative focus, and the syntax all contribute to the reader's identificatory wishes for warmth, safety, and security. When these wishes, apparently realized, are abruptly frustrated, the resultant anger fosters an experience of outside authority—whether fictional destiny or social institution—as cruel and implacable. The power which anger confers upon frustrating authority, in turn, increases the experience of powerlessness through which the reader, identified with the hero/victim, confronts his own vulnerability. Thus the transient identification with the hero is reinforced and the cycle of wish, frustration, and anger renewed. This reciprocal relationship between literary structure and the affect—conscious or not—that that structure evokes in the reader is an essential and complex element in the esthetic experience of *Candide*.

Notes

1. Ira O. Wade, *The Intellectual Development of Voltaire* (Princeton, N.J.: Princeton University Press, 1969), pp. 683–84.

2. Among those who objectify response and for whom an objective reader follows logically: Jonathan Culler, *Structuralist Poetics* (Ithaca, N.Y.: Cornell University Press, 1975); Wolfgang Iser, *The Implied Reader: Patterns of Communication in Prose Fiction from Bunyan to Beckett* (Baltimore, Md.: Johns Hopkins University Press, 1974), pp. 274–93; Lowry Nelson, Jr., "The Fictive Reader and Literary Self-Reflexiveness," in Peter Demetz, Thomas H. Greene, Lowry Nelson, Jr., eds., *The Disciplines of Criticism* (New Haven, Ct.: Yale University Press, 1968), pp. 173–91. Among those who hold response and the reader to be subjective: Robert Crosman, "Do Readers Make Meaning?" in Susan R. Suleiman and Inge Crosman, eds., *The Reader in the Text* (Princeton, N.J.: Princeton University Press, 1980), pp. 149–64; David Bleich, *Subjective Criticism* (Baltimore, Md.: Johns Hopkins University Press, 1978); Norman N. Holland, *5 Readers Reading* (New Haven, Ct.: Yale University Press, 1975). For an excellent general survey of varieties of reader-response criticism, see Susan R. Suleiman, "Introduction" in Susan R. Suleiman and Inge Crosman, eds., *The Reader in the Text*, pp. 3–45.

3. Sigmund Freud, "Creative Writers and Daydreaming" (1907), included in this book.

4. Hans Sachs, *The Creative Unconscious: Studies in the Psychoanalysis of Art* (Cambridge, Mass.: Science-Art Publishers, 1942), pp. 11–54.

5. David M. Beres and Jacob A. Arlow, "Fantasy and Identification in Empathy," *Psychoanalytic Quarterly* (1974), 43:26–50.

6. See Gail S. Reed, "Towards a Methodology for Applying Psychoanalysis to Literature," *Psychoanalytic Quarterly* (1982), 51:19–42.

7. Albert D. Hutter, "The High Tower of His Mind: Psychoanalysis and the Reader of 'Bleak House,' " *Criticism* (1977), 29:296–316, p. 313.

8. On "unpleasure" see Freud, "Instincts and their Vicissitudes," *The Standard Edition*, edited by James Strachey (London: Hogarth Press and the Institute of Psychoanalysis, 1957), 14:111–40, p. 136.

9. Freud, "The Future Prospects of Psychoanalytic Therapy" (1910), *Standard Edition* 12:144–45.

10. For recent writing about countertransference see, among others, Peter Giovacchini, *Treatment of Primitive Mental States* (New York: Jason Aronson, 1979), pp. 477–95; Otto Kernberg, *Borderline Conditions and Pathological Narcissism* (New York: Jason Aronson, 1975), pp. 49–69; Robert Langs, ed., *Classics in Psychoanalytic Technique* (New York: Jason Aronson, 1981), pp. 139–347; Harold Searles, *Collected Papers on Schizophrenia and Related Subjects* (New York: International Universities Press, 1965), pp. 192–215, 349–80, 521–59, *passim;* D. W. Winnicott, "Hate in the Countertransference" (1947), in *Through Paediatrics to Psycho-Analysis* (New York: Basic Books, 1975), pp. 194–203.

11. For a suggestion of where more objective evidence of collective response

may be found, see Reed, "Towards a Methodology for Applying Psychoanalysis to Literature."

12. See, for example, Amy Marsland, "Voltaire: Satire and Sedition," *Romanic Review* (1966), 57:35–40; Christopher Thacker, introduction to *Candide ou l'Optimisme: Edition Critique* (Geneva: Droz, 1968); Jacques Vanden Heuval, *Voltaire dans ses Contes* (Paris: Armand Colin, 1967), p. 264.

13. For example, Richard A. Brooks, *Voltaire and Leibniz* (Geneva: Droz, 1964), pp. 106–7; William Bottiglia, *Candide, Analysis of a Classic,* 2nd ed. rev. (Geneva: Institut et Musée Voltaire, 1964), pp. 109–10; Henri Coulet, "La Candeur de Candide," *Annales de la Faculté des Lettres et Sciences Humaines d'Aix,* (1960), 34:87–99, p. 95; John Pappas, "*Candide* Rétrécissement ou Expansion?" *Diderot Studies* (1968), 10:241–63, pp. 241–43; Roy S. Wolper, "Candide, Gull in the Garden?" *Eighteenth Century Studies* (1969), 3:265–77.

14. Voltaire, *Candide ou l'Optimisme, Edition Critique,* edited by René Pomeau (Paris: A. G. Nizet, 1959), XXII, p. 185. Further citations will be given in the text and will include chapter and page number.

15. Henri Coulet, "La Candeur de Candide."

16. Gérard Genette, *Figures III* (Paris: Editions du Seuil, 1972), pp. 206ff. Genette's reciprocal term is "zero degree focalization." I have used omniscience in its place for stylistic not theoretical reasons.

17. For a differently oriented discussion of chapter division see Michael Danahy, "The Nature of Narrative Norms in *Candide,*" in Theodore Besterman, ed., *Studies on Voltaire and the Eighteenth Century* (Banbury, Oxfordshire: The Voltaire Foundation, 1973), vol. 114, pp. 113–40.

18. See Martin Price, *To the Palace of Wisdom: Studies in Order and Energy from Dryden to Blake* (1964; rept. Garden City, N.Y.: Doubleday, 1965), p. 314.

14.

John Keats' Psychology
of Creative Imagination

Stanley A. Leavy, M.D.

IN A LETTER TO his brothers written in December 1817, when he
was twenty-two years old, John Keats wrote: "I had not a dispute but a
disquisition with Dilke [a member of his intimate circle], on various subjects; several things dovetailed in my mind, & at once it struck me, what
quality went to form a Man of Achievement especially in Literature &
which Shakespeare possessed so enormously—I mean *Negative Capability*,
that is when man is capable of being in uncertainties, Mysteries, doubts,
without any irritable reaching after fact and reason—"[1]

The striking phrase underscored by Keats does not recur as such in
his writings. Its sense however appears frequently as one of the essential
points in his understanding of the workings of the creative mind, and
consideration of it may serve as an entrance into Keats' theory of creativity that can perhaps be best summed up in another phrase: "That which
is creative must create itself" (1:374). This theory seems to me to deserve
attention not only in view of the literary achievement of Keats, but with
regard to certain implications for psychoanalysis latent in the poet's
expressions.

Keats contrasted men of "negative capability" with "consequitive"

From *The Psychoanalytic Quarterly* (1970), 39:173–97. Copyright © 1970 *The Psychoanalytic
Quarterly*. Reprinted by permission.

men (1:218), like his friend and publisher John Taylor, whom he respects as reasoners, philosophers, with thoroughly logical minds—but at their most developed polar opposites from himself, and above all from his supreme ideal, Shakespeare. At one time or another Keats varied in his estimation of the importance of knowledge as such, at times reproaching himself for his lack of knowledge and complaining, a few months after he wrote the "negative capability" letter, now in a letter to Taylor, that he knew nothing, had read nothing, and meant "to follow Solomon's directions of 'get Wisdom—get understanding'" (1:271). Knowledge—and here meaning the knowledge of science and philosophy—was "needful" and helped "by widening speculation, to ease the Burden of the Mystery." Nevertheless he also had to confess elsewhere that he had "never yet been able to perceive how any thing can be known for truth by consequitive reasoning," and he wonders in a letter to Benjamin Bailey whether "even the greatest Philosopher ever arrived at his goal without putting aside numerous objections" (1:185), that is, without having to overlook the doubts which would inevitably creep in to corrupt his certainties if he had not already closed himself to them. For just as "philosophy" intends to reach a certain assurance about things within the limitations imposed by logical thought, so the poetic mind is open— as one of Keats' biographers has defined "Negative Capability"[2]—to "tolerance for ambiguity," or in the words of another biographer—"the heart's hunger for settlement, for finality, cannot be answered unless we shut ourselves off from the amplitude of experience, with all its contradictory diversity."[3] Keats put the whole thing tersely in a letter to J. H. Reynolds: "Axioms in philosophy are not axioms until they are proved upon our pulses" (1:279).

The contrast implied in these thoughts is that existing between reason and imagination, and rather to the credit of the latter than the former. If we accept as a functional meaning of "reason" something like "the capacity to think clearly" we do not run into any contradiction with "imagination," but familiarly the notion of reason includes its critical actions at their most stringent. Reason by such extension of meaning is antipoetical, interposing syllogistic thinking in such a fashion that all tendencies toward symbol and metaphor are excluded unless they are so labeled,—and being so labeled they are reduced from poetry to technical prose. Imagination on the other hand is free, having shaken off the shackles of logic; it sees the identity of opposites, the middle between being and not-being, the overlap between approximated images and ideas, and admits the full reality of "secondary" qualities, not acknowledging the primacy of the statistical and the quantifiable. If imagination finds its pathological form in delusion, reason, more insidiously because more respectably, is represented symptomatically in constricted, rationalizing thought which may eventuate in the strait jacket of obsessionalism. Imagination, intrepid in its admission of all "uncertainties, Mysteries, doubts" is exposed to the possibility of terror as well as wonder, but the poet must let go and trust the "pulses" of his private experience. Yet Keats also recognized that in so far as "reason" led to increased knowledge of the objective world, it enhanced rather than limited imagination by "widening speculation." To use the concepts of our own time, it is consonant with Keats' point of view to assert that we may be as imaginative in our interpretation of atomic particles as in reliving a pastoral tradition.

Keats said to Bailey, his friend studying for Holy Orders, "I am certain of nothing but the holiness of the Heart's affections and the truth of Imagination" and "The Imagination may be compared to Adam's dream [in Paradise Lost]—he awoke and found it truth" (1:184–85). The relations between imagination and dream, and the connection of both with the objective world, are recurrent themes in the poems as well as the letters of Keats; in his effort to make real the world of fantasy and dream, a struggle existed there that he could not fully resolve. If he saw in the writing of "Endymion," his long early poem, a "Regular stepping of the Imagination towards a Truth" and a progress in the direction of

fellowship divine
A fellowship with essence, till we shine
Full alchymized and free of space— (1:218)

nevertheless he was also to understand that this progress beyond the mortal "bourne" cannot be realized within the limitations imposed by the human condition, and some of his greatest poems embody the attempt and the failure.[4]

Becoming familiar with these and certain others of Keats' psychological ideas, it struck me how remarkably they prefigure and also illuminate psychoanalytic concepts of creative imagination. No reader of the letters of Keats will take them for the statement of a systematic psychology, which it will already be apparent would have been quite foreign to

Keats' mind. Nor are the ideas themselves original with Keats. In abstract form they derive from the philosophical idealism of his time through the principal mediation of the writings and lectures of his older friend, the critic William Hazlitt.[5] Sometimes the ideas are no more than quotations from Hazlitt;[6] sometimes the borrowings from the speculations of other romantic poets, especially Coleridge and Wordsworth, are equally apparent. What confers a peculiar validity on Keats' ideas is their intimate association with the writing of his poems, and with their latent content. If they are bound to the romantic-idealist attitude to life, and also to Keats' highly personal understanding of that attitude, they were subjected to the irreplaceable test of poetic practice. In short, use of Keats' ideas on creativity depends on our willingness to concede that the poet possessed an exceptional access to the working of his own mind permitting him to know what he was doing and how he did it. I am therefore quite deliberately using Keats' ideas as if they were themselves, so to speak, "psychoanalytic interpretations" of the data of experience. I am making almost no attempt to "analyze" Keats by uncovering the unconscious intentions of his ideas; if anything the thrust is in the opposite direction, to determine what the poet's experience as *he* understood it may do for psychoanalysis. That he borrowed some of his ideas from others and assimilated them into himself as his experience dictated is only further evidence that he was convinced of their pertinence to what he knew directly.

Almost all Keats' ideas, not only the psychological ones, that reached expression in prose did so in his letters, a magnificent collection of materials for autobiography, bountifully disclosing the inner life of the poet in a stage intermediate between experience and poetry. There are critics who claim as high literary value for the letters as for the poems, but such considerations aside it is intensely interesting that one of the most enduring poets seems to have been able to catch and to put into simple prose some of the secrets of his own creative ability, and by extension the poetic process in general. The letters that have been preserved cover the whole period of his creative life (1817–1821) and are among many other things a commentary on it.

"Negative capability" then would be a capacity to give free rein to the imagination. The disparate, absurd, inchoate, illogical, impossible would not present stop-signs. It can be taken for granted that equipped with this gift any person might attain hitherto unrecorded—because personally unique—imaginings. All that prevents that from happening is the restraint ordinarily imposed in the face of "uncertainties, Mysteries, doubts" and a need for the security of "fact and reason"; it is these that balk the flight of fancy. They induce sobriety, make for order, propriety, punctuality, accomplishment, but—this is what counts—they block the way to truth. Unhappily, while "many have original Minds who do not think it" (1:231), only a few have the confidence to put down in tangible signs the record of what they have discovered with their fancy; the rest escape the experience by sliding into conformity with custom. A truly "complex mind," Keats said, would be "one that is imaginative and at the same time careful of its fruits," and would exist "partly on sensations partly on thought," qualities he generously attributed at that point to his rather unsubtle friend Bailey, and which are more appropriately assigned to Keats himself (1:186).

The contribution of imagination to the acquiring of significant new knowledge has by now become a commonplace, which it does not appear to have been in Keats' day. But it is not primarily knowledge of the kind we relate to scientific understanding that Keats refers to here in any case. If any common phrase will designate it, "truth" is "existential" knowledge, and that is what our grasping for security inhibits. A barrier exists between the person and his experience; it becomes too rapidly detached, cold, past and passed-by, the memory lacking the enrichment of imaginative reconstruction within himself. The poetic experience—if not the poetic gift—is universally possible, but the conduct of life is antipoetic. Bergson's distinction between intuitive and discursive knowledge has been usefully applied with reference to this problem,[7] but how familiar a ring it has, and how much it sounds like the analysis of certain kinds of character resistance!

There is reason enough for the "resistance." While making its daring and even dangerous venture "beyond its proper bound," going too far, and yet still within the confines of mortality, the imagination reveals to the soul the "eternal fierce destruction" of nature (1:262). The risk must be taken since there is no other approach to truth. There are further tragic implications: from Keats' metaphysical position, the attainment of truth in its fullness remains outside mortal life, and Keats had only spasmodic faith in any other sort of life. As it is, only approximations of truth can be made (the reasons for this depend on certain other ideas of Keats which also call for examination), but it is the emotion aroused by ceaseless striving toward the imaginative grasp of that which is, and the inevitable failure of the attempt, that enriches and deepens poetry. Set free on its impossible task, the imagination does all it can "to add a mite to that mass of beauty which is harvested from these great materials, by the finest spirits, and put into etherial existence for the relish of our fellows." Yet—he was visiting the Lake District when he wrote thus to his brother Tom—it was just there, surrounded by natural beauty, that he felt limits to his own mind too: "I live in the eye; and my imagination, surpassed, is at rest" (1:301).

What is this power of imagination to reach truth? Keats is specific about this. For one thing he accepts without question the proposition that knowledge is not just the impression of the objective world on the mind, but an active interchange between the mind and its objects, amounting to a union between the knower and the known, the percipient and the perceived, the subject and the object. He wrote precisely about this unitive process as he witnessed it in his own mind. "No sooner am I alone than shapes of epic greatness are stationed around me" and "according to my state of mind I am with Achilles shouting in the trenches, or with Theocritus in the Vales of Sicily" (1:403, 404). Far from being in union with literary images alone, he also finds himself one with the sparrow picking about the gravel (1:186), and, according to his friend Richard Woodhouse, he could even "conceive of a billiard ball that it may have a sense of delight in its own roundness, smoothness, volubility and the rapidity of its motion" (1:389). Surely that is a convincing example of imagination set free by "negative capability," and, as is the rule with Keats, the sanity of the projective thinking is guaranteed by the humor of the statement. Imaginative union of another sort appears in a letter in which Keats writes of an exotic young woman, Jane Cox, whom he had met at the home of his friends the Reynoldses:

She is not a Cleopatra; but she is at least a Charmian.—When she comes into the room she makes an impression the same as the Beauty of a Leopardess. I always find myself there at ease with such a woman; the picture before me always gives me life and animation which I cannot feel with any thing inferiour— I am at such times too much occupied in admiring to be awkward or on a tremble. I forget myself entirely *because I live in her* (1:395).

He added that he was not in love with her and had lost "but one night's sleep" thinking of her.

Whatever the nature of the attraction he felt toward Jane Cox, in this passage he refers to something closer to a form of identification than to sensual love, or perhaps to that form of identification which may be an unrecognized part of sensual love. But the point of it is that imagination made possible empathic participation in the existence of other persons and other objects generally. The poet is the man of particularly strong empathic development:

> 'Tis the man who with a bird,
> Wren or Eagle, finds his way to
>   All its instincts; he hath heard
> The Lion's roaring, and can tell
>   What his horny throat expresseth . . .[8]

As an objective statement about the external world, all such claims are absurd. As a declaration of preconditions for knowledge they may stand on firmer ground, and psychoanalytically, with especial concern for *personal* knowledge, they demand a hearing.

The power of unitive imagination, or empathy, is not accorded equally to all men. It is to be found in men who "have not any individuality, any determined Character" (1:184). This rather surprising idea, which at first sounds only like an example of the paradoxical "rodomontade" for which Keats was celebrated among his friends, is on the contrary one to which he clung steadfastly, and which is another fixed part of Keats' psychology. He found it a preeminent attribute of Shakespeare, and he refers to it many times in his letters. He wrote to Woodhouse in October 1816 (in reply to Woodhouse's earnest injunction that he not carry out his threat to abandon poetry because it was so poorly received by the public):

As to the poetic Character itself—it is not itself—it has no self—it is everything and nothing. It has no character—it enjoys light and hate; it loves in gusto, be it foul or fair, high or low—It has as much delight in conceiving an Iago as an Imogen. What shocks the virtuous philosopher, delights the camelion Poet—A Poet is the most unpoetical of anything in existence; because he has no identity—Not one word I ever utter can be taken for granted as an opinion growing out of my identical nature—the identity of everyone begins to press upon me. (1:386–87)

And even *this* "opinion," he added, might not be his own but that of "some character in whose soul I now live."

A life without "identity" of its own, fused with the things of its experience and the creatures of its imagination, is a life of "allegory" such as Shakespeare led, "and his works are the comments on it" (2:67). This apodictic expression notwithstanding, Keats could also write that human life is passed in a "Vale of Soul-making" (2:102) in which men are not "souls" until they acquire identities, till each one is personally himself, and that "takes a world of Pains and troubles." And further, the soul "is a world of itself and has enough to do in its own home" (2:146). The contradiction is at least partly resolved if we read Keats' meaning to be that it is not the innate or early fixed character of a man that makes him a creative person but rather his openness to new formative experiences, in the absence of a determinately ordered character-structure. Keats at twenty-two soberly recommended "a very gradual ripening of the intellectual powers" as the basis of "great productions," a comment which he follows with an instance from his own experience: "I sat down yesterday to read King Lear once again the thing appeared to demand the prologue of a Sonnet, I wrote it & began to read" (1:214). How much is condensed in that experience! In the absence of "identity" Keats had lived long both with and *as* the characters of Shakespeare's imagination, and the poem comes into being suddenly under the inspiration of Shakespeare, whom he had already long regarded as "the presider" over his poetic life. (1:142)

The outward movement of the poet's mind then is unimpeded because of certain peculiarities in his "identity," a term that we can take over from Keats into our own language with no change in its meaning. The nonpoetical mind is more bound by habit; it clings to its past interpretations, because they are so much a part of it. It is defended against novely from the objective world, but it is more important that it is intolerant of incursions from the inner world, which would disrupt its form. The gradually developed mind of the poet is one in which earlier formed impressions are freer to exist, and remain available for the working of the released, active imagination. Less confident than the average man about *who* he is, the poet's ego goes out to meet its objects, seeking union with them, becoming them. Keats borrows again, this time from Edmund Spenser, in selecting a metaphor to describe the nature of the union:

> The noble heart that harbors vertuous thought,
> And is with child of glorious great intent,
> Can never rest, until it forth have brought
> Th' eternal Brood of Glory excellent. (1:134)

The creative mind then is here likened to the pregnant womb. In his own famous sonnet Keats began:

> When I have fears that I may cease to be
> Before my pen has glean'd my teeming brain . . . (1:222)

As a result of the adventure of the ego-without-identity of the poet, his mind has achieved empathic union with its objects, and he is unable to rest (in the letter in which Spenser is quoted, Keats was referring literally to insomnia) until the delivery of the "child" has taken place. Incidentally, the equivocal nature of the child with which the heart is pregnant is amply demonstrated by the company kept by this sonnet: it is preceded in the letter in which it first appeared by some bawdy verses of no great merit ("O blush not so") and some pretentious doggerel ("Hence Burgundy, Claret & port"). It is as if the poet, while able, as Keats surely was, to tell the difference between the valuable and the trivial in his own work, still had an affection for whatever had been conceived in and by his mind.

The "conception" of poetry is a bisexual process. The bee and the flower he said "receive a fair guerdon" of one another, and, perhaps with Tiresias in mind, he asks, "who shall say between Man and Woman which is the most delighted?" (1:232). If at one point he concludes: "Let us open our leaves like a flower and be passive and receptive" we recall on the other hand his account of the active progress of the imagination into the life of the sparrow, or of "Charmian," or into the roundness of the billiard ball, for a more complete picture of the way that the released imagination is able to produce poetry. There is an active, willed grasping of and entrance into the images which have imprinted themselves on the poet's mind as sensations, and which have continued to live within him. "Passivity" is not inactive spongelike quiescence, but, after the manner of "negative capability," a withholding of judgment on the images so eagerly collected, from reading, scenery, art, and especially human nature.

It has recently been shown how certain works of painting and sculpture influenced Keats' poetry.[9] Paintings in which Greek mythological themes were represented were prominent, as in some of the work of Poussin, and the embodiment of poetic themes in visible elements had a powerfully stimulating effect on the poet. Attitude, coloring, associations among the figures on canvas or in stone became part of the perceptual material on which his imagination could work. For all its grand themes, however, art had no more significance than the rest of the mass of experiences which Keats elaborated into his magical constructions. He could be as lyrical in his letters about the taste of claret, or of a nectarine, as about the Elgin marbles. His reading, of Shakespeare foremost, but also of lesser writers and especially Robert Burton, was absorbed in his thought. One can trace the preconscious associations of his writing and his reading and the impressions made on him by persons around him. A direct affiliation lies between the manifest images of a poem and certain concrete sensory experiences—from the taste of claret to the "beaker of Hippocrene," from nursing his dying brother Tom to "the fever and the fret," from the sight of the Elgin marbles to the sonnet on them and to the Grecian Urn. The transformation imposed by and on the perceptions, the real work of the poet, is the result of their elaboration through both conscious and unconscious mental activity. Keats described, he said, in contrast to Byron, not what he saw but what he imagined (2:200). Keats' best work is loaded with the imagery of vision as well as other sensory modalities and the particularity of perception is what distinguishes him from other poets. Rhetoric, generalization are of more importance in others, and perhaps it is for this reason that we are able to see an affinity between Keats' psychological ideas and those of psychoanalysis, which is likewise concerned with the details of experience and their psychic transformation.

If we distinguish two kinds of "unconscious" mental processes, literary criticism (to the extent to which it is psychological) may be said to be engaged with the explication of one of them, namely the "preconscious." Social attitudes, personal philosophy, artistic usages, or even quite deep personal intentions may be far from explicit statement in a poem, but the characteristic ambiguity of poetic language permits the critic to discover them latent in highly overdetermined interrelationships among the parts of the poem. Sometimes we may feel that such relationships are read into the poem to suit the interests of the critic; while that may be so, it is wrong to make this a general proposition, because to deny the existence of latent meaning, or to deny that it can be rationally investigated, suggests not only that critics merely rediscover their projected fantasies, but also that poets are not so creative as they actually are.

Psychoanalysis is not unlike criticism in its approach to the "texts"; we often refer to the "dream-text" as if it were a literary work. The main difference is one of "depth" in the psychoanalytic meaning of the word; a perhaps oversimplified distinction might be made between those elements latent in the work which were once at least subliminally conscious and those which were always unconscious in adult life. Gittings, in his admirable recent biography of Keats and earlier in his study limited to the single great creative year of the poet, has made it his special task to trace the preconscious sources of a very large number of Keats' poetic images and ideas.[10] Having as they do the merit of a superabundance of convincing material, it is the more significant that such studies do not tell us very much about the psychological process whereby the materials of experience are transformed into poetry. Nor on the other hand are we always satisfied with psychoanalytic works which do make a claim to explain as well as to describe the creative process. Does Keats himself have anything to tell us when we consider his observations on creativity to be spontaneous but essentially "psychoanalytic" insights into the nature of the poet's art?

Even the poet is unble to admit into consciousness just anything at all that is stirring in his mind. In Keats' letters, for example, we may find associations of ideas which serve to deny the fear and proximity of death, which he was at other times more prepared to acknowledge consciously. "Negative capability" enables the poet to withhold making up his mind; he practices a sort of laissez-faire with respect to any and all images that are admitted. But just as the free associations of the analysand and the analyst are the source of the unconscious content and not that content itself, so the poet's ideas are uninhibited, but still subject to censorship, and they may serve other defensive purposes as well.

Even Keats was unable to offer a prescription to help us become poets, and we cannot find in his letters the answer to the all-important question how to acquire "negative capability." Psychoanalytic patients learn the meanings of their associations, including the meaning of the intrusions of unexpected ideas into their consciousness, tolerated long enough and possessing enough intensity to attract other words to themselves. Experience teaches us that the pedagogic influence at work is the proven interest of the analyst, and his abstinence from judgment. Patients are as much surprised that such trivial "rags and tags" of ideas that they produce are tolerated, as they are about the neutral reception accorded to memories and fantasies of which they are ashamed. Perhaps teachers and other guardians of the growing poet help in a similar way, by safeguarding inner freedom of imagery in all its childish delicacy from becoming stultified through defensiveness and conformity to conventional formulations. Keats' own delight in metaphor, his physical enactment of it, in fact, was appreciated by his early friend Charles Cowden Clarke. But it is also likely that the fostering of imaginative freedom is itself an intrapsychic phenomenon, and that teachers like analysts can only assist its evolution. In such extreme cases as that of Keats it may originate in intensities of sensation at which we can only guess, imperiously sweeping aside logical objections until the ego is of experience to reawaken a wide mass of preconsciously and unconsciously withheld memories and refocus them into new clusters. While the defensive structure is weaker than it is in other kinds of personality, the tenacity of the hold on earlier objects which have become internalized is also less. Does that mean that objects are not strongly cathected libidinally by the poet so that he has to go in search of new objects for that reason, as is said of actors? That is very doubtful indeed, and Keats's life illustrates the contrary. But it does seem, on the basis of Keats's observation or self-observation, that for all the strength of the libidinal cathexis, poets do not feel themselves to be "formed," they are perpetually "fetal," or as Goethe once put it more modestly, "pubertal." (One cannot help remarking that what is true of the poet might also be true of the poet manqué, a much more numerous class.)

It is especially to be noted that the instigation to inner development is found in the "World of Pains and troubles," in Keats' thought, in the inevitability of disappointment, and, again translating, the inevitability of the internalization of bad as well as good objects. The poet is the seeker of experience par excellence; the universal human need to make a world for oneself in him finds the special expression of verbal organization, so that he creates objects that organize his own ego and provide organizing ideas for others.

Keats defines poetic internalization allusively and yet with the clearest explicitness in the first of his great odes, the "Ode to Psyche." Through the medium of intricate condensations in his adaptation of the myth of Cupid and Psyche, Keats at once gives homage to the creative spirit *and* erects a temple to the spirit within himself:

Yes, I will be thy priest, and build a fane
  In some untrodden region of my mind,
Where branched thoughts, new grown with pleasant pain,
  Instead of pines shall murmur in the wind:

    . . . .

And in the midst of this wide quietness
A rosy sanctuary will I dress
With the wreath'd trellis of a working brain,
  With buds, and bells, and stars without a name,
With all the gardener Fancy e'er could feign,
Who breeding flowers, will never breed the same . . .[11]

The richness of condensation and illusion in these lines invokes and yet renders futile attempts at exhaustive analysis, like all true art. In the earlier part of the poem, the myth narrated by Apuleius in his *Metamorphoses* is as though recollected by sculptures and paintings probably seen by the poet in London, all the while tinctured by the religion of beauty as it was understood by the romantics. Precise observation of nature, romantic nostalgia, contemporary neurological theory, erotic longing, are bound together by the poet's ego into a new constellation of introjects, having among its meanings the meaning that poetic art is itself a refashioning of the world as it is absorbed into the "psyche." I do not think that we would be turning the "Ode to Psyche" to an "Ode to Psychology" by seeing it this way, as perhaps the culmination of the poet's efforts to give expository form to the creative experience as he had lived it. The creative act is personified in the "gardener Fancy," who alongside his homage to the spirit exists "without the working brain," which I take to be also the "teeming brain" of the sonnet, "When I have fears—" and also, in the lines of Spenser quoted from Keats' letter earlier, "the heart . . . with child of glorious great intent." Because the identity of the poet is fluid, he can become and remain at once the "gardener" and the "sanctuary," and having psychically possessed the object, move on "and never breed the same." The sexual tone of the process is pitched climactically in the last line of the ode, when Psyche's window is opened "to let the warm Love in."[12]

With varying degrees of definitiveness and permanence, "objects" are intended by the ego, and endowed with its cathexes. The ego forms and is formed by them, as the infant unwittingly plays a part in forming the maternal attitudes with which in turn he unites to form his own primary identity. The difficult psychoanalytic problem that faces us at this point is obviously one regarding motivation: what engages the poet so relentlessly in this way, so that the universal need to make a world for oneself is turned into an active process which—except during fallow periods, themselves a part of the whole—the creative artist cannot let go?

Such questions, which come down to the psychology of artistic talent or artistic genius, resolve themselves into two aspects, only one of which is really germane: it does not get us anywhere to discover that the poet, like everyone else, is beset by mental conflict. The peculiarity of his species is that he makes poems, not that he has conflicts. I do not mean that we ought to belittle the efforts of psychoanalysts to demonstrate the nature of the conflicts (I am using that word to represent psychopathological situations in general) from the evidence left by the poet. On the contrary it seems to me that as in Keats' case we have a lot to learn, for the very reason that the poet, the word-man, leaves a more persuasive record of his inner experience than we can hope to find elsewhere.

To get some idea of what the specific psychic qualities of the poet are, in Keats' understanding of them, I must revert to some concepts which have already been suggested. Keats had a literal meaning in mind when he wrote that he went to Scotland, on the trip with Brown, in search of "new Objects," but he might just as well have been writing psychologically. The poet's ego seeks objects, a function which is universal, but which here is unique in respect to the fate of the representations of these objects. The ego that so actively seeks them out is also passive to them, it is both the "bee" and the "flower," the "gardener" and the "fane," the "man" and the "woman." Endymion is both the lover in pursuit of Cynthia, his object, and the sleeping shepherd discovered by her. Exposed as he is to such an abundance of psychic experience, and entering as he does into transient but intense fusions with his images in the empathic moment, he requires, summarily speaking, only one further property for the poem to be the form in which he internalizes his experience; namely the words. While by themselves an abundance of words might make one a lexicographer, not a poet, when "the shadow of the object" falls on the ego of the poet (it is no accident that this phrase with its implications for melancholia occurs in connection with Keats) it does so in a way that distinguishes the poet. It may be—and here I confess that my source does not give me direct support—that the poet's abundant stock of words becomes accessible to him and flows so freely because the psychic barrier between unconscious images and the pre-conscious verbal cathexis of them is attenuated, as another aspect of "negative capability."

The making of poems is the poet's way of completing the process of internalization of the world of experience. He may or may not be more driven to making an imaginal world for himself than others, but for him building that world and articulating it in words are inseparable. While in a literal sense the persistent unconscious engram or memory of any perception is an internalized object, a part of the inner milieu which can possibly be returned to consciousness, it is the word that classifies and defines the engram, making it a part of the self, the poet's enduring inner structure with a past, a present, and a possible future. And, moreover, through verbalization of his inner world in all its utmost privacy, the poet has something to give to other men, "to add a mite to that mass of beauty which is harvested from these great materials."

Notes

1. *The Letters of John Keats 1814–1821*, edited by Hyder Edward Rollins (Cambridge: Harvard University Press, 1958), 1:193. Subsequent volume numbers and page references will appear in the text.

2. Aileen Ward, *John Keats, the Making of a Poet* (New York: Viking Press, 1963), p. 161.

3. Walter Jackson Bate, *John Keats* (Cambridge: Harvard University Press, 1964), p. 242.

4. Earl R. Wasserman, *The Finer Tone: Keats' Major Poems* (Baltimore: Johns Hopkins University Press, 1953).

5. Bate, *John Keats*, pp. 232 ff.

6. William Hazlitt, *The Round Table*, 3rd ed. (London: John Templeman, 1817).

7. Walter Jackson Bate, *Negative Capability* (Cambridge: Harvard University Press, 1939).

8. *The Poetical Works of John Keats*, edited by H. W. Garrod (London: Oxford University Press, 1961), pp. 393–94.

9. Ian Jack, *Keats and the Mirror of Art* (London: Heinemann, 1954).

10. Robert Gittings, *John Keats* (London: Heinemann, 1968); *John Keats, The Living Year* (London: Heinemann, 1954).

11. *Poetical Works of Keats*, pp. 211–12.

12. See Harold Bloom, "The 'Ode to Psyche' and the 'Ode on Melancholy' " in Walter Jackson Bate, ed., *Keats, A Collection of Critical Essays* (Englewood Cliffs, N.J.: Prentice-Hall, 1964).

15.

Henry James' Dream of the Louvre, "The Jolly Corner," and Psychological Interpretation

Cushing Strout

THE JAMES FAMILY compellingly attracts our intellectual interest because of its rich mixture of influentially productive genius and disabling emotional conflict, both amply documented. William and Henry were themselves interested in psychological matters of motivation, especially in states of mind bordering on the abnormal. Characteristically, each has left us a report of a nightmare, and each has turned his personal experience to professional account. Just as the philosopher took notes on his bizarre nightmare of disassociated identity and used them in an essay on mysticism in a philosophical journal,[1] so did the novelist recount in his autobiography what he called "the most appalling yet most admirable nightmare" of his life.[2]

The novelist described the dream in his autobiography, *A Small Boy*

From *The Psychohistory Review* (1979), 8(1–2):47–52. Copyright © 1979 *The Psychohistory Review*. Reprinted by permission.

and Others (1913), without indicating when it took place. The nightmare replayed in the dreamer's mind a vivid scene of his visit to Paris in 1855 when he was not yet a teenager. It was his first visit to the Louvre with his tutor and his older brother, William, and the *Galerie d'Apollon* had especially impressed him. As an old man he remembered the scene as vividly incarnating not only the "glory" of art, but also of "history and fame and power."[3] It also gave him a "heart-shaking" prevision of "the kind of life, always of the queer so-called inward sort" that he was destined to have. His "small scared consciousness," the old man tells us, felt a mixture of "alarm and bliss" at this prophecy, suggested by the blend of "splendour and terror" in the gallery's profusion of esthetic and historical symbols, which thereafter made this palace of art "interchangeable" with "the house of life."[4] In his nightmare of "many years later" James recognized the polished parqueted floor of the gallery in the Louvre, which had first suggested an idea of style to the twelve-year-old boy. In the "dream-adventure" the hall was cleared for the fearsome pursuit of a "dimly descried figure," retreating in terror of the dreamer, who only a moment before had been "abjectly" defending the door against the apparition but now had turned the tables, "surpassing him for straight aggression and dire intention." The lightning of a thunderstorm revealed not only the remembered Louvre, but also, as he recalled it, his "young imaginative life in it of long before."[5]

James never wrote about any connection between this dream and his fiction, yet a parallel exists. About the turn of the century William Dean Howells had suggested to James that he capitalize on his talents for writing ghost stories and for dramatizing the "international theme" by fusing them together in a single tale. James eagerly snapped up the idea of an "international ghost" at a time in his life when he was faced with the need to recover from the disastrous failure of his attempts to write for the theater. His "international ghost" was to be the hero of his uncompleted, posthumous *The Sense of the Past*, and its "germ idea" involved a young American who, in going back into an earlier time in English history, becomes a source of terror to others, rather than a victim of his own fear.[6] This idea of 1900 may have drawn some inspiration from the "dream-adventure," or helped to inspire it, because the essential plot involves the same reversal.

James temporarily abandoned this novel, but in 1908 he published "The Jolly Corner," a short story of which the "intimate idea," he wrote six years later in his notebooks, was "turning the tables" on a ghost, a "haunting apparition otherwise qualified to appall *him;* and thereby winning a sort of victory by the appearance, and the evidence, that this personage or presence was more overwhelmingly affected by him than he by *it.*"[7] In this respect James described the dream, the story, and the novel in the same terms. James' biographer, Leon Edel, plausibly suggests that the dream of the Louvre may have happened in 1910 when the novelist noted waking up in London's Reform Club, feeling greatly relieved from his debilitating depression.[8] There is no way, however, to be sure whether the dream or the stories came first.

"The Jolly Corner" taps several emotionally powerful themes. Its hero is a kind of Prodigal Son who returns piously to his birthplace, having left America "in the teeth of [his] father's curse." He is obsessed with the idea of who he might have been had he never left. For everyone, revisiting childhood scenes and wondering about a lost ambition, the road not taken can have a compelling fascination. Moreover, the story also engages us with the idea of the alter ego as a buried negative identity, which we fail to recognize in ourselves even when others can see its presence.

The overlapping of James' dream and "The Jolly Corner" is suggested by the bare bones of the plot in so far as it involves a man haunted by the ghost of a double whom he finally confronts in the front hall of his old house. Because the hero, Spencer Brydon, is a returned expatriate, many critics have seen him as a simple surrogate for James, who had recently revisited America before writing the story. Superficially, the story seems to justify the idea that Brydon's horror at the appearance of the ghost is confirmation of James' choice of Europe, but the more sensitive readings have responded to the maimed features of the ghost as a symbolic reflection of the hero's own selfish, dilettantish life. The meaning of his experience, when he recovers from the faint induced by confronting the ghost and finds himself in the arms of a female confidante, an old New York friend, Alice Staverton, has further divided the critics. For some he has achieved self-knowledge by discovering a love for her, while recognizing his false self in the ghost; for others he has become reconciled with his other self through Alice's acceptance of him; while a recent reading suggests that he has become his double and that his nocturnal passage through the house has turned him, encouraged by Alice, into a New York real estate operator, ready to sacrifice his old

New York birthplace to developers. I believe that neither recognition, reconciliation, nor conversion are adequate or accurate terms for Brydon's relation to his double.

To clarify our understanding of the story it is useful to keep in mind Edel's observation that the dream differs from "The Jolly Corner" because the hero, instead of conquering the ghost, is finally "overwhelmed" and collapses into unconsciousness.[9] The dreamer is more courageous in expressing his aggression, which is appropriate to the conflation in James's mind of the *Galerie d'Apollon* with Napoleon. (Not only do the words rhyme, but the gallery's cabinets contain among other royal jewels the crown of the first Napoleon.) In 1915, following a stroke, James fell into an impersonation of the emperor by dictating letters in his name, one of them about redecorating the Louvre.[10] It is not surprising therefore that he associated the gallery with history, fame, and power, as well as with art. With respect to aggression, in one sense the story *is* like the dream because the hero's obsession is the idea, shared by Alice, that his alter ego would have had power.

The story also contains the dream's idea of a haunted man who "turned the tables" and became himself, "in the apparitional world, an incalculable terror," as the hero reflects; but "he didn't too much insist, truly, on that side of his privilege."[11] This dramatic feature of the dream is only a passing thought in the story. Rather than breaking open a closed door and making hot pursuit, he actually listens outside the door that may shield the ghost and tries to suggest a truce: " 'You affect me as by the appeal positively for pity; you convince me that for reasons rigid and sublime—what do I know?—we both of us should have suffered. . . . So rest for ever and let *me*.' " He starts to descend, but feeling an impulse soon afterwards to retrace his steps to the closed door, he realizes that if he should find it open, "it would all too abjectly be the end of him." He would fling himself out the window he had left open, for the open door would mean that "the agent of his shame—for his shame was the deep abjection—was once more at large and in general possession; and what glared him thus in the face was the act that this would determine for him." The ghost, then, is connected with a dreaded shame that "he hung back from really seeing."[12]

Significantly, on his descent Brydon tries "to imagine himself a knight of romance," but in trying "to think of something noble, as that his property was really grand, a splendid possession," he realizes that he is instead taking a "clear delight" in a decision to redevelop the building, "to sacrifice it" by letting in "the builders, the destroyers."[13] Having thus shamefully become a developer, he then confronts the ghost in the front-hall vestibule, burying his face behind raised hands, as if his countenance were "buried as for dark deprecation." What Brydon sees in the ghost of his other self is proof that "*he*, standing there for the achieved, the enjoyed, the triumphant life, couldn't be faced in his triumph." Brydon's dream of success through power is realized in the form of a nightmare about a maimed monster whose shame has to be hidden by his covering hands. Yet Brydon sees no connection between this monster and himself: "the face was the face of a stranger." He collapses from the menace of "a life larger than his own."[14]

By this imaginative use of the idea of a double James has told us truths about his hero's double nature. Before analyzing these meanings, we should recall the dream again because the critic's view of its meaning is likely to condition any discussion of the story. Edel begins by calling all attempts to interpret the nightmare as "gratuitous speculation," but he then goes on to interpret it for six pages and to declare that James used it as the germ of "The Jolly Corner." (Four volumes later, however, Edel suggests instead that the dream probably happened two years after the publication of the story.) Edel is persuaded that the dream reflects Henry's rivalry with his older brother, who was assured in French and the world of art, as Henry in those early years was not. In recounting the dream, Edel notes, Henry recalls that he undertook his first visit to the Louvre with his brother, and the autobiography records Henry's persistent sense of being junior to William. B. D. Horwitz has extended this sibling-rivalry theme to indict James for being unable to face (except in his dream) the ambivalent "violence and love" he felt for his brother, and Horwitz concludes that a desolated sense of "lost emotional life" finds only a "substitute triumph" in Henry's art. Richard Hall has speculated a scandalous step further by seeing in the novelist a repressed and thwarted incestuous love for William.[15] In this spirit one might more plausibly cast a modish light on the dream by seeing it as incorporating the dreamer's guilty fear of elements in himself, especially of aggressive feelings toward those he loves, compensated for narcissistically by a fantasy of omnipotence. James' avowed sense of "glory" in the Louvre would then suggest the fantasies indulged by the "grandiose self" of pathological narcissism.

These readings merely use the dream, however, to illustrate some-body's psychoanalytic theory, and without the benefit of having the patient's free associations to the dream material, evidence indispensable to clinical judgment. They minimize as well James' freedom from the bor-derline crises suffered by his father, his brother William, and his sister Alice, as well as his extraordinary productivity and generous treatment of his siblings and friends. Horwitz condemns the stories for being a "reversal or denial" of a "realistic solution"—that is, direct confrontation of James' anxieties. Horwitz then infers that because he could not incor-porate the "other self figured by his brother or by the young men whom he adopted as friends and proteges, James was subject to severe bouts of self-doubt and depression." [16] Paradoxically, this psychologizing treats the dream as "realistic" and the stories as evasions, mere rationalizations of "psychic death." I shall argue just the reverse: that the dream is, clas-sically, a wishful fantasy—the story an intelligent and subtle self-critical treatment of it—and I shall connect James' depressions with his voca-tional conflict rather than his erotic life. Freud wisely emphasized both love and work as psychic imperatives, but it is extraordinary how reluc-tant literary-psychological commentators have been to respond to Erik-son's complaint, now twenty years old, that the problem of work is the most neglected problem in psychoanalysis, both in theory and practice.

For a biographer the crucial clues to the dream must be what James says about it, what personal context he puts it in, what he makes out of it as an artist and autobiographer. In his autobiography James connects the Louvre's gallery of his childhood visit with an ambivalent "prevision" of the kind of "queer so-called inward sort" of life that he was to have as an artist, the palace of art becoming mixed up in his mind ever after with the "house of life." It is the place where he associates art with "history and fame and power," and the Napoleonic ambiance of the gilded hall colors James' magisterial artistic ambition, reflected in his legendary title of Master and his final delusion of being Napoleon. In his view, as Stephen Donadio has pointed out, "the power of the artist must there-fore be seen as of a kind with that of conquerors and heads of state." [17] The dream, which uses this setting to fantasize the reversal of a threat-ened defeat, may plausibly be linked (without theoretical dogmatizing) to the actual vocational events that had plunged James into depression: his commercial failure in the London theater, shockingly climaxed by that evening in 1895 when he was savagely booed on the stage of *Guy Domville*, or the revival fifteen years later of his theatrical ambitions and his gloom about the reception of his New York Edition. His wish-fulfillment turns the tables on those who rejected him, and the person who was made to feel like a frightened small boy becomes triumphant in a setting where art reverberates with the glory of Napoleonic conquest.

Critics who move too directly from James' life to his story, how-ever, blur some differences between Brydon and his creator, even though they share many features. Edel is helpful in suggesting that the idea of the ghost as a capitalist builder connects with the "enterprising side" of James as an architect of his New York Edition; but it is his theatrical ambition that is more to the point of a troubled seeking for profitable success. Edel emphasizes sibling rivalry by seeing the story's concern with an alter ego as pointing to the self that "had tried to live in his brother's skin, but could not shed it, and the self that reflected his crea-tivity." Edel's effort to read the story as "laying the ghost of his old rivalry with William" builds upon Saul Rosenzweig's Freudian interpre-tation of James' writing as a sublimation of a castration-anxiety caused by an identification with a crippled father. For Rosenzweig the ghost is James' "unlived life," and he lays this ghost by overcompensation through his active war work for the English cause.[18] These theories exploit the story without finding confirmation in its details or doing justice to its subtleties. James did write a story, "The Blast in the Jungle," about a man who recognizes too late his own failure to participate in life by taking the risks of commitment, and it is tempting to see Brydon as another version of this inactive character, one dreaming of a life of ac-tion.

But, contra Rosenzweig, Brydon *has* lived; the point is that he has " 'followed strange paths and worshipped strange gods' " in pursuing a " 'selfish frivolous scandalous life.' "[19] Furthermore, to see sibling ri-valry in the plot is to make the ghost a surrogate for William James. Though he also had trouble with his eyes, William never confused prag-matism with the idea of commercial success. The novelist himself never made this vulgar error, not only because he admired his brother, but because he felt a deep sympathy with the tenor of his philosophy. Read-ing *Pragmatism*, Henry wrote his brother, "I was lost in the wonder of the extent to which all my life I have (like M. Jourdain) unconsciously pragmatised. You are immensely and universally *right*."[20] Edel fails to note also that it is James, not Brydon, who recognizes the ghost's mirroring meaning.

A failing of these psychoanalytic explanations is that they do not try hard enough to comprehend the story as a drama of irony before they situate it biographically. E. D. Hirsch, Jr., pertinently quotes a sociologist, Lucien Goldmann, on a relevant procedural issue: " 'The illumination of a meaningful structure constitutes a process of comprehending it; while insertion of it into a vaster structure is to explain it.' "[21] To comprehend the point of a story is not the same thing as to explain the generating circumstances of its creation. The distinction is especially important when the story, as in the case of "The Jolly Corner," incorporates so much biographical material. "Reading it as biography has, as usual with James," Peter Buitenhuis has remarked, "been the main source of critical confusion about it."[22] The imagery of the house and the final scene of the hero returning to consciousness in the arms of Alice have engendered much critical "psycho-babble" about wombs, surrogate mothers, and symbolic rebirth, rather than historical awareness that the idea of "the encountered *Doppelgänger* was a popular one in late nineteenth-century literature," including famous stories by Stevenson, Wilde, and Conrad.[23]

The distortion in the conflation of James and Brydon is serious because it blurs a crucial point in the plot: Brydon himself metaphorically shares the "ruined sight" of the ghost in seeing nothing of himself in the maimed creature ("Such an identity fitted his at *no* point, made its alternative monstrous").[24] Yet it is Alice Staverton who earlier points out to him, with "an irony without bitterness" derived from her having imagination: " 'In short you're to make so good a thing of your sky-scraper that, living in luxury on those ill-gotten gains, you can afford for a while to be sentimental here!' "[25] She knows, as he never does, that the monster is also the person he has been, living off the leasing of his house and a renovated apartment building, for his obsession with the idea of the powerful man he might have been expresses a flaw in his character: " 'you don't care for anything but yourself.' "[26] As Alice half-seriously suggests, if he had stayed in America, he might have invented the sky-scraper; at least on his return to America there already has begun to stir in one "compartment of his mind" a "capacity for business and a sense for construction."[27] James has portrayed a hero fascinated with the idea of an alter ego whose nature he cannot see in himself. There is no final recognition of self-knowledge for Brydon; only Alice knows the truth about him.

The main problem in comprehending the point of the story comes at the end when Brydon recovers consciousness in Alice's arms and speaks of having come back to "knowledge." It is not self-recognition of his own maimed personality because he still obtusely denies any connection between the "beast" and himself (" 'But it's not me.' "). Alice points out that she not only pitied but accepted and liked the "black stranger," because he suggested somehow to her that Brydon wanted *her*. Picking up on this cue, Brydon begins to see by a "dim light" when he recognizes that though the ghost may have "a million a year," he does not have Alice. At this point, when she is embraced, Alice ironically humors his blindness about the ghost (" 'And he isn't—no, he isn't—you!' "). On this ironic line the story ends.

Adeline Tintner's new reading that Alice has encouraged his obsession and induced him to become a New York real estate operator, rather than a caretaker of his old house, ignores the Hawthornian way in which his love for Alice constitutes transcendence of his former egotism, just as she represents a link with the old pre-modern New York. Brydon wakes up, James tells us, like a man who "has gone to sleep on news of a great inheritance, and then after dreaming it away, after prophaning it, with matters strange to it," now has only to "watch it grow" in a "serenity of certitude."[29] This simile suggests a return to sanity rather than to a continuation of his nocturnal, panic-stricken decision to abandon his house to the developers, a profanation of his inheritance. In his dream-ridden obsession Brydon momentarily abandoned his inheritance, while James in his nightmare had courageously routed his enemy. But to see Brydon as finally converted to the commercialism of New York makes a mockery out of his sense of having been restored to life. This reading turns the plot of James' dream upside down. The hidden other self possessing the dreamer—Mr. Hyde taking over Dr. Jekyll—is another story, indeed, one already told and quite incompatible with James' own view that "The Jolly Corner" (like his dream) used the conceit of the haunted man enjoying a victory over the haunter.

But if the problems of comprehension must come first, those of explanation have their own rights. The literary biographer is necessarily more than just a close reader of his subject's stories. He must treat each story as a historical document in the life of the subject, marking out some point in the process of the person's and the writer's development. From this point of view we need to see "The Jolly Corner" in the context of James' life-circumstances. Edel is certainly right when he says the story has much to do with James' "ambivalence about his Americano-European."[30] Spencer Brydon is himself an "international ghost," or double, in *some* respects, for his creator.

Psychologically, it is probably not accidental that (as Freud would appreciate) the hero left New York at twenty-three and returned at fifty-six, thirty-three years later. James himself decisively left America for France when he was thirty-two (the reverse of twenty-three) and published this story thirty-three years later at the age of sixty-five (the reverse of fifty-six). This mirroring (perhaps unconscious) is appropriate to an alter ego, and Brydon's dream of a career in which he would have enjoyed commercial power is analogous to James' own persistent and doomed wish for a commercial success in the theater. In the character of Alice Staverton—who is for Brydon an emotional link with his youth in an older, more attractive America, rapidly being supplanted by sky-scrapers, immigrants, and commercialism—James found a fictional way of dealing with *The American Scene*'s counterpoint between his repulsion from modern America and his lyrical nostalgic memories. By making her sympathetic to the dreamed-of other self whom Brydon rejects, James provides a qualifying foil for Brydon's harshly negative condemnation of modern New York because her tolerance seems to have an insider's wisdom beyond his expatriated understanding. For her the ghost is also a missed opportunity, a figure in her dreams.

The strongest evidence for the Brydon/James connection is the parallel imagery in *The American Scene* (published a year before "The Jolly Corner") where James narrates his troubled return to his old home and his discovery that his birthplace is blocked out by a high structure, which makes him feel he has been "amputated" of "half" his history—a reminder that the ghost is missing two fingers, as if "shot away." Moreover, at Ellis Island, where the immigrants give a shock to his sense of national consciousness by implictly requiring him to share it with them, he speaks of seeing "a ghost in his supposedly safe old house." Like his hero, James was deeply shocked by changes in his old New York, sky-scrapers being for him "monsters of the mere market," lacking all historical associations. James tells us in his autobiography that his first idea of style came from the parqueted floor of the *Galerie d'Apollon*, while he has Brydon confess that he found it first in the black and white tiles in the hall of his family house, which he recognizes when he wakes from his faint. Brydon's awakening memory parallels the artist's recognition of the Louvre's floor in awaking from his nightmare. Adeline R. Tintner, in a photographic essay on James' use of New York buildings in his later stories, observes that the black and white tiles, like many other details about Brydon's house, reflect the actualities of a still-surviving friend's house where James had resided during his trip in 1904–5. To establish the locus of the story Tintner shrewdly notes that James wrote Mrs. Mary Cadwalader Jones of Greenwich Village to tell her how in his writing he found the hours spent there living again, his "spirit gratefully haunting them always or rather how insidiously *turning the tables* they, the mystic locality itself, *haunt and revisit my own departed identity*" (italics hers).[31] This phrasing also reveals the repetition of the idea of his nightmare and of his story, thus connecting emotionally the house of his friend, the gallery of his nightmare, and the four-story brownstone of his hero.

These biographical connections are manifest. But, standing in this biographical light, we may raise more controversial queries. What balance does the story strike in resolving the author's feelings about the competing attractions of America and Europe in his own history? Does Brydon's embrace of Alice, the name of James' sister and sister-in-law, reflect an emotional identification with America, biographically expressed in Edel's point that all of James' work after "The Jolly Corner" was "intimately related to his American past"?[32] Or does the repulsive image of modern New York in the tale reflect James' earlier decision, after his return from America to England in 1905, to burn forty years of accumulated papers?[33] Ambivalent feelings animate the story. We may speculate responsibly that he had personal motives for adding his own fictional example to "the sudden plethora of dual-personalities stories in the nineties," the widespread revival of the Gothic form "to explore the dark side of human nature."[34] James' link with Stevenson's famous story is a close one. As an admiring friend, he was much distressed when Stevenson died in Samoa during the rehearsal period of James' *Guy Domville*, his crucial failure in the London theater. By contrast, Stevenson's *Dr. Jekyll and Mr. Hyde* had run up huge circulation figures. These associations might well help influence James' decision after his American trip to tell a story of a hidden self, preoccupied with power, as a response to Howells' suggestion in 1900 of an "international ghost."

In terms of the "international theme" in James' own life, the ironies in the story prohibit our reading it as countenancing an unambiguous, simple choice between America or Europe, for it reflects the same division between lyrical nostalgia for the American past and fascinated criticism of the American present that defines the author's own feelings in *The American Scene*. Moreover, the story's criticism of Brydon's hidden drive for economic power functions autobiographically as James' criticism of his own hankering for profitable success. Yet we may still wonder about the biographical reason for James' decision to make his hero an unperceptive person needing the guidance of a woman with an emotional interest in him. The strength of the story, however, lies in this interesting complication, for it creates a dialogue between the hero and Alice that is full of dramatic irony for the reader, who has the pleasure of reading between the lines in a way that the hero notably fails to do.

This critical point is not a psychological one. The question deserves a nonbiographical answer. I think we must grant the novelist compelling aesthetic reasons for this difference from his dream, qualifying the heroism of his dreamer in a way that is more appropriate to a story than to the melodramatic wish-fulfillment of the "dream-adventure." Lionel Trilling has applauded the genius of having a dream that not only represents guilty fear as the price of the dreamer's arrogation, James' imperious view of the artist, but also dramatizes the triumphant overcoming of fear "in the very place where he had his imperious fantasy."[35] Psychologically, Trilling is surely right. But the plot of a successful dream is not likely to be artistically suitable for the plot of a story. Making his story only partially autobiographical, James made it more subject to artistic control and the vehicle for a subtle use of the double to portray a failure of self-knowledge, qualified by a milder victory than James himself enjoyed in his dreams. His creative recovery from the depressing failure of his theatrical ambitions was more heroic than anything Spencer Brydon ever does, and part of that heroism was his ability to find a fictional way of criticizing his own fantasy of popular success. In this sense the plot of "The Jolly Corner" contains a nightmare that is as "admirable" in artistic terms as the artist's own nightmare was "admirable" in psychological terms.

There is no evidence that James ever noticed either the similarity or the differences between the autobiographical dream and his hero's hallucinated voyage through his birthplace. What he did see was that the idea of turning the tables on a ghost (conceived for a novel) was incorporated in "The Jolly Corner," though he was more accurate in referring to using a "scrap of that fantasy" than in speaking of that "scrap" as the story's "intimate idea." But James himself saw the basic point when he reminded himself not to be artistically inconvenienced by the overlapping. "I have free use of everything I originally caught at in that connection."[36]

In one of the prefaces to the collected and revised edition of his works he spoke of there being more to say about the composition of "The Jolly Corner" than space allowed, "almost more in fact than categorical clearness might see its way to."[37] As a result, he said nothing, a reticence suggesting that the story had emotional roots not easy to uncover, like the nightmare itself. But it is not the frightening of the ghost that makes the strongest link between the dream and the story. It is the setting of the Louvre's parqueted floor,[38] its childhood association with art and power, the visit's prevision in the "small scared consciousness" of the artist having a future life of the "queer so-called inward sort." Brydon's sense of his early home's tiled floor has a similar ambiance of style and this displaced detail, transferred from childhood Paris to childhood New York, is not incongruous because the emotional theme of an ambivalent vision of power links the dream and the story.

The strongest claim for the dream of the Louvre is that James' fiction, "taken as a whole, becomes a series of paradigms of that dream." In this perspective the polarities of "passivity and aggression" define the recurrent themes of his stories. Daniel J. Schneider's *The Crystal Cage* persuasively shows how much of the fiction is colored and structured by James' ambivalent response to this type of conflict. Unfortunately, Schneider mistakenly calls it a "childhood dream" and qualifies his own theory by the admission that the theme of "turning the tables" appears only in the later fiction.[39] The crucial polarity for James first appears, I suggest, not in the dream, but in his youthful love letter mourning the death of Minny Temple in 1870. "It's the *living* ones that die; the writing ones that survive," he observed to his brother William, referring to the last letters from her.[40] The odd phrasing for this context unintentionally betrays his own persistent sense of the writer's life as a passive, detached seeing, isolated from the vulnerabilities of ordinary relationships. The dream of the Louvre reverses that passivity, because artistic ambition as imperial as James' has its own aggressive intention.

Placing "The Jolly Corner" in the light of the author's later career, we can now reconnect the dreamer and the writer. Two years after the story's publication James experienced a revival of his theatrical ambition, which brought with it a debilitating depression that prevented two of his plays from being produced.[41] Whatever the date of his dream, one thing is clear: in reality he did not fully exorcise the ghost in his soul. James saw the flaw in Spencer Brydon, but the artist could not eliminate his hero's wish for power from his own consciousness, tantalized as it was by the delusory dream of a Napoleonic conquest through popular success on the stage. His story testifies to a consciousness capable of criticizing egotistical detachment, self-absorption, and commercial ambition. But writing that story did not free him from the wish reflected in his dream. The triumphs of art, unlike dreams of victory, are always achieved within the limitations of reality.

Notes

1. I have analyzed William James' crisis and work in "William James and the Twice-Born Sick Soul," *Daedalus* (1968), 97 (3):1062–82 and "The Pluralistic Identity of William James: A 'Psycho-historical' Reading of *The Varieties of Religious Experience*," *American Quarterly* (1971), 23:135–52.

2. Henry James, *Autobiography*, Frederick W. Dupee, ed. (New York: Criterion Books, 1956), p. 196.

3. *Ibid.*

4. *Ibid.*, p. 198.

5. *Ibid.*, pp. 196–97.

6. F. O. Matthiessen and Kenneth B. Murdock, eds., *The Notebooks of Henry James* (New York: Oxford University Press, 1947), p. 300.

7. *Ibid.*, pp. 367–68.

8. Leon Edel, *Henry James: The Master, 1901–1916* (Philadelphia: Lippincott, 1972), pp. 442–47.

9. Leon Edel, *Henry James: The Untried Years, 1843–1870* (Philadelphia: Lippincott, 1953), pp. 67–79.

10. Stephen Donadio, *Nietzsche, Henry James, and the Artistic Will* (New York: Oxford University Press, 1978), pp. 228–36.

11. Napier Wilt and John Lucas, eds., "The Jolly Corner," *Americans and Europe: Selected Tales of Henry James* (Boston: Houghton Mifflin, 1965), p. 425.

12. *Ibid.*, p. 433.

13. *Ibid.*, p. 434.

14. *Ibid.*, p. 435–36.

15. Edel, *The Untried Years*, pp. 68–80; B. D. Horwitz, "The Sense of Desolation in Henry James," *Psychocultural Review* (1977), 1(4):388–91; Richard Hall, "An Obscure Hurt," *New Republic* (1979), 180(17–18):25–31, 25–29.

16. Horwitz, "Sense of Desolation in Henry James," pp. 487, 479.

17. Donadio, *Nietzsche, James, and the Artistic Will*, p. 255.

18. Edel, *The Master*, pp. 315–16; "The Ghost of Henry James," *Partisan Review* (1944), 11(4):436–55.

19. Peter Buitenhuis, *The Grasping Imagination: The American Writings of Henry James* (Toronto: Toronto University Press, 1970), p. 217.

20. F. O. Matthiessen, ed., *The James Family* (New York: Knopf, 1961), p. 343.

21. Eric Hirsch, *The Aims of Interpretation* (Chicago: University of Chicago Press, 1976), p. 2.

22. Buitenhuis, *Writings of Henry James*, p. 212.

23. *Ibid.*, p. 219.

24. Wilt and Lucas, eds. "The Jolly Corner," p. 436.

25. *Ibid.*, p. 417.

26. *Ibid.*, p. 421.

27. *Ibid.*, p. 414.

28. *Ibid.*, p. 441.

29. *Ibid.*, p. 437; Adeline Tintner, "Landmarks of 'The Terrible Town': The New York Scene in Henry James' Last Stories," *Prospects* (1976), 2:406.

30. Edel, *The Master*, p. 315.

31. W. H. Auden, ed., *The American Scene* (New York: Scribner's, 1946), pp. 85 and 91; Tintner, "Henry James' Last Stories," pp. 406–8.

32. Edel, *The Master*, p. 317.

33. Leon Edel, ed., *The Ghostly Tales of Henry James* (New Brunswick, N.J.: Rutgers University Press, 1948), p. 723.

34. Masao Miyoshi, *The Divided Self: A Perspective on the Literature of the Victorians* (New York: New York University Press, 1969), p. 294.

35. Lionel Trilling, "The Princess Cassamassima," *The Liberal Imagination: Essays on Literature and Society* (New York: Harcourt Brace, 1976 [1950]), p. 83.

36. Matthiessen and Murdock, eds., *Notebooks*, pp. 364, 367, 368.

37. Richard P. Blackmur, introduction to *The Art of the Novel: Critical Prefaces* (New York: Scribner's, 1946), p. 262.

38. For an evocative photograph of the *Galerie d'Apollon* in the Louvre see Harry I. Moore, *Henry James* (New York: Viking Press, 1974), p. 19.

39. Daniel J. Schneider, *The Crystal Cage: Adventures of the Imagination in the Fiction of Henry James* (Lawrence: Regents Press of Kansas, 1978), pp. 36–37, 67.

40. Matthiessen, ed., "To William James, March 29, 1870," *The James Family*, p. 256.

41. Percy Lubbock, ed., *The Letters of Henry James* (New York: Scribner's, 1920), 2:6.

16.

The Woolfs' Response to Freud: Water Spiders, Singing Canaries, and the Second Apple

Jan Ellen Goldstein

WHEN QUEEN VICTORIA DIED IN 1901, a rebellion was already beginning against Victorianism. Among its leaders were the Bloomsbury group, an informal coterie of writers, artists, and intellectuals. Taking the radical new ethics of G. E. Moore as their battle cry, they proclaimed and exemplified new personal and artistic freedoms in the decade before the First World War. Young Lytton Strachey, for example, became a persuasive spokesman for enlightened attitudes toward sexual behavior and was held responsible for a sudden flourishing of homosexual activity among Cambridge undergraduates.[1] In 1910 Roger Fry organized the first Postimpressionist Exhibition and introduced the new movement in French painting to a generally indignant English public; to compound the shock, the ladies of Bloomsbury attended a ball in honor of the oc-

From *Psychoanalytic Quarterly* (1974), 43:438–76. Copyright © 1974 Jan Ellen Goldstein. Reprinted by permission.

casion dressed in Gauguin-inspired Tahitian sarongs.[2] One member of the group recalls the high spirit and heady self-image of Bloomsbury in those years: "We were the forerunners of a new dispensation; we were not afraid of anything."[3]

By the 1920s, and even before, Bloomsbury became identified with that potent and imported ideology of anti-Victorian rebellion—Freudianism. They were, in fact, important lay disseminators of the "new psychology," as it was called, in England.

"MOORISM" AND FREUDIANISM

The philosophy of the Cambridge don G. E. Moore made the strongest of impressions on Bloomsbury: it colored their minds, said Leonard Woolf as indelibly as the climate of India colors the face of a Tamil.[4] Philip Rieff has noted that "Freud begins where G. E. Moore leaves off in the famous last chapter of *Principia Ethica*."[5] Rieff is not here speaking literally, of any direct influence exercised by Moore upon Freud, but figuratively, of a goal they shared and of Freud's more forceful and direct means of attaining it. That goal was, in Rieff's phrase, "to defend the private man" against the often excessive demands which society makes upon him for conformity to its public norms. People in sympathy with Moore, it might be inferred from Rieff's remarks, would be likely to find Freud congenial as well. This was precisely the case with Bloomsbury.

Before the appearance of Freud in English thought, Bloomsbury had deployed Moore's ethics in a campaign in defense of "the private man." Moore had stipulated that personal affection and esthetic enjoyment were the only true goods in human experience and the only genuine justifications for the performance of duty;[6] therefore Bloomsbury could challenge the authority of their duty-bound Victorian elders and fault them for emotional impoverishment and lack of intimacy. The Moorist value system led Bloomsbury, of their own accord, to modes of self-examination that anticipated the Freudian. For the purpose of improving their personal relationships, they devised, while undergraduates at Cambridge around the turn of the century, "the method," a "compulsory . . . third degree psychological examination" which they carried out on one another so as to reveal what each "was really like."[7]

233

The similarity between "Moorism" and Freudianism can be put in other terms. Moore oriented his ethics around subjective psychology. In his canon, the good was a "state of consciousness" involving not only *cognition* of a beautiful inanimate or human object but also an *emotion* "appropriate" to that beauty.[8] The individual was thus obliged to turn inward, to examine his emotions with some subtlety, to learn to articulate them to himself. In making introspection an ethical necessity, Moore was part of the *fin de siècle* trend toward non-religious introspection (another exemplar is Henri Bergson) which found its fullest elaboration and systematization in Freud.

Thus Moore, whose magnum opus appeared in 1903, prepared a significant group of English intellectuals for receptivity to Freud. But there were also ways in which he represented a very different world view from that of Freud, a world view much more in harmony with the Victorian. The innovative anti-Victorian tendencies in Moore impelled his disciples toward Freud, but his conservative tendencies militated against a full acceptance of psychoanalysis.

Among these conservative tendencies was Moore's unshakeable faith in the rationality of human nature. He focused his ethics on the affective life, but he was able to achieve this daring departure from nineteenth-century ethical theory only by the compromise measure of endowing the affective life with rational traits. When Moore spoke of an emotion "appropriate" to its object, he was expecting an extraordinary degree of precision from the emotions: they must be simple and clear, not uneasy amalgams of contradictory emotions. . . . When John Maynard Keynes reminisced about Bloomsbury in 1938, he plainly labeled the Moorist outlook he and his friends had shared as "intellectually pre-Freudian,"[9] "a purer, sweeter air by far than Freud cum Marx"[10] and one which kept them sheltered from the crucial insights of the twentieth century. . . . The members of Bloomsbury were, said Keynes, "water-spiders, gracefully skimming, as light and reasonable as air, the surface of the stream without any contact at all with the eddies and currents underneath."[11]

THE FORMAL TIES BETWEEN BLOOMSBURY AND FREUD

Still it was Bloomsbury, so ambivalent in its modernism yet so dedicated to ushering in the "new dispensation," which played a major role in bringing Freud to the English. The initial and closest ties to the psychoanalytic movement were forged by peripheral members of the group: James and Alix Strachey, Adrian and Karin Stephen.

James Strachey, Lytton's younger brother and later the editor of the Standard Edition of Freud, became interested in psychoanalysis shortly before the war, but it was not until 1920 that he and his wife Alix made the decision to study it professionally. They then took up residence in Vienna and within a year had sufficiently impressed Freud that he requested them to translate a series of his clinical papers. That project led to further familiarity: they were soon visiting Freud regularly on Sunday afternoons to discuss not only problems of translation but "whatever problems we want to." [12] By the summer of 1921, when they returned to England and vacationed in Cumberland with Lytton and his friends, they were wholly absorbed in their new work. Writing to Virginia Woolf, Lytton described James as uninterested in rustic outings and preferring to stay at home "balanced upon a horsehair sofa, reading the psychopathology of dreams by Dr. Varendonck." [13] The vignette suggests that, with such a presence in their midst, psychoanalytic theory was reaching the other members of Bloomsbury. Certainly it reached Lytton, whose psychological interpretations in his 1928 biography of Elizabeth and Essex can be traced directly to the tutelage he received from his brother and sister-in-law. [14]

Adrian Stephen, Virginia Woolf's younger brother, had been studying medieval law when, in the early twenties, he "suddenly threw the Middle Ages and law out the window and became . . . a qualified doctor and a professional psychoanalyst." [15] He was joined by his wife, Karin Costelloe Stephen, who, as one of Henri Bergson's first supporters in the English philosophical community, had earlier shown her receptivity to the concept of an unconscious mind.

Through their friendship with James Strachey, Leonard and Virginia Woolf also became involved in the psychoanalytic movement. In 1924, after quarrels with Otto Rank put an end to the plan by which all English psychoanalytic texts were to be published in Austria, Strachey and Ernest Jones approached the Hogarth Press, [16] founded by the Woolfs only seven years before and dedicated to the principle of "refusing to publish anything unless we thought it worth publishing." [17]

A LIFELONG ILLNESS

Virginia Woolf avoided Freudianism at the time of her nervous breakdown in 1913–1915. She continued to avoid it in all her subsequent bouts with mental illness, up to and including the final one which led to her suicide in 1941.

Her illness had a long history. When her mother died in 1895, Virginia, aged thirteen, suffered her first breakdown.[18] Barely recovered in 1897, she went through another period of acute distress, this one apparently precipitated by the furtive sexual advances of her doting half brother, George Duckworth.[19] A third serious breakdown followed in 1904, after she had nursed her father through his long last illness. She attempted suicide and heard "those horrible voices"—birds singing Greek choruses, King Edward using foul language in the garden.[20] As she became a novelist, her now chronic depressions began to attach themselves to her writing, the downward swing coinciding with the correction and return of the galleys when, as she later described it, "I must wean my mind from it [the finished work] . . . and prepare another creative mood":[21] at this point the prospect of the novel's imminent release to the critics also threatened her.[22] The 1913 breakdown was the prototype of this situation: her first novel, *The Voyage Out*, had just been completed. In addition, there was a renewed sexual disturbance. During her honeymoon in the fall of 1912, she had found herself repelled by sexual love.[23] The combined stresses of literary production and marriage forced her, for the fourth time in her life, over "the border which divides what we call insanity from sanity."[24]

Psychoanalysis was available in London in 1913. Ernest Jones had begun practicing it there in 1906,[25] and, although clashes with the medical establishment sent him into voluntary exile in Canada in 1908, he made annual visits to London and returned there permanently in 1913.[26] Dr. David Forsyth became a full-time analyst several years before the war, as did Dr. M. D. Eder, a London-born Jew active in Fabian socialist politics.[27] The London Psycho-Analytical Society, a branch of the international association, was founded in 1913. Although it was a less formidable organization than its name might imply (of fifteen original members, only four were psychoanalytic practitioners), its existence attested to the growing interest in Freudian therapy in the English capital.

"In 1913," Leonard Woolf wrote some fifty years later, "the state of knowledge with regard to nervous and mental diseases was desperately meagre." [28] He has recorded all the doctors whom Virginia consulted during the breakdown of 1913–1915: George Savage, Maurice Craig, T. B. Hyslop, Henry Head, Maurice Wright. [29] The first three appear in Ernest Jones' portrait of turn-of-the-century Harley Street as the successive superintendents of London's Bethlehem Hospital ("Bedlam"). All had taken up the private practice of psychiatry upon retirement from this post. Jones has only contempt for the triumvirate of Savage, Craig, and Hyslop: their treatment was limited to signing "the necessary certificates" and entrusting their patients "to expensive hospitals where they would periodically visit them." [30] Henry Head was one of the most famous neurologists of his day and the editor of *Brain*. Maurice Wright, who had once treated Leonard for a nervous tremor of the hands, utilized the technique of suggestion. [31] Though Head and Wright were more forward-looking mental specialists than the other three, [32] their advice to Virginia Woolf in 1913–1915 was identical with the others': that she go to a nursing home for a few weeks and stay in bed, resting and eating. [33]

Virginia's ailment was diagnosed as "neurasthenia," [34] or nervous exhaustion, the catchall "diagnosis of fashion" among the genteel classes of Europe and America since the 1870s. [35] The treatment prescribed for her was standard for neurasthenics—the Weir Mitchell treatment, or rest cure as it was popularly called. The name is misleading because rest was only ancillary in Mitchell's conception of the cure. The cardinal element was nutrition, deliberate overfeeding to stabilize the irregular brain cells supposedly responsible for the illness. [36] The Weir Mitchell treatment was thus based upon a "onesidedly materialistic" medical outlook: the body could influence the mind but not vice versa; the mind was only an emanation from the brain, an organ function, and so mental disturbance clearly must be tackled in the brain. [37] Evidence that Virginia Woolf submitted herself to this treatment can be found in her letters to Lytton Strachey. In the fall of 1915, when her long illness seemed to be finally over: "I really am all right and weigh 12 stone!—three more than I've ever had, and the consequence is I can hardly toil uphill, but it's evidently good for the health. I look forward to being rid of the nurse soon." [38] And again in 1921 the process is repeated: "All sorts of plagues descended on me. I'm now recovered, gained 6 lbs." [39]

Though the popularity of the Weir Mitchell treatment declined sharply with the coming of suggestive therapies and psychoanalysis, [40]

Virginia Woolf stuck with it till the end. The former superintendent of Bethlehem, Maurice Craig, was "for the rest of Virginia's life the mental specialist to whom we went for advice when we wanted it";[41] and his handbook, *Nerve Exhaustion*, indicates the kind of advice he must have given her. He was a thoroughgoing conservative, not implacably hostile to Freudian therapy but extremely wary of it, believing that many patients did not have "the mental stability to stand the strain" of the "distressing ideas" it brought to light.[42] He was furthermore convinced that nervous breakdowns were conditions of the total body, requiring direct physical treatment and not merely the Freudians' "clearing up of amnesias."[43] On the other hand, he was unequivocally in favor of "therapeutic" weight gain. In 1940 Virginia's doctor was Octavia Wilberforce, who happened also to run a farm with a herd of Jersey cows. Since food was scarce during the war, Dr. Wilberforce brought the prescribed milk and cream to Virginia once a week.[44]

Despite the cheeriness of her remarks to Lytton Strachey on the benefits of overeating, her account in *Mrs. Dalloway* of Septimus Smith's war neurosis and ultimate suicide suggests her more fundamental dissatisfaction with the Weir Mitchell treatment.[45] The tragicomic irrelevance of that treatment to the patient's mental suffering emerges in the interior monologue of the eminent, prosperous, and complacent Harley Street neurologist, Sir William Bradshaw: "When a man comes into your room and says he is Christ (a common delusion) . . . and threatens, as they often do, to kill himself, you invoke proportion; order rest in bed; rest in solitude; silence and rest; rest without friends, without books, without messages; six months' rest; until a man who went in weighing seven stone six comes out weighing twelve."[46] Sir William, says Virginia Woolf, "penalized despair."[47] But, however bitterly it was expressed in her novel, this dissatisfaction with traditional psychiatry did not function for her as an incentive to seek psychoanalysis.

If she clung to an old-fashioned treatment, she likewise clung to an old-fashioned conception of her illness. As late as 1933, the Freudian notion that physical symptoms can have psychic causes was alien to her. In her journal she wrestled with the problem of the origin of her recurrent symptoms:

While I was forcing myself to do Flush my old headache [the earliest warning of a breakdown] came back—for the first time this autumn. Why should the Ps. [Pargiters, the working title of *The Years*] make my heart jump; why should Flush stiffen the back of my neck? What connection has the brain with the body? Nobody in Harley Street could explain, yet the symptoms are purely physical.[48]

In the same year she toyed with the applicability of a Freudian conception of mental breakdown to her own situation—only to reject it. She had read, as soon as it was published, Geoffrey Faber's biography of Cardinal Newman, *Oxford Apostles*. Faber had, as one member of Bloomsbury put it, approached his subject "armed with psychoanalysis."[49] The book included analyses of Newman's dreams and childhood fantasies and, what caught Virginia Woolf's attention, a hypothesis about the cause of his periodic nervous collapses. They were not, Faber maintained, induced by overwork,[50] the generally accepted cause of neurasthenia before Freud. Rather, they were the result of a repressed conflict between two tendencies in Newman's personality, one assertive and ambitious, the other wanting to be dominated and bent on failure.[51] Faber stressed that this conflict remained "out of sight," penetrating Newman's consciousness only in the veiled form of a religious struggle between self-will and obedience to God. Virginia Woolf responded to these ideas in her journal:

I've been reading Faber on Newman; compared his account of a nervous breakdown; the refusal of some pàrt of the mechanism; is that what happens to me. Not quite. Because I'm not evading anything. I long to write The Pargiters.[52]

Here and at other points in her journal, when Virginia Woolf speculates on the cause of her depressions, she does hit upon conflict as a plausible explanation. But it is conflict between activities in the real world: "the effort to live in two spheres—the novel and life";[53] or conflict within the conscious mind: "the strife and jar . . . [of] 2 types of thought, the critical, the creative."[54] The idea of repressed conflict—the idea, in essence, of not knowing her own mind—is flatly denied and apparently very distasteful to her.

KNOWLEDGE OF FREUD

How much did Virginia Woolf know about Freud? She did not read any of his works until December 1939. Reading Freud was a stint she set herself, a deliberate and self-disciplined divergence from her natural propensity to read literature. Her journal records:

Began reading Freud last night; to enlarge the circumference: to give my brain a wider scope: to make it objective; to get outside. Thus defeat the shrinkage of age. Always take on new things.[55]

Prior to 1939 she was, of course, by no means ignorant of Freud. Replying in 1931 to the inquiry of a German scholar who was making an assessment of the influence of Freudianism on English novelists, she stated that she was acquainted with psychoanalysis "only in the ordinary way of conversation":[56] but she neglected to say that, with a brother and sister-in-law who were psychoanalysts and James and Alix Strachey as friends, this conversation was far from ordinary. Her journal for 1923 indicates that Adrian even discussed his own analysis with her.[57] For about two decades before 1939, references to Freud are scattered throughout her nonfictional writings, and from these her opinions of the Freud she knew at second hand can be pieced together.

FEELINGS ABOUT PSYCHOANALYTIC THERAPY

Her first explicit mention of Freudianism occurs in 1920 in her brief anonymous review of J. D. Beresford's novel, *An Imperfect Mother*.[58] At the outset she "hazard[s] the opinion" that the author "has acted the part of stepfather to some of the very numerous progeny of Dr. Freud." She is correct: Beresford had studied Freud extensively under the watchful eye of Dr. M. D. Eder and had recently advocated the application of psychoanalytic theory to the novel.[59] The results of his literary policy appropriately form the subject of Virginia Woolf's review, which is entitled "Freudian Fiction." But she strays once from her main point to remark upon psychoanalysis as a therapy:

This [plot] is strictly in accordance with the new psychology which in the sphere of medicine claims to have achieved positive results of great beneficence. A patient who has never heard a canary sing without falling down in a fit can now walk through an avenue of cages without a twinge of emotion since he has faced the fact that his mother kissed him in the cradle. The triumphs of science are beautifully positive.

This remark might better be described as a minor outburst: not only is it gratuitous, but the sudden profusion of bizarre imagery and the sarcastic rendition of what the Freudians are able to tell a person about himself bespeak a conglomeration of powerful emotions impelling Virginia Woolf here. In calling "the triumphs of science . . . beautifully positive," she is making an implicit comparison between the psychoanalyst's confidence in his end-product and her own ambivalence about it—an ambivalence expressed in the hypothetical case she presents. While the fit is certainly pathological, it is, after all, brought on by a thing of delicate beauty; and according to the Moorist canon, responsiveness to beauty is one of the primary goals of life. If the only given alternative is to be "without a twinge of emotion" when canaries are singing, Virginia Woolf might well prefer to eschew medical "beneficence" and retain the "sickness." (And in only slightly disguised form, it does seem to be her own sickness, with its aural hallucinations of singing birds, that she has in mind.)

Certainly the emotional numbness she here associates with a psychoanalytic cure would be anathema to her. She reveled not only in insensitivity but in hypersensitivity:

A change of house makes me oscillate for days. And that's life: that's wholesome. Never to quiver is the lot of Mr. Allinson, Mrs. Hawkesford and Jack Squire.[60]

Furthermore, this desirable hypersensitivity seemed to her the obverse of depression—and inextricably bound up with it. "If we didn't . . . tremble over precipices," the same entry in her journal continues, "we should never be depressed, I've no doubt; but already should be faded, fatalistic and aged." Hence to root out the depression through psychoanalytic therapy would be to lose the other side as well, to render one's emotional life monochromatic.

In even more explicit ways, she associates her illness with her artistic capabilities:

These curious intervals in life—I've had many—are the most fruitful artistically—one becomes fertilized—think of my madness at Hogarth—and all the little illnesses—that before I wrote the Lighthouse for instance. Six weeks in bed now would make a masterpeice of Moths.[61]

Similarly, in another entry, her "returning health" after a "nervous breakdown in miniature" is "shown by the power to make images; the suggestive power of every sight and word is enormously increased."[62] Virginia Woolf's distrust of psychoanalysis is thus based in part on her own version of the age-old identification of genius and insanity. (Her hypothetical patient is "afflicted" with an artistic hypersensitivity; had she chosen a case of horse phobia or hand-washing compulsion for her example, the illness itself would have no redeeming value and her argument against the psychoanalytic cure would lose its force.) While many writers sought psychoanalysis during the 1920's in order to conquer writing blocks or generally improve their writing,[63] probably just as many feared that it would adversely affect their creativity.

Human integrity requires that the private realm or illness remain inviolable. Virginia Woolf's firm statement of this tenet has direct if unintended bearing upon her attitude toward psychoanalysis:

> We do not know our own souls, let alone the souls of others. Human beings do not go hand in hand the whole stretch of the way. There is a virgin forest, tangled, pathless, in each. Here we go alone and like it better so. Always to be accompanied, always to be understood, would be intolerable.[64]

By implication, then, the cooperative exploration entailed by psychoanalytic therapy is not for Virginia Woolf the "defense of the private man" that Philip Rieff would have it; it is instead an intolerable companionship and an unjustifiable assault upon privacy.

FEELINGS ABOUT PSYCHOANALYTIC THEORY

To say that Virginia Woolf did not want to entrust her illness to a psychoanalytic practitioner is not to say that she found the psychoanalytic theory of mental functioning utterly erroneous. In matters not related to her own illness she could find the psychoanalytic perspective, even when applied to herself, valid and illuminating; and a clear example of this occurs in her feminist essay, *A Room of One's Own*. During an imaginary visit to the British Museum, where she does some fruitless research on the cause of the dearth of female writers throughout history, Virginia Woolf sits down to brood and finds that she is "unconsciously, in my listlessness" drawing a picture. It is a picture of the Enemy: Professor von X engaged in writing his magisterial tome, *The Mental, Moral and Physical Inferiority of the Female Sex;* and he looks angry. Virginia Woolf analyzes the doodle at length:

> Drawing a picture was an idle way of finishing an unprofitable morning's work. Yet it is in our idleness, in our dreams, that the submerged truth sometimes comes to the top. A very elementary exercise in psychology, not to be dignified by the name of psychoanalysis, showed me, on looking at my notebook, that, the sketch of the angry professor had been made in anger. Anger had seized my pencil while I dreamt. But what was anger doing there? Interest, confusion,

amusement, boredom—all these emotions I could trace and name as they succeeded each other throughout the morning. Had anger, the black snake, been lurking among them? Yes, said the sketch, anger had.[65]

The picture is thus treated as a bit of "psychopathology of everyday life," a minor eruption of the unconscious into behavior which can then be used to explore the inner self. It works for Virginia Woolf as a kind of diagnostic test, informing her of the anger that had remained utterly outside awareness. Her identification of her act of automatic drawing[66] as a kind of waking dream reveals her degree of psychoanalytic sophistication: "The mechanism of . . . chance actions," wrote Freud in 1901, "can be seen to correspond in its most essential points with the mechanism of dream-formation."[67] Virginia Woolf has also here indicated a qualified belief in Freudian dream theory: "in our dreams . . . the submerged truth *sometimes* comes to the top."[68]

What is notably absent from this interpretation is the sexual content that Freud usually discovered in slips and random actions. Virginia Woolf must have found Freud's sexual emphasis distasteful, alarming, and unassimilable. Critics have frequently commented upon the avoidance of sexual love in her novels; she herself confided in her journal that the world she created in her fiction was "vague & dream like . . . , without love, or heart, or passion, or sex and is the only world I really care about."[69] The "dark places of psychology" which appealed to her in Joyce and other modern novelists had, by her definition, no connection at all with unruly bodily instincts. "Mr. Joyce," she said, "is spiritual; he is concerned at all costs to reveal the flickering of that innermost flame which flashes its messages through the brain."[70]

This powerful self-protective tendency to desexualize certainly helps to account for her long delay in directly confronting Freud through reading him. Yet Virginia Woolf was also far from openly accusing Freud, as so many did from the first announcement of his theories in the 1890's straight through to the 1930's, of prurience and pansexualism. This was not the Bloomsbury style. Bloomsbury had always stood for sexual freedom. Swept up in its pre-war libertine rebelliousness, Virginia Woolf went swimming naked with Rupert Brooke in response to his challenge,[71] wore a sarong at the Postimpressionist Ball, typed Lytton Strachey's bawdy *Ermyntrude and Esmerelda*, and assured him she would be delighted to type anything else "chaste or otherwise."[72] She could not sustain this kind of spontaneity. But despite the sexual repression and maladjustment more basic to her nature, she no doubt assented intellectually to Bloomsbury's anti-Victorian sexual attitudes—and to Freud's investigations of the sexual impulse. She permitted herself but one oblique jibe against the Freudian insistence upon the universality of sexual motivation. Pondering an anonymous woman seated opposite her in a railway car, trying to fathom the mysteries of her character, Virginia Woolf resoundingly rejected a Freudian interpretation. "They would say she kept her sorrow, suppressed her secret—her sex they'd say—the scientific people. But what flummery to saddle *her* with sex!"[73]

PSYCHOANALYSIS AND ART

Given the high, quasi-religious place of art in Bloomsbury's scheme, they were bound to take umbrage at Freud's depiction of the artist as a clever neurotic able, by a roundabout process, to turn his fantasies of "honour, power, wealth, fame and the love of women"[74] into the means of their own realistic fulfilment. Roger Fry responded to Freud in 1924 with *The Artist and Psycho-Analysis,* an indignant lecture which later won Ernest Jones' respect as a representative and "most incisively expressed" critique of Freud's views.[75] Fry's arguments were echoed in *The Nation* by his fellow Bloomsburyan Clive Bell and Leonard Woolf offered his opinions on the subject in 1923 and 1924.[76]

Virginia Woolf, however, never became embroiled in this theoretical debate on the nature and sources of artistic creativity. Her interest in the relationship of Freudianism and art was practical; what, she wanted to know, would be the impact of psychoanalysis upon the novelist's *craft?* She held that in novel writing the salient quality and the main challenge were the creation of character. "Men and women write novels because they are lured on [by] . . . a little figure who rises before them saying 'My name is Brown. Catch me if you can.' " Or, even more pointedly, "It is to express character . . . that the form of the novel, so clumsy, verbose and undramatic, so rich, elastic and alive, has been evolved."[77] Thus it was only natural that, when faced with new psychological theories purporting to explain human character, she should voice a concern about whether and how they could be incorporated into the novel. She was not, at the outset, optimistic.

Virginia Woolf never came to an appreciation of Freud as "healer," but toward the end of her life she did paint an optimistic picture of the salutary effects of Freudianism on future (though not present) literature. Her journal shows that this revised assessment, which she wove into a lecture already in progress, was a sudden, fresh insight resulting directly from her reading of Freud. . . .

The similarities between Freud's dream work and Virginia Woolf's "work done by unconsciousness" are unmistakable. While Freud himself never drew an explicit analogy between the dream work and the process of artistic creation, the analogy was prevalent among literary intellectuals.[78] In so far as Virginia Woolf is reflecting this analogy, she has made a significant shift of emphasis. Her "under-mind" corresponds to the Freudian *pre*conscious: it sifts the day's residues, relegating some to temporary forgetfulness but not repressing them in the technical sense. Though Virginia Woolf has chosen to call this "under-mind," "unconsciousness," the repressed sexual content of the true Freudian unconscious, the crucial factor in Freud's dream work has exercised no influence on the sifting and reshaping of the material. The water-spider habits of Bloomsbury are in evidence here: although Virginia Woolf is willing to go below the surface of the mind, she will not go the whole way down. She has domesticated the unconscious.

"All through the nineteenth century, down to August 1914," Virginia Woolf wrote in "The Leaning Tower," the class divisions of society were so fixed that writers, comfortably ensconced in ivory towers of middle-class birth and expensive education, were unconscious of them. This unconsciousness was artistically fruitful: it enabled writers to create characters who were not types but individuals; because writers did not see the "hedges that divide classes," they could see "the human beings who dwelt within the hedges." With the social upheavals of the First World War, however, came the rude shock of class consciousness. Hence the dominant metaphor of the lecture: the writers' tower began to lean. Whatever else this experience may have meant, it was artistically stultifying. The new generation—writers such as Auden, Spender, Isherwood—discovered themselves powerless to create characters. They began perforce to write about themselves in autobiographical plays, poems, and novels; they became "great egotists."

For Virginia Wolf, "great egotism," or constant self-analysis, is another form of too much consciousness, and, like too much consciousness of the social structure, it is unconducive to the production of great works of literature. But Virginia Woolf believes that its *delayed* effects will be enormously beneficial; and in this context, her one unequivocal affirmation of Freud occurs:

Consider how difficult it is to tell the truth about oneself—the unpleasant truth. . . . The nineteenth-century writers never told that kind of truth, and that is why so much nineteenth-century writing is worthless; why for all their genius, Dickens and Thackeray seem so often to write about dolls and puppets, not about full-grown men and women; why they are forced to evade the main themes and make do with diversions instead. If you do not know the truth about yourself, you cannot tell it about other people.

The leaning-tower writer has had the courage at any rate . . . to tell the truth, the unpleasant truth, about himself. . . . By analysing themselves honestly, with help from Dr. Freud, these writers have done a great deal to free us from nineteenth-century suppressions. The writers of the next generation may inherit from them . . . that unconsciousness which . . . is necessary to writers. . . . For that great gift of unconsciousness the next generation will have to thank the creative and honest egotism of the leaning tower group.[79]

This "Freudian manifesto" is in some ways a backhanded one. Virginia Woolf can appreciate Freudianism only by looking beyond it, to a time when people will no longer have to focus upon Freudian insights but can act, and especially create, upon an assimilated knowledge of them. No doubt there is an implicit squeamishness about the insights themselves here, a desire to bypass them—as Virginia Woolf did for so many years. Nonetheless, her dialectic of too much consciousness yielding renewed unconsciousness seems to me sensible as an approach to the literary use of Freud (since neither simulating a pre-Freudian innocence nor directly transposing Freudian constructs into the novel, in Beresford's fashion, can produce viable literature). The dialectic is also true to Freud's own spirit. Freud did not regard the self-absorption required by psychoanalysis as a good in itself but rather saw "the turning outward that signified freedom from inwardness as . . . the resolution of neurosis."[80] In "The Leaning Tower," then, Virginia Woolf can be said to have depicted the self-absorption of the writers of the thirties as a symptom of a general cultural neurosis; but she credits psychoanalysis with the eventual cure as well.

It is noteworthy that she distances herself from this affirmation of Freud. Her own generation is labeled as the upright tower school: only their successors, the leaning tower school, faced Freud head on, told the "unpleasant truth" about themselves; and only the leaning tower school's successors will reap the ultimate rewards of Freudianism. Very accurately, Virginia Woolf leaves her audience with the impression that she has been a nonparticipant observer of the Freudian revolution, that she is herself almost untouched by it.

A SELF-PROCLAIMED FREUDIAN

Lacking the genius of his wife, Leonard Woolf was endowed with innumerable talents and had a richly variegated career as civil servant in Ceylon, publisher, book reviewer, essayist, fiction writer, political theorist, and adviser to the Labour Party. Not the least of his contributions was his nurturance of his wife: his constant attentiveness to her mercurial psychological states and his ability to provide the emotional environment in which she could function creatively. Woolf was a "penniless Jew"—the description is Virginia's at the time of their engagement[81]—a socioeconomic background unique among the members of Bloomsbury but compensated for in his case by a Cambridge education. Between 1960 and 1969, he wrote a five-volume autobiography: he emerges there as a man without artifice, garrulous but understated, engaging in his candor. "The perfectly candid man," Stephen Spender called him,[82] and it is hard to disagree. However, on the subject of Freudianism, ambiguities and self-deceptions to creep into Woolf's position.

In the autobiography, Woolf presents himself as a Freudian. He repeatedly and conspicuously invokes the theories of Freud to interpret his past experiences, bolster his opinions, probe the personalities of his contemporaries. Thus, to cite a few examples, a prank played on Woolf in 1904 now becomes, in light of "Jokes and Their Relation to the Unconscious" (from which Woolf quotes a half page), not an expression of fun but of hostile impulses which could not be overtly acted out because of the requirements of "civilization."[83] Similarly the contradictory character of H. W. Massingham, Editor of *The Nation* in the 1920s, now seems to demonstrate a connection typically found in pacifists between their political beliefs and the sadistic "goings on down among their ids in their unconscious"; nor does Woolf exempt his own left-wing and humanistic politics from this diagnosis.[84] And describing a second cousin of Virginia whom he met in 1912, Woolf notes that "Madge worshipped her father [the literary critic John Addington Symonds] as so many daughters have since the time of Electra, in a way which was not fully understood until the second eating of the apple on the tree of knowledge by Sigmund Freud."[85]

The avowal of Freudianism is also made explicitly in the autobiography and its historical origin stated. Woolf was, he tells us, won over to the doctrines of Freud at almost the earliest possible moment: within a year after the first of Freud's books appeared in English translation. In June 1914 he was asked to review *The Psychopathology of Everyday Life* for a short-lived periodical called *The New Weekly;* being conscientious, he read *The Interpretation of Dreams* (published in England in 1913) as well. His response, as he reported it some fifty years later, was glowingly favorable: "I am, I think not unreasonably, rather proud of having in 1914 recognized and understood the greatness of Freud and the importance of what he was doing at a time when this was by no means common."[86] The evidence of the 1914 review corroborates this. Woolf there praises the exceptional qualities of Freud's mind: his power to discern a coherent pattern in a great mass of detail, "his sweeping imagination more characteristic of the poet than the scientist." Woolf is aware that many people will find Freud "too far fetched," and, declining to discuss this verdict fully in the small space allotted him, he simply asserts, "categorically and confidently," that "there is a substantial amount of truth in the main thesis of Freud's book and that truth is of great value."[87]

In recording this bit of personal and English cultural history, Woolf has, with characteristic scruple, taken pains to guard against inaccuracy and the common tendency to "credit [one]self . . . mistakenly"; he has, he makes a point of saying, not merely trusted his memory of the 1914 review, but has unearthed the actual document and quoted it. Still, other factors call his Freudianism into doubt. Ironically, the most forceful bit of counterevidence is contained in the very passage in which he discussed the 1914 review—or rather, in the placement of that passage in the rest of the book. It comes sandwiched between accounts of the two stages of Virginia's breakdown; and it is brought up in relation to a 1914 Fabian conference at which Woolf met Walter Lippmann for the first time. Lippmann was one of the first popular advocates of psychoanalysis in America, and the two men "somehow or other . . . got onto the subject of Freud, psychoanalysis, and insanity" and discovered that they shared a deep rapport. In true Bloomsbury fashion, Woolf recalls his exhilaration at their intimacy, at having found someone who could "go below . . . the usual surface of conversation . . . with complete frankness."[88] But he fails to make any connection between the *content* of their conversation (and his reading and endorsement of Freud) and the anxious search for medical help for Virginia that occupies him only a few pages before and again a few pages later. The degree of dissociation is rather startling. However great Woolf's intellectual admiration for Freud at this point, it clearly did not extend into the personal, practical sphere of even considering psychoanalytic treatment for Virginia.

Nor is his intellectual praise for Freud, taken alone, free of difficulties. In the first place, the very equanimity of the 1914 review raises suspicion. Nowhere does it show Woolf grappling with Freud's assertion that, even in normal minds, unconscious processes interfere with and indeed undermine conscious functioning. This assertion was, after all, at loggerheads with Woolf's own intellectual foundations in Moorist rationalism; and if he did, as he claims, realize the "importance" of Freud, he could not have done so without a personal intellectual upheaval. His ready and unruffled acceptance of psychoanalysis in 1914 seems to have been a casual one, prompted by his true acuity of judgment about Freud's stature as a thinker and by a Bloomsburyan broad-mindedness and interest in the psychological realm, but ultimately predicted upon Woolf's failure to grasp the implications of the texts before him.

Furthermore, it is by reference to the 1914 review alone that Woolf establishes his credentials as one of the Freudian avant-garde; but when the researcher ventures outside the autobiography and looks at Woolf's other book reviews (in *The New Statesman* during the First World War and in *The Nation* from 1923 to 1930), it appears that his 1914 affirmation of Freud was an isolated one. The wartime book reviews, several on psychological topics, never mention Freud. One in 1916 makes a blanket assertion of the "singular unsuccess of psychologists"[89]; and the favorable notice given later that year to Wilfred Trotter's *Instincts of the Herd in Peace and War* shows no awareness that Trotter, who had earlier introduced Ernest Jones to the work of Freud, was now a Freudian revisionist whose "herd instinct" was postulated as an explicit emendation of psychoanalytic instinct theory.[90] Woolf's *Nation* column, "The World of Books," begun in the 1920's when Freudianism had just become a topic of intense popular interest, reveals a much greater awareness of Freud but, at the same time, a caution far removed from the pro-Freudian protestation of the autobiography. A remark about the "possible truth" of psychoanalysis, weighted to the positive side by Woolf's admission that "the heat which psychoanalysis generates in the arguments of those who disagree with it is a very strong argument in its favor,"[91] is typical of this period.

LEONARD WOOLF'S FREUD

Why then does Woolf present himself as a Freudian so insistently in his autobiography? Toward the end of his life, I think he had arrived at a personal conception of Freud that was wholly congenial to his own way of thinking, if not wholly faithful to Freud's. This "Freud" provided him with a modern, up-to-date authority for some of his favorite ideas.

Into *Principia Politica*, the third volume of *After the Deluge*, Freud makes a sudden and dramatic entrance. Taking no notice of his absence from the previous two volumes, Woolf now calls Freud one of the three "dominating intellectual influence[s]" in the modern world and cites as his "most fundamental and far-reaching" contribution his elucidation of the origin of the "sense of sin."[92] In this assessment, Woolf has clearly overlooked Freud the clinician and has fastened upon Freud the philosopher of *Civilization and Its Discontents* who had declared his "intention to represent the sense of guilt as the most important problem in the development of civilization." Feeling "sinful," Freud says, is the "devout" person's terminology for feeling guilt.[93]

Freud's analysis of the "sense of sin" is of such importance to Woolf because of its bearing on Woolf's concept of civilization, a concept all the more essential to him because of his own life experience of two world wars. According to *Principia Politica*, the "sense of sin" has always been the primary motor of the history of the West. From it sprang the idea of God, the necessary agent of punishment for sinful man. Divine vengeance furnished the model for the first political regimes, which sanctioned cruel and barbarous punishment. Diametrically opposed to the sense of sin, trying to assert itself against it, is the human impulse toward "civilization." For Woolf, civilization is the ascendancy of the rational faculty; and, within the individual and collective psyche, the rational faculty is capable of being totally paralyzed by the sense of sin. Thus the initial progress to civilization was made by the ancient Greeks precisely because they were able to escape their sense of sin "for a time—

alas too short a time"; and civilization collapses whenever, as has happened twice in the twentieth century, the sense of sin regains the upper hand.[94]

For Woolf, Freud is a staunch and effective ally of this precious and precariously based civilization. He has shown, Woolf tells us, that "the sense of sin is universal in human beings," that it develops inevitably from infantile sexual feelings and oedipal conflict, that its sources "remain in unconsciousness" from whence they now and then erupt, unsuspected and "with devastating results."[95] The implication is that Freud's objective scientific dissection of the sense of sin enables us to cope with sin more competently, robs sin of its magical and sinister hold over the human mind, and helps our civilized rationality to remain in control of our primitive religious impulse.

Thus, while in his laudatory paraphrases of Freud, Woolf seems to accept the fatal inevitability of the sense of sin, he gradually strays from this pessimistic view. In the next chapter of *Principia Politica*, he is still in agreement with the Freudian view that civilization requires instinctual renunciations: this is a favorite idea which recurs throughout his autobiography. But he now states that human beings "can learn" to make these renunciations without developing a sense of sin or guilt, that it is possible to substitute for the latter "the sanctions of love . . . and reason." This substitution, Woolf implies, can be made by the institutions of socialization: the family—by refraining, for example, from corporal punishment for bed wetting: and the primary school—by refraining from overly strict discipline and from inculcation of the sense of "duty."[96] Woolf has here diluted the Freudian conception of guilt and made it much more tolerable and manageable. For Freud love cannot be so simply substituted for guilt because it is bound up in the very origin of guilt. And the institutions of socialization can do little to counter the development of the sense of guilt: "Experience shows," wrote Freud, "that the severity of the super-ego which a child develops in no way corresponds to the severity of the treatment which he has himself met with."[97] Thus Woolf's "Freudianism" shifts Freud's emphases significantly. Whereas Freud regards civilization as necessitating the control of aggressive impulses and thereby producing the sense of guilt, Woolf's "civilization" requires control of both aggressive impulses and sense of guilt (or sin). Since Woolf deems this dual control feasible, his true "civilization" is without discontents.

Moreover Leonard Woolf has, like Virginia, domesticated the unconscious. In a passage in *Principia Politica*, he erroneously attributes to Jung ideas expressed by Freud as early as *The Interpretation of Dreams* and then proceeds to emend these ideas. It is not true, he says, that "there is no verbal, conceptual or logical reasoning in the dreams or unconscious of modern man." Utterly ignoring Freud's distinction between the contents of the unconscious itself and the final manifest dream, Woolf argues that the unconscious is at least partly rational because in dreams "we speak and are spoken to; we have general and abstract ideas; we act because we have understood the abstract or general ideas in something that has been said; we think in words and therefore 'reason.' "[98] This is an extraordinary distortion of the bedrock of Freudian theory for a man who claims to be a Freudian. Though Leonard Woolf could refer to psychoanalytic theory as "the second eating of the apple on the tree of knowledge," it is apparent that he could partake of the fruit without being fully expelled from the Eden of sweet Moorist rationalism.

Notes

1. See Michael Holroyd, *Lytton Strachey: A Critical Biography*, vols. 1 and 2 (New York: Holt, Rinehart & Winston, 1967, 1968), 1:208.
2. See Quentin Bell, *Bloomsbury* (London: Weidenfeld & Nicholson, 1968), p. 43.
3. John Maynard Keynes, "My Early Beliefs" from *Two Memoirs* (London: Rupert Hart-Davis, 1949), p. 82.
4. Leonard Woolf, *Beginning Again: An Autobiography of the Years 1911 to 1918* (New York: Harcourt, Brace & World, 1964), p. 25.
5. Philip Rieff, *Freud: The Mind of a Moralist* (New York: Viking Press, 1959), p. 261.
6. G. E. Moore, *Principia Ethica* (Cambridge: The University Press, 1903), p. 189.
7. Leonard Woolf, *Sowing: An Autobiography of the Years 1880 to 1904* (New York: Harcourt, Brace & World, 1960), p. 127.
8. G. E. Moore, *Principia Ethica*, pp. 189–90.
9. Keynes, *Two Memoirs*, p. 100.
10. *Ibid.*, p. 92.
11. *Ibid.*, p. 103.
12. Holroyd, *Lytton Strachey*, 2:442.
13. James Strachey and Leonard Woolf, eds., *Letters: Virginia Woolf and Lytton Strachey* (New York: Harcourt, Brace, 1956), p. 132.
14. *Ibid.*

15. Leonard Woolf, *Downhill All the Way: An Autobiography of the Years 1919 to 1939* (New York: Harcourt, Brace & World, 1967), p. 164.

16. Ernest Jones, *The Life and Work of Sigmund Freud* (New York: Basic Books, 1957), 3:36–37.

17. L. Woolf, *Beginning Again*, p. 255.

18. See Quentin Bell, *Virginia Woolf: A Biography* (New York: Harcourt, Brace, Jovanovich, 1972), 1:44.

19. *Ibid.*, p. 45.

20. *Ibid.*, pp. 89–90.

21. Leonard Woolf, ed., *A Writer's Diary: Being Extracts from the Diary of Virginia Woolf* (New York: Harcourt, Brace, 1953), p. 252.

22. L. Woolf, *Beginning Again*, p. 149.

23. See Bell, *Virginia Woolf*, 2:5–6.

24. L. Woolf, *Beginning Again*, p. 76.

25. Ernest Jones, *Free Associations: Memories of a Psycho-Analyst* (New York: Basic Books, 1959), p. 162.

26. *Ibid.*, p. 229.

27. *Ibid.*, pp. 228–29.

28. L. Woolf, *Beginning Again*, p. 159.

29. *Ibid.*, p. 160.

30. Jones, *Free Associations*, p. 123.

31. L. Woolf, *Sowing*, p. 28.

32. Head later attempted to explain the Freudian theory of repression neurophysiology (Jones, *Free Associations*, p. 134) and Wright became an associate member of the British Psycho-Analytical Society in 1919 (see "Reports of the International Psycho-Analytical Association: History of the British Psycho-Analytical Society," *International Journal of Psychoanalysis* (1920), 1:118). But by the time of these occurrences, their roles in Virginia Woolf's care had already terminated.

33. L. Woolf, *Beginning Again*, p. 156.

34. *Ibid.*, p. 148.

35. See Walter Bromberg, *Man Above Humanity: A History of Psychotherapy* (Philadelphia: J. B. Lippincott, 1954), p. 152.

36. See Ernest Jones, *Treatment of the Neuroses: Psychotherapy from Rest Cure to Psychoanalysis* (New York: Schocken Books, 1963), pp. 24–25.

37. See Jones, *Free Associations*, p. 155.

38. J. Strachey and L. Woolf, eds., *Letters*, p. 70.

39. *Ibid.*, p. 133.

40. See Bromberg, *Man Above Humanity*, p. 155.

41. L. Woolf, *Beginning Again*, p. 160.

42. Maurice Craig, *Nerve Exhaustion* (London: J. & A. Churchill, 1922), pp. 122–23.

43. *Ibid.*, pp. 125–26.

44. Leonard Woolf, *The Journey Not the Arrival Matters: An Autobiography of the Years 1939–1969* (New York: Harcourt, Brace & World, 1970), p. 87.

45. Virginia Woolf, *Mrs. Dalloway* (New York: Harcourt, Brace, 1925).

46. *Ibid.*, pp. 149–50.

47. *Ibid.*, p. 150.

48. L. Woolf, *A Writer's Diary*, p. 188.

49. Francis Birrell, "A Very English Centenary," *New Statesman & Nation* (1933), n.s. 6, p. 78.

50. Geoffrey Faber, *Oxford Apostles: A Character Study of the Oxford Movement* (New York: Scribner's, 1934), p. 51.

51. *Ibid.*, pp. 177–79.

52. L. Woolf, *A Writer's Diary*, pp. 202–3.

53. *Ibid.*, p. 203.

54. *Ibid.*, p. 176.

55. *Ibid.*, p. 309.

56. See Reinald Hoops, *Der Einfluss der Psychoanalyse auf die englische Literatur.* Anglistiche Forschungen, LXXVII, 1934, p. 147.

57. See Bell, *Virginia Woolf*, 2:116.

58. Virginia Woolf, "Freudian Fiction," in *Contemporary Writers* (New York: Harcourt, Brace & World, 1965).

59. J. D. Beresford, "Psycho-Analysis and the Novel," *London Mercury* (1920), vol. 1.

60. L. Woolf, *A Writer's Diary*, p. 63.

61. *Ibid.*, p. 143.

62. *Ibid.*, p. 96.

63. Frederick J. Hoffman, *Freudianism and the Literary Mind*, 2d ed. (Baton Rouge: Louisiana State University Press, 1957), pp. 71–72.

64. Virginia Woolf, *On Being Ill* (New York: Harcourt, Brace, 1948), p. 14.

65. Virginia Woolf, *A Room of One's Own* (New York: Harcourt, Brace, 1929), pp. 52–53.

66. The experiments of the Surrealists with automatism, which were being conducted in Paris during the 1920s, may have been in Virginia Woolf's mind. The Surrealists regarded these experiments as direct extensions of psychoanalytic technique. See Cardinal, Roger, and Short, *Surrealism: Permanent Revelation* (London: Studio Vista, 1970).

67. Sigmund Freud, *The Psychopathology of Everyday Life* (1901), *Standard Edition*, p. 277.

68. V. Woolf, *A Room of One's Own.*

69. Bell, *Virginia Woolf*, 1:126.

70. Virginia Woolf, "Modern Fiction" in *The Common Reader* (New York: Harcourt, Brace, 1925), pp. 215, 214.

71. See Stephen Spender, "The Perfectly Candid Man," *New York Review of Books* (1970), 14:29.

72. J. Strachey and L. Woolf, eds., *Letters*, p. 60.

73. Virginia Woolf, "An Unwritten Novel," in *A Haunted House and Other Short Stories* (New York: Harcourt, Brace, 1948), p. 13.

74. Sigmund Freud, "Introductory Lectures on Psycho-Analysis," part III, "General Theory of the Neuroses," *Standard Edition* (1915–1917), p. 376.

75. Roger Fry, *The Artist and Psycho-Analysis* (London: Hogarth Press, 1924); Jones, *The Life and Work of Sigmund Freud*, p. 409.

76. Clive Bell, "Dr. Freud on Art," *Nation & Athenaeum* (1924), 36:690–91; Leonard Woolf, "The Daydream," *Nation & Athenaeum* (1923), 34:346; "Poetry and Dreams," *Nation & Athenaeum* (1924), 36:18.

77. Virginia Woolf, "Mr. Bennett and Mrs. Brown," in *The Captain's Death Bed and Other Essays* (New York: Harcourt, Brace, 1923), pp. 94, 102.

78. See L. Woolf, "Poetry and Dreams."

79. Virginia Woolf, "The Leaning Tower," in *The Moment and Other Essays* (New York: Harcourt, Brace, 1948), pp. 148–49.

80. Philip Rieff, *The Triumph of the Therapeutic: Uses of Faith After Freud* (New York: Harper & Row, 1969), p. 190.

81. See Bell, *Virginia Woolf*, 2:2.

82. Spender, "The Perfectly Candid Man," p. 23.

83. Leonard Woolf, *Growing: An Autobiography of the Years 1904–1911* (New York: Harcourt, Brace & World, 1962), p. 14.

84. L. Woolf, *Downhill All the Way*, p. 95.

85. L. Woolf, *Beginning Again*, p. 73.

86. *Ibid.*, p. 167. Woolf is also accurate about the rarity of his position in 1914. In fact, the first extended discussion of Freud in a nontechnical publication in England did not occur until 1912, in the journal, *The New Age*. See Wallace Martin, *The New Age under Orage: Chapters in English Cultural History* (Manchester: Manchester University Press, 1967), pp. 140–41.

87. Leonard Woolf, "Everyday Life," *New Weekly* (1914), 1:412.

88. L. Woolf, *Beginning Again*, p. 168.

89. Leonard Woolf, "Crowds and Their Leaders," *New Statesman* (1916), 6:398.

90. Leonard Woolf, "The Inhuman Herd," *New Statesman*, (1916), vol. 7.

91. L. Woolf, "Poetry and Dreams."

92. Leonard Woolf, *Principia Politica: A Study of Communal Psychology* (London: Hogarth Press, 1953), pp. 41, 65.

93. Sigmund Freud, "Civilization and Its Discontents" (1930), *Standard Edition*, 11:134, 124.

94. L. Woolf, *Principia Politica*, p. 65.

95. *Ibid.*, pp. 65–66.

96. *Ibid.*, pp. 113, 131.

97. Freud, "Civilization and Its Discontents," 11:132, 130.

98. L. Woolf, *Principia Politica*, p. 121.

PART IV

THREE VIEWS
OF KAFKA

Franz Kafka's personality, talent, and works have provided inexhaustible material for psychoanalytic commentary and criticism. His conflicted childhood—dominated by a powerful father and a submissive mother, traumatized by the birth and death of two brothers before he was five years old, and aggravated by his mother's responses to them—has been dissected from every conceivable perspective, if only because Kafka's literary works are so full of dreams and symbolism, transformations, and mutliple meanings, ironies, and insights, that they promise, more than most, to illuminate the relationship between art and creativity. Because Kafka died at the age of forty-one, knew for years that he would succumb to tuberculosis, and wrote about his illness as well as about his problems with women in his many letters and diaries, his life has seemed more accessible than that of other geniuses. And Kafka's cultural background, so similar to Freud's, his contemporaneity with the "birth" of psychoanalysis, and the willingness of family and friends to talk to neighbors have offered an especially vast territory for exploration.

Among the many approaches to understanding Kafka, Erich Fromm's interpretation of *The Trial* as a work of art written in symbolic dream language is a marvelous example of criticism that looks to the work to know its creator. Fromm begins by questioning the meaning of Joseph K.'s arrest, noting that K. is aware of being arrested by the police as well as of being blocked in his development. And he juxtaposes components of the story and uses of words and of feelings to indicate how these corresponded to dreams which could have been dreamt by an individual like Kafka, who was "aware that he was wasting his life and rotting away fast," who "humanely speaking was almost dead, but could continue his life as a bank official just the same." Fromm discusses the "authoritarian conscience," whose virtue is obedience and greatest crime disobedience. Fromm finds them both in the novel—symbolically represented, respectively, as the Inspector and the Priest, and in the court, the judges, and assistants. K.'s confusion, his dilemma, and his inability to find his way alone (parallel to Kafka's own life) ends in a nightmare—a nightmare which "for the first time [allowed] K. to be aware of his greediness and of the sterility of his life . . . [and which] only in the terror of dying gave him the power to visualize the possibility of love and friendship and, paradoxically . . . for the first time, faith in life."

Margarete Mitscherlich-Nielsen also focuses on Kafka's conflicts, and on the ambiguities in his texts. By likening her interpretation of this written text to a psychoanalytic case description, she alerts us to the subjectivity of the literary interpreter who, like the psychoanalyst, brings his own prejudices to the situation, and to the application of this subjectivity in analytic transference and countertransference. By "using his understanding and intuition," the analyst is able "to penetrate to the unconscious meanings of literary or biographic texts . . . [which] may broaden the general understanding of how an individual psyche perceives and copes with private and collective events." And this is what "lures" the analyst into literary criticism. By examining Kafka's childhood, Mitscherlich-Nielsen hopes to illuminate questions such as why Kafka deemed *Metamorphosis* an indiscretion, and why he likened writing both to "the most important thing in the world," and to "a form of prayer." Kafka's early life is reconstructed by consideration of his parents' preoccupations, personalities, and relationship; Kafka's feelings of anxiety and loneliness are explored—as well as his lifelong friendship with Max Brod, and his closeness to his sister Ottla. Mitscherlich-Nielsen not only applies her psychoanalytic expertise to these questions, but also to outside influences such as Prague anti-Semitism, and responses to his writing. Thus, paternal and maternal social status, along with "the systematic destruction of myself"—due to childhood experience—and feelings of self-hatred are shown to relate to early narcissism, and to the wish for fusion with the mother—which was reinacted by K. and other characters, and in his interaction with women. Accounting for many previous analytic commentaries on Kafka, Mitscherlich-Nielsen finds Heinz Kohut's theory of the "narcissistically damaged" person who suffers from hypochondriacal anxieties and fragmentation of the self among the most applicable. Craving maternal understanding (which only Ottla and Felice managed to supply) is traceable to Kafka's early object-relations, to the inability to break from his parents and to the "profound lack of self-confidence, pre-oedipal aggressions and fixations." The stories owe their effect to Kafka's ability to transform his repetition compulsion, with the help of "new, brilliantly conceived imagery and fantasies"—and to the resonance these evoke in his readers. For the understanding from unconscious to unconscious, between author and reader, concludes Mitscher-lich-Nielsen, is direct and yet protects the reader's mind through the nature of the descriptions.

Ronald Hayman might maintain, too, that writing protects Kafka from himself. In storytelling, Kafka "talked to himself about himself," and in his diaries external events could not be held apart from their fictional elaborations, nor dreams and fantasies from stories. Hayman's new contributions to Kafkaiana are based on previously unknown letters and thus allow for a new perspective. We now know that "Kafka's letters contain about fifty times as many words as the fiction published with his consent," that for many years he wrote in secret, and that he found it easier to communicate in the third person than in the first. For Kafka it was more important to write than to be read, notes Hayman, for it allowed one half of him to take the risk of reaching out, and the other to hide under the bedclothes. While Hayman compares this to the schizophrenic, who feels the separation of the self and the body, and refers to incidents of splits in the fiction, using clinical terminology, he refrains from the type of analysis which psycholanalysts Fromm or Mitscherlich-Nielsen engage in. Hayman's thrust is literary and social; he focuses on the anti-Semitic prejudices and incidents which must have upset Kafka's life, which must have exacerbated his already intense free-floating anxieties, and diverted them to the fiction. This essay's strength, it seems, derives from Hayman's sharp analytic insights, which, however, are not couched in terms of a clinical diagnosis. Hayman does point out that it must have been Kafka's identification as a Jew which reduced him to tears upon reading Arnold Zweig's *Ritualmord in Ungarn;* his vegetarianism may have been connected to the revulsion he felt against his paternal grandfather's occupation as ritual butcher; and his "sense of being guilty and innocent at the same time was shared by other potential victims of anti-Semitism." How his sensitivity to noise, his hypochondria, and his

Jewishness served as the raw material for *The Trial* and *The Castle*, and how these, in turn, changed during his life, are sources of further insights for Hayman, and are connected to Kafka's "struggle for existence even if his body was beyond repair." "K.'s obsession about penetrating the castle," Hayman writes, "reflects Kafka's relentless determination to go wherever his writing led him, to colonize as much as he could of the world inside his head, even if it meant defying the God who did not want him to write."

The three contributions in this section touch on most of the questions surrounding Kafka, but others continue to be raised as the more peripheral influences—of teachers, neighbors, or coworkers—continue to be explored.

17.

Franz Kafka

Erich Fromm

AN OUTSTANDING EXAMPLE of a work of art written in symbolic language is Kafka's *The Trial*. As in so many dreams, events are presented, each of which is in itself concrete and realistic; yet the whole is impossible and fantastic. The novel, in order to be understood, must be read as if we listened to a dream—a long complicated dream in which external events happen in space and time, being representations of thoughts and feelings within the dreamer, in this case the novel's hero, K.

The novel begins with a somewhat startling sentence: "Someone must have been telling lies about Joseph K., for without having done anything wrong he was arrested one fine morning."[1]

K., we might say, begins the dream with an awareness that he is "arrested." What does "arrested" mean? It is an interesting word which has a double meaning. To be arrested can mean to be taken into custody by police officers and to be arrested can mean to be stopped in one's growth and development. An accused man is "arrested" by the police, and an organism is "arrested" in its normal development. The manifest story uses "arrested" in the former sense. Its symbolic meaning, however, is to be understood in the latter. K. has an awareness that he is arrested and blocked in his own development.

In a masterful little paragraph, Kafka explains why K. was arrested. This is how K. spent his life:

From Erich Fromm, *The Forgotten Language* (New York: Holt, Rinehart, and Winston, 1951). Copyright 1951 © 1979 Erich Fromm. Reprinted by permission.

turn from mimesis

That spring K. had been accustomed to pass his evenings in this way: after work whenever possible—he was usually in his office until nine—he would take a short walk, alone or with some of his colleagues, and then go to a beer hall, where until eleven he sat at a table patronized mostly by elderly men. But there were exceptions to this routine, when, for instance, the Manager of the Bank, who highly valued his diligence and reliability, invited him for a drive or for dinner at his villa. And once a week K. visited a girl called Elsa, who was on duty all night till early morning as a waitress in a cabaret and during the day received her visitors in bed.

It was an empty, routinized life, sterile, without love and without productiveness. Indeed, he was arrested, and he heard the voice of his conscience tell him of his arrest and of the danger that threatened his personality.

The second sentence tells us that "his landlady's cook, who always brought him his breakfast at eight o'clock, failed to appear on this occasion. That had never happened before." This detail seems unimportant. In fact, it is somewhat incongruous that after the startling news of his arrest such a trivial detail as his breakfast not having come should be mentioned; but, as in so many dreams, this seemingly insignificant detail contains important information about K.'s character. K. was a man with a "receptive orientation." All his strivings went in the direction of wanting to receive from others—never to give or to produce.[2]

He was dependent on others, who should feed him, take care of him, and protect him. He was still a child dependent on his mother—expecting everything from her help, using her and manipulating her. As is characteristic of people of this orientation, his main concern was to be pleasant and nice so that people, and in particular women, would give him what he needed; and his greatest fear was that people might become angry and withhold their gifts. The source of all good was believed to be outside, and the problem of living was to avoid the risk of losing the good graces of this source. The result is an absence of the feeling of his own strength and intense fear of being threatened with desertion by the person or persons whom he is dependent upon.

K. did not know who accused him or what he was accused of. He asked: "Who could these men be? What were they talking about? What authority could they represent?" A little later, when he talked with the "Inspector," a man higher up in the hierarchy of the court, the voice became somewhat more articulate. K. asked him all sorts of questions having nothing to do with the main question of what he was accused of, and in answering him the Inspector made a statement which contained one of the most important insights that could be given K. at that point—and for that matter to anyone who is troubled and seeks help. The Inspector said, "However, if I can't answer your questions, I can at least give you a piece of advice; think less about us and of what is to happen to you, think more about yourself instead." K. did not understand the Inspector's meaning. He did not see that the problem was within himself, that he was the only one who could save him, and the fact that he could not accept the Inspector's advice indicated his ultimate defeat.

This first scene of the story closes with another statement by the Inspector which throws a great deal of light on the nature of the accusation and of the arrest.

"You'll be going to the Bank now, I suppose?" "To the Bank?" asked K. "I thought I was under arrest? . . . How can I go to the Bank, if I am under arrest?" "Ah, I see," said the Inspector, who had already reached the door. "You have misunderstood me. You are under arrest, certainly, but that need not hinder you from going about your business. You won't be hampered in carrying on the ordinary course of your life." "Then being arrested isn't so very bad," said K., going up to the Inspector. "I never suggested that it was," said the Inspector. "But in that case it would seem there was no particular necessity to tell me about it," said K., moving still closer.

Realistically, this could hardly happen. If a man is arrested, he is not permitted to continue his business life as usual nor in fact, as we see later, any of his other ordinary activities. This strange arrangement expressed symbolically that his business activities and everything else he did were of such a nature as not really to be touched by his arrest as a human being. Humanely speaking, he was almost dead, but he could continue his life as a bank official just the same, because this activity was completely separated from his existence as a human being.

K. had a vague awareness that he was wasting his life and rotting away fast. From here on, the whole novel deals with his reaction to this awareness and with the efforts he makes to defend and to save himself. The outcome was tragic; although he heard the voice of his conscience, he did not understand it. Instead of trying to understand the real reason for his arrest, he tended to escape from any such awareness. Instead of helping himself in the only way he could help himself—by recognizing the truth and trying to change—he sought help where it could not be found—on the outside, from others, from clever lawyers, from women whose "connections" he could use, always protesting his innocence and silencing the voice that told him he was guilty.

Perhaps he could have found a solution had it not been for the fact that his moral sense was confused. He knew only one kind of moral law: the strict authority whose basic commandment was "You must obey." He knew only the "authoritarian conscience," to which obedience is the greatest virtue and disobedience the greatest crime. He hardly knew that there was another kind of conscience—the humanistic conscience—which is our own voice calling us back to ourselves.[3]

In the novel, both kinds of conscience are represented symbolically: the humanistic conscience by the Inspector and later by the Priest; the authoritarian conscience by the court, the judges, the assistants, the crooked lawyers, and all others connected with the case. K.'s tragic mistake was that, although he heard the voice of his humanistic conscience, he mistook it for the voice of the authoritarian conscience and defended himself against the accusing authorities, partly by submission and partly by rebellion, when he should have fought for himself in the name of his humanistic conscience.

The "court" is described as despotic, corrupt, and filthy; its procedure not based on reason or justice. The kind of lawbooks the judges used (shown him by the wife of an attendant) were a symbolic expression of this corruption. They were old dog-eared volumes, the cover of one was almost completely split down the middle, the two halves were held together by mere threads. "How dirty everything is here!" said K., shaking his head, and the woman had to wipe away the worst of the dust with her apron before K. would put out his hand to touch the books. He opened the first of them and found an indecent picture. A man and a woman were sitting naked on a sofa, the obscene intention of the draftsman was evident enough, yet his skill was so small that nothing emerged from the picture save the all-too-solid figures of a man and a woman sitting rigidly upright and, because of the bad perspective, apparently finding the utmost difficulty even in turning toward each other. K. did not look at any of the other pages, but merely glanced at the title page of the second book. It was a novel entitled, *How Grete Was Plagued by Her Husband Hans*. "These are the lawbooks that are studied here," said K. "These are the men who are supposed to sit in judgment on me."

Another expression of the same corruption was that the attendant's wife was used sexually by one of the judges and one of the law students and that neither she nor her husband was permitted to protest. There is an element of rebelliousness in K.'s attitude toward the Court and a deep sympathy in the Law-Court Attendant who, after having given K. "a confidential look such as he had not yet ventured in spite of all his friendliness," said, "A man can't help being rebellious." But the rebelliousness alternated with submission. It never dawned upon K. that the moral law is not represented by the authoritarian court but by his own conscience.

[margin note: K = Kant!]

To say that this idea never dawns upon him would not be quite correct. Once toward the end of his journey he came as close to the truth as he ever did. He heard the voice of his humanistic conscience represented by the priest in the Cathedral. He had gone to the Cathedral to meet a business acquaintance to whom he was to show the city, but this man had not kept the appointment and K. found himself alone in the Cathedral, a little forlorn and puzzled until suddenly an unambiguous and inescapable voice cried: "Joseph K.!"

K. started and stared at the ground before him. For the moment he was still free, he could continue on his way and vanish through one of the small dark wooden doors that faced him at no great distance. It would simply indicate that he had not understood the call, or that he had understood it and did not care. But if he were to turn round he would be caught, for that would amount to an admission that he had understood it very well, that he was really the person addressed, and that he was ready to obey. Had the priest called his name a second time K. would certainly have gone on, but since there was a persistent silence, though he stood waiting a long time, he could not help turning his head a little just to see what the priest was doing. The priest was standing calmly in the pulpit as before, yet it was obvious that he had observed K.'s turn of the head. It would have been like a childish game of hide-and-seek if K. had not turned right round to face him. He did so, and the priest beckoned him to come nearer. Since there was now no need for evasion, K. hurried back—he was both curious and eager to shorten the interview—with long flying strides toward the pulpit. At the first rows of seats he halted, but the priest seemed to think the distance still too great, he stretched out an arm and pointed with sharply bent forefinger to a spot immediately before the pulpit. K. followed this direction too; when he stood on the spot indicated he had to bend his head far back to see the priest at all. "You are Joseph K.," said the priest, lifting one hand from the balustrade in a vague gesture. "Yes," said K., thinking how frankly he used to give his name and what a burden it had recently become to him; nowadays people he had never seen before seemed to know his name. How pleasant it was to have to introduce oneself before being recognized! "You are an accused man," said the priest in a very low voice. "Yes," said K. "So I have been informed." "Then you are the man I seek," said the priest. "I am the prison chaplain." "Indeed," said K. "I had you summoned here," said the priest, "to have a talk with you." "I didn't know that," said K. "I came here to show an Italian round the Cathedral." "A mere detail," said the priest. "What is that in your hand? Is it a prayer book?" "No," replied K., "it is an album of sights worth seeing in the town." "Lay it down," said the priest. K. pitched it away so violently that it flew open and slid some way along the floor with disheveled leaves. "Do you know that your case is going badly?" asked the priest. "I have that idea myself," said K. "I've done what I could, but without any success so far. Of course, my first petition hasn't been presented yet." "How do you think it will end?" asked the priest. "At first I thought it must turn out well," said K., "but now I frequently have my doubts. I don't know how it will end. Do you?" "No," said the priest, "but I fear it will end badly. You are held to be guilty. Your case will perhaps never get beyond a lower Court. Your guilt is supposed, for the present, at least, to have been proved." "But I am not guilty," said K.; "It's a misunderstanding. And, if it comes to that, how can any man be called guilty? We are all simply men here, one as much as the other." "That is true," said the priest, "but that's how all guilty men talk." "Are you prejudiced against me too?" asked K. "I have no prejudices against you," said the priest. "I thank you," said K.; "but all the others who are concerned in these proceedings are prejudiced against me. They are influencing even outsiders. My position is becoming more and more difficult." "You are misinterpreting the facts of the case," said the priest. "The verdict is not so suddenly arrived at, the proceedings only gradually merge into the verdict." "So that's how it is," said K., letting his head sink. "What is the next step you propose to take in the matter?" asked the priest. "I'm going to get more help," said K., looking up again to see how the priest took this statement. "There are several possibilities I haven't explored yet." "You cast about too much for outside help," said the priest disapprovingly, "especially from women. Don't you see that it isn't the right kind of help?" "In some cases, even in many, I could agree with you," said K., "but not always. Women have great influence. If I could move some women I know to join forces in working for me, I couldn't help winning through. Especially before this Court, which consists almost entirely of petticoat-hunters. Let the Examining Magistrate see a woman in the distance and he almost knocks down his desk and the defendant in his eagerness to get at her." The priest drooped over the balustrade, apparently feeling for the first time the oppressiveness of the canopy above his head. What could have happened to the weather outside? There was no longer even a murky daylight; black night had set in. All the stained glass in the great window could not illumine the darkness of the wall with one solitary glimmer of light. And at this very moment the verger began to put out the candles on the high altar, one after another. "Are you angry with me?" asked K. of the priest. "It may be that you don't know the nature of the Court you are serving." He got no answer. "These are only my personal experiences," said K. There was still no answer from above. "I wasn't trying to insult you," said K. And at that the priest shrieked from the pulpit! "Can't you see anything at all?" It was an angry cry, but at the same time sounded like the involuntary shriek of one who sees another fall and is startled out of himself.

The priest knew what the real accusation against K. was, and he also knew that his case would end badly. At this point K. had a chance to look into himself and to ask what the real accusation was, but, consistent with his previous orientation, he was interested only in finding out where he could get more help. When the priest said disapprovingly that he casts about too much for outside help, K.'s only response was fear that the priest was angry. Now the priest became really angry, but it was the anger of love felt by a man who saw another fall, knowing he could help himself but could not be helped. There was not much more the priest could tell him. When K. moved in the direction of the doorway, the priest asked, "Do you want to leave already?" Although at that moment K. had not been thinking of leaving, he answered at once, "Of course, I must go. I'm the assistant manager of a Bank, they're waiting for me. I only came here to show a business friend from abroad round the Cathedral." "Well," said the priest, reaching out his hand to K., "then go." "But I can't find my way out alone in this darkness," said K.

K.'s was indeed the tragic dilemma of the person who could not find his way alone in the darkness and who insisted that only others could guide him. He sought help but he rejected the only help the priest could offer him. Out of his own dilemma he could not understand the priest.

He asked, "Don't you want anything more to do with me?" "No," said the priest. "You were so friendly to me for a time," said K., "and explained so much to me, and now you let me go as if you cared nothing about me." "But you have to leave now," said the priest. "Well, yes," said K., "you must see that I can't help it." "You must first see that I can't help being what I am," said the priest. "You are the prison chaplain," said K., groping his way nearer to the priest again; his immediate return to the Bank was not so necessary as he had made out; he could quite well stay longer. "That means I belong to the Court," said the priest. "So why should I make any claims upon you? The Court makes no claims upon you. It receives you when you come, and it relinquishes you when you go."

The priest made it quite clear that his attitude was the opposite of authoritarianism. While he wanted to help K. out of love for his fellow men, he himself had no stake in the outcome of K.'s case. K.'s problem, in the priest's view, was entirely his own. If he refused to see, he must remain blind—because no one sees the truth except by himself.

What is so confusing in the novel is the fact that it is never said that the moral law represented by the priest and the law represented by the court are different. On the contrary, in the manifest story the priest, being the prison chaplain, is part of the court system. But this confusion in the story symbolizes the confusion in K.'s own heart. To him the two are one, and just because he is not able to distinguish between them, he remains caught in the battle with the authoritarian conscience and cannot understand himself.

One year elapsed after K. had the first inkling of his arrest. It was now the evening before his thiry-first birthday and his case had been lost. Two men came to fetch him for the execution. In spite of his frantic efforts, he had failed to ask the first question. He had not found out what he was accused of, who accused him, and what was the way to save himself.

The story ends, as so many dreams do, in a violent nightmare. But while the executioners went through the grotesque formalities of preparing their knives, K. had for the first time an insight into his own problem. "I always wanted to snatch at the world with twenty hands, and not for a very laudable motive, either. That was wrong, and am I to show now that not even a whole year's struggling with my case has taught me anything? Am I to leave this world as a man who shies away from all conclusions? Are people to say of me after I am gone that at the beginning of my case I wanted it to finish, and at the end of it wanted it to begin again? I don't want that to be said."

For the first time K. was aware of his greediness and of the sterility of his life. For the first time he could see the possibility of friendship and human solidarity:

His glance fell on the top story of the house adjoining the quarry. With a flicker as of a light going up, the casements of a window there suddenly flew open; a human figure, faint and insubstantial at that distance and that height, leaned abruptly far forward and stretched both arms still farther. Who was it? A friend? A good man? Someone who sympathized? Someone who wanted to help? Was it one person only? Or were they all there? Was help at hand? Were there some arguments in his favor that had been overlooked? Of course there must be. Logic is doubtless unshakable, but it cannot withstand a man who wants to go on living. Where was the Judge whom he had never seen? Where was the High Court, to which he had never penetrated? He raised his hands and spread out all his fingers.

While all his life K. had been trying to find the answers, or rather to be given answers by others, at this moment he asked questions and the right questions. It was only the terror of dying that gave him the power to visualize the possibility of love and friendship and, paradoxically, at the moment of dying he had, for the first time, faith in life.

Notes

1. This and all subsequent quotations are from Franz Kafka, *The Trial*, definitive edition revised, translated by Willa and Edwin Muir (New York: Knopf 1937). Copyright 1937, © 1956 and renewed 1965 by Alfred A. Knopf, Inc. Reprinted by permission of the publisher.

2. See the description of the receptive orientation in the author's *Man for Himself* (New York: Rinehart, 1947).

3. See the chapter on humanistic and authoritarian conscience in *Man for Himself.*

18.

Psychoanalytic Notes on Franz Kafka

Margarete Mitscherlich-Nielsen

TO MANY OF FRANZ KAFKA'S READERS his works seem strangely "abstracted," like exact and detailed descriptions of a world that yet remains oddly remote. Had Kafka been a writer of less extraordinary gifts, he could not have found images and descriptive devices for processes that so many people sense obscurely within themselves; one would probably shrink back from his texts with their depictions of cruelty, torture, and desolation.

A great deal of research has been done and a great deal written about Kafka. Much of the interest he provokes is prompted by the contradiction between the gentleness of the person and his excursions into cruel fantasies. The considerations I offer here may help to explain this puzzling ambiguity; they certainly do not claim to impart definitive insights. At most they are reflections on the ways in which individual and collective traumata may have influenced the course of Kafka's life and the development of his talent. In this essay, I have been concerned mainly with his biography and have drawn on his letters and diaries and on his

From paper presented to the Freiburg Psychoanalytisches Seminar in 1976 and originally published in *Psyche* (1977), no. 31, pp. 60–83; also in *Psychocultural Review* (1979), 3 (1):1–24. Translated by Beverley R. Placzek. Copyright © 1979 Margarete Mitscherlich-Nielsen. Reprinted by permission.

literary work primarily in order to understand his conflicts and the way in which, psychically, he dealt with experience.

Naturally, attempts of this sort also involve some transmutation of the texts by the person who reads them: inevitably one brings one's own particular turn of mind to bear in choosing among them, absorbing, understanding, and interpreting them. Any assimilation of a written text, whether a work of literature or a psychoanalytic case description, is subject to the specific defensive attitudes, expectations, and fantasies of the analyst or critic. The more willing one is to acknowledge and recognize that there is ultimately no such thing as an objective critique, nor in fact any total psycho-physical reality that is not subjectively perceived and processed, the less likely one will be to succumb to pseudo-factuality or rationalization.

The interpretative method I use is based on perceptions deriving from psychoanalytic practice and the direct observation of children and adolescents. Some people will condemn this procedure, since the analysand's transference, which normally serves as a guideline and corrective, is not available to the analyst who attempts to interpret literary works and biographical information. Clearly, psychoanalytic interpretation of literary texts—that is, the distillation of their unconscious and symbolic meaning—compares only to a limited extent with the work of clinical interpretation. In the treatment situation, how one interprets the material presented by the analysand is determined in a way characteristic to psychoanalysis by the sound of the voice, the mood, the body-posture, etc. accompanying it, as well as by the feelings and associations it evokes in the analyst. The analysand's transference and the analyst's countertransference serve to sharpen perception of the unconscious meanings in the clinical-analytic "text." For all its unavoidable repetition of fundamental conflicts and defensive attitudes, this text is constantly being transformed by the analyst's interpretations and the influence these exert on the analysand's relation to himself and to the analyst. Through the psychic interaction of the analytic partners that governs the analytic process, dimensions of empathy and understanding evolve which are simply not available for use in interpreting literary texts or biographical information. So it is not without some reason that we analysts are often asked how we justify stretching what we have learned from clinical analysis over onto such a different domain. In answer, we can only point out how fruitful many of the previous applications of psychoanalytic knowledge have been, starting with those of Freud himself. The analyst, using his understanding and intuition in a very specific way, strives to penetrate to the unconscious meanings of literary or biographical texts—texts which, moreover, are often complex and cryptic, the work of peculiarly articulate and usually highly sensitive people. In so doing, he may broaden the general understanding of how an individual psyche perceives and copes with private as well as collective events.

It is, I believe, chiefly this possibility, touching as it does also on the analyst's understanding of himself, which lures him over and over again to apply his learning in areas that lie beyond the boundaries of his clinical knowledge.

Thomas Mann said of Franz Kafka: "He was a dreamer and his compositions are often dreamlike in conception and form; they imitate the oppressive, illogical absurdity of dreams, those mysterious shadow-pictures of actual life, so exactly as to be laughable."[1] It is true. Like dreams, Kafka's works are illogical and timeless—although they remind one rather more of nightmares. The sober clarity, brevity, and realistic precision of the descriptions are in marked contrast to the unusual, fantastic, oppressive, cruel and painful, often incomprehensible contents of the stories. Ways of thinking and experiencing that as a rule stay buried deep in the unconscious are described with uncanny accuracy. And so, for all the apparent absurdity of what is depicted, the same feelings of weird reality are aroused in the reader as assail us at night when we dream—such feelings as also permeate the hallucinatory fantasies of children and psychotics. But in spite of the humor and irony of which Kafka was occasionally capable, these writings have little to do with laughter. Commenting in a letter to Kafka about *Meditation*, the Viennese poet Otto Stoessl finds it "full of very pertinent humor, turned inward as it were, . . . the humor of a healthy frame of mind."[2] Concerning which Kafka remarks to Felice: "He also writes about my book *(Meditation)* but with such a complete lack of understanding that for a moment I thought the book must be really good, since—even in a man as discerning . . . as Stoessl—it can create that kind of misunderstanding."[3] Kafka, like Rilke, D. H. Lawrence, and many others, was writing autobiography, although he was communicating his experience on another level. He called his story "Metamorphosis" an indiscretion.[4] With writing, he tried to give shape to his internal reactions, to his psychic efforts at working through his experiences, and to lay hold of the anxieties, fantasies and recollections emerging from his unconscious. By means of projective identification he was apparently able to transform himself into the personages of his stories and through them to express his misery, his pain, and his dread—and also his indifference, coldness, and hatred—far more accurately than he could ever have done in his real person or through his real object relations.

To him writing was "the most important thing in the world . . . the way his delusion is important to the madman."[5] Elsewhere, he alluded to "writing as a form of prayer."[6] In the end, however, all his attempts at curing himself by writing were unavailing to save him from the tuberculosis that brought about his early death. In a letter to Max Brod about the onset of his tuberculosis, he remarked: " 'Things can't go on this way,' said the brain, and after five years the lungs said they were ready to help."[7]

A review of Kafka's life, particularly of his childhood, may help us to gain access to his psychic structure and to his frequently puzzling behavior. Here I rely mainly on Klaus Wagenbach's carefully compiled biography of Kafka's youth; it is both more objective and more complete than that of Max Brod.[8] Kafka himself was aware of the bearing of his childhood and youth.

Kafka was born in Prague on July 3, 1883. His father, Hermann Kafka, had owned a notions and tailors' supplies store there since 1882. He was of Czech-Jewish proletarian origin. Hermann Kafka's father was a butcher; his family lived in very modest circumstances, often suffering actual want. Kafka's mother, Julie Loewy, was the daughter of a prosperous brewer and belonged to the wealthy and cultivated German-Jewish provincial middle class. Franz Kafka was born on the boundary between Prague's poverty-stricken Jewish ghetto and the richer middle-class Jewish quarter where his mother had lived before her marriage. His father had spoken Czech at home but sent his children to German schools, since in those days to belong to the small German upper class offered greater prospects of advancement. For Hermann Kafka, who in his childhood had suffered so many humiliations, to climb into the exalted realm of the bourgeoisie was the focus of all aspirations.

Franz was the oldest of six children. After him two brothers (Georg and Heinrich) were born, both of whom died in infancy, the one at a year and a half, the other at six months. Kafka experienced the birth and death of these two brothers between the time he was two and the time he was five. For his mother the psychic stress of the death of these two sons must have been particularly great, as she herself had early been exposed to traumatic experiences of loss. When she was three years old she had lost her mother, who died of typhus, and, when she was four, her grandmother had committed suicide. The work of mourning—which ultimately leads to the healing of psychic wounds left by the death of close relatives—is beyond the powers of a child that age. Often after such losses—as the findings of Martha Wolfenstein have shown[9]—a lurking notion is formed that "if I am as good and lovable as my parents expect, they will come back to me." Kafka's mother, who was the second oldest child and the only girl among five brothers, had early had to undertake the duties of a mother. This constellation probably reinforced her unconscious psychic need to be lovable in order to persuade the mother who had died to return. It may also be assumed that this was *one* of the reasons why, later, she was almost incapable of defending herself against the tyrannical emotional demands made on her by her husband. Since Hermann Kafka claimed his wife's total energy and concern, it is hardly likely that after the loss of the two sons he would have granted her adequate opportunity for her work of mourning, for a temporary withdrawal into herself and her grief.

The early death of his brothers and his mother's reaction to their loss—probably warding off emotion on the surface but deeply depressed beneath—must have had a profound effect on Kafka, to which, I think, insufficient consideration has been given. I see in it the beginning of his later psychic disturbances, his separation anxieties, his contact difficulties, death-wishes, and self-alienation. As we gather from her letter to Felice, his mother suffered very much over her son's way of life, which, she felt, was ruining his health. She was particularly attached to this her sole remaining son. Given her life history, one must assume that Kafka's abuse of his health aroused not only her concern but also great underlying anxiety and feelings of guilt. It is possible that unconsciously Kafka, by living as he did, wished to make her worry and grieve as much over him as she had over the brothers who had died.

When he was six years old, Kafka was sent to school. That same year a sister, Elli, was born; a year later another sister, Valli; and two years after that his youngest sister, Ottla, who later became his favorite. Those first years of his life must have been of traumatic importance for Kafka: he was exposed to the oppressive vitality of his father and had to endure the illness and death of his two brothers. At the same time his mother—on the basis, as we assume, of her own traumatization in early childhood—acquiescing totally in the social norm, yielded submissively to the tyranny of her husband. Kafka's own description of himself is of someone "whose education basically took place in a lonely, too cold or too hot boy's bed."[10]

Throughout his first years, external unrest was added to these inner perturbations. Kafka's parents, having moved to Prague, were constantly in search of an apartment and location for their shop that would be appropriate to the particular stage of their slow social climb. In seven years they moved at least four times.

As he remembers it, Franz was brought up essentially by a cook, a housekeeper and, later, by a governess. During the day his mother helped his father in the shop; in the evening she came home late, so that for days on end he hardly saw her at all.

He describes her as "illimitably good," but attributes to her "the part of a beater during a hunt" led by his father.[11] Surely this must mean that she was weak and that, for all her love and her desire to help, she was able neither to protect him effectively nor to respond to him emotionally according to his particular needs. That she tried to protect him—as she later did his sisters, too—from their irascible father is confirmed by numerous accounts. Nevertheless, it is obvious that the relationship to her husband, the need to placate his ever-impending fits of anger, remained always at the center of her interest and endeavors.

Although he had few real learning difficulties in school, subjectively Kafka suffered from the feeling that his boundless incapacity might be recognized at any moment, and he would be expelled. He started writing during the first years of high school (about 1897/1898). In this he encountered nothing but rejection or indifference from his father; and from most of the other members of the family, too (except now and again from his sisters), he got little understanding. His mother considered it a pastime, as her touching letter to F. B. shows. However, he did not leave off writing—almost the only activity that afforded him any sort of relief and happiness.

From his early childhood on, Franz Kafka was dogged by feelings of anxiety and loneliness. Later, he made a virtue of necessity: loneliness became for him the precondition for pursuing what he saw as "the most productive direction for my being to take"[12]—namely, writing.

275

But despite his timidity, his inner loneliness, despite what he himself described as his "coldly imaginative" nature,[13] Kafka was not as solitary as all that. We know that in his school days, there were already friendly contacts which meant a lot to him. With his sisters he could be spontaneous, even exuberant. He staged regular theatrical performances with them, read aloud to them and, while he was doing so, felt freer than at almost any other time. His intimate relation to his sister Ottla is well known. But even beyond the family there were always people who loved and admired him. His correspondence was widespread and in part of great intensity. His close friendship with Max Brod lasted till the end of his life. The warmth, mobility, and expressiveness of his features have often been described. And yet, what a classmate said of him was surely also accurate:

We were all very fond of him and thought highly of him, but we could never become quite intimate with him; somehow there was always a glass wall around him. With his quiet friendly smile he was open to the world but himself he kept shut away. . . . What has stayed in my mind is the picture of a tall, slight boyish person, who looked so quiet, who was kind and friendly, who gave generous recognition to everyone else, and yet himself somehow always remained remote and alien.[14]

His original intention had been to study literature, philosophy, and sociology after graduating from high school. But he soon gave that up and, probably in compliance with his father's wishes, settled on the study of law. This meant that—according to Kafka himself—he could remain indifferent, and required only "that in the few months before the exams, and in a way that told severely on my nerves, I was positively living, in an intellectual sense, on sawdust which had, moreover, been chewed for me in thousands of other people's mouths."[15] A year after passing the state law examination, he got a job at the Workers' Accident Insurance Institute. He stayed there, highly regarded by his colleagues and superiors, until his retirement a few years before his early death. He impressed all those who knew him as a particularly friendly, humorous, stable, and gentle person—characteristics that were in marked contrast to what he felt about himself and to what went on in his imagination. Only those close to him were given ample evidence of his tensions, anxieties, feelings of alienation and discontent. His relations to women, in particular, were overshadowed and almost always destroyed by his contradictory needs and feelings, his insoluble psychic conflicts, and his repetition compulsions—as one can see from his life history, his works, his diaries, and his letters.

In August 1914, when he was thirty-one years old, Kafka had to leave home for the first time. Although he felt extremely unhappy there, he would probably never have left of his own accord. Only the need to make room for his oldest sister and her children, who moved in with the parents during the war, induced him to look for a room outside the family home. None suited him; everywhere he was disturbed by noise. Only in his sister Ottla's house did he sometimes feel comfortable. Not until the last years of his life, and only because of his tuberculosis, did he manage to live away from Prague for a while. When, in 1917, he became ill, he felt it rather as a relief with regard to his inner distress: ". . . until finally, under the strain of the superhuman effort of wanting to marry . . . blood came from the lung."[16] From then on, he worked in the insurance company only sporadically, living either at his sister Ottla's house or with his parents in Prague. In 1923, he moved to Berlin for a short time.

Kafka never married. Twice he got engaged to Felice Bauer, but dissolved his engagement definitively after five years. A further attempted engagement, to Julie Wohrysek, also came to grief. And the course of his relationship with Milena Jesenska, which at first was extremely passionate, was also ultimately negative. He could always bear closeness only for a short time. In the second year of his friendship with Milena, her presence and even her letters threw him into such a state of inner agitation that he had to ask her neither to write to him nor to visit him. And yet he not only gave her his diaries to read, he also let her keep them. Slight discords were to him enormously important. In a letter to Milena, he describes his first sexual encounter with a shop-girl. She "had made a tiny repulsive gesture (not worthwhile mentioning), had uttered a trifling obscenity (not worthwhile mentioning),"[17] but this nevertheless prompted him to turn away from her abruptly after the second encounter.

His sexual relations to women were exceedingly difficult. His sister Ottla was probably the only woman whose presence had a soothing effect on him, whose tenderness and understanding were always welcome. In September 1917, he wrote to Max Brod: "I live with Ottla in a good minor marriage; marriage not on the basis of the usual violent high currents but of the small windings of the low voltages."[18] Or: "Ottla is

literally bearing me up on her wings through the difficult world."[19] Heinz
Politzer (1975) has shown us what Kafka meant by "the usual violent
high currents." In his diaries Kafka speaks of "coitus as punishment for
the happiness of being together."[20] Increasingly he turned Ottla into his
mother; in the year before his death he cried out for her, calling her his
"big mother." In September 1917, he wrote to Max Brod: "In any case,
my attitude toward the tuberculosis today resembles that of a child cling-
ing to the pleats of its mother's skirts."[21] In spite of his desperate attempts, Kafka did not succeed in marrying. To him sexuality was often
something that aroused anxiety, and in this the "trifling obscenity" played
a large part. He spoke of the "bursting sexuality of . . . women. Their
natural impurity."[22] That on the other hand the "obscenity" of sexuality
was particularly attractive to him made for insoluble conflicts. Many of
the women with whom he had sexual relations belonged to the lowest
social strata and were involved in sexual relations with several men; degradation was their daily bread. In the last year of his life he lived with
Dora Diamant, a young Eastern-European Jewess. Although she was
more than twenty years younger than he, she showed him a maternal
tenderness like that of his sister Ottla. We must perhaps assume that
only as a very sick man could he allow himself both to arouse and also
to accept a woman's maternal tenderness. At any rate, for the first time
he did not find the decision to marry and have children difficult. He
asked for Dora's hand and was surprised when the rabbi, to whom her
father went for advice, opposed this unequal marriage between a very
young woman and a mortally sick man without further explanation.

Looking more closely at the unvarying repetition of Kafka's conflicts
and at his specific—though mostly warded off—needs, we discover that
there is one trait they have in common, namely a repressed yearning for
a tender all-comprehending mother who would admire and protect him.
Though repressed, this yearning broke through again and again. The
desire for symbiotic fusion, which appears clearly in his longing for death,
was always reactivated when, in any intimate relation with a woman,
the first disappointments arose—which, given his over-sensitivity and
ambivalence, were almost inevitable. To protect himself against these
regressive tendencies, he exaggerated his need for solitude; this, to be
sure, led him back by roundabout routes symbolically to the womb, or
reinforced his identification with the mother. "This writing is the most
important thing in the world to me (in a way that is horrible to everyone

around me), . . . the way her pregnancy is important to a woman.[23] When disappointments and misunderstandings first started between him and Felice, he wrote to her: "I have often thought that the best mode of life for me would be to sit in the innermost room of a spacious locked cellar with my writing things and a lamp. Food would be brought and always put down far away from my room outside the cellar's outermost door. The walk to my food in my dressing gown, through the vaulted cellars, would be my only exercise. I would then return to my table, eat slowly and with deliberation, then start writing again at once. From what depths I would drag it up. Without effort."[24]

Kafka's biographers (Wagenbach, Brod, and many psychoanalytic authors) have concerned themselves chiefly with the oedipal and post-oedipal period in Kafka's development. They ascribe his disorders to his father's inability to understand the boy's feelings or they blame specifically his upbringing in a materialistically oriented family striving primarily for advancement and success. The schools, too, are blamed, where mean-minded nationalistic teachers, aiming solely at the transmission of concrete knowledge, offered little that was attractive. Also, the difficult maternal inheritance—there was much depression and eccentricity among the Loewys—has been drawn on to explain Kafka's psychic plight. Kafka himself repeatedly stressed that he belonged more to the Loewy side of the family than to the Kafkas. He attributed many of his problems to his Jewishness. He was vividly aware of the peculiar situation of the German-Jewish minority in Prague, their linguistic and personal isolation—they belonged neither to the Germans nor to the orthodox Jews: as Germans living in enmity with the Czechs and as Jews exposed to the anti-Semitism of the Germans. Kafka's father was interested in the Jewish religion only insofar as it served his upward-striving needs. It is impossible to estimate how much Kafka suffered from the dearth of believable ideals in his upbringing—a dearth which reinforced his feelings of inner emptiness and of his own meaninglessness and worthlessness.

Franz K.—like all small children—must have harbored death wishes toward rivals who deprived him prematurely of his mother's attention. When such wishes become reality—and both Franz's brothers died—they often contribute to lasting, deep-seated feelings of guilt. Guilt feelings that cannot be traced to any recognizable real cause play a salient role in Kafka's life and in his work. And here it should be remembered that his mother was herself already burdened by her own childhood experiences of loss, from which we may conclude that she had difficulty working through the death of those two sons. Kafka's identification with his mother—he himself becomes pregnant, gives birth to works—we see as resulting from his early temporary emotional loss of her. And identification with a depressive mother who was warding off her mourning also meant internalizing her depression.

There evolved that "systematic destruction of myself"—to quote Kafka on the consequences of his childhood experience—which he then continued under his own stage direction "like a horrible instrument of torture." Interest in torture, the transformation of agony into pleasure, is to be found frequently in his writing (in "The Penal Colony," as in the *Diaries*). "This morning, for the first time in a long time, the joy again of imagining a knife twisted in my heart."[25] "Yes, torturing is extremely important to me, I'm preoccupied with nothing but being tortured and torturing."[26] He suffered greatly from the fact that the basic emotions he felt toward people were fear, indifference, and cold-heartedness. The ability to feel pain and sorrow was therefore particularly important to him. "But we need books that affect us like a disaster, that grieve us deeply, like the death of someone we loved more than ourselves, like being banished into forests far from everyone, like a suicide. A book must be the axe for the frozen sea inside us."[27] He complained a great deal: "My peculiarity was not accorded any recognition." "All I felt was the injustice done to me, I went to bed sadly, and here were the beginnings of that hatred which has in a certain respect determined my life in relation to my family and hence my life as a whole."[28]

In Kafka's letter to his father, and also in his letters to Felice, it is impossible to overlook the fact that behind his self-reproaches there are accusations. In his famous letter, he accuses not only his father; because of his profound ambivalence, he does not spare his mother either. "So we find the key to the clinical picture: we perceive that the self-reproaches are reproaches against a loved object which have been shifted away from it onto the patient's own ego."[29] As in the melancholiac, in Kafka too, object relations are built up on a narcissistic basis. What has taken place is "an identification of the ego with the object that has been relinquished . . . so that the object-cathexis, when obstacles come in its way, can regress to narcissism."[30]

In a conversation with Janouch, Kafka declared: "Love always inflicts wounds which never heal, because love always appears hand in hand with filth."[31] In spite of this negative statement, his sexual needs were at times very strong. We know of frequent visits to brothels and to prostitutes. With Max Brod he often visited nightclubs where relationships to semi-prostitute girls of the lower classes were initiated.

Sometimes, as he writes to Max Brod, the body of almost every girl tempted him; then again he tells of wandering through the streets of a red-light district and mentions that it was actually the older prostitutes to whom he was drawn, women who in daylight, when he watched them at their everyday tasks, were without any sexual attraction whatsoever. Occasionally—as in the novel *The Castle* where they are represented by Frieda—incestuous desires broke through. Also in "Fragments" there is a passage which is revealing in this regard: " 'Mother?' I asked, smiling. 'If you like—' she said. 'But you're much younger than Father, aren't you?' I said. 'Yes,' she said, 'much younger; he might be my grandfather and you my husband.' "[32]

For men like Kafka, according to White, oedipal desires are above all an expression of oceanic longings for union with the mother. Every woman, if she represented the mother for him, reawakened such longings; this also accounted for his inability to unite "pure" desexualized love with love that was "filthy" and sexual. There is plenty of evidence for Kafka's longing for symbiotic fusion. For instance, he wrote to Milena, whom at times he addressed as mother: "Last night I dreamt about you. What happened in detail I can hardly remember, all I know is that we kept merging into one another, I was you, you were me."[33] Unlike White, I believe that such desires served to ward off disappointments that were already setting in, and that they emerged in Kafka only when, for instance, Felice or Milena were unable to respond to him as he wished. Felice was quite clearly a transference figure who evoked extravagant hopes in Kafka. The letters he wrote to her in the first months remind one in some ways of Freud's exchange of letters with Fliess. Canetti speaks of "the dialogues that Kafka was conducting with himself by way of her."[34] To be sure—far more so than was ever true of Freud's relation to Fliess—Felice was for Kafka a highly ambivalently loved self-object. Kafka's relation to himself and his self-objects, which represent an internalizing of the early mother-child relation and its functions, was, as we know, extremely precarious. His earliest psychic structure was shaped by what he had internalized of the maternal functions. And because the mother's—presumed—latent depression was reinforced by the death of both his brothers, this was not conducive to the formation of any feeling of inner security or a strong ego. On the contrary, it is at the root of his self-hate. For him to have achieved a new beginning, more trusting internalizations of new relatinships would have required from Felice a degree of empathy of which few women would have been capable—and certainly not she.

In view of the content of several of Kafka's stories ("In the Penal Colony," *The Castle*, "Metamorphosis," etc.) White's interpretation is persuasive. According to him, Kafka perceived the primal scene as a sadistic act in which the mother was wounded or in the course of which the parents destroyed one another. Often, in his diaries, intercourse is described as a sadistic battle. "One of the most effective means of seduction that Evil has is the challenge to struggle. It is like the struggle with women which ends in bed."[35] Pregenital sadistic impulses also undoubtedly contributed to making the sex act so anxiety-provoking and so unsatisfying to Kafka.

Many people took Kafka's world to be a vision of what later was to befall the Jews in Hitler's camps and crematoria. Kohut sees in Kafka's works the depiction of a world increasingly incapable of compassion.[36] Kafka's descriptions of an alienated, unfathomable, incomprehensible, and unreal world represent—according to Kohut—the predominant psychic problems with which the man of tomorrow will have to cope. Kohut speaks of narcissistic disturbances such as those shown by Kafka, of a fragmentation of the self, as being caused by the false empathy of self-objects (the primary relational figures, most often the parents). The narcissistically damaged person is unable to free himself from these pathogenic and later internalized self-objects. All subsequent interpersonal relations are sucked into their wake. The respective objects are not perceived as having an independent existence but as a part of the self. In the "Letter to his Father,"[37] it becomes apparent that for Kafka both parents represent externalized, warded-off components of his own personality. The attempts he made to use friends as "bridges to the world" in order not to sink completely into his own narcissistic world were not always successful: his childhood friend Oskar Pollak (to whom he once wrote, "For me, you were, along with much else, also something like a window through which I could see the streets"[38]) found himself, in contrast to Max Brod, unable to fulfill this task.

Hypochondriacal anxieties indicating a fragmentation of the self were marked in Kafka: he suffered from a fear that he would lose his hair, that he would lose his eyesight; a slightly deformed toe was the source of numerous complaints; he was possessed by fear of infection, etc. The complaints with which he plagued Brod, Felice, and others were infinite; his chronic sleeplessness and frequent fierce headaches are well known. The excessive sensitivity of his skin and his exaggerated sensitivity to noise also gave him trouble. All these symptoms became unbearably intensified when he tried to tie himself to a woman. As he wrote: "This manifests itself in the fact that from the moment when I make up my mind to marry I can no longer sleep, my head burns day and night, life can no longer be called life. I stagger about in despair. . . . It is the general pressure of anxiety, of weakness, of self-contempt."[39] This was true for Felice and perhaps also for Julié, but no longer for Dora. Upon closer examination, it would seem that this state was the consequence of disappointed expectations of which he himself was not conscious. We might say, with Kohut, that because his "narcissistic-exhibitionistic" needs "were lacking in adequate confirming responses ("mirroring")," Kafka's evolving self received an insufficient amount of that narcissistic cathexis which normally produces reassurance and "the cohesion of the self."[40] His urge to fill the inner void in order to feel that he was alive thus became unduly strong. At times, even in the very earliest years of his childhood, Kafka felt that alienation and coldness which later, in tones of inner loathing and bitter complaint, he confided to his diary. And yet, at the same time, he also wrote: "In me, by myself, without human relationship, there are no visible lies. The limited circle is pure."[41] The wish to be alone, not to have to endure the "filth" of intimate relations, the desire to descend into the depths of himself remained throughout his life a defense mechanism which fostered his productivity as an author. "I can still have passing satisfaction from works like 'A Country Doctor,' provided I can still write such things at all (very improbable). But happiness only if I can raise the world into the pure, the true, the immutable."[42] Apparently only Ottla and Dora were able to adopt toward him an attitude of maternal understanding and closeness that evoked no conflicts but soothed him and stabilized his self-esteem.

Does this mean that in Kafka creativity—"truly original thought"— was (as Kohut assumes of all creativity) nourished mainly by self-grandiosity rather than by idealizing narcissistic energies? Was it, in him, a narcissistic neurosis which evolved out of a narcissistic deficit, a lack of narcissistic "mirroring"? Or were early conflicts in him, too, the source of his feelings of alienation? Unlike Kohut, White depicts Kafka's narcissistic development as resulting from serious conflicts with his father. Kernberg, too, sees a close connection between narcissism and object-related conflicts. He holds that in particular very early, deep-seated, conflict-laden aggressions lead to the development of narcissistic personality disorders. Again according to White, in "The Judgment" Kafka reveals the two conflicting sides of his personality, the friend in Russia standing for total withdrawal and pure narcissism and Georg for the component in Kafka's make-up which attempted to overcome his lack of contact by marrying Felice Bauer. The father fixation of his withdrawn self, the yearning for his father hidden behind his isolation, are projected onto the father: it is the father who yearns for the friend who has emigrated to Russia. Kafka's submerged homosexual desires can be expressed only through projection: he has the father rage against his own fiancée. In "The Judgment," as in "Metamorphosis," the son is at first portrayed as the strong one who gives support to the weak father. However, all this soon proves to be deceptive and the relationships are reversed. As the son grows weaker, the father grows strong, in fact, almost omnipotent. In both stories, by destroying himself, the hero strengthens the family. But at the same time, as is particularly clear in "The Judgment," he savors his self-destruction and the implicit accusation against the people closest to him or against "the ones up there." Thus, suicide is not shown primarily as deserved self-punishment nor simply as an act of aggression against the self which basically is aimed at someone else, as Freud regarded it. What is in the foreground in Kafka's case is the masochistic libidinization of suicide, and its significance as a yearning for reunification with the mother. In a remark addressed to Brod, Kafka compared suicide to "a powerful ejaculation."

I should like here to discuss narcissism above all as a developmental stage, in order to substantiate my view of the genesis of Kafka's psychic distress. Roughly speaking, the narcissistic phase encompasses the period when the child is as yet unable to distinguish between the self and the object. At about eighteen months, the internalization of the mother, that is, self- and object-representations, have been established to the point where, with the help of slowly evolving object constancy, the child learns to endure temporary separations from the mother. (I refer the reader here to the investigations of Mahler and Furer, René Spitz, James and

Joyce Robertson.)[43] The development of a stable sense of one's own worth also depends on the maturity and inner consistency of the self-representations.

In his second year, Kafka experienced his mother's pregnancy and the birth of a younger brother. It is to be assumed that during this period his mother, who was greatly overtaxed in every respect, must have neglected him to a considerable degree—at least emotionally. And the disturbance in his contacts and internalizations probably became deeper with the birth of the second brother and the death of both brothers in the course of the following three years. Kafka's later psychopathology bears the earmarks of a disturbance in the separation-individuation phase such as Mahler describes. The inability to mourn, and thus the inability gradually to free himself from the primary objects in order to enter into new object relations, determined his behavior throughout his life. He could not break away from his parents, was unable to marry, and suffered inordinately from anxiety, a profound lack of self-confidence, preoedipal aggressions, and fixations. In his object relations—despite all his kindness and friendliness—he remained focused upon himself. At intervals the boundaries between self and object became blurred without, however, there ever being any psychotic misapprehension of reality. The response evoked by conflicts between the wish for surrender and the need for direct contact on the one hand, and an easily aroused ambivalence on the other, was a regressive desire for fusion or narcissistic retreat. Aggressions were sexualized, and he sought to cope with losses by means of conflict-laden identifications. His self-centeredness, his almost unfulfillable hopes, and his ambivalence problems had their greatest effect on his relations to women. I assume that his father, who in spite of his tyrannical moods was probably more spontaneous in his contacts, should for Kafka have replaced the depressive mother. Statements in which he compares his writing to pregnancy or birth may be interpreted as restitution wishes aimed at recalling his two brothers to life or as attempts, by identification with his mother, to master his dependence on this all-powerful being.

But what then accounts for the widespread effect of Kafka's stories? Almost all of them communicate something uncanny, cruel, or incomprehensible, and many of them end with the hero's committing suicide or being tortured to death. White tries to show that notwithstanding all the cruelty, confusion, and torment, these stories provide a secret fulfillment of libidinal drives. Thus, for Kafka, death symbolizes a sexual culmination, representing the fulfillment both of masochistic homosexual impulses ("The Judgment") and of oceanic wishes for fusion. However, it seems to me that White overlooks the fact that this very sort of fantasized drive fulfillment served as a defense against anxiety-producing early death wishes against his brothers and, later, against his father. Furthermore, these fantasies were meant to cope with the overwhelming separation- and annihilation-anxieties that arose when these younger brothers became ill and died, and his mother—in consequence of these events—withdrew from him emotionally. The father showed no sympathy for the situation of mother and child; on the contrary, he made matters worse by his egocentric lack of understanding. This, in my view, furnished the source of Kafka's conflicts and the disturbances in his capacity to relate, as well as of the warped instinctual development with which they were combined.

Kafka, like so many artists before and after him, was unable throughout his life to solve the conflict between dependence and the desire to be alone. He evidently did not manage to build up a transitional object in the sense of a creative unification of contradictory urges, to integrate his need for dependence with his need for autonomy. He remained locked into an endless repetition of self-destructive defenses against infantile traumata and the regressive or perverse drive-fulfilling fantasies and unbridgeable disturbances of communication that resulted. And yet, insofar as it could be converted into writing, his repetition compulsion did not have the senseless unvarying character of traumatic neuroses. By means of new, brilliantly conceived imagery and fantasies, which also reached out to touch the fantasies of numerous readers, he was able to depict the incurable misunderstandings between himself and his surroundings, and in particular between himself and his parents. By writing down what even to him was uncanny and almost incomprehensible and in this way setting up a communication with potential readers, the inner void from which at other times he suffered so often and so bitterly was filled, so that in the periods when he was productive he could feel almost happy.

That nevertheless in his will he demanded the destruction of most of his work may be an expression of the fact that ultimately, from his point of view, all his attempts at coping with his unresolved guilt problems, his aggression and his inability to love, to overcome his self-alienation, to lift the world into the realm of "the pure, the true, and the immutable" had remained unavailing.

A nightmare is formed, Freud holds, when within the dream itself the fulfillment of forbidden desires is punished by anxiety. As in a nightmare, Kafka's stories, too, evoke sufficient anxiety in the reader to permit the return of forbidden instinctual impulses without overwhelming feelings of guilt developing. Furthermore, the omnipotence fantasies present in all Kafka's works compensate for the impotence of the victims. And the reader, by identification with the author, becomes master over the life and death of his negative heroes. Kafka, who accepted the value norms and lifestyles of his milieu without inwardly approving of or often even understanding them, suffered from a type of psychic self-alienation which is not uncommon and which can be set off by childhood experiences such as his. Deep-seated disturbances of contact with the primary relational figures are the rule in such cases. The masterly portrayal of the disturbances in his self-definition and of his inability either to defend himself against or to integrate internalizations which he felt to be false, explains, I believe, the widespread resonance Kafka has found among his readers. From unconscious to unconscious the understanding between author and reader is direct. But the nature of the description protects the conscious mind of the reader, keeps him from being overwhelmed by his own forbidden wishes, by unbearable anxieties and feelings of utter desolation.

Notes

1. Quoted in Klaus Wagenbach, *Franz Kafka in Selbstzeugnissen und Bilddokumenten* (Reinbek bei Hamburg: Rowohlt-Verlag, 1965), p. 144.

2. Franz Kafka, *Letters to Felice* (New York: Schocken Books, 1973), p. 178.

3. *Ibid.*, p. 177.

4. Originally, Kafka had intended to group the stories "The Stoker," "The Judgment," and "Metamorphosis" in a single volume to be entitled *The Sons.* Later, Kafka wanted to put "The Judgment," "Metamorphosis" and "The Penal Colony" together under the title *Punishment.* One has the impression that his productivity increased with his need for punishment following the dissolution of his first engagement to Felice Bauer: soon thereafter, in August 1914, he began work on *The Trial*, then, in October 1914, among other things he wrote "The Penal Colony." Only upon his renewed attempts to marry did the kind of self-destruction that was so crippling to his productivity re-emerge, the "years of

torment, the terrible double life, from which probably only insanity will find a way out." Klaus Wagenbach, *Franz Kafka: Eine Biographie seiner Jugend, 1883– 1912* (Berne, Switzerland: Franke-Verlag, 1958), p. 151.

5. Frank Kafka, *Letters to Friends, Family, and Editors* (New York: Schocken Books, 1977), p. 323.

6. Kafka, *Dearest Father* (New York: Schocken Books, 1954), p. 312.

7. Kafka, *Letters*, p. 138.

8. Wagenbach, *Franz Kafka: Eine Biographie*; M. Brod, *Franz Kafka: A Biography* (New York: Schocken Books, 1960).

9. Martha Wolfenstein, "How is Mourning Possible?" *The Psychoanalytic Study of the Child* (1966), 21:93–129.

10. *Letters*, p. 362.

11. *Dearest Father*, p. 157.

12. *The Diaries of Franz Kafka* (New York: Schocken Books, 1948), 1:211.

13. *Dearest Father*, p. 178.

14. Wagenbach, *Eine Biographie*, p. 269.

15. *Dearest Father*, p. 181.

16. *Ibid.*, p. 179.

17. Kafka, *Letters to Milena* (London: Secker & Warburg, 1953), p. 164.

18. *Letters*, p. 141.

19. *Ibid.*, p. 137.

20. *Diaries*, 1:296.

21. *Letters*, p. 138.

22. *Diaries*, 1:294.

23. *Letters*, p. 323.

24. Kafka, *Letters to Felice*, p. 156.

25. *Diaries*, 1:129.

26. *Letters to Milena*, p. 216.

27. *Letters*, p. 16.

28. *Dearest Father*, p. 203.

29. Sigmund Freud, "Mourning and Melancholia," *Collected Works*, Standard Edition (London: Hogarth Press, 1916), 14:248.

30. *Ibid.*, p. 249.

31. G. Janouch, *Conversations with Kafka* (New York: New Directions, 1971), p. 179.

32. *Dearest Father*, p. 282.

33. *Letters to Milena*, p. 207.

34. E. Canetti, *Kafka's Other Trial: Letters to Felice* (New York: Schocken Books, 1974), p. 15.

35. *Dearest Father*, p. 35.

36. H. Kohut, "The Future of Psychoanalysis," *Annual of Psycho-analysis* (1975), 3:325–340.

37. *Dearest Father*, pp. 138–196.

38. *Letters*, p. 9.

39. *Dearest Father*, pp. 189–190.

40. H. Kohut, "Thoughts on Narcissism and Narcissistic Rage," *The Psychoanalytic Study of the Child* (1972), 27:370, 362.

41. *Diaries*, 1:300.

42. *Ibid.*, 2:187.

43. M. S. Mahler and Manuel Furer, *On Human Symbiosis and the Vicissitudes of Individuation* (New York: International Universities Press, 1968); M. S. Mahler, "On the First Three Subphases of the Separation-Individuation Process," *International Journal of Psycho-Analysis* (1972), 53:333–38; Mahler, "Symbiosis and Individuation: The Psychological Birth of the Human Infant," *The Psychoanalytic Study of the Child* (1974), 29:89–106; Mahler, F. Pine, and A. Bergman, *The Psychological Birth of the Human Infant* (New York: Basic Books, 1975); Renée A. Spitz, *No and Yes: On the Genesis of Human Communication* (New York: International Universities Press, 1957); Mahler, *A Genetic Field Theory of Ego Formation: Its Implications for Pathology* (New York: International Universities Press, 1959); Mahler and G. Cobliner, *The First Year of Life* (New York: International Universities Press, 1965); Mahler, "The Evolution of Dialogue," in Max Schur, ed., *Drive, Affects, Behavior*, (New York: International Universities Press, 1965), 2:170–90; James and Joyce Robertson, "Young Children in Brief Separation: A Fresh Look," *The Psychoanalytic Study of the Child* (1971), 26:264–315.

19.

Kafka and the Mice

Ronald Hayman

READING THROUGH KAFKA'S published work in roughly chronological order, I soon saw that there could be no question of separating fiction from introspection. For Kafka, storytelling was one way—not easy, but less difficult than others—of talking to himself about himself. He wrote fragments of narrative into his diary, and it would be impossible to separate external events from fictional elaborations of them, or dreams and fantasies from stories. The confusion is a prerequisite of the lucidity he achieves. Inside the maze he chalks wonderfully clear lines on the ground, but only by dint of keeping his eyes off the walls. It would be pointless to inquire what they are made of.

The earliest surviving attempt to distill abjection into allegory occurs in a letter Kafka wrote when he was nineteen years old. (Because it was in a letter he could not destroy it, as he did other early fictions.) The alter ego is so ashamed of his height that he sits with his legs dangling outside the window. With clumsy, skinny, spidery fingers, he is knitting woollen socks, almost skewering his gray eyes on the needles. A well-dressed visitor jabs him, as he speaks, in the stomach, but when he is left alone he weeps, perhaps from self-pity, wiping his eyes with the socks that he is knitting.

Kafka's letters contain (at a rough guess) fifty times as many words as the fiction published with his consent, and they constitute the only

From *Partisan Review* (1981), 48(3):355–65. Copyright © 1981 *Parisan Review*. Reprinted by permission.

part of his oeuvre that does not pose the problem: Whom was he writing for? After showing his work to Oskar Pollak, who was his closest friend when he was twenty, he went on writing in secret for several years. He had met Brod in 1902 but did not show him any of his work or even admit that he was writing until about 1906, and Brod could not remember being allowed to read any of it until 1909.

Not that Kafka was writing entirely for himself in the stories or entirely for his correspondents in the letters. As with a forty-page letter to his father, which he never delivered, he compulsively sketched gestures of communication, only to leave them uncompleted. Perhaps he was writing to the people (and especially to the women) who looked at him with an indifference he found intolerable. It was too painfully reminiscent of the childhood in which his mother had had unlimited time for her husband but almost none for her son. There is a revealing passage in "Wedding Preparations in the Country" when the narrator, who is not a writer or involved in storytelling, reflects about how much easier it is to tell a story about oneself in the third person than in the first. The word "story" occurs to him when he sees a woman looking at him or perhaps just looking in his direction. If only he could explain everything to her. "But all the work one does gives one no right to expect loving treatment from everybody, on the contrary, one's alone, quite remote, and only an object of curiosity." The non sequitur is never brought into focus, but the fantasy behind it is that if only the woman could be made to listen, if only everything could be explained to her, nothing about him would strike her as odd or unlovable. Later the same fantasy and the same need would drive Kafka to write over a quarter of a million words of self-explanation to Felice Bauer. Physically she did not attract him, and most of the time he did not want her physical presence, but not having her love was almost unbearable.

Perhaps the question "Whom was he writing for?" is a secondary one. What mattered was to keep writing, even if what he wrote was never read again, even by himself. Writing was a means of protecting himself by splitting himself into two halves. One half can go out and take all the risks, while the other half stays safe and snug, hiding under the bedclothes. Raban—the name (raven) hints at his relation to Kafka (*kavka* means jackdaw)—can do what Kafka did as a child: "I can send my body with clothes on. If it totters out through the door of my room, the tottering betrays not fear but its nothingness. Nor is it excitement if it stumbles on the steps, travels sobbing into the country, and eats its evening meal there in tears. For I myself am all this time in bed, tucked up cosily under the yellow-brown blanket. . . . For I'm still dreaming." This is comparable to what, for the schizophrenic, can feel like a separation between self and body. The real self is held back so violently that it comes to feel disembodied, while the body becomes the center of what D. W. Winnicott calls "the false self." The disembodied self is confined to purely mental activity, while the body can go out and confront other people, without jeopardizing the integrity of the real self. But for Kafka, the self that stays behind is the one in the greater danger, having no solid corporality to protect it from the magical transformations that imagination can induce. "I have, as I lie in bed, the form of a large beetle, a stag-beetle or a cock-chafer, I believe. . . . Then I'd pretend it was a matter of hibernating, and press my little legs to my paunchy body. And whisper a few words, instructions, to my sad body, which is close by me, and crooked. I've soon finished. It bows, goes hastily and it will do everything as well as can be, while I rest." This is from "Wedding Preparations," written seven years before *Metamorphosis*. He has split himself like an amoeba: the self to be asserted is detached from the self that abdicates.

That Kafka's father played a leading role in inducing this anxiety is cogently suggested by the forty-page letter written when Kafka was thirty-three years old. As evidence the letter is valid but incomplete, not because it leaves the father's view out of account—it does not—but because it ignores the anti-Semitism which tended to foster guilt feelings and played a part in habituating Kafka to siding against himself. In 1882, the year before he was born, a professor of theology at Prague University published an article maintaining that the Jews were committed by their religion to working for the destruction of all Christians and all their property. The slander was repeated in a book, August Rohling's *Der Talmudjude*, and in a spate of rabidly anti-Semitic leaflets, which coincided with the first in a series of damaging allegations that Jews were perpetrating ritual murder. In 1883 there was a trial in Tisz-Eszlar, a Hungarian village, where Jews were accused of slaughtering a Christian girl. Allegations of ritual murder followed at irregular intervals. One of the most damaging was made in 1899 when an unemployed Jew, Leopold Hilsner, was indicted for killing Anežka Hrůzová at Polná, in northeastern Bohemia. The idea that her blood had been used in Passover matzos was encouraged in pamphlets, newspaper articles, and speeches, especially after the post mortem reports that the body had lost large quantities of blood. In October mobs rampaged through the old city in Prague, overturning stalls and attacking shops, while similar incidents occurred in many Moravian towns. In Prague Jews were attacked on the streets, windows were broken in their shops and houses; when Kafka was nearly ten, a servant girl's body was found in the Elbe near Kolin, where his uncle Philip lived, and rumor had it that her Jewish master and his friends had murdered her in order to use her blood in the matzos. Rioting ensued. As the grandson of a ritual slaughterer (*schochet*) Kafka must have been particularly sensitive to the anti-Jewish hysteria whipped up by the allegation; seventeen years later when he read Arnold Zweig's play *Ritualmord in Ungarn* (*Ritual Murder in Hungary*), he was reduced to tears. Based loosely on the Hilsner scandal, the play centers on a boy who falsely denounces his father and coreligionists. Finally he knifes himself in a synagogue. Kafka's vegetarianism may have had one of its roots in revulsion at the idea of his father's father's daily activity— ritually slitting the throats of animals, hacking up their bodies, feeding his family with money earned from butchering. The butcher's knife will be recurrent in Kafka's nightmares, daydreams, and fictions. "The regular diet of my imagination is fantasies like this one: I'm lying outstretched on the floor, sliced up like roast meat, and with my hand I am slowly pushing a slice towards a dog in the corner." He also started to write a story himself about ritual murder in Odessa but destroyed the manuscript. But anti-Semitic incidents are virtually never mentioned in Kafka's diaries or letters, even when he is attempting an exhaustive catalog of childhood events that caused psychological damage.

If he had the feeling that he was constantly "under surveillance," it must have been partly because of these, though mainly because his nagging father never desisted for long from his diatribe. Humiliatingly denounced, even in the presence of friends and strangers, Kafka retained the feeling he'd had as a child of being arbitrarily condemned and punished without having done anything wrong. This sense of being guilty and innocent at the same time was shared, to some extent, by other potential victims of anti-Semitism, caught as they were in the crossfire between pan-Germanism and Czech nationalism.

Like K. in *The Castle*, Kafka would never be able to graft himself into local society; nor could he seal himself off from it:

The forsaken solitary who still wants now and then to attach himself somewhere, the man who, depending on the time of day, the changing state of the weather, of his business, and so on, may need to catch sight of a friendly arm, he could cling to—he can't hold out for long without a window looking out on the street. And if he feels no desire for anything at all, and only, as a weary man, leans on his window-sill with his gaze shifting between sky and passers-by, if he wants nothing and his head's slightly thrown back, even then the horses below will draw him down into their traffic of carts and noise, so ultimately into human concord. ("The Street Window")

Windows and doors are abnormally important in Kafka's work because he could never feel proprietorial about space: it was always a matter of surveying alien territory or trespassing on it. He often daydreamed about leaving Prague, but until he was thirty-one years old he never managed (except for a few months in 1914 when there was no room for him) to move out of his parents' flat into a room of his own. His bedroom was like a corridor. His parents had to walk through it to get from the living room to their bedroom, and if his mother saw Kafka's jacket hanging up with a letter sticking out of the pocket, she was quite liable to fish it out and read it. She did that with one of Felice's letters, and then asked Felice to use her influence on Franz to make him eat more and sleep more.

I doubt whether anyone has been more sensitive to noise than Kafka was, and we will never quantify the agony he suffered from family shouting matches, laughter, doors slamming, taps running, household objects being dropped. There is the occasional pointer to this in the diaries, but except for one oblique remark—that he felt like vomiting when he saw the matrimonial bed, the bed linen no longer clean, the carefully laid out nightshirts—there is no pointer to the sound that must have been nearly unbearable. Hermann Kafka was not the sort of man who would feel obliged to respect his sensitive son's nervous system by inhibiting or even modifying the noises he wanted to make while coupling with his wife. We know the walls were thin enough for Kafka to hear if his father coughed in bed, so he must have heard a great deal besides coughing. Possibly that is one of the reasons he evolved the insane and exhausting routine of trying to sleep in the late afternoon after he had come home from the office and had something to eat. Then he tried to rouse himself into writing and go on until the small hours of the morning. Defying his congenital weakness, though only too aware of it, he was trying, in effect, to crowd two short days into every one. His routine was more comfortable and more productive when he found a room of his own in 1915, but as soon as he had the hemorrhage, just over two years later, he gave up trying to live on his own. For about eight months he stayed in the country with his sister Ottla, and after that lived with his parents again for five years. Apart from eight months in a mountain sanatorium and three more months with Ottla after she had married, he went on living in his father's flat until nine months before he died. So he could never feel that a house or a flat or even a room belonged to him. Throughout all the stints of freedom he had outside what he came to think of as a prison, it was always a mtter of living as Ottla's guest or renting a restricted space in somebody's else's property. He never even had a rented flat that was properly self-contained. This must have a lot to do with the way that Josef K. in *The Trial* knows himself to be under arrest though free to move from one place to another. And in *The Castle*, to stay in the village at all, K. has to be both devious and defiant. When he is given a job as caretaker in the school, he has to misuse space by sleeping in a classroom. When he tries to accost the castle official Klamm by waiting inside his sledge, he is like a frightened schoolboy steeling himself to go out of bounds. He can never feel "This space is mine. This is my territory." And neither could Kafka.

During office hours he was surrounded by non-Jews: it was exceptional for a Jew to be employed by the Workers' Accident Insurance Association. But from school days onwards, his friends, almost without exception, were Jewish. Even the sociable Brod had scarcely any non-Jewish friends. That Kafka was uneasy about this may be inferred from the critique he wrote in his diary (March 1911) of Brod's novel *Jüdinnen* (*Jewesses*). Kafka complains about the absence of non-Jewish observers to put the Jewishness into perspective, and, unflatteringly, he compares the Jewish ladies with lizards. However happy we are to watch an individual lizard on an Italian footpath, we'd be horrified to see hundreds of them crawling over each other in a pickle jar. There was no non-Jewish observer to put his social life into perspective.

Though he lived in a Jewish world, Kafka began by feeling himself to be an outsider to the Jewish religion. Its rituals, he wrote in 1911, were "on their very last legs . . . have only a historical character." On his rare visists to synagogue, he felt alienated from the Eastern European Jews, who were less assimilated than their Western coreligionists in manners, habits, clothing, hair style, and language. Most of the Easterners spoke Yiddish; the more orthodox still wore long sidelocks. Possibly Kafka's initial hostility to the work of Martin Buber was partly a hostility to Eastern Jews, for what Buber was doing in his books was presenting them to the West by translating into literature the oral tradition of Hassidic stories which merged religion, mysticism, and folklore. A turning point in Kafka's development as a writer and as a Jew was the arrival of the Yiddish actors in 1911. Their performances and his friendship with the leading actor, Yizchak Löwy, changed his attitude to the Yiddish language, to Jewish rituals, and to Hassidism. In 1912 he started reading books on Yiddish literature and Judaism, as well as attending events organized by the Bar Kochba society. By the time he met Buber in 1913, Kafka had already taken his first step—in *Metamorphosis*—towards the kind of animal legend he was to write later, a kind which has affinities with the Hassidic tales Buber had translated. Their influence on Kafka's work was merging with that of the Yiddish theater. And in December 1914 he wrote the legend of the doorkeeper, which he incorporated into *The Trial*. Despite the cathedral setting, the matrix of the story is Judaic. There is no description of the building in which the gate (Tor) is situated; all we are told is: "Before the law stands a doorkeeper," and what he says about other doorkeepers implies that the building is as large as a castle or a palace. In the upper world, according to some Cabalistic parables, there are seven palaces, each guarded by hosts of gatekeepers, and God sits at the highest point, surrounded by awesome mystery.

At the beginning of 1917 Brod wrote to Buber that Kafka was drifting "unawares into Judaism." In the spring Kafka wrote "The Great Wall of China" in a style that sometimes parodies Talmudic commentary. Though the wall never becomes a mere symbol for the Law, Kafka was now tackling the problem of how it was evolved, and at the same time writing a miniature history of the Jews in the Diaspora. One of Kafka's greatest enthusiasms in the last few years of his life was for the study of modern Hebrew, and his only symbiotic relationship with a woman was also a relationship with the traditions of Eastern European Judaism. Dora Dymant's father was an Orthodox Polish Jew and one of Kafka's earliest conversations with her culminated in her reading from Isaiah in Hebrew. Kafka's parents disapproved of her, looking down on her in the way most Western Jews looked down on Easterners, but with her help he found the courage to defy his father and live with her in

Berlin. Meeting Brod in August 1923, shortly before he left Prague, he read out the curses from Leviticus and said that he wanted *tefillin*, the phylacteries used by Orthodox Jews for prayers every morning except the Sabbath. And during 1923 he borrowed his parents' Hebrew prayerbook.

His struggle for faith was a struggle to salvage his existence even if his body was beyond repair. "Believing means: releasing what's indestructible, in the self, or better: releasing the self, or better: being indestructible, or better: being." He was reading the periodical *Der Jude* (*The Jew*) and taking pleasure in its antimaterialism. One writer called the Bible sacramental and the world excremental. We are separated from God, wrote Kafka, on two sides: by the Fall and by the Tree of Life. Paradise remains intact and immune to the curse laid on mankind. This was why "Human judgment of human actions is true and futile—first true and then futile."

In Kafka's last three years (1921–1924) the imagery of ghosts and spirits became recurrent in his writing. He seemed to be unaware of how much sediment the Yiddish plays had left in his imagination, and while the Hassidic tales and the Cabala were invaluable to his fiction, they had also dragged him back into premodern premises. Writing about his illness, Kafka often used transcendental language, suggesting—at least half seriously—that scientific concepts made the malaise harder to cure than the idea of possession did. Was it not still an open question whether weakness caused evil spirits to invade the body or whether "weakness and illness are already a stage in possession, the preparation of the human body as a bed for unclean spirits to copulate in"? At the same time he was thinking of himself as being personally assaulted by God. In his diaries God is never mentioned by name, but on the 10th or 11th of February, 1922, he wrote, "New attack by G." A few sentences later, reversing the image, he equates God not with the enemy but with the general who is leading the despairing multitudes through mountain passes no one else can find in the snow. Superstitious, he wanted to stop short of activating its potential. "We can't escape the ghosts we release into the world," he told Gustav Janouch. "Again and again evil returns to its point of departure." The same anxiety, no doubt, lay behind his instructions to Brod that all his writing must be destroyed. Dora Dymant testifies: "Time and again he said to me, 'I wonder if I've escaped the ghosts.'

. . . He wanted to burn everything he'd written in order to free his soul from these 'ghosts.' What he really wanted to write was to come afterwards, only after he had gained his 'liberty.' "

As Kafka says in one version—not finally used—of the opening to *The Castle*, "I've a difficult task in front of me, and I've dedicated my whole life to it. I do this gladly, without asking for pity from anyone. But because it's all I have—the task I mean—I ruthlessly reject anything that may distract me. I tell you, I can be mad in my ruthlessness." This may be too explicit, but a more decisive reason for suppressing it was that it points too revealingly at the correspondence between K.'s task and Kafka's. K.'s obsession about penetrating the castle reflects Kafka's relentless determination to go wherever his writing led him, to colonize as much as he could of the world inside his head, even if it meant defying the God who did not want him to write. His task involved him in besieging the forbidden castle, making contact with the Absolute, confronting the unconfrontable, looking God in the face and then doing his best to break the Second Commandment by constructing a graven image. He must defy all the doorkeepers.

In his last story "Josefine the Singer, or the Mouse People," the main focus is social. The narrator's primary interest is in the relationship between the prima donna and the people; one of Kafka's underlying concerns is with his own relationship with the Jewish people and Jewish culture. The mouse people is described as "nearly always on the move, scuttling to and fro for reasons that often aren't clear," and also as "not only childish but in some respects prematurely old, childhood and old age don't come to us as to others." Many of Kafka's Jewish contemporaries had also been deprived of a normal childhood and a normal maturity. But his links with the Jewish people were more negative than he would have liked; given respite from harassment, the mice dream "as if they could stretch and relax in the great warm bed of the community."

The mouse people had "always, somehow or other saved itself, though not without sacrifices which fill historical researchers with horror." (Who but Kafka could have compared Jews and mice so tellingly that the parable looks prophetic?) Perhaps one reason for Kafka's earlier antipathy towards Buber's rendering of Hassidic legends was that they implied a folkish solidarity; what embarrassed him now was awareness of his indebtedness to them. The only oblique acknowledgment occurs in this story: Josefine denies any connection between her art and folk-squeaking, smiling with brazen arrogance when anyone points out the similarity. But the story raises the question of whether Kafka may sometimes have wished his fiction to serve the same function as folk art (or as Yiddish theater): when the mass mouse audience listens attentively to Josefine, the squeaking "comes almost like a message from the people to the individual." Josefine believes that she protects the people. If her art does not drive away the evil, at least it gives others the strength to bear it. Kafka could not seriously believe that his fiction would have this effect, but he could seriously play with the idea.

PART V

TWO VIEWS

OF CARROLL

THERE ARE MANY INTERPRETATIONS of Lewis Carroll's works, and especially of his *Alice in Wonderland* and *Through the Looking-Glass*, but we have chosen two very different Freudian approaches—by the English literary critic William Empson and by the French psychoanalyst/philosopher Gilles Deleuze. Their premises are very divergent; the former relies on traditional analysis of themes, symbolism, and meanings, and the latter assimilates structural linguistics to his own preoccupations linking the language of schizophrenics to that of poets (both make up new words, frequently based on similarities and differences of sounds and sense). Deleuze's focus is on Alice's use of words, *non-sense* components of which he compares to Artaud's "breathscreams" and to the defensive and anti-phobic nature of schizophrenic "contraction"; he dismisses classical psychoanalysis as "content with designating cases, analyzing personal histories, or diagnosing complexes."

Empson finds too little psychoanalytic criticism of the Alices, attributing it to symbolism inviting interpretations in bad taste; the shift to the "*child*-become-judge" allowed the author to make covert judgments. He locates Darwinist ideas in Carroll's treatment of Alice's tears, and in the salt water which is "the sea from which life arose"; in the *Looking-Glass*, too, "there are ideas about progress at an early stage of the journey of growing up." Both books, Empson argues, "are topical; whether you call the result allegory or 'pure nonsense' it depends on ideas about progress and industrialization." Symbolism is employed subtly to show the contradictions in the social order, as well as in personal relations, and is particularly full of irony in Carroll's pictures of animals—whether the prince's dog, the snapdragon fly, or the gnat. Freudian themes are even stronger in connections between the death of childhood and the development of sex, and in those concerning new knowledge with its concomitant conflicts about growing up and remaining a child, of warding off death through eternal childhood. When the Alice stories are interpreted as dreams, Freudian themes—from falling into a hole to birth trauma, from fetus position to swimming in tears—abound. Symbolic pleasures, narcissistic indulgence, the desire to include all sexuality in the girl child, the cat representing intellectual detachment, and many more examples are given to indicate the constant presence of opposing impulses—in the work and in its creator. Social customs, assumptions, and class distinctions as well are examined from the child's perspective, upsetting conventions, particularly the upper-class convention of little girls as "creatures of such refinement that they could only live on weak tea with cream in it." The notions that "the perfect lady can gain all the advantages of contempt without soiling herself by expressing or even feeling it," and that the "life of highest refinement must be allowed a certain avid infantile petulance" are associated by Carroll with death, and loneliness. Virtue and intelligence are both lonely, concludes Empson, and hiding behind snobbery and good manners appears to obfuscate this fact, and to make life in our insane world possible.

Gilles Deleuze's Alice as well pictures the contradictions in modern society. Instead of focusing on oppositions within themes, such as manners, intelligence, customs, he emphasizes the oppositions themselves, and how the latter are expressed through language. In this way he finds new contradictions in the text, demonstrating the structuralists' notions of the openness of all texts. Deleuze's association of Lewis Carroll and Antonin Artaud itself builds on the notion that the reader's associations to existing texts make up for new texts which, in turn, draw on the cultural unconscious. The imaginative connections created by Deleuze himself, which allow him to elaborate on these two very different literary figures, and whose use of language Deleuze then compares to the language used by schizophrenics, make this essay an example of the best of French criticism. But insofar as this type of criticism relies more on the critic's associations than on literary traditions, or on the social and personal circumstances of the writer's life and development, its idiosyncratic components differentiate it from what literary criticism was thought to be all about. The emphasis on the use of words, and the fact that Artaud did translate Carroll—choosing the words in French—tends to legitimate Deleuze's argument, at least within the current French-oriented context. Artaud's assessment of Lewis Carroll as a "pervert, a minor pervert, who limits himself to the creation of a surface language and does not sense the true problem of language in its depth," is the theme Deleuze explores at length. Artaud's and Carroll's preoccupation with alimentary and excremental matters is associated with the frequent eating/speaking dualities of schizophrenics. Both Carroll and Artaud are known to have had mental breakdowns, thus prompting the customary questions about the role of mental illness in creativity. Yet, by concentrating on the language of the works, and particularly on the alliterations, double meanings, and non-sense syllables, that is, on phonetic elements which are then linked to both *language-affect* and *language-effect*, Deleuze manages to introduce another level of analysis—the linguistic level Lacan superimposes on traditional psychoanalysis. Simply put, Deleuze finds that language is changed, that through a series of transformations, "speaking has collapsed onto eating . . . non-sense has ceased to give meaning at the surface . . . that Being, which is nonsense, has teeth." Hence he can conclude that unlike other psychoanalytic criticism, which finds schizoid fragments either in Alice or in other surface elements of the stories, or that which concentrates only on the "depth" of Artaud's organ-oriented symbolisms, these authors must be treated as similar in their concerns and different in their means of expression. Deleuze "would not give one page of Antonin Artaud for all of Carroll. . . . [although] Carroll, on the other hand, remains the master . . . of surfaces [on which] the entire logic of meaning is held." In a way, this assessment, also, replicates the arguments between current Anglo-Saxon and French criticism—between description of emergent knowledge and the search for unconscious structures.

20.

Alice in Wonderland: The Child as Swain

William Empson

IT MUST SEEM a curious thing that there has been so little serious criticism of the Alices, and that so many critics, with so militant and eager an air of good taste, have explained that they would not think of attempting it. Even Mr. De la Mare's book, which made many good points, is queerly evasive in tone. There seems to be a feeling that real criticism would involve psychoanalysis, and that the results would be so improper as to destroy the atmosphere of the books altogether. Dodgson was too conscious a writer to be caught out so easily. For instance it is an obvious bit of interpretation to say that the Queen of Hearts is a symbol of "uncontrolled animal passion" seen through the clear but blank eyes of sexlessness; obvious, and the sort of thing critics are now so sure would be in bad taste; Dodgson said it himself, to the actress who took the part when the thing was acted. The books are so frankly about growing up that there is no great discovery in translating them into Freudian terms; it seems only the proper exegesis of a classic even where it would be a shock to the author. On the whole the results of the analysis, when put into drawing room language, are his conscious opinions; and if there was no other satisfactory outlet for his feelings but the special one fixed in his books the same is true in a degree of any original artist. I shall use psychoanalysis where it seems relevant, and feel I had better begin by saying what use it is supposed to be. Its business here is not to discover a neurosis peculiar to Dodgson. The essential idea behind the books is a shift onto the child, which Dodgson did not invent, of the obscure tradition of pastoral. The formula is now "*child*-become-judge," and if Dodgson identifies himself with the child so does the writer of the primary sort of pastoral with his magnified version of the swain. (He took an excellent photograph, much admired by Tennyson, of Alice Liddell as a ragged beggar girl, which seems a sort of example of the connection.) I should say indeed that this version was more open to neurosis than the older ones; it is less hopeful and more a return into oneself. The analysis should show how this works in general. But there are other things to be said about such a version of pastoral; its use of the device prior to irony lets it make covert judgments about any matter the author was interested in.

There is a tantalizing one about Darwinism. The first Neanderthal skull was found in 1856. *The Origin of Species* (1859) came out six years before *Wonderland*, three before its conception, and was very much in the air, a pervading bad smell. It is hard to say how far Dodgson under cover of nonsense was using ideas of which his set disapproved; he wrote some hysterical passages against vivisection and has a curious remark to the effect that chemistry professors had better not have laboratories, but was open to new ideas and doubted the eternity of hell. The 1860 meeting of the British Association, at which Huxley started his career as publicist and gave that resounding snub to Bishop Wilberforce, was held at Oxford where Dodgson was already in residence. He had met Tennyson in '56, and we hear of Tennyson lecturing him later on the likeness of monkeys' and men's skulls.

The only passage that I feel sure involves evolution comes at the beginning of *Wonderland* (the most spontaneous and "subconscious" part of the books) when Alice gets out of the bath of tears that has magically released her from the underground chamber; it is made clear (for instance about watering places) that the salt water is the sea from which life arose; as a bodily product it is also the amniotic fluid (there are other forces at work here); ontogeny then repeats phylogeny, and a whole Noah's Ark gets out of the sea with her. In Dodgson's own illustration as well as Tenniel's there is the disturbing head of a monkey and in the text there is an extinct bird. Our minds having thus been forced back onto the history of species there is a reading of history from the period when the Mouse "came over" with the Conqueror: questions of race turn into the questions of breeding in which Dodgson was more frankly interested, and there are obscure snubs for people who boast about their ancestors. We then have the Caucus Race (the word had associations for Dodgson with local politics; he says somewhere, "I never go to a Caucus without reluctance"), in which you begin running when you like and leave off when you like, and all win. The subtlety of this is that it supports Natural Selection (in the offensive way the nineteenth century did) to show the absurdity of democracy, and supports democracy (or at any rate liberty) to show the absurdity of Natural Selection. The race is not to the swift because idealism will not let it be to the swift, and because life, as we are told in the final poem, is at random and a dream. But there is no weakening of human values in this generosity; all the animals win, and Alice because she is Man has therefore to give them comfits, but though they demand this they do not fail to recognize that she is superior. They give her her own elegant thimble, the symbol of her labor, because she too has won, and because the highest among you shall be the servant of all. This is a solid piece of symbolism; the politically minded scientists preaching progress through "selection" and *laissez-faire* are confronted with the full anarchy of Christ. And the pretense of infantalism allows it a certain grim honesty; Alice is a little ridiculous and discomfited, under cover of charm, and would prefer a more aristocratic system.

In the *Looking-Glass* too there are ideas about progress at an early stage of the journey of growing up. Alice goes quickly through the first square by railway, in a carriage full of animals in a state of excitement about the progress of business and machinery; the only man is Disraeli dressed in newspapers—the new man who gets on by self-advertisement, the newspaper-fed man who believes in progress, possibly even the rational dress of the future.

> . . . to her great surprise, they all *thought* in chorus (I hope you understand what *thinking in chorus* means—for I must confess that *I* don't), "Better say nothing at all. Language is worth a thousand pounds a word."
>
> "I shall dream of a thousand pounds tonight, I know I shall," thought Alice.
>
> All this time the Guard was looking at her, first through a telescope, then through a microscope, and then through an opera-glass. At last he said, "You're travelling the wrong way," and shut up the window and went away.

This seems to be a prophecy; Huxley in the Romanes lecture of 1893, and less clearly beforehand, said that the human sense of right must judge and often be opposed to the progress imposed by Nature, but at this time he was still looking through the glasses.

But the gentleman dressed in white paper leaned forward and whispered in her ear, "Never mind what they all say, my dear, but take a return ticket every time the train stops."

In 1861 "many Tory members considered that the prime minister was a better representative of conservative opinions than the leader of the opposition" (D.N.B.). This seems to be the double outlook of Disraeli's conservatism, too subtle to inspire action. I think he turns up again as the unicorn when the Lion and the Unicorn are fighting for the Crown; they make a great dust and nuisance, treat the common-sense Alice as entirely mythical, and are very frightening to the poor king to whom the Crown really belongs.

"Indeed I shan't," Alice said rather impatiently. "I don't belong to this railway journey at all—I was in a wood just now—and I wish I could get back there!"

When she gets back to the wood it is different; it is Nature in the raw, with no names, and she is afraid of it. She still thinks the animals are right to stay there; even when they know their names "they wouldn't answer at all, if they were wise." (They might do well to write nonsense books under an assumed name, and refuse to answer even to that.) All this is a very Kafka piece of symbolism, less at ease than the preceding one; *Wonderland* is a dream, but the *Looking-Glass* is self-consciousness. But both are topical; whether you call the result allegory or "pure nonsense" it depends on ideas about progress and industrialization, and there is room for exegesis on the matter.

The beginning of modern child sentiment may be placed at the obscure edition of *Mother Goose's Melodies* (John Newbury, 1760), with "maxims" very probably by Goldsmith. The important thing is not the rhymes (Boston boasts an edition of 1719. My impression is that they improved as time went on) but the appended maxims, which take a sophisticated pleasure in them. Most are sensible proverbs which the child had better know anyway; their charm (mainly for the adult) comes from the unexpected view of the story you must take if they are not to be irrelevant.

Amphion's Song of Eurydice.

I won't be my Father's Jack,
I won't be my Father's Jill,
I won't be my Fiddler's Wife,
And I will have music when I will.

T'other little Tune,
T'other little Tune,
Prithee Love play me
T'other little Tune.

MAXIM.—Those Arts are the most valuable which are of the greatest Use.

It seems to be the fiddler whose art has been useful in controlling her, but then again she may have discovered the art of wheedling the fiddler. The pomp of the maxim and the childishness of the rhyme make a mock pastoral compound. The pleasure in children here is obviously a derivative of the pleasure in Macheath; the children are "little rogues."

Bow wow wow
Whose dog art Thou?
Little Tom Tinker's Dog.
   Bow wow wow.

Tom Tinker's Dog is a very good Dog; and an honester Dog than his Master.

Honest ("free from hypocrisy" or the patronizing tone to a social inferior) and *dog* ("you young dog") have their *Beggar's Opera* feelings here: it is not even clear whether Tom is a young vagabond or a child.

This is a pleasant example because one can trace the question back. Pope engraved a couplet "on the collar of a dog which I gave to His Royal Highness"—a friendly act as from one gentleman to another resident in the neighborhood.

I am his Highness' dog at Kew.
Pray tell me, sir, whose dog are you?

Presumably Frederick himself would be the first to read it. The joke carries a certain praise for the underdog; the point is not that men are slaves but that they find it suits them and remain good-humored. The dog is proud of being the prince's dog and expects no one to take offense at the question. There is also a hearty independence in its lack of respect for the inquirer. Pope took this from Sir William Temple, where it is said by a fool: "I am the Lord Chamberlain's fool. And whose are you?" was his answer to the nobleman. It is a neat case of the slow shift of this sentiment from fool to rogue to child.

Alice, I think, is more of a "little rogue" than it is usual to say, or than Dodgson himself thought in later years:

loving as a dog . . . and gentle as a fawn; then courteous—courteous to *all*, high or low, grand or grotesque, King or Caterpillar . . . trustful, with an absolute trust.

and so on. It depends what you expect of a child of seven.

She had quite a long argument with the Lory, who at last turned sulky, and would only say, "I am older than you, and must know better"; and this Alice would not allow without knowing how old it was, and as the Lory positively refused to tell its age, there was no more to be said.

Alice had to be made to speak up to bring out the points—here the point is a sense of the fundamental oddity of life given by the fact that different animals become grown-up at different ages; but still if you accept the Lory as a grownup this is rather a pert child. She is often the underdog speaking up for itself.

The book also keeps to the topic of death—the first two jokes about death in *Wonderland* come on pages 3 and 4—and for the child this may be a natural connection; I remember believing I should have to die in order to grow up, and thinking the prospect very disagreeable. There seems to be a connection in Dodgson's mind between the death of childhood and the development of sex, which might be pursued into many of the details of the books. Alice will die if the Red King wakes up, partly because she is a dream product of the author and partly because the pawn is put back in its box at the end of the game. He is the absent husband of the Red Queen who is a governess, and the end of the book comes when Alice defeats the Red Queen and "mates" the King. Everything seems to break up because she arrives at a piece of *knowledge*, that all the poems are about fish. I should say the idea was somehow at work at the end of *Wonderland* too. The trial is meant to be a mystery; Alice is told to leave the court, as if a child ought not to hear the evidence, and yet they expect her to give evidence herself.

"What do you know about this business?" the King said to Alice.

"Nothing," said Alice.

"Nothing *whatever?*" persisted the King.

"Nothing whatever," said Alice.

"That's very important," the King said, turning to the jury. They were just beginning to write this down on their slates, when the White Rabbit interrupted: "*Un*important, your Majesty means, of course," he said in a very respectful tone, but frowning and making faces as he spoke.

"*Un*important, of course, I meant," the King hastily said, and went on to himself in an undertone, "important—unimportant—unimportant—important—" as if he were trying which word sounded best.

There is no such stress in the passage as would make one feel there must be something behind it, and certainly it is funny enough as it stands. But I think Dodgson felt it was important that Alice should be innocent of all knowledge of what the Knave of Hearts (a flashy-looking lady's man in the picture) is likely to have been doing, and also important that she should not be told she is innocent. That is why the king, always a well-intentioned man, is embarrassed. At the same time Dodgson feels that Alice is right in thinking "it doesn't matter a bit" which word the jury write down; she is too stable in her detachment to be embarrassed, these things will not interest her, and in a way she includes them all in herself. And it is the refusal to let her stay that makes her revolt and break the dream. It is tempting to read an example of this idea into the poem that introduces the *Looking-Glass.*

> Come, hearken then, ere voice of dread,
>   With bitter summons laden,
> Shall summon to unwelcome bed
>   A melancholy maiden.

After all the marriage bed was more likely to be the end of the maiden than the grave, and the metaphor firmly implied treats them as identical.

The last example is obviously more a joke against Dodgson than anything else, and though the connection between death and the development of sex is I think at work, it is not the main point of the conflict about growing up. Alice is given a magical control over her growth by the traditionally symbolic caterpillar, a creature which has to go through a sort of death to become grown-up, and then seems a more spiritual creature. It refuses to agree with Alice that this process is at all peculiar, and clearly her own life will be somehow like it, but the main idea is not its development of sex. The butterfly implied may be the girl when she is "out" or her soul when in heaven, to which she is now nearer than she will be when she is "out"; she must walk to it by walking away from it. Alice knows several reasons why she should object to growing up, and does not at all like being an obvious angel, a head out of contact with its body that has to come down from the sky, and gets mistaken for the Paradisal serpent of the knowledge of good and evil, and by the pigeon of the Annunciation, too. But she only makes herself smaller for reasons of tact or proportion; the triumphant close of *Wonderland* is that she has outgrown her fancies and can afford to wake and despise them. The *Looking-Glass* is less of a dream product, less concentrated on the child's situation, and (once started) less full of changes of size; but it has the same end; the governess shrinks to a kitten when Alice has grown from a pawn to a queen, and can shake her. Both these clearly stand for becoming grown-up and yet in part are a revolt against grown-up behavior; there is the same ambivalence as about the talking animals. Whether children often find this symbolism as interesting as Carroll did is another thing; there are recorded cases of tears at such a betrayal of the reality of the story. I remember feeling that the ends of the books were a sort of necessary assertion that the grown-up world was after all the proper one: one did not object to that in principle, but would no more turn to those parts from preference than to the "Easter Greeting to Every Child that Loves Alice."

To make the dream story from which *Wonderland* was elaborated seem Freudian one has only to tell it. A fall through a deep hole into the secrets of Mother Earth produces a new enclosed soul wondering who it is, what will be its position in the world, and how it can get out. It is in a long low hall, part of the palace of the Queen of Hearts (a neat touch), from which it can only get out to the fresh air and the fountains through a hole frighteningly too small. Strange changes, caused by the way it is nourished there, happen to it in this place, but always when it is big it cannot get out and when it is small it is not allowed to; for one thing, being a little girl, it has no key. The nightmare theme of the birth trauma, that she grows too big for the room and is almost crushed by it, is not only used here but repeated more painfully after she seems to have got out; the rabbit sends her sternly into its house and some food there makes her grow again. In Dodgson's own drawing of Alice when cramped into the room with one foot up the chimney, kicking out the hateful thing that tries to come down (she takes away its pencil when it is a juror), she is much more obviously in the fetus position than in Tenniel's. The White Rabbit is Mr. Spooner to whom the spoonerisms happened, an undergraduate in 1862, but its business here is as a pet for children which they may be allowed to breed. Not that the clearness of the framework makes the interpretation simple; Alice peering through the hole into the garden may be wanting a return to the womb as well as an escape from it; she is fond, we are told, of taking both sides of an argument when talking to herself, and the whole book balances between the luscious nonsense world of fantasy and the ironic nonsense world of fact.

I said that the sea of tears she swims in was the amniotic fluid, which is much too simple. You may take it as Lethe in which the souls were bathed before rebirth (and it is their own tears: they forget, as we forget our childhood, through the repression of pain) or as the "solution" of an intellectual contradiction through Intuition and a return to the Unconscious. Anyway it is a sordid image made pretty; one need not read Dodgson's satirical verses against babies to see how much he would dislike a child wallowing in its tears in real life. The fondness of small girls for doing this has to be faced early in attempting to prefer them, possibly to small boys, certainly to grownups; to a man idealizing children as free from the falsity of a rich emotional life their displays of emotion must be particularly disconcerting. The celibate may be forced to observe them, on the floor of a railway carriage for example, after a storm of fury, dabbling in their ooze; covertly snuggling against mamma while each still pretends to ignore the other. The symbolic pleasure of dabbling seems based on an idea that the liquid itself is the bad temper which they have got rid of by the storm and yet are still hugging, or that they are not quite impotent since they have at least "done" this much about the situation. The acid quality of the style shows that Dodgson does not entirely like having to love creatures whose narcissism takes this form, but he does not want simply to forget it as he too would like a relief from "ill temper"; he sterilizes it from the start by giving it a charming myth. The love for narcissists itself seems mainly based on a desire to keep oneself safely detached, which is the essential notion here.

The symbolic completeness of Alice's experience is I think important. She runs the whole gamut; she is a father in getting down the hole, a fetus at the bottom, and can only be born by becoming a mother and producing her own amniotic fluid. Whether his mind played the trick of putting this into the story or not he has the feelings that would correspond to it. A desire to include all sexuality in the girl child, the least obviously sexed of human creatures, the one that keeps its sex in the safest place, was an important part of their fascination for him. He is partly imagining himself as the girl child (with these comforting characteristics) partly as its father (these together make *it* a father) partly as its lover—so it might be a mother—but then of course it is clever and detached enough to do everything for itself. He told one of his little girls a story about cats wearing gloves over their claws: "For you see, 'gloves' have got 'love' inside them—there's none outside, you know." So far from its dependence, the child's independence is the important thing, and the theme behind that is the self-centered emotional life imposed by the detached intelligence.

The famous cat is a very direct symbol of this ideal of intellectual detachment; all cats are detached, and since this one grins it is the amused observer. It can disappear because it can abstract itself from its surroundings into a more interesting inner world; it appears only as a head because it is almost a disembodied intelligence, and only as a grin because it can impose an atmosphere without being present. In frightening the king by the allowable act of looking at him it displays the soul force of Mr. Gandhi; it is unbeheadable because its soul cannot be killed; and its influence brings about a short amnesty in the divided nature of the Queen and Duchess. Its cleverness makes it formidable—it has very long claws and a great many teeth—but Alice is particularly at home with it; she is the same sort of thing.

The Gnat gives a more touching picture of Dodgson; he treats nowhere more directly of his actual relations with the child. He feels he is liable to nag at it, as a gnat would, and the gnat turns out, as he is, to be alarmingly big as a friend for the child, but at first it sounds tiny because he means so little to her. It tries to amuse her by rather frightening accounts of other dangerous insects, other grownups. It is reduced to tears by the melancholy of its own jokes, which it usually can't bear to finish; only if Alice had made them, as it keeps egging her on to do, would they be at all interesting. That at least would show the child had paid some sort of attention, and he could go away and repeat them to other people. The desire to have jokes made all the time, he feels, is a painful and obvious confession of spiritual discomfort, and the freedom of Alice from such a feeling makes her unapproachable.

The purpose of a dream on the Freudian theory is simply to keep you in an undisturbed state so that you can go on sleeping; in the course of this practical work you may produce something of more general value, but not only of one sort. Alice has, I understand, become a patron saint of the Surrealists, but they do not go in for Comic Primness, a sort of reserve of force, which is her chief charm. Wyndham Lewis avoided putting her beside Proust and Lorelei to be danced on as a debilitating child cult (though she is a bit of pragmatist too); the present-day reader is more likely to complain of her complacence. In this sort of child cult the child, though a means of imaginative escape, becomes the critic; Alice is the most reasonable and responsible person in the book. This is meant as charmingly pathetic about her as well as satire about her elders, and there is some implication that the sane man can take no other view of the world, even for controlling it, than the child does; but this is kept a good distance from sentimental infantilism. There is always some doubt about the meaning of a man who says he wants to be like a child, because he may want to be like it in having fresh and vivid feelings and senses, in not knowing, expecting, or desiring evil, in not having an analytical mind, in having no sexual desires recognizable as such, or out of a desire to be mothered and evade responsibility. He is usually mixing them up—Christ's praise of children, given perhaps for reasons I have failed to list, has made it a respected thing to say, and it has been said often and loosely—but he can make his own mixture; Lewis' invective hardly shows which he is attacking. The praise of the child in the Alices mainly depends on a distaste not only for sexuality but for all the distortions of vision that go with a rich emotional life; the opposite idea needs to be set against this, that you can only understand people or even things by having such a life in yourself to be their mirror; but the idea itself is very respectable. So far as it is typical of the scientist the books are an expression of the scientific attitude (*e.g.*, the bread-and-butter fly) or a sort of satire on it that treats it as inevitable.

The most obvious aspect of the complacence is the snobbery. It is clear that Alice is not only a very well-brought-up but a very well-to-do little girl; if she has grown into Mabel, so that she will have to go and live in that poky little house and have next to no toys to play with, she will refuse to come out of her rabbit hole at all. One is only surprised that she is allowed to meet Mabel. All through the books odd objects of luxury are viewed rather as Wordsworth viewed mountains; meaningless, but grand and irremovable; objects of myth. The whiting, the talking leg of mutton, the soup tureen, the tea tray in the sky, are obvious examples. The shift from the idea of the child's unity with nature is amusingly complete; a mere change in the objects viewed makes it at one with the conventions. But this is still not far from Wordsworth, who made his mountains into symbols of the stable and moral society living among them. In part the joke of this stands for the sincerity of the child that criticizes the folly of convention, but Alice is very respectful to conventions and interested to learn new ones; indeed the discussions about the rules of the game of conversation, those stern comments on the isolation of humanity, put the tone so strongly in favor of the conventions that one feels there is nothing else in the world. There is a strange clash on this topic about the three little sisters discussed at the Mad Tea Party, who lived on treacle. "They couldn't have done that, you know," Alice gently remarked, "they'd have been ill." "So they were," said the Dormouse, "*very* ill." The creatures are always self-centered and argumentative, to stand for the detachment of the intellect from emotion, which is necessary to it and yet makes it childish. Then the remark stands both for the danger of taking as one's guide the natural desires ("this is the sort of thing little girls would do if they were left alone") and for a pathetic example of a martyrdom to the conventions; the little girls did not mind *how* ill they were made by living on treacle, because it was their rule, and they knew it was expected of them. (That they are refined girls is clear from the fact that they do allegorical sketches.) There is an obscure connection here with the belief of the period that a really nice girl is "delicate" (the profound sentences implied by the combination of meanings in this word are *a*) "you cannot get a woman to be refined unless you make her ill" and more darkly *b*) "she is desirable because corpselike"); Dodgson was always shocked to find that his little girls had appetites, because it made them seem less pure. The passage about the bread-and-butter fly brings this out more frankly, with something of the willful grimness of Webster. It was a creature of such high refinement that it could only live on weak tea with cream in it (tea being the caller's meal, sacred to the fair, with nothing gross about it).

A new difficulty came into Alice's head.

"Supposing it couldn't find any?" she suggested.
"Then it would die, of course"
"But that must happen very often," Alice remarked thoughtfully.

"It always happens," said the Gnat.

After this, Alice was silent for a minute or two, pondering.

There need be no gloating over the child's innocence here, as in Barrie; anybody might ponder. Alice has just suggested that flies burn themselves to death in candles out of a martyr's ambition to become Snapdragon flies. The talk goes on to losing one's name, which is the next stage on her journey, and brings freedom but is like death; the girl may lose her personality by growing up into the life of convention, and her virginity (like her surname) by marriage; or she may lose her "good name" when she loses the conventions "in the woods"—the animals, etc., there have no names because they are out of reach of the controlling reason; or when she develops sex she must neither understand nor name her feelings. The Gnat is weeping and Alice is afraid of the wood but determined to go on. "It always dies of thirst" or "it always dies in the end, as do we all"; "the life of highest refinement is the most deathly, yet what else is one to aim at when life is so brief, and when there is so little in it of any value." A certain ghoulishness in the atmosphere of this, of which the tight lacing may have been a product or partial cause,[1] comes out very strongly in Henry James; the decadents pounced on it for their own purposes but could not put more death wishes into it than these respectables had done already.

Alice willingly receives social advice like "curtsey while you're thinking what to say, it saves time," and the doctrine that you must walk away from a queen if you really want to meet her has more point when said of the greed of the climber than of the unself-seeking curiosity of the small girl. Or it applies to both, and allows the climber a sense of purity and simplicity; I think this was a source of charm whether Dodgson meant it or not. Alice's own social assumptions are more subtle and all-pervading; she always seems to raise the tone of the company she enters, and to find this all the easier because the creatures are so rude to her. A central idea here is that the perfect lady can gain all the advantages of contempt without soiling herself by expressing or even feeling it.

This time there could be no mistake about it; it was neither more nor less than a pig, and she felt that it would be quite absurd for her to carry it any further. So she set the little creature down, and felt quite relieved to see it trot quietly away into the wood. "If it had grown up," she said to herself, "it would have made a dreadfully ugly child, but it makes rather a handsome pig, I think."

And she began thinking over other children she knew, who might do very well as pigs, and was just saying to herself, "if only one knew the right way to change them—" when she was a little startled by seeing the Cheshire Cat on the bough of a tree a few yards off.

The Cat only grinned when it saw Alice. It looked goodnatured, she thought: still it had very long claws and a great many teeth, so she felt that it ought to be treated with respect.

The effect of cuddling these mellow evasive phrases—"a good deal"— "do very well as"—whose vagueness can convey so rich an irony and so complete a detachment, while making so firm a claim to show charming good will, is very close to that of Wilde's comedy. So is the hint of a delicious slavishness behind the primness, and contrasting with the irony, of the last phrase. (But then Dodgson feels the cat deserves respect as the detached intelligence—he is enjoying the idea that Alice and other social figures have got to respect Dodgson.) I think there is a feeling that the aristocrat is essentially like the child because it is his business to make claims in advance of his immediate personal merits; the child is not strong yet, and the aristocrat only as part of a system; the best he can do if actually asked for his credentials, since it would be indecent to produce his pedigree, is to display charm and hope it will appear unconscious, like the good young girl. Wilde's version of this leaves rather a bad taste in the mouth because it is slavish; it has something of the naïve snobbery of the high-class servant. Whistler meant this by the most crashing of his insults—"Oscar now stands forth unveiled as his own 'gentleman' "—when Wilde took shelter from a charge of plagiarism behind the claim that a gentleman does not attend to coarse abuse.

Slavish, for one thing, because they were always juggling between what they themselves thought wicked and what the society they addressed thought wicked, talking about sin when they meant scandal. The thrill of *Pen, Pencil and Poison* is in the covert comparison between Wilde himself and the poisoner, and Wilde certainly did not think his sexual habits as wicked as killing a friend to annoy an insurance company. By their very hints that they deserved notice as sinners they pretended to accept all the moral ideas of society, because they wanted to succeed in it, and yet society only took them seriously because they were connected with an intellectual movement which refused to accept some of those ideas. The Byronic theme of the man unable to accept the moral ideas of his society and yet torn by his feelings about them is real and permanent, but to base it on intellectual dishonesty is to short-circuit it; and leads to a claim that the life of highest refinement must be allowed a certain avid infantile petulance.

Alice is not a slave like this; she is almost too sure that she is good and right. The grownup is egged on to imitate her not as a privileged decadent but as a privileged eccentric, a Victorian figure that we must be sorry to lose. The eccentric though kind and noble would be alarming from the strength of his virtues if he were less funny; Dodgson saw to it that this underlying feeling about his monsters was brought out firmly by Tenniel, who had been trained on drawing very serious things like the British Lion weeping over Gordon, for *Punch*. Their massive and romantic nobility is, I think, an important element in the effect; Dodgson did not get it in his own drawings (nor, by the way, did he give all the young men eunuchoid legs) but no doubt he would have done so if he had been able. I should connect this weighty background with the tone of worldly goodness, of universal but not stupid charity, in Alice's remarks about the pig: "I shall do my best even for you; of course one will suffer, because you are not worth the efforts spent on you; but I have no temptation to be uncharitable to you because I am too far above you to need to put you in your place"—this is what her tone would develop into; a genuine readiness for self-sacrifice and a more genuine sense of power.

The qualities held in so subtle a suspension in Alice are shown in full blast in the two queens. It is clear that this sort of moral superiority involves a painful isolation, similar to those involved in the intellectual way of life and the life of chastity, which are here associated with it. The reference to *Maud* (1855) brings this out. It was a shocking book; mockery was deserved; and its improper freedom was parodied by the flowers at the beginning of the *Looking-Glass*. A taint of fussiness hangs over this sort of essay, but the parodies were assumed to be obvious (children who aren't forced to learn Dr. Watts can't get the same thrill from parodies of him as the original children did) and even this parody is not as obvious as it was. There is no doubt that the flowers are much funnier if you compare them with their indestructible originals.

The Tiger Lily was originally a Passionflower, but it was explained to Dodgson in time that the passion meant was not that of sexual desire (which he relates to ill-temper) but of Christ; a brilliant recovery was made after the shock of this, for *Tiger-Lily* includes both the alarming fierceness of ideal passion (chaste till now) and the ill-temper of the life of virtue and self-sacrifice typified by the governess (chaste always). So that in effect he includes all the flowers Tennyson named. The willow tree that said Bough-Wough doesn't come in the poem, but it is a symbol of hopeless love anyway. The pink daisies turn white out of fear, as the white ones turn pink in the poem out of admiration. I don't know how far we ought to notice the remark about beds, which implies that they should be hard because even passion demands the virtues of asceticism (they are also the earthy beds of the grave); it fits in very well with the ideas at work, but does not seem a thing Dodgson would have said in clearer language.

But though he shied from the Christian association in the complex idea wanted from "Passion-Flower" the flowers make another one very firmly.

"But that's not *your* fault," the Rose added kindly: "you're beginning to fade, you know—and then one can't help one's petals getting a little untidy." Alice didn't like this idea at all: so, to change the subject, she asked "Does she ever come out here?" "I daresay you'll see her soon," said the Rose. "She's one of the thorny kind." "Where does she wear the thorns?" Alice asked with some curiosity. "Why, all round her head, of course," the Rose replied. "I was wondering *you* hadn't got some too. I thought it was the regular rule."

Death is never far out of sight in the books. The Rose cannot help standing for desire but its thorns here stand for the ill-temper not so much of passion as of chastity, that of the governess or that involved in ideal love. Then the thorns round the queen's head, the "regular rule" for suffering humanity, not yet assumed by the child, stand for the Passion, the self-sacrifice of the most ideal and most generous love, which produces ugliness and ill-temper.

The joke of making romantic love ridiculous by applying it to undesired middle-aged women is less to be respected than the joke of the hopelessness of idealism. W. S. Gilbert uses it for the same timid facetiousness but more offensively. This perhaps specially nineteenth-century trick is played about all the women in the Alices—the Ugly Duchess who had the aphrodisiac in the soup (pepper, as Alice pointed out, produces "ill-temper") was the same person as the Queen in the first draft ("Queen of Hearts and Marchioness of Mock Turtles") so that the Queen's sentence of her is the suicide of disruptive passion. The Mock Turtle, who is half beef in the picture, with a cloven hoof, suffers from the calf love of a turtledove; he went to a bad school and is excited about dancing. (He is also weeping for his lost childhood, which Dodgson sympathized with while blaming its exaggeration, and Alice thought very queer; this keeps it from being direct satire.) So love is also ridiculous in young men; it is felt that these two cover the whole field (Dodgson was about thirty at the time) so that granted these points the world is safe for chastity. The danger was from middle-aged women because young women could be treated as pure like Alice. Nor indeed is this mere convention; Gilbert was relying on one of the more permanent jokes played by nature on civilization, that unless somewhat primitive methods are employed the specific desires of refined women may appear too late. So far as the chaste man uses this fact, and the fact that men are hurt by permanent chastity less than women, in order to insult women, no fuss that he may make about baby women will make him dignified. Dodgson keeps the theme fairly agreeable by connecting it with the more general one of self-sacrifice—which may be useless or harmful, even when spontaneous or part of a reasonable convention, which then makes the sacrificer ridiculous and crippled, but which even then makes him deserve respect and may give him unexpected sources of power. The man playing at child cult arrives at Sex War here (as usual since, but the comic Lear didn't), but not to the death nor with all weapons.

The same ideas are behind the White Queen, the emotional as against the practical idealist. It seems clear that the *Apologia* (1864) is in sight when she believes the impossible for half an hour before breakfast, to keep in practice; I should interpret the two examples she gives as immortality and putting back the clock of history, also Mass occurs before breakfast. All through the Wool and Water chapter (milk and water but not nourishing, and gritty to the teeth) she is Oxford; he life of learning rather than of dogmatic religion. Every one recognizes the local shop, the sham fights, the rowing, the academic old sheep, and the way it laughs scornfully when Alice doesn't know the technical slang of rowing; and there are some general reflections on education. The teacher willfully puts the egg a long way off, so that you have to walk after it yourself, and meanwhile it turns into something else; and when you have "paid for" the education its effects, then first known, must be accepted as part of you whether they are good or bad. Oxford as dreamy may be half satire half acceptance of Arnold's "adorable dreamer" purple patch (1865).

Once at least in each book a cry of loneliness goes up from Alice at the oddity beyond sympathy or communication of the world she has entered—whether that in which the child is shut by weakness, or the adult by the renunciations necessary both for the ideal and the worldly way of life (the strength of the snobbery is to imply that these are the same). It seems strangely terrible that the answers of the White Queen, on the second of these occasions, should be so unanswerable.

We are back to the crucial topic of age and the fear of death, and pass to the effectiveness of practice in helping one to believe the impossible; for example that the aging Queen is so old that she would be dead. The helplessness of the intellect, which claims to rule so much, is granted under cover of the counterclaim that since it makes you impersonal you can forget pain with it; we do not believe this about the Queen chiefly because she has not enough understanding of other people. The jerk of the return to age, and the assumption that this is a field for polite lying, make the work of the intellect only the game of conversation. Humpty Dumpty has the same embarrassing trick for arguing away a suggestion of loneliness. Indeed about all the rationalism of Alice and her acquaintances there hangs a suggestion that there are after all questions of pure thought, academic thought whose altruism is recognized and paid for, thought meant only for the upper classes to whom the conventions are in any case natural habit; like that suggestion that the scientist is sure to be a gentleman and has plenty of space which is the fascination of Kew Gardens.

The Queen is a very inclusive figure. "Looking before and after" with the plaintive tone of universal altruism she lives chiefly backwards, in history; the necessary darkness of growth, the mysteries of self-knowledge, the self-contradictions of the will, the antinomies of philosophy, the very Looking-Glass itself, impose this; nor is it mere weakness to attempt to resolve them only in the direct impulse of the child. Gathering the more dream rushes her love for man becomes the more universal, herself the more like a porcupine. Knitting with more and more needles she tries to control life by a more and more complex intellectual apparatus—the "progress" of Herbert Spencer; any one shelf of the shop is empty, but there is always something very interesting—the "atmosphere" of the place is so interesting—which moves up as you look at it from shelf to shelf; there is jam only in the future and our traditional past, and the test made by Alice, who sent value through the ceiling as if it were quite used to it, shows that progress can never reach value, because its habitation and name is heaven. The Queen's scheme of social reform, which is to punish those who are not respectable before their crimes are committed, seems to be another of these jokes about progress:

"But if you *hadn't* done them," the Queen said, "that would have been better still; better, and better, and better!" Her voice went higher with each "better" till it got to quite a squeak at last.

There is a similar attack in the Walrus and the Carpenter, who are depressed by the spectacle of unimproved nature and engage in charitable work among oysters. The Carpenter is a Castle and the Walrus, who could eat so many more because he was crying behind his handkerchief, was a Bishop, in the scheme at the beginning of the book. But in saying so one must be struck by the depth at which the satire is hidden; the queerness of the incident and the characters takes on a Wordsworthian grandeur and aridity, and the landscape defined by the tricks of facetiousness takes on the remote and staring beauty of the ideas of the insane. It is odd to find that Tenniel went on to illustrate Poe in the same manner; Dodgson is often doing what Poe wanted to do, and can do it the more easily because he can safely introduce the absurd. The Idiot Boy of Wordsworth is too milky a moonlit creature to be at home with Nature as she was deplored by the Carpenter, and much of the technique of the rudeness of the Mad Hatter has been learned from Hamlet. It is the ground bass of this kinship with insanity, I think, that makes it so clear that the books are not trifling, and the cool courage with which Alice accepts madmen that gives them their strength.

This talk about the snobbery of the Alices may seem a mere attack, but a little acid may help to remove the slime with which they have been encrusted. The two main ideas behind the snobbery, that virtue and intelligence are alike lonely, and that good manners are therefore important though an absurd confession of human limitations, do not depend on a local class system; they would be recognized in a degree by any tolerable society. And if in a degree their opposites must also be recognized, so they are here; there are solid enough statements of the shams of altruism and convention and their horrors when genuine; it is the forces of this conflict that make a clash violent enough to end both the dreams. In *Wonderland* this is mysteriously mixed up with the trial of the Knave of Hearts, the thief of love, but at the end of the second book the symbolism is franker and more simple. She is a grown queen and has acquired the conventional dignities of her insane world; suddenly she admits their insanity, refuses to be a grown queen, and destroys them.

"I can't stand this any longer!" she cried, as she seized the table-cloth in both hands: one good pull, and plates, dishes, guests, and candles came crashing down together in a heap on the floor.

The guests are inanimate and the crawling self-stultifying machinery of luxury has taken on a hideous life of its own. It is the High Table of Christ Church that we must think of here. The gentleman is not the slave of his conventions because at need he could destroy them; and yet, even if he did this, and all the more because he does not, he must adopt while despising it the attitude to them of the child.

Note

1. It was getting worse when the Alices were written. In what Mr. Hugh Kingsmill calls "the fatal fifties" skirts were so big that the small waist was not much needed for contrast, so it can't be blamed for the literary works of that decade.

21.

The Schizophrenic and Language: Surface and Depth in Lewis Carroll and Antonin Artaud

Gilles Deleuze

THE PRESENCE OF ESOTERIC WORDS and portmanteau words has been pointed out in the rhyming chants of little girls, in poetry, and in the language of madness. Such an amalgamation is troubling, however. A great poet can write in a direct relation to the child that he was and the children that he loves; a madman can produce a great body of poetry in direct relation to the poet that he was and has not ceased to be. This in no way justifies the grotesque trinity of child, poet, and madman. We must be attentive to the displacements which reveal a profound difference beneath superficial resemblances. We must note the different functions and depths of *non-sense* and the heterogeneity of portmanteau words,

From Gilles Deleuze, *Logique du sens* (Paris: Editions de Minuit, 1969). Translated and condensed in *Textual Strategies: Perspectives in Post-Structuralist Criticism*, Josué V. Harari, ed. (Ithaca, N.Y.: Cornell University Press, 1979). Copyright © 1979 Cornell University Press. Reprinted by permission.

which do not authorize grouping together those who invent them or even those who employ them. A little girl can sing "pimpanicaille" (in French, a mixture of "pimpant" + "nique" + "canaille"), a poet write "frumious" (furious + fuming) or "slithy" (lithe + slimy), and a schizophrenic say "perspendicacious" (perpendicular + perspicacious)[1]: we have no reason to believe that the problem is the same because of superficially analogous results. There can be no serious association of the little elephant Babar's song with Artaud's breathscreams, "Ratara ratara ratara Atara tatara rara Otara otara katara."[2] Let us add that the logicians' error when speaking of non-sense is to give disembodied examples which they construct laboriously for the needs of their demonstration, as if they had never heard a little girl sing, a great poet recite, or a schizophrenic speak. Such is the poverty of these "logical" examples (except in the case of Russell, who was inspired by Lewis Carroll). Here, again, the inadequacies of the logicians do not authorize us to construct a new trinity in opposition to theirs, however. The problem is a clinical one: that of the displacement from one mode of organization to another, or of the formation of a progressive and creative disorganization. The problem is also one of criticism, that is, of determining differential levels at which change occurs in the form of non-sense, in the nature of portmanteau words, in the dimension of language as a whole.

We would like to consider two great poetic texts containing such traps of resemblance: Antonin Artaud confronts Lewis Carroll first in an extraordinary transcription—a counter equivalence—of Carroll's "Jabberwocky" and then in one of his letters written from the insane asylum in Rodez. Reading the opening stanza of "Jabberwocky" as it was rendered into French by Artaud, one has the impression that the first two lines still correspond to Carroll's criteria, and conform to the rules of other French translations of Carroll.[3] Beginning with the last word of the second line, however, a displacement, and even a central, creative breakdown, occurs, one which transports us to another world and to a completely different language. In fright we recognize this language without difficulty: it is the language of schizophrenia. Caught up in grammatical syncopes and overburdened with gutturals, even the portmanteau words seem to have another function. At the same time, we see the distance separating Carroll's language, which is emitted at the surface, from Artaud's language, which is hewn from the depths of bodies—a distance which reflects the difference between their problems. We then understand the full significance of Artaud's declarations in one of the letters from Rodez:

I did not do a translation of "Jabberwocky." I tried to translate a fragment of it, but it bored me. I never liked the poem, which always seemed to me to smack of affected infantilism. . . . *I do not like surface poems or languages* which smell of happy leisure moments and intellectual triumphs. . . . One can invent one's language and make pure language speak with an a-grammatical meaning, but this meaning must be valid in itself, it must come from anguish. . . . "Jabberwocky" is the work of a profiteer who wanted—while filled with a well-served meal—to fill up intellectually on others' suffering. . . . When one digs into the shit of the individual being and his language, the poem must necessarily smell bad; "Jabberwocky" is a poem that its author has taken special pains to keep outside the uterine being of suffering into which all great poets have dipped, and from which, delivering themselves into the world, they smell bad. In "Jabberwocky" there are passages of fecality, but it is the fecality of an English snob who curls the obscene in himself like ringlets around a hot curling iron. . . . It is the work of a man who ate well, and you can smell it in his writing. (9:184–86)

In short, Artaud considers Lewis Carroll a pervert, a minor pervert, who limits himself to the creation of a surface language and does not sense the true problem of language in its depth—the schizophrenic problem of suffering, of death, and of life. Carroll's games seem puerile to him, his nourishment too worldly, even his fecality hypocritical and too well-bred.

Let us briefly consider *Alice*. A strange evolution takes place throughout all of Alice's adventures. One can sum it up as the conquest or discovery of surfaces. At the beginning of *Alice in Wonderland*, the search for the secret of things and events goes on in the depths of the earth: in deeply dug wells and rabbit holes, as well as in the mixtures of bodies which penetrate each other and coexist. As one advances in the narrative, however, the sinking and burrowing movements give way to lateral, sliding movements: from left to right and right to left. The animals of the depths become secondary, and are replaced by playing card characters, characters without thickness. One might say that the former depth has spread itself out, has become breadth. Here lies the secret of the stammerer (Carroll)—it no longer consists in sinking into the depths, but in sliding along in such a way that depth is reduced to nothing but the reverse side of the surface. If there is nothing to see behind the curtain, it is because everything visible (or rather, all possible knowledge) is found along the surface of the curtain. It suffices to follow the curtain far enough and closely enough—which is to say superficially enough—in order to turn it inside out so that right becomes left, and vice versa. Consequently, there are no adventures of Alice; there is but *one* adventure: her rising to the surface, her disavowal of the false depths, and her discovery that everything happens at the borderline. For this reason, Carroll abandoned the first title that he had in mind, *Alice's Adventures Underground*.

This is even more true of *Alice's* sequel, *Through the Looking-Glass*. Events, in their radical difference from things, are no longer sought in the depths, but at the surface: a mirror that reflects them, a chess board that "flattens" them to a two-dimensional plane. By running along the surface, along the edge, one passes to the other side; from bodies to incorporeal events. The continuity of front and back replaces all levels of depth. In *Sylvia and Bruno*, Carroll's major novel, one witnesses the completion of this evolution: a stretching machine elongates even songs; the barometer neither rises nor falls, but moves sideways, giving horizontal weather; Bruno learns his lessons backward and forward, up and down, but never in depth; and Fortunatus' purse, presented as a Moebius strip, is made of handkerchiefs sewn together "in the wrong way," so that its external surface is in continuity with its internal surface, and inside and outside become one.

This discovery that the strangest things are on the surface or, as Valéry would say, that "the skin is deepmost" ("le plus profond, c'est la peau"), would be unimportant if it did not carry with it an entire organization of language: Carrollian language. It is clear that, throughout his literary work, Carroll speaks of a very particular type of thing, of *events* (of growing, shrinking, eating, cutting, and so on), and he interprets the nature of these events in a strange manner whose equivalent one finds only in the logic of the Stoics.

This abstractly presented schema of the logic of the Stoics comes to life in Carroll's work. As he said in an article entitled "The Dynamics of a Parti-cle," "*plain superficiality* is the character of a speech." Throughout Carroll's work, the reader will encounter: 1) exits from tunnels in order to discover surfaces and the incorporeal events that are spread out on these surfaces; 2) the essential affinity of events with language; 3) the constant organization of the two surface series into the dualities eating/speaking, consumption/proposition, and designation/expression; and 4) the manner in which these series are organized around a paradoxical element, which is expressed sometimes by a hollow word, sometimes by an esoteric word, and sometimes by a portmanteau word whose function is to fuse and ramify these heterogeneous series.[4] In this way "snark" ramifies an alimentary series ("snark" is of animalish origin, and belongs therefore to the class of consumable objects) and a linguistic series ("snark" is an incorporeal meaning); "Jabberwocky" subsumes an animal and a conversation at the same time; and finally, there is the admirable gardener's song in *Sylvia and Bruno*, in which each couplet brings into play two different types of terms that elicit two distinct perceptions: "He thought he saw . . . He looked again, and found it was. . . ." The couplets develop two heterogeneous series: one of animals, of beings, or of consumable objects described according to physical and sensory (sonorous) qualities; the other, of symbolic objects and characters, defined by logical attributes which are bearers of meaning.[5]

The organization of language described above must be called poetic, because it reflects that which makes language possible. One will not be surprised to discover that events make language possible, even though the event does not exist outside of the proposition that expresses it, since as an "expressed" it does not mix with its expression. It does not exist prior to it and has no existence by itself, but possesses an "insistence" which is peculiar to it. "To make language possible" has a very particular meaning. It signifies to "distinguish" language, to prevent sounds from becoming confused with the sonorous qualities of things, with the noisiness of bodies, with their actions and passions, and with their so-called "oral-anal" determinations. What makes language possible is that which separates sounds from bodies, organizes them into propositions, and thus makes them available to assume an expressive function. Without this surface that distinguishes itself from the depths of bodies, without this line that separates things from propositions, sounds would become inseparable from bodies, becoming simple physical qualities contiguous with them, and propositions would be impossible. This is why *the organization of language is not separable from the poetic discovery of surface*, or from Alice's adventure. The greatness of language consists in speaking only at the surface of things, and thereby in capturing the pure event and the combinations of events that take place on the surface. It becomes a question of reascending to the surface, of discovering surface entities and their games of meaning and of non-sense, of expressing these games in portmanteau words, and of resisting the vertigo of the bodies' depths and their alimentary, poisonous mixtures.

Let us consider another text, far removed from the genius of Artaud and the surface games of Carroll, one whose beauty and density lie in the clinical realm.[6] This text concerns a schizophrenic language student who experiences an eating/speaking duality, and who transposes it into propositions, or rather, into two sorts of language: his mother tongue (English), which is essentially *alimentary* and excremental, and foreign languages, which are essentially *expressive* and which he strives to acquire. In order to hinder the progress of his study of foreign languages, his mother threatens him in two equivalent ways: either she waves before him tempting but indigestible foods packaged in cans, or else she jumps out at him suddenly and abruptly speaks English to him before he has time to plug his ears.

He fends off this double threat with a set of ever more perfected procedures. He eats like a glutton, stuffs himself with food, and stomps on the cans, all the while repeating several foreign words. At a deeper level, he establishes a resonance between the alimentary and the expressive series, and a conversion from one to the other, by translating English words into foreign words according to their phonetic elements (consonants being the most important). For example, *tree* is converted by use of the *R* that reappears in the French vocable (*arbre*), and then by use of the *T* which reappears in the Hebrew term. Finally, since the Russians say *devero* (tree), one can equally transform *tree* into *tere*, *T* then becoming *D*. This already complex procedure gives way to a more generalized one when the idea occurs to the schizophrenic student to employ certain associations: *early*, whose consonants (*R* and *L*) raise particularly delicate problems, is transformed into French expressions dealing with time like *suR Le champ, de bonne heuRe, matinaLement, dévoRer L'espace*, or even into an esoteric and fictive word of German consonance, *uRLich*.

Here, again, what is it that gives us the impression that this language is both very close to, and yet totally different from, Carroll's? Are we talking of a different organization of language, or something worse and more dangerous? One is reminded of Artaud's vehement denunciation of Carroll: "I do not like surface poems or languages." Consequently, how could Carroll appear to Artaud as anything but a well-mannered little girl, sheltered from all the problems of the depths?

The discovery that *there is no more surface* is familiar to and experienced by any schizophrenic. The great problem, the first evidence of schizophrenia, is that the surface is punctured. Bodies no longer have a surface. The schizophrenic body appears as a kind of body-sieve. Freud emphasized this schizophrenic aptitude for perceiving the surface and the skin as if each were pierced by an infinite number of little holes.[7] As a result, the entire body is nothing but depth; it snatches and carries off all things in this gaping depth, which represents a fundamental involution. Everything is body and corporeal. Everything is a mixture of bodies and, within the body, telescoping, nesting in and penetrating each other. It is all a question of physics, as Artaud says: "We have in the back filled vertebra, which are pierced by the nail of pain, and which through walking and the effort of lifting, become cans by being encased upon each other."[8] A tree, a column, a flower, a cane pushes through the body; other bodies always penetrate into our body and coexist with its parts. As there is no surface, interior and exterior, container and content no longer have precise limits; they plunge into universal depth. From this comes the schizophrenic way of living contradictions: either in the deep cleavage that traverses the body, or in the fragmented parts of the body which are nested in each other and whirl around. Body-sieve, fragmented body, and dissociated body form the first three dimensions of the schizophrenic body—they give evidence of the general breakdown of surfaces.

In this breakdown of the surface, all words lose their meaning. They may retain a certain power of designation, but one which is experienced as empty; a certain power of manifestation, but experienced as indifferent; a certain signification, but experienced as "false." But words, in any case, lose their meaning, their power to set down or express incorporeal effects (events) distinct from the body's actions and passions. All words become physical and affect the body immediately. The process is of the following type: a word, often of an alimentary nature, appears in capital letters printed as in a collage that fixes it and divests it of its meaning. Yet as the pinned word loses its meaning, it bursts into fragments, decomposes into syllables, letters, and above all into consonants which act directly on the body, penetrating it and bruising it. We have seen this in the case of the schizophrenic language student: the mother tongue is emptied of its meaning at the same time that its *phonetic elements* gain an uncommon power to inflict pain. Words cease to express attributes of the state of things. Their fragments mix with unbearable sonorous qualities and break into parts of the body where they form a mixture, a new state of things, as if they themselves were noisy, poisonous foods and encased excrements. The organs of the body become defined and determined as a function of the decomposed elements which affect and attack them.[9] In this process of passion, a pure *language-affect* is substituted for the *language-effect:* "All Writing is Pig-Shit," says Artaud (1:120); that is, all fixed, written words are decomposed into noisy, alimentary, and excremental fragments.

In this way an awesome primary order, namely, language-affect, replaces the organization of language. It is within this primary order that the schizophrenic fights and strives to affirm the rights of another sort of word over the passion-word. It is henceforth less a matter for the schizophrenic of recuperating meaning than of destroying words, of warding off affects, or of transforming the body's painful passion into a triumphant action. All this takes place in the depths beneath the punctured surface. The language student offers an example of the means by which the painful splinters of words in the mother tongue are converted into actions through foreign languages. Just as, earlier, the power of wounding was in the phonetic elements affecting the encased or dislocated parts of the body, so victory now can be obtained only by establishing breath-words, scream-words in which all values are exclusively tonic and non-written. To these values corresponds a superior body, a new dimension of the schizophrenic body. The body has become a superior organism without parts, one that functions entirely by insufflation, inhaling, evaporation, and transmission of fluids.[10]

This determination of the active process, in opposition to the process of passion, doubtless seems insufficient at first. Indeed, fluids seem no less maleficent than fragments. But they seem so only because of the action/passion ambivalence. It is here that the contradiction experienced in schizophrenia finds its true point of application: passion and action are the inseparable poles of an ambivalence only because the two languages that they form belong inseparably to the body, to the depths of bodies. One is therefore never sure that the ideal fluids of a partless organism do not carry with them parasitic worms, fragments of organs and solid foods, and remnants of excrements; one can even be certain that maleficent powers use fluids and insufflations in order to make fragments of passion pass into the body. The fluid is necessarily corrupted, but not by itself—only by the other pole, from which it is inseparable. Nevertheless, the fact remains that it represents the active pole, or the state of perfect mixture, in opposition to the encasing and bruising of imperfect mixtures, which constitute the passive pole. In schizophrenia there is a way of living the distinction between two corporeal mixtures, the partial mixture, which corrupts, and the total and liquid mixture, which leaves the body intact. In the insufflated fluid or liquid element there is the unwritten secret of an active mixture that is like the liquefying "principle of the Sea," in opposition to the passive mixtures of the encased parts. It is in this sense that Artaud transforms the Humpty Dumpty poem about the sea and the fishes into a poem about the problem of obedience and command.[11]

This second language, this process of action, is defined in practice by an overload of consonants, gutturals, and aspirates, as well as interior apostrophes and accents, breaths, and scansions, and a modulation which replaces all the syllabic and even literal values. It is a matter of making an action out of a word by rendering it indecomposable, impossible to disintegrate: language without articulation. Here, however, the bond is a palatalized, an-organic principle, a block or mass of sea. In the case of the Russian word *devero* (tree), the language student rejoices over the existence of a plural—*derev'ya*—in which the interior apostrophe ("yod," the linguists' soft sign) seems to assure him of a fusion of the consonants. Instead of separating them and making them pronounceable, one could say that the vowel reduced to the "yod" makes the consonants indissociable by liquefying them, that it leaves them unreadable, and even unpronounceable, but it turns them into vocal outbursts in a continuous breath. The outbursts are welded together in the breath, like the consonants in the sign which liquefies them, like the fish in the mass of the sea, like the bones in the blood of the organless body, or like a sign of fire, a wave "that hesitates between gas and water," as Artaud said.[12] These outbursts become sputterings in the breath.

When Antonin Artaud says in his "Jabberwocky": "Up to the point where rourghe is to rouraghe to rangmbde and rangmbde to rouarghambde," it is precisely a question of articulating, insufflating, or palatalizing a word, causing it to blaze out so that it becomes the action of a partless body, rather than the passion of a fragmented organism. It is a question of turning the word into a consolidated, indecomposable mass of consonants by using soft signs. In this language one can always find equivalents for portmanteau words. For "rourghe" and "rouarghe," Artaud himself indicates *ruée* (onslaught), *roue* (wheel), *route* (route), *règle* (rule), *route à régler* (a route to be regulated). (One can add le Rouergue, the region of Rodez in which Artaud happened to be.) In the same way, when he says "Uk'hatis" (with the interior apostrophe), he indicates *ukhase* (ukase), *hâte* (haste), and *abruti* (idiot), and adds "a nocturnal jolt beneath Hecate which means the moon pigs thrown off the straight path" (9:167).

However, at the very moment in which the word appears to be a portmanteau word, its structure and the commentary adjoined to it persuade us of something entirely different: Artaud's "Ghoré Uk'hatis" are not equivalent to the "pigs who have lost their way," to Carroll's "mome raths," or to Parisot's "verchons fourgus." They do not function on the same level. Far from assuring a ramification of series according to meaning, they bring about a chain of associations between tonic and consonantal elements, in a region of infra-meaning, according to a fluid and burning principle that absorbs or actually resorbs the meaning as it is produced: Uk'hatis (or the strayed moon pigs), is K'H (*cahot*—jolt), 'KT (*nocturne*—nocturnal), H'KT (*Hécate*—Hecate).

The duality of schizophrenic words has not received adequate attention. It consists of *passion-words which explode in wounding phonetic values*, and *action-words which weld together inarticulated tonic values*. These two types of words develop in relation to the state of the body, which is either fragmented or organless. They also refer to two types of theater— the theater of terror and passion, and the theater of cruelty, which is essentially active—as well as two types of non-sense, passive and active: the non-sense of words emptied of meaning, which decompose into phonetic elements, and the non-sense of tonic elements which form indecomposable words that are no less empty. In both these cases everything happens below meaning, far from the surface. It is here a matter of under-meaning (*sous-sens*), of un-meaning (*insens*), of *Untersinn*, which must be distinguished from the non-sense at the surface. In both of its aspects, language is, to quote Hölderlin, "a sign empty of meaning." It is still a sign, but one that merges with an action or passion of the body.

This is why it is insufficient to say that schizophrenic language is defined by an incessant and mad sliding of the signifying series onto the signified series. In fact, no series remains at all; both have disappeared. They now exist only in appearance. "Speaking" has collapsed onto "eating," and into all the imitations of a "chewing mouth," of a primitive oral depth. Non-sense has ceased to give meaning at the surface; it absorbs, it engulfs all meaning from both sides, that of the signifier and that of the signified. Artaud says that Being, which is nonsense, has teeth.

In the surface organization which we described earlier as secondary, physical bodies and sonorous words were at the same time separated and articulated by an incorporeal borderline—that of meaning, which represents the pure "expressed" of words, on the one side, and logical attributes of bodies on the other. It follows then, that although meaning results from the body's actions and passions, it is a result that is different in nature (is neither action nor passion), and that protects sonorous language against being confused with the physical body. In the primary order of schizophrenia, on the contrary, there is no duality except that between the actions and passions of the body; language is both of these at the same time and is entirely resorbed into the body's gaping depths. There is no longer anything to prevent propositions from collapsing onto bodies and mixing their sonorous elements with the olfactive, gustative, digestive, and excremental affects of bodies. Not only is there no longer any meaning, but there is no longer any grammar or syntax, nor even any articulated syllabic, literal, or phonetic elements. Antonin Artaud can entitle his essay "An Antigrammatical Endeavor against Lewis Carroll."[13] Carroll needs a very strict grammar, one responsible for preserving the inflexion and articulation of words as separated from the flexion and articulation of bodies, if only by mirrors that reflect these words and "send" a meaning back to them. For this reason we can oppose Artaud and Carroll, point by point—the primary order in opposition to the secondary organization. Surface series of the "eating/speaking" type really have nothing in common with those poles of the depths that apparently resemble them. The two configurations of non-sense, which, at the surface, distribute meaning between different series, have nothing to do with the two descents of non-sense (*Untersinn*) that pull, engulf, and resorb meaning. The two forms of stuttering—clonic and tonic—have only the most superficial analogy with the two schizophrenic languages. The break at the surface has nothing in common with the deep cleavage (*Spaltung*). Even portmanteau words have entirely heterogeneous functions.

One can find a schizoid "position" in the child before he rises to or conquers the surface. In addition, one can always find schizoid fragments at the surface itself, since its role is precisely that of organizing and displaying elements that have come from the depths. Still, it is no less erroneous and condemnable to confuse the conquest of the surface in the child, the breakdown of the surface in the schizophrenic, and the mastery of surfaces by a "minor pervert." Lewis Carroll's work can always be turned into a kind of schizophrenic tale. Some English psychoanalysts have rashly done so, pointing out the telescopings and encasings of Alice's body, her manifest alimentary (and latent excremental) obsessions, the fragments that designate morsels of food as well as "choice morsels," the collages and labels of alimentary words that are quick to decompose, the losses of identity, the fishes in the sea, and so on. One may also ask what sort of madness is represented clinically by the Mad Hatter, the March Hare, and the Dormouse. In the opposition between Alice and Humpty Dumpty,[14] one can always recognize the two ambivalent poles: fragmented organs/organless body, body-sieve/superior body. Artaud himself had no other reason at first for confronting the Humpty Dumpty text. But it is at this moment that Artaud's warning rings out: "I did not do a translation. . . . I never liked the poem. . . . I do not like surface poems or languages."

Bad psychoanalysis has two ways of deceiving itself: it can believe that it has discovered identical subject matters, which necessarily can be found everywhere, or it can believe that is has found analogous forms which create false differences. In doing either, psychoanalysis fails on both grounds: those of clinical psychiatry and literary criticism. Structuralism is right in reminding us that form and content matter only within the original and irreducible structures in which they are organized. Psychoanalysis should have geometric dimensions rather than merely consisting of personal anecdotes. It is first of all the organization and the orientation of these geometric dimensions, rather than reproductive materials or reproduced forms, that constitute both life and sexuality. Psychoanalysis should not be content with designating cases, analyzing personal histories, or diagnosing complexes. As a psychoanalysis of meaning, it should be geographic before being anecdotal: it should distinguish between different regions. Artaud is neither Carroll nor Alice. Carroll is not Artaud, Carroll is not even Alice. Artaud plunges the child into an extremely violent alternative between corporeal passion and action that conforms to the two languages of depth. Either the child must not be born, which is to say, must not leave the chambers of his future spinal column, upon which his parents fornicate (which amounts to an inverse suicide)—or else he must become a fluid, "superior," flaming body, without organs or parents (like those whom Artaud called his "daughters" yet-to-be-born).

Carroll, on the contrary, awaits the child in accordance with his language of incorporeal meaning. He awaits her at the moment at which the child leaves the depths of the maternal body without yet having discovered the depths of her own body, that brief moment of surface when the little girl breaks the surface of the water, like Alice in the pool of her own tears. Carroll and Artaud are worlds apart. We may believe that the surface has its monsters (the Snark and the Jabberwock), its terrors and its cruelties which, though not from the depths, nevertheless have claws and can snatch laterally, or even pull us back into the depths whose dangers we thought we had averted. Carroll and Artaud are nonetheless different; at no point do their worlds coincide. Only the commentator can move from one dimension to the other, and that is his great weakness, the sign that he himself inhabits neither. We would not give one page of Antonin Artaud for all of Carroll; Artaud is the only person to have experienced absolute depth in literature, to have discovered a "vital" body and its prodigious language (through suffering, as he says). He explored the infra-meaning, which today is still unknown. Carroll, on the other hand, remains the master or the surveyor of surfaces we thought we knew so well that we never explored them. Yet it is on these surfaces that the entire logic of meaning is held.

Notes

1. "Perspendicacious" is a portmanteau word used by a schizophrenic to designate spirits that are suspended above the subject's head (perpendicular) and that are very perspicacious. Mentioned in Georges Damas, *Le Surnaturel et les dieux d'après les maladies mentales* (Paris: Presses Universitaires de France, 1946), p. 303.

2. Antonin Artaud, *Oeuvres complètes* (Paris: Gallimard, 1970), 9:188. Henceforth, references will be to the volume and page of this edition. [All translations are those of the editor, Josué Harari.] Breath-screams are used in Artaud's theater of cruelty as a means of preventing spectators from relating to the "intellectual" content of language. [The scream is a specific system of breathing derived from the cabala, and is designed to free the feminine or repressed side of the self.—HARARI.]

3. The original text of "Jabberwocky" which Humpty Dumpty explicates is found in *Through the Looking-Glass*, in Lewis Carroll, *Complete Works* (New York: Modern Library, 1936), p. 215, and goes as follows:

'Twas brillig, and the slithy toves
Did gyre and gymble in the wabe
All mimsy were the borogoves,
And the mome raths outgrabe.

Artaud's version (taken from "L'Arve et l'aume, tentative anti-grammaticale contre Lewis Carroll," 9:156–174) is as follows:

Il était roparant, et les vliqueux tarands
Allaient en gibroyant et en brimbulkdriquant
Jusque là où la rourghe est à rouarghe à rangmbde et rangmbe à rouarghambde:
Tous les falomitards étaient les chats-huants
Et les Ghoré Uk'hatis dans le grabugeument.

Whereas Henri Parisot's translation (see Lewis Carroll, Seghers ed.) reads:

Il était grilheure; les slictueux toves
Gyraient sur l'alloinde et vriblaient;
Tout flivoreux allaient les borogoves;
Les verchons fourgus bourniflaient.
—HARARI

4. An esoteric word can be defined as the point of convergence of two different series of propositions. A first type of esoteric word is limited to a contraction of the syllabic elements of a proposition ("y'reince" for "your royal highness"). Another type is concerned with affirming, within the esoteric work, the conjunction and the coexistence of two series of heterogeneous propositions. (Snark = shark + snake). Finally, there exists a third type of esoteric word—which is the contraction of several words and thus englobes several meanings. The essential characteristic of the portmanteau word is that it is based on a strict *disjunctive synthesis*. Its function always consists of ramifying the series in which it is placed (frumious = fuming + furious *or* furious + fuming).—HARARI.

5. The song of the gardener, in *Sylvia and Bruno*, is made up of nine verses, eight of which are in the first volume, the ninth appearing in *Sylvia and Bruno Concluded*, ch. 20. We quote here two of the verses.—HARARI.

He thought he saw an Albatross
 That fluttered round the lamp;
He looked again, and found it was
 A Penny-Postage-Stamp. (p. 347)

He thought he saw an Argument
 That proved he was the Pope:
He looked again, and found it was
 A Bar of Mottled Soap. (p. 701)

6. Louis Wolfson, *Le Schizo et les langues* (Paris: Gallimard, 1971). On this subject see the introduction written by Deleuze to Wolfson's book and the articles by Alain Rey ("Le Schizolexe," *Critique* [1970], Nos. 279–80) and Jeffrey Mehlman ("Portnoy in Paris," *Diacritics* [1972], vol. 2).—HARARI.

7. "The Unconscious," in *Metapsychology* (1915). Citing the cases of two patients one of whom perceives his skin, and the other his sock, as systems of small holes in continual risk of expansion, Freud shows that this symptom is peculiar to schizophrenia, and could belong neither to a hysteric nor to an obsessional neurotic.

8. In *La Tour de feu*, April 1961.

9. On the subject of organ-letters, see Artaud, "Le Rite de Peyotl," in *Les Tarahumaras* (9:32–38)—HARARI.

10. See Artaud's superior, or "organless" body made only of bone and blood: "No mouth No tongue No teeth No larynx No esophagus No stomach No belly No anus I will reconstruct the man that I am" (*Oeuvres complètes* 84:102).

11. Compare Carroll's and Artaud's versions of the same poem—Ed.

But he was very stiff and proud:
He said, 'You needn't shout so loud!"

And he was very proud and stiff:
He said, 'I'd go and wake them, if—'
I took a corkscrew from the shelf:
I went to wake them up myself.

And when I found the door was locked,
I pulled and pushed and kicked and knocked.

And when I found the door was shut,
I tried to turn the handle, but—(Carroll, p. 220)

He who is not does not know
The obedient one does not suffer.

It is for him who is to know
Why total obedience
Is that which has never suffered

When the being is what disintegrates
Like the mass of the sea.

. . .

God only is that which obeys not,
All other beings do not yet exist,
And they suffer.

. . .

The being is he who imagines himself to be
To be enough to dispense with himself
From learning what the sea wants . . .

But every little fish knows it. (Artaud, 9:171–72; Harari's translation)

12. "One feels as if one is inside a gaseous wave which emits an incessant crackling from all sides. Things are released, as from what was your spleen, your liver, your heart, or your lungs; they escape untiringly, and burst in this atmosphere which hesitates between gas and water, but which seems to call things to itself and to command them to regroup. . . . What escaped from my spleen or my liver was in the shape of letters from a very ancient and mysterious alphabet chewed by an enormous mouth" (9:32–33).—HARARI.

13. "And I will add that I have always despised Lewis Carroll (see my letters from Rodez concerning the 'Jabberwocky'): for me this was an antigrammatical endeavor not *following* Carroll, but *against* him" (9:273–74).—HARARI.

14. See *Through the Looking-Glass*, in which Humpty Dumpty introduces himself as an egg, or a body without organs, and reproaches Alice for the organic differentiation of her face, which he judges to be too ordinary.

PART VI

THE FRENCH CONNECTION

THE ESSAYS IN the following section have all been influenced, in large measure, by French psychoanalysis, that is, by Jacques Lacan's reading of Freud, which itself owes much to structural linguistic theory. Like Lévi-Strauss, Lacan followed Saussure, who had postulated language as a self-sufficient system that is both complete and historical at every moment. Because binary relationships are said to exist between the *signifier* (sound-image) and the *signified* (concept), between *langue* (language system) and *parole* (individual speech), between *phonemic* (recognized) levels of speech and abstract systems of signs (they have their own built-in oppositions), between *metaphor* and *metonymy*, the method of structural linguistics is based on the mediation between these dualisms. Given the complexity of psychic phenomena addressed by Freud, such as reaction formation, defenses, oppositions, and transformations which occur in the relations between unconscious and conscious meaning, Lacan thought that the Saussurean method would prove a valuable tool to apprehend the structure of every psyche, including Freud's. Thus the various accepted meanings, for example, of Freud's own dreams, which had "fathered" psychoanalysis, could be broadened; and psychoanalysis itself could become even more complex—or at least more French. Lacan was certain that Freud who, like any other writer, had to put down myr. ads of simultaneous impressions sequentially, can be improved upon if only we examine his texts through "chains of signifiers." Such a reading allowed him to discover as yet unknown components of Freud's mind, components which allegedly went into the creation of psychoanalysis. In other words, he could free associate to Freud for the benefit of the discipline.

Literary critics adapting this view of psychoanalysis do not always refer to Lacan, or even to the structure of language, but many of the notions about the relationships between readers and writers, between readers and texts, or about word play, derive from the new connections he made between language and psychoanalysis. For Lacan also argued that the language Freud used is more important than classical Freudians or critics have thought it to be, that *what* Freud wrote was not as consequential as *how* he wrote it, so that only a textual rereading which recognizes a dialectical relationship between parts of sentences, sections of works, early and late works, and between words and their language, can explain what he really meant. Since Freud's unconscious was involved in his writing, and is also the basis of psychoanalysis itself, Lacan believed that we must mine it, in order to improve psychoanalytic understanding.

Although he agreed with Freud that the unconscious can never be fully explored, Lacan was sure that his own method would accomplish this task better than any other. In the area of literary criticism, the French structuralists and deconstructionists and their American followers have favored linguistic and textual criticism. They differ from earlier formalists in their search for new meanings and associations; they no longer regard the text as necessarily having any fixed meanings.

Leo Bersani was only minimally influenced by the French innovations. But the way in which the themes of art, love, prostitution, inpotence, androgyny, and divinity are connected in his book on *Baudelaire and Freud* is reminiscent of some of the works of Roland Barthes. Particularly Bersani's use of language, with its jolts and daring, with its wish to shock, and with its clever juxtapositions, approaches the edge of its subject, attempts to read the white spaces, as Barthes would put it. Psychoanalytic knowledge is taken for granted, whether Bersani talks of "the shattering of the artist's integrity . . . as a momentous sexual event," of "psychic penetrability fantasized as sexual penetrability," or of "poetic inspiration . . . transforming the poet from a man into a woman." But the framework of this psychoanalysis is different, and it is also tinged by French Marxism, when he says that "sexual energy may not be the opposite of art, but the only version of art which the lower classes are capable of producing," or that "screwing is the lyricism of the masses." His emphasis on oppositions and on transformations is based on Saussurean linguistics, and on the dialectical mediation between words, concepts, and meanings which allows for new associations and conclusions. Hence Bersani can generalize from Baudelaire that "the artist is intrinsically an unanchored self," and that "psychic identity is also dissipated by the very force with which it is projected toward others in the same way that the orgasm dissipates the intensity of our sexual desire for others." This technique allows him to conclude that the poet's passivity transforms him into a woman.

Geoffrey Hartman's essay takes the French connection for granted, as he begins by stating that every literary narrative hides another one. The importance which Lacan attached to naming is evident in Hartman's notion of the psyche's vulnerability as extending into the bowels of languages, from images to the calling out of a name. An individual's name places that person, endows him with his family qualities and position, sets the conditions of the formation of his self, and of his relationship with others. Focusing on the structure of Genet's view of the Annunciation, Hartman uses the connection between the meaning of words and what these words might signify, to show how "Denunciation is converted to Annunciation," and how Derrida's destructuring of language, or its decentering, is rooted in this tradition. The emphasis on sound, as well as on meaning, symbolism, and alliteration, that is, on spoken language rather than on what is written alone, multiplies the many associations: we no longer question their correctness because every association is valid, and the critic's imagination determines the subtleties and complexities of his work. Hartman tells us that he addresses the truth of language itself, and that verbal associations belie the possibility of closure. They tend to be spontaneous, accidental, and idiosyncratic. Using Lacanian premises, he hypothesizes that "literature is the elaboration of a specular name," which itself "is always already a fiction," since it is rooted in the *mirror stage*. The latter reference is to Lacan's theory that the child's first view of itself in a mirror between six and eighteen months, although immediately repressed, allegedly determines all future self-images. Hartman's focus in this essay, however, is on Walter Benjamin and on how his autobiography is determined by such a specular name, or by the aura surrounding it, and by all the associations to it. As he proves this point, with associations Benjamin made in his dreams and his work, he shows the necessity of psychoanalytic language—read structurally.

René Girard compares Freud's ideas on artists' narcissism—"the condition of a subject who prefers never to get out of himself, even when he appears to do so"—to those of Proust's. Girard argues that in Proust's "actual practice as a novelist in *Jean Santeuil,* we will find only material that appears to confirm Freud's conception of narcissism and its privileged application to both the artist and the work of art." But in *Remembrance of Things Past* the fictional substance of desire is found to be different, shifting to what would correspond to Freud's notion of more mature love, that is, to "object love." Selecting incidents in *Remembrance,* Girard shows how words like *autonomy* and *self-sufficiency* tend to recur, and how Proust, like Freud, implies that the maturity of the old is in having renounced part of their narcissism. Still, with Proust "there is no such thing as voluntary renunciation," even though "desire can be both self-oriented and other-oriented." Girard compares theoretical differences and the differences between the protagonists in *Jean Santeuil* and in *Remembrance* to reveal the relative inferiority of the former in comparison to the latter, on the basis of what Freud called "intact narcissism." Just as Freud argued that he had renounced part of his own narcissism to make the invention of psychoanalysis possible, maintains Girard, so Proust was able to place the narrator in the position of the rejected outsider only in the later (and superior) work. Beyond this, Girard, following Freud, argues that a certain amount of narcissism must remain in everyone, but that Freud's model, unfortunately, is deficient—more metaphoric than scientific. This allows him to conclude that "Freud is obviously a greater poet and Proust a greater analyst of desire," and to discuss the quality of metaphors both of them use. Literary critics are either for Freud or against him; those who are Freudian never regard Freud's texts themselves as the raw material for theoretical insights, and those who are not ignore the centrality of desire in fiction. But, continues Girard, "literature and psychoanalysis need *each other*"; they must "establish a dialogue of equals." Although Freud himself constantly assumed this connection, this formulation mirrors Lacan's—from the literary rather than the clinical perspective.

Lacan, as we know, analyzed literary texts, and his essay on Poe's "The Purloined Letter" has been quoted by every structuralist literary critic. This is why Serge Doubrovsky can say, "don't worry, I won't redo this act, nor will I play or replay some instance of the card," in his comment on Sartre's *La Nausée.* Doubrovsky focuses on the card game in the novel, reading some of its meanings with the help of a metalanguage, which "begins where customary criticism leaves off," so that what "is insignificant begins to signify." This type of reading calls for free association to every idea, and for a textual reading that juxtaposes not only ideas and narrative, but encourages the reader, in this case Doubrovsky, to associate to Sartre's novel. Since Doubrovsky knows a great deal about literature and psychoanalysis, his analysis, based only on two remarks by Roquentin about his dream of a *nauseating* vagina, opens up many new questions. The web woven by this type of reading, in this case between Sartre, *La Nausée*, and Doubrovsky, can be most provocative. The unveiling of hidden desire, that is of sexuality and eroticism, is its major aim. The contribution of French psychoanalysis, in simple terms, is its stripping away of the morality of Freud's own time, of sexual insinuation and unconscious wishes, whose traces can be found in texts. Hence sexual fantasies, homosexuality, and the way authors deal with them—consciously and unconsciously—are associated to as in psychoanalytic dream analysis, in order to unveil the full meaning. Whether the reader is titillated, disgusted, or indifferent upon reading that Roquentin's "entire body had become *the female organ*," or that "from the minute I become unable to prove that I am a man, *I am immediately transformed into a woman*," all readers are inevitably involved. Doubrovsky's essay goes beyond this general interest of French psychocriticism, insofar as he brings in classical psychoanalytic theory to show how "having averted obsession with sodomization, Roquentin has yet to confront the threat of castration, in order that the well-known 'masculine protest' be complete." This is effected, according to Doubrovsky, to the extent that drawing the *nine of hearts* (*neuf* is also "new"), in the resolution of the young man's fantasy, indicates that "you are not 'given' masculinity, you have to 'take' it yourself, that is, undertake it." But in keeping with French criticism, the essay's conclusion is open-ended—itself a text for further comments. Julia Kristeva, literary and linguistic scholar, and a key member of the *Tel Quel* group, also became a Lacanian psychoanalyst. This background explains the ease with which she takes for granted the relation between these various special fields that other people often question. It also explains the difficulties most people may have in knowing what her references are all about. *Jouissance*, for instance, translated as pleasure or enjoyment, has been much discussed by French writers, especially by Roland Barthes, for whom this word subsumed all the unwritten associations a reader might make to a text, including erotic and fantasy responses. Linking these to psychoanalytic ideas of defense mechanism, reaction formations, or transformations—in their Lacanian ramifications—Kristeva brings in her own associations to "The Father, Love, and Banishment"—associations more concerned with femininity than masculinity. Intrinsic to these associations, also, is the central idea of the deconstructionists that every uttered reality is immediately false, and, in turn, needs to be deconstructed. There never is a final truth, only an approximation to it. Thus Kristeva can maintain that "a man experiences love and simultaneously puts it to the test on the death of his father," or that "the father's sublime Death, and thus *Meaning*, merges with the son's 'self.' " Central to such statements, of course, is the acceptance of the Oedipus complex, and of the importance of an individual's own development within his or her language and family. Using Beckett's reference to banishment as standing "above/beyond a life of love," and arguing that "the myth of the bachelor writer," in Beckett, "comes close to Marcel Duchamp's dry humor," Kristeva makes other connections as well, to virginity, Proust, and Kafka. Beckett, Kristeva maintains, writes against Joyce by "ascetically rejecting the latter's . . . *jouissance*." Kristeva then moves on to free associate to the various roles of the mother. But, simplification is anathema to Kristeva's enterprise which, along with all the neo-Lacanian endeavors, insists on the openness of the text—an openness which leads her to "the true guarantee of the last myth of modern times, the myth of the feminine."

22.

Artists in Love

Leo Bersani

Love is the desire to prostitute oneself.
. . . .
What is art? Prostitution.[1]

What is love?
The need to go outside oneself.
Man is an adoring animal.
To adore is to sacrifice oneself and to prostitute oneself.
Thus all love is prostitution.

The most prostituted being is the Supreme Being, God Himself,
since for every individual he is the friend above all others, since he
is the common, inexhaustible reservoir of love. (1286–87)

A woman is hungry and she wants to eat. Thirsty and she wants to
drink.
She is in heat and she wants to be screwed.
What admirable qualities!
Woman is *natural*, that is to say abominable. (1272)

The more man cultivates the arts, the less he can get a hard-on.
A more and more apparent divorce takes place between the spirit
and the brute.
Only the brute has no trouble getting a hard-on, and screwing is
the lyricism of the masses.

To screw is to aspire to enter into another person, and the artist
never goes outside himself. (1295–96)

LEO BERSANI

ART, LOVE, PROSTITUTION, IMPOTENCE, ANDROGYNY, AND DIVINITY: Baudelaire frequently seems to be proposing a fundamental identity among all these terms. In the aphoristic prose of the *Journaux intimes*, he makes a strikingly unstable effort to locate the sexuality of art. From the enigmatic pronouncements just quoted, we can, however, infer a kind of fantasy-logic. Art resembles love in that both the lover and the artist go outside themselves; they lose themselves in others. This is not merely poetic empathy. Baudelaire is anxious to describe something more radical than a sympathetic projection into other people's lives. And his feelings about the prostitution of self inherent in love and art vary wildly. In the prose poem "Les Foules," Baudelaire praises "that ineffable orgy, that holy prostitution of the soul which, in an act of poetry and charity, gives itself entirely to the unexpected and to the unknown" (244). But in "Le *Confiteor* de l'Artiste" (also from the *Petits Poèmes en prose*), the very energy of an ecstatic loss or drowning of the self in "the immensity of the sky and the sea" at the end of an autumnal afternoon "creates a malaise and a positive suffering. My excessively taut nerves now transmit only screaming and painful vibrations" (232). Finally, in the passages quoted a moment ago from the *Journaux intimes*, the artist's availability to others is linked to the "abominable naturalness" of women. Both love and art are natural activities ("Man is an adoring animal"), and, with his usual ambivalence toward the idea of nature, Baudelaire characterizes the lover's and the artist's desires to prostitute themselves as both a holy and a degrading openness. What exactly is the nature of this openness?

In his essay on Constantin Guys, "Le Peintre de la vie moderne," Baudelaire tells the story of a friend—now "a famous painter"—who, as a child, would watch his father getting dressed and "contemplate, with both dazed astonishment and joy, the muscles of his arms, the gradations of his skin coloring tinged with pink and yellow, and the bluish network of his veins." Baudelaire suggests that the child's essentially artistic contemplation of the world is the equivalent of a violent appropriation of the self by forms alien to it: "The spectacle of external life was already filling him with respect and taking hold of his mind [Le tableau de la vie extérieure le pénétrait déjà de respect et s'emparait de son cerveau]. Form already obsessed him and possessed him." Before anything new, the child's (and the artist's) gaze is "fixed" and expresses an "animal-like ecstasy [l'oeil fixe et animalement extatique]." The self is suddenly possessed, filled up, even shaken by a scene from the world. "I will venture

348

further; I maintain that inspiration is related to *cerebral congestion*, and that every sublime thought is accompanied by a nervous shock or jolt [une secousse nerveuse], which varies in strength and which reverberates even in the cerebellum" (1159).

Artistic attention produces ecstasy and dissipates the self's integrity. "To go outside oneself" is equivalent to allowing the self to be penetrated, to having it invaded, congested, and shattered by the objects of its attention. Now the idea of the artist's prostitution covers two radically different experiences in Baudelaire. On the one hand, the artist-prostitute's "ineffable orgy" of openness to the world corresponds to a narcissistic appropriation of the world. The self is "lost" only to be relocated everywhere. In part, the description of Constantin Guys as "homme des foules" designates prostitution as a narcissistic strategy. "To be away from home, and yet to feel everywhere at home; to see the world, to be at the center of the world and remain hidden from the world, these are some of the lesser pleasures of those independent, passionate, impartial spirits who can be described only awkwardly in language. The observer is a *prince* who enjoys being incognito everywhere." When this observer rushes into the crowd, it is, as in Poe's story "The Man of the Crowd," in order to pursue a stranger who seems to be his double; Poe's convalescent hero, evoked by Baudelaire in "Le Peintre de la vie moderne," is fascinated by a man who reproduces his own passionate interest in crowds (1160, 1158). But Baudelaire also speaks, in the essay on Guys, of the artist being shattered by otherness. He is penetrated, congested, and shaken by the heterogeneity of "the spectacle of external life." The artist is excited *by and into* alien images. There is then the possibility that by prostituting himself, the artist, like the lover, will be "sacrificing" himself—or, more exactly, sacrificing a certain wholeness or integrity for the sake of those pleasurable nervous shocks which accompany the release of desiring energies by scenes from external life.

In the *Journaux intimes*, the shattering of the artist's integrity is also seen as a momentous sexual event. In order to be possessed by alien images, the artist must open himself in a way which Baudelaire immediately associates with feminine sexuality. Psychic penetrability is fantasized as sexual penetrability, and in glorifying "the cult of images" as "my great, my unique, my primary passion," Baudelaire is also confessing a passion which may change him into a woman (1295). Michel Butor has taken the opposite position, maintaining that images of masculine sexuality are linked to the fact of being a poet for Baudelaire. But this connection has less to do with the poet's intrinsic nature than with the will necessary for composition, and especially for publication. It is true, as Butor says, that Baudelaire associates will with virility, but the loss of virility cannot be reduced to a loss of will. Instead, will is a kind of secondary virility which struggles against a much more fundamental devirilization. For Butor, the decision of Baudelaire's family in 1844 to appoint a legal guardian who would dole out his inheritance to him for the rest of his life "devirilized" Baudelaire.[2] But the passages we are looking at from the *Journaux intimes* suggest that the very nature of poetic inspiration is enough to transform the poet from a man into a woman. The "abominable" feature of women is that they are "natural," and the examples of their closeness to nature all have to do with their appetite to absorb (food, drink, and the penis). They would seem to be characterized by an animal ecstasy very much like that ecstatic openness which, in "Le Peintre de la vie moderne," Baudelaire finds in children and in artists.

The paradoxical final consequence of this line of (fantasy) reasoning is that the very sexuality of art desexualizes the artist. The last passage from the *Journaux intimes* quoted at the beginning of this essay is ambiguous in this respect. "The more man cultivates the arts, the less he can get a hard-on." But the reasons which Baudelaire gives for this sexual debilitation seem to go against what we have just been saying. Art would now seem to belong to the domain of the spiritual; the artist gradually loses contact with his bodily appetites because of a divorce between his flesh and his spirit. The idea of going outside oneself reappears in this passage, but now it is connected with the antithesis of artistic activity, with carnal appetites. Sex, brutishness, the absence of art, and going outside oneself all belong together; on the other side, there is impotence, spirituality, art, and a permanent self-containment (the artist never leaves himself).

But even here the antithesis is somewhat qualified by the suggestion that sexual energy may not be the opposite of art, but the only version of art which the lower classes are capable of producing. Sex *is* art, but art takes the form of sex only in the masses: "Screwing is the lyricism of the masses." The "opposition" between the activities of the flesh and those of the spirit may turn out to be a continuous scale of expression for a single impulse. Furthermore, the assertion of the artist's self-pro-

350

tective immobility is in such profound contradiction not only with other theoretical statements, but also with so much of Baudelaire's poetry, that we may suspect it to be a defense against Baudelaire's most powerfully felt experience of art. In "Le Peintre de la vie moderne," Baudelaire significantly hesitates to call Guys a dandy because of the very quality which accounts for his being an artist: his "insatiable passion" to see and to feel, to lose himself in crowds ("Sa passion et sa profession, c'est d'épouser la foule"). It is by his inability to remain "insensitive" (or self-contained) that Guys "detaches himself violently from dandyism" (1160).[3] We may therefore conclude that behind the explicit statement from the *Journaux* which we have just considered, there is a hidden assertion: the sexual explosiveness of artistic activity (rather than its "spirituality") renders the artist impotent. The constant in Bauldelaire's thought would be the idea of a connection between art and the loss of virility. At times, it is the sublimity of art which accounts for this loss; at other times—and, I think, much more interestingly—the artist loses his virile identity *through* an obscene openness to external reality which makes him an artist but which also makes him—a woman.[4]

The artist is intrinsically an unanchored self. The energy with which he penetrates the world (or is penetrated by the world) sets him afloat among alien forms of being. And, because they repeat the poet's exceptional openness, God and lovers similarly partake of the exhilarating risks of problematic being. In love and in art, identity floats. Its wholeness can be shattered, as we have begun to see, in various ways. The self may be invaded by scenes from the world to the point of not being able to maintain any distance from them, to the point of being entirely absorbed in them. Psychic identity is also dissipated by the very force with which it is projected toward others in the same way that the orgasm dissipates the intensity of our sexual desire for others. Or, conversely, consciousness adopts an ecstatic passivity before the "spectacle of external life," a passivity which in itself transforms the poet into a woman. The *Journaux intimes* are thus exceptionally suggestive about the relation between poetic production and sexuality. For Baudelaire, the esthetic imagination is inseparable from erotic intensities and shifting sexual identities. His work is, as a result, an extraordinarily rich document about both the nature of sensual pleasure in poetic activity and the psychic dislocations implicit in poetic (erotic) fantasy.

Notes

1. Charles Baudelaire, *Oeuvres complètès*, edited by Y.-G. Le Dantec and Claude Pichois (Paris: Pléiade, 1961), p. 1247. All quotations from Baudelaire will be from this edition, and page references will be given in the text. All prose translations are my own.

2. Michel Butor, *Histoire extraordinaire, essai sur un rêve de Baudelaire* (Paris: Gallimard, 1961), pp. 40–42.

3. Speaking of the same passage, Sartre writes: "it is clear that dandyism represents a higher ideal than poetry"; it is Baudelaire's "sterile wish" for something beyond poetry (Jean-Paul Sartre, *Baudelaire* [Paris: Gallimard, 1947], pp. 183, 196).

4. Baudelaire's attitude toward the artist's dual sexuality is not always negative. In *Les Paradis artificiels*, he speaks of "a delicate skin, a distinguished accent, a kind of androgynous quality" acquired by men raised principally by women ("L'homme qui, dès le commencement, a été longtemps baigné dans la molle atmosphère de la femme"). Without these qualities, "the roughest and most virile genius remains, as far as artistic perfection is concerned, an incomplete being" (444–45). Butor sees the *mundus muliebris* as the "necessary theater" in which the artist, by an act of will, conquers his virility—and his artistic powers. The devirilized male artist who desires women is, as Butor nicely concludes, a lesbian, and lesbians for Baudelaire are "the very symbol of the apprentice poet, of the poet who has not yet published" (*Histoire extraordinaire*, pp. 79, 85–86).

23.

Psychoanalysis:
The French Connection

Geoffrey H. Hartman

EVERY LITERARY NARRATIVE contains another narrative: however continuous or full the one seems to be, the other is discontinuous and lacunary. Jean-Luc Nancy has called this "other" narrative the "discours de la syncope." Given that our minds tend to overestimate, even when wary or ashamed of it, fictional writing, the reader is usually forced into the position of having to recover the "discours de la syncope," that is, the precariousness of all transitions, or the undecidability of fiction's truth. Every story is like Isabel's in Melville's novel *Pierre*, and every authoritative title or naming should be treated on the analogy of "Pierre, or the Ambiguities."

Yet this deepening sense of an endless or ungrounded or non-continuous discourse is not purely cautionary or destructive. There is something we can take away with us: a perception similar to that offered by myths and positive interpretation. Our vision of the psyche's vulnerability broadens and intensifies; it extends into the bowels of language, from images to names and to the pathos that insistently attends the giving or calling out of a name. However different the Gothic gloom of Melville's *Pierre* and Faulkner's *Absalom, Absalom*, both novels turn on the seductive

From Geoffrey H. Hartman, *Saving the Text* (Baltimore, Md.: Johns Hopkins University Press, 1981). Copyright © 1981 Johns Hopkins University Press. Reprinted by permission.

centrality of a scene of recognition—of naming and acknowledgment. The concepts of vocation, initiation, and identity run parallel yet subordinate to that central hinge that Aristotle in the *Poetics* already discerned as essential to Greek tragedy.

The desire for a "here and now," fixed image or defining word, mystic portrait or identity-imposing story, is not dissociable, according to psychiatry, from family romance: the recognition scene is always a displaced or sublimated family scene. It is no different with the Christian scandal of the "Presence of the Word" (*logos spermatikos*) in the Immaculate Conception, or more precisely, in the Annunciation. Let me, therefore, recenter these reflections on the most famous scene of nomination in our culture: the Annunciation.

There are, of course, other scenes that show the word of God coming to earth with vocational force. But this episode is particularly relevant to Genet because it "magnifies" a woman; indeed, Mary's hymn, called the Magnificat after its Latin version, and recorded in Luke, has become part of Christian liturgy. Not only is the Presence of the Word in this scene of nomination also the Word of the Presence ("Hail, O favored one, the Lord is with you," Luke 1:28), but the transcendental signifier, as we might truly call it, issues in a Magnificat because it takes away a curse: of infertility, and more generally, in reference to woman, of impure, because infertile, menstruation. Mary's condition, moreover, could have shamed her (Matthew 1:18–20, Luke 1:24), but through the intervention of the angelic word a potential denunciation becomes an annunciation.

In Genet, profanely, the same structure holds. Denunciation is converted to Annunciation; the curse (perhaps that of being born of woman, or male seed considered as impure, as a menstrual flow, *unless* made fertile in the woman) is taken away; and the Magnificat of a convict's style results. How "you are a thief" should become functionally equivalent to the sanctifying "you are with child" is the psychic puzzle that Sartre and Derrida try to resolve.[1]

It is not by chance that Derrida should choose to continue through Genet his critique of the "closure" imposed on thought or language by the so-called logocentric tradition. Within that closure even miracles have their limits: virgin birth, or fullness (of grace) must be female. A male parthenogenesis is "inconceivable," even as miracle, except through the ultimate veil of theologic mystery. Scenes of nomination that affect men

354

in scripture tend in fact, as with Abraham, to be a call for child sacrifice. But Freudian pornosophy has the bad taste to raise the question of whether the artist's work is not a male childbirth, and his book a "proles sine matre nata" (Montesquieu).

"You are a thief" can only stand for "you are with child" if, at some level, Genet is trying to steal the womb itself—whereas he can at most, if we trust Ferenczi's bioanalysis, steal *into* the womb and give something to that death in order to live.[2] Genet is not successful in modifying even imaginatively the logocentric enclosure: he simply erects a subversive, symmetrical counterpart, the image of male fullness of grace, "L'annonce fait à Jean-Marie." Sound reasoning on his flowery or anthographic style must include the thought that flowers such as the lilies of the field or those associated with the Annunciation are pure in the sense that Hegel caught when he posits a nonagonistic "religion of flowers": they can grow and multiply as if by grace, without the curse of labor (cf. Genesis 3:16ff.). The commandment, by place the first in the Bible, "Be fruitful and multiply," is death to hear, as Adam remarks in Milton's *Paradise Lost* (10:731), for it means, after the Fall, a multiplying of deaths or, as for Genet, *genitality with no grace except as it "blesses" a woman.* His family of thieves and murderers is erected in vain opposition to the survival of the "onto-theologic" model in secular society.

Genet's mirror image of the Holy Family, then, expresses a reversal rather than a transvaluation of values. Given the conservative character of the institution of language, it is doubtful that there could be transvaluation. We can reverse or trope catachresically, we can deploy all the subversive flowers in the anthology of speech, or we can reverse in another sense, by deconstruction, and expose the fallacy that every great artist's mind passes on itself—the result remains a secret recognition scene. As Genet himself has written: "The world is turned inside out like a glove. It happens that I am the glove and I understand at last that on the day of judgment God will call me with my own voice: 'Jean, Jean.' "[3] Or Lacan: "The Word always subjectively includes its own reply. . . . The function of Language is not to inform but to evoke. What I seek in the Word is the response of the other. . . . In order to find him, I call him by a name which he must assume or refuse in order to reply to me." "The allocution of the subject entails an allocutor . . . even if he is speaking 'off' or 'to the wings.' He addresses himself to *ce (grand) Autre* whose theoretical basis I have consolidated."[4]

Even the most deliberate counterannunciation yet conceived, Mallarmé's mirror scene in the *Herodiade*, can only use the language of flowers against itself. "Vous mentez, o fleur nue de mes lèvres." Herodiade's specular cries know they have no issue. Devoted to sterility, Herodiade is Mary's opposite in the drama of the logos that eventuates so curiously in Genet's (or Derrida's) image of the mother as "bourreau berceur." The logos as the *relève* (*Aufhebung*/fulfillment) of metaphor reifies metaphor and suppresses language fertility. Christ and Herod become co-conspirators in this Genet-ic massacre.

"Vous mentez," that denunciation so often addressed to the artist, is now, in the Nietzsche-(Wilde)-Derrida line of thinking, the only annunciation. It is addressed to language itself, "fleur nue de nos lèvres." Lacan, following Heidegger, is tempted to ground language, or the symbolic realm, in that peculiar mendacity, or error, or untruth. The second part of *Being and Time* (especially paragraphs 54–60) contains an analysis of the elusiveness of the quest for truth in terms of self-identity. Such a quest is based on a *Sich-Verhören*, a word that in German denotes at one and the same time our attempt to know the truth by taking the self into custody and interrogating it, and the failure of that attempt, since a mishearing or mistaking of what has been said is inevitable. Language gives the lie to the ego's capture of a specular identity just as it gives the lie to itself. The genuine logos is always a dia-logos; and the guardian spirit of the symbolic and differential realm is a Father barring the image's closure of dialogue, of stilling prematurely what one might call, after Hegel, the *elaboration* of the negative.

Yet to ground something in untruth is still to ground it. Is a true untruth better than an untrue truth? The dialectics become dizzying or Ibsenian. Truth (*vérité*) remains, moreover, an important word for Lacan, and Derrida objects to it, as Adorno to a Heidegger-influenced "jargon of authenticity." It might also be observed that the symbolic father (or Derrida's counterpart, the spectral mother), while a reformulation of Freud's dead primal father of *Totem and Taboo*, has no more clinical or verifiable reality than the "fair Lady of Shallot" in Tennyson's poem of that name, who seems to be both victim and guardian of the specular capture Lacan posits. This allusion shows, however, that a *sort* of evidence exists, even if contaminated by the very realm—literature or art—being limited by scientific definition.[5]

Derrida is very aware of this contamination, which he deconstructs rather than denies or delimits. He does not place language, by theoretical fiat, on the side of the symbolic and against the specular realm of the absolute or totalizing illusion. Language is not a "cause" that cures (a "talking cure") by drawing the mirror image into the discourse of the Other. Though Derrida views language as a School of Virtue chastening the eternally narcissistic ego, he sees no triumph of the therapeutic by means of a language that is itself infected by a sickness unto death he has labeled logo-centrism.

"I am half-sick of shadows," says the Lady of Shallot, and turns from her mirror to the reality of advent. She did not know that by her avertedness, by staying within representation, she had postponed death. The most art can do, as a mirror of language, is to burn through, in its cold way, the desire for self-definition, fulness of grace, presence; simply to expose the desire to own one's own name, to inhabit it numinously in the form of "proper" noun, words, or the signatory act each poem aspires to be. Though Tennyson's Lady, unlike Mallarmé's Herodiade, "knows not what the curse may be" as she helps to weave Tennyson's language, the result is the same: a negative scene of nomination. She becomes in death what she was without knowing it in life: a floating signifier.

> Under tower and balcony,
> By garden-wall and gallery,
> A gleaming shape she floated by,
> Dead-pale between the houses high,
> Silent into Camelot.
> Out upon the wharfs they came,
> Knight and burgher, lord and dame,
> And round the prow they read her name,
> *The Lady of Shallot.*

My reference to Tennyson suggests that a *sortie* from the textual involution of the French sphere is possible. Derrida has himself tried interpreting Poe, who is comparable to Tennyson, yet does not provide a true exit because French commentary has been investing him since Baudelaire and Mallarmé. The trouble with Tennyson is that his poetic

357

dream-work seems at first no work at all. It is so easy, so unlabored—deceptively "idle," to use a charged word of his own—when held beside Mallarmé's. Poem and lady remain immaculate though web, mirror, or spell may break. Such impassibility is perhaps part of the infection, an unresolved narcissism of festering lily or psyche. Yet this liaison between specular and poetic is precisely what fosters the illusion of completeness and so the attractive fetish we call a poem. For a moment the et cetera of language is absorbed into that fetish: remnant and rhyme coincide.

Derrida, however, does not allow himself even so much dallying with closure. The rhyming properties of language, the sonic rings and resonances always potentially there, are like Poe's "The Bells" (cited by him) and their telltale symptoms of a vertiginous *glissement* of language toward an uncontrollable echoing: a mad round of verbal associations or signifier-signifying signifiers. The anxiety roused by language *as* language is that this echoing movement cannot be economized, that it is a fluid curse, a telling that is merely that of time, whose wasting becomes a trolling: *Glas*.

His adventure is
having been *named*.
    —Sartre, *Saint Genet*

. . . the difficulty begins with the name.
    —Ralph Waldo Ellison, "Hidden Name and Complex Fate"

The subject too, if he can appear to be
the slave of language, is all the more
so of a discourse in the universal
movement, in which his place is
already inscribed at birth, if only
by virtue of his proper name.
    —Lacan, "The Agency of the Letter in the Unconscious or
      Reason since Freud"

My hypothesis, inspired by French reflections, that literature is the elaboration of a specular name, is not meant to encourage a new substantialism of the word. Since the specular name is always already a fiction—hidden or forgotten or canceled, or motivated unconsciously by a life that dies into allegory—it can determine autobiographical quests only in the manner of Plato's theory of anamnesis. The quest, as it becomes lifelong and remains indeterminate, recuperates esoteric traditions: stories about the magic of names, anagrammatic events of various kinds, scenes of nomination or annunciation, and generally, to steal the title of Karl Abraham's early essay, "the determining force of names."

Gershom Scholem has published a strange name fantasy of Walter Benjamin's, written at Ibiza, Spain, in 1933.[6] I would like to conclude with it. It involves Paul Klee's picture *Angelus Novus* (a personal icon for Benjamin, who owned it) and the ancient tradition of the natal genius or personal angel whose name is hidden but who represents one's true identity and secret self. Benjamin's allegory, close in some respects to a Kafka parable and in other respects to a Baudelaire prose poem, was deeply linked to his situation at that time: his troubled relation to women, his Jewish ancestry, and his sense of being born under Saturn (he had written *The Origin of German Tragedy* and was steeped in Baudelaire). Scholem's beautiful and thorough interpretation has brought this out in a definitive way, and I cannot add to what he has said.

My interest lies elsewhere; in Benjamin's fantasy as a particularly revealing example of how autobiography is determined by the idea of a hidden—spectral or specular—name. I will quote only the opening paragraphs, which constitute about half of this interesting document, but they suffice to show how Benjamin verges on a complex scene of nomination: an angelus-annunciation that turns not only on the magical force of an occult name but also on what might happen when that name is or must be betrayed.

Agesilaus Santander

When I was born the thought came to my parents that I might perhaps become a writer. Would it not be good, then, if not everybody noticed immediately that I was a Jew. That is why they gave me in addition to the name by which I was called [*Rufnamen*] two further, exceptional ones, from which it couldn't be perceived either that a Jew bore them or that they belonged to him as first names [*Vornamen*]. Forty years ago no parents could have proved more far-seeing. What they considered a remote possibility has come true. Except that the precautions by which they meant to counter fate were set aside by the one most concerned. That is to say, instead of making it public together with his writings, he treated it as the Jews the additional name of their children which remains secret. Indeed, they only communicate it to them when they reach manhood. Since, however, this manhood can occur more than once in a lifetime, and the secret name may remain the same and untransfigured only for the pious, so to whoever is not pious the change of name might be revealed all at once, with the onset of a new manhood. Thus with me. But it remains the name, nevertheless, which binds together the vital forces in strictest union, and which must be guarded against the unauthorized [*Unberufenen*].

Yet this name is not at all an enrichment of the one it names. On the contrary, much falls away from his image when that name becomes audible. His image loses above all the gift of appearing to be human. In the room I occupied in Berlin, before he stepped—armed and encased—out of my name into the light, he fixed his picture on the wall: New Angel. The Kabbala relates that in every instant [*Nu*] God creates a numberless number of new angels, all of whom are only destined, before they dissolve into nothing, to sing for a single moment the praise of God before His throne. Such an angel the New one pretended to be before he would name himself.

What emerges with startling clarity is the *aura* of being named or imaged. Benjamin also said: "Things made of glass have no 'aura' " ("Die Dinge aus Glas haben keine 'Aura' "). So the world he projects in his Romance of Being Named resists translucence or glassification: the very word "Agesilaus" strikes one as the opposite of the word "Glas"—it contains g-l-a-s, in fact, and becomes, as it were, its antonym. Recalling Benajmin's interest in anagrams Scholem suggests that the title of his fantasy should be deciphered as "Der Angelus Satanas" (The Angel Satan), and he links it to the "New Angel" of Klee's picture that continued to haunt Benjamin. (See, especially, the ninth of his "Theses on the Philosophy of History," written not long before his death.) But one should add that the insistence of this picture in the writer's life is itself "demonic": it reveals a specular fixation on Benjamin's part, and seems to be transposed from German Romantic fiction or the gothic novella. However we unriddle it, "Agesilaus Santander" remains an abracadabra phrase that aims at reviving the aura of names, or of a naming with ritual and fixative power.

I doubt, then, that this title is decipherable in a single way. The difference in sound shape, for example, between Agesilaus and Angelus (Novus) could foreground the syllable "laus," to remind us of the Latin word for praise; if so, a relation might suggest itself between "Age"/"Ange" plus "laus" and the cabalistic angel whose essence is to praise God a single moment, an "Augen"-blick.

Other decipherings may be possible, but I will try only one more. Benjamin thinks of himself as a refugee: he has abandoned the orthodoxy of his fathers; he is in Spain, from which the Jews were expelled and a former home of the cabalists, whose mystical reflections on names was known to him through Scholem; the Nazis have come to power; and he ponders angels whose essence is not permanence but transience, whose newness is their nowness, or their flight from *Nu* to *Nichts*, as they praise and wait to be dissolved. Considering, then, that this scholar was doomed to wander, if not to flee, and that his major work had been on seventeenth-century German literature, might he not have remembered the poet of that era who took the pseudonym "Angelus Silesius" for his *Der Cherubinischer Wandersmann* (The Cherub Wanderer), a collection of epigrammatic mystical verses? "Agesilaus," though a real and not a made-up name, seems to scramble "Angelus Silesius" into a single word, and Santander could suggest the mixed Santa/Satanic quality of Benjamin the pilgrim or some desired relation to Southern (Spanish and cabalistic) rather than Northern spirit of place through the name of this town.

What we are given, then, is the aura of a name: "Agesilaus Santander" is the quintessence of an anagram rather than a univocally decipherable writing. The scrambling is permanent and the meanings we recover are fugitive constructions, like the "new angels" in contrast to the old. The name may even accuse the maker of the name: it is "satanic" also in that. For it stands as the product of an artificial mysticism that evokes an "aura artificiel" in the manner of Baudelaire's "paradis artificiel." It betrays a fallen aura, mere aroma of aura, the whiff of a Turkish cigarette and eastern mysteries. Like "Xanadu" and "Kubla Khan" the name is an authentic fake, a given or proper name consumed by the imagination, the scar of a signature that belongs to no one. "Its traits had no human likeness." Benjamin's fantasy could be part of a book on hashish he meant to write. He continued to look, patiently and yet in flight, to the origin of all names in the garden God had planted eastward of Eden. Psychoanalysis: the Eden connection.

Notes

1. Sartre's book on Genet, originally published in 1952, is translated by Bernard Frechtman as *Saint Genet: Actor and Martyr* (New York: G. Braziller, 1963). I refer chiefly to the section "A Dizzying Word" in book 1, which contains the story of Genet's "specular capture" (Lacan's, not Sartre's, phrase) by the identity-imposing words "You are a thief." Freud's remarks on the "language of flowers" in *The Interpretation of Dreams* are found in the Standard Edition of the *Complete Psychological Works* (London: Hogarth Press, 1953–74), 4:319–25, and 5:652.

2. Sandor Ferenczi's bioanalysis is in his *Thalassa: Toward a Theory of Geni-*

tality, first published in German in 1924. An important step in the French reception of the book was Nicolas Abraham's edition for the "Petite Bibliothèque Payot" in 1962.

3. Jacques Derrida, *Glas* (Paris: Galilée, 1974), p. 220b. Translations from *Glas* are my own. The reference after each quotation is to the page and column (a left, b right) of *Glas*.

4. Several essays by Lacan are available in translation; Antony Wilden's *The Language of the Self* (Baltimore: Johns Hopkins University Press, 1968), contains a fully annotated version of the famous "Discours de Rome." I quote from Wilden's translation. A fine Lacanian study, directly focused on literature and relevant to *Glas*, is that of J. Laplanche, *Hölderlin et la question du père* (Paris: Presses Universitaires de France, 1961). Other analysts influenced by Lacan or D. W. Winnicott or both, who have done work to interest English readers, are André Green and J.-B. Pontalis.

5. On wounding and naming, see L. Brisman, " 'At Thy Word': A Reading of *Romeo and Juliet*," *Bulletin of the Midwest MLA* (1975), 8:21–35; also Norman Holland, "A Touching of Literary and Psychiatric Education," *Seminars in Psychiatry* (1973), 5:287–99. On the psychic import of names, the following sources may prove interesting: Sigmund Freud, *Totem and Taboo*, ch. 4, the section on "Nominalist Theories"; Karl Abraham's short essay of 1911, "Über die determinierende Kraft des Namens." Jean Starobinski has edited Saussure's notebooks, recovering his theory of the anagrammatic (hypogrammatic) generation of certain hermetic verses (*Les Mots sous les mots* [Paris: Gallimard, 1971]). See also Jacques Derrida, *De la grammatologie* (Paris: Editions Minuit, 1967), pp. 157ff., "La Guerre des noms propres." This book has been translated by G. Spivak as *Of Grammatology* (Baltimore: Johns Hopkins University Press, 1976). Also Dwight Culler, *Tennyson* (New Haven: Yale University Press, 1977), ch. 1, "Tennyson, Tennyson, Tennyson." The amphibious relations between proper and common nouns are deepened by the work of Nicolas Abraham and Maria Torok on cryptonomy in *Le Verbier de l'homme aux loups* (Paris: Aubier-Flammarion, 1976). This is preceded by "Fors," an essay by Derrida translated in *Georgia Review* (1977), 31:64–120.

6. Gershom Scholem's "Walter Benjamin und sein Engel," containing the *Agesilaus Santander* text in its two versions, is found in *Zur Aktualität Walter Benjamins*, edited by Siegfried Unseld (Frankfurt am Main: Suhrkamp, 1972). I quote the second version of Benjamin's text and have modified the translation by W. J. Dannhauser in *Denver Quarterly* (1974), 9:9–12. There is some word-play that cannot be rendered in translation; it includes perhaps an allusion to the fact that as a name "Walter Benjamin" seems to contain two first names (Benjamin, the family name, being also a common first name). The German word for first name, "Vorname" is homophonous with "Vornahme," that is, "project" or "resolution." Benjamin's concept of the "aura" is described at length in "The Work of Art in the Age of Mechanical Reproduction," originally published in 1936, available in translation in *Illuminations*, edited by Hannah Arendt (New York: Schocken Books, 1969).

24.

Narcissism: The Freudian

Myth Demythified by Proust

René Girard

IN HIS *On Narcissism: An Introduction*, Freud defines this notion as
the attitude of a person who treats himself as an object of sexual love.
He can also detect, he believes, an "object narcissism" in which the subject turns his libido not directly toward himself but toward love objects
that "resemble" this subject too much to qualify as "real" objects. These
objects must be viewed as mere appendages of the subject. Narcissism,
in other words, is the condition of a subject who prefers never to get out
of himself, even when he appears to do so.[1]

Freud likes to think in terms of a fixed quantity of libidinal energy
that can be directed either toward the self, or a substitute of the self, on
the one hand, or toward a "real" object, different enough from the subject, on the other. In the first case—narcissism—the libidinal energy goes
in a circle, so to speak; it stays with the subject or returns to it. As a
result this subject may be said to be self-contained or self-sufficient,
whereas in the second case—"true object love"—the libidinal energy is
discharged outside. The self is "diminished," "impoverished."

Still according to *Narcissism*, it is normal for children to be highly
narcissistic; even adults should retain a certain degree of narcissism but

From René Girard, *Psychoanalysis, Creativity, and Literature*, Alan Roland, ed. (New York:
Columbia University Press, 1978). Copyright © 1978 Columbia University Press. Reprinted by permission.

not too much. An excessively narcissistic adult can be said to be "immature." Freud considers women and artists as especially prone to excessive narcissism. The notion of narcissism plays a major role in Freud's theory of art and the artist.

In the nineteenth century and in the first half of the twentieth, there is a large amount of philosophical and literary theory that corresponds rather closely to the views of Freud on the affinity between artists and the self-sufficiency labeled by him "narcissism." A major difference, however, is that in many pronouncements by artists and writers, the condition described by psychoanalysis as excessively and pathologically narcissistic is presented as a positive asset, even as an ideal toward which the artist must strive if he has not yet truly achieved it. Between philosophers such as Fichte or Stirner, some major romantic and symbolist poets, and a prose writer like André Gide in twentieth-century France, we had many differences, of course, but we find also a common element; it could be summed up as a deliberate embrace and celebration of some or all features of "excessive narcissism." We often hear from these writers that loved objects are desirable and poetic only insofar as they become reflections of the poet's self. As soon as it is no longer suffused with subjective passion and imagination, reality becomes banal, vulgar, disappointing.

When Marcel Proust expresses himself directly in regard to desire, as if he were a psychologist, rather than through his fiction, he shares the narcissistic or individualistic ideology that was still widespread among intellectuals and artists during his lifetime. People, he writes, love primarily themselves, and they seek themselves in the objects of their desire. They endow the desired object with a mystery and beauty that really flows from themselves. The superior self radiates enough energy to transfigure commonplace reality into its own image, turning it into poetry. Only when the genuine *otherness* of outside reality breaks through to us does disenchantment occur. Reality does not come up to the high expectations of the self; it is less beautiful, less rich, less authentic, less substantial than the self's own private projections.

If we read the theoretical pronouncements on the nature of the self and of desire in *Remembrance of Things Past*, the great masterpiece Proust wrote and published in the last ten years of his life, we find that they often remain very much as before. As long, therefore, as we base our judgment on Proust's theoretical pronouncements, wherever they may come from, or on his actual practice as a novelist in *Jean Santeuil*, we will find only material that appears to confirm Freud's conception of narcissism and its privileged application to both the artist and the work of art.

The only place where things are different is also the one that counts most from a literary standpoint, Proust's practice as a novelist in the great masterpiece. There, the fictional substance is quite new as far as desire is concerned; it no longer corresponds to the narcissistic model. It is the desire of a self that feels extremely "impoverished," even destitute. The word "impoverishment" is actually used by Proust, just as it is used by Freud in *Narcissism*, in connection with "anaclytic" or "object love." We may suppose, therefore, that between the two novels, Proust has shifted from "narcissism" to "object love." The fact, after all, should not surprise us since the Proust of the later novel is older than the Proust of the earlier one. "Object love" is constantly described by Freud as "more mature" than "narcissistic love."

This idea seems strengthened at first by the type of object that fascinates the narrator as well as the other characters in *Remembrance of Things Past*. Love-objects always give an impression of "blissful autonomy" or "self-sufficiency." They correspond to Freud's idea of "intact narcissism." It is no longer the subject of desire that is narcissistic as in the earlier novel, but its object. This sounds like a paradox but, if we turn back to *Narcissism*, we will see that the same paradox is present in Freud, too, and that it is a paradox of "anaclytic" or object desire.

It seems very evident that one person's narcissism has a great attraction for those others who have renounced part of their own narcissism and are seeking after object-love; the charm of a child lies to a great extent in his narcissism, his self-sufficiency and inaccessibility, just as does the charm of certain animals which seem not to concern themselves about us, such as cats and the large beasts of prey. In literature, indeed, even the great criminal and the humorist compel our interest by the narcissistic self-importance with which they manage to keep at arm's length everything which would diminish the importance of their ego. It is as if we envied them their power of retaining a blissful state of mind—an unassailable libido-position which we ourselves have since abandoned. The great charm of the narcissistic woman has, however, its reverse side; a large part of the dissatisfaction of the lover, of his doubts of the women's love, of his complaints of her enigmatic nature, have their root in this incongruity between the types of object-choice.[2]

If we go to the great descriptions of desire, in *Remembrance of Things Past*, Proust is going to look even more "mature" and Freud even more astute than the one and the other did up to this point. Down to almost every detail, it seems, everything corresponds to that "great attraction" that "one person's narcissism" exerts upon those "who have renounced part of their own narcissism and are seeking after object-love."

Let us turn to a famous passage in *Within a Budding Grove:* the first encounter by Marcel, the narrator, with a group of girls he calls *la petite bande.* The scene is in the resort town of Balbec—Cabourg—in Normandy. Marcel's attention becomes immediately attracted by the adolescents because of the tightly knit appearance they give, and their contemptuous indifference toward anyone but each other.

> Though they were now separately identifiable, still the mutual response which they gave one another with eyes animated by self-sufficiency and the spirit of comradeship, in which were kindled at every moment now the interest now the insolent indifference with which each of them sparkled according as her glance fell on one of her friends or on passing strangers, that consciousness, moreover, of knowing one another intimately enough always to go about together, by making them a "band apart" established between their independent and separate bodies, as slowly they advanced, a single atmosphere making of them a whole as homogenous in its parts as it was different from the crowd through which their procession gradually wound.
>
> For an instant, as I passed the dark one with the fat cheeks who was wheeling a bicycle, I caught her smiling, sidelong glance, aimed from the centre of that inhuman world which enclosed the life of his little tribe, an inaccessible, unknown world to which the idea of what I was could certainly never attain nor find a place in it.[3]

Words like "autonomy" and "self-sufficiency" recur several times in the course of the description which extends in the novel over ten pages. There is not one feature in one writer which does not have its counterpart in the other. The girls, of course, are neither "great criminals" nor "humorists" but their behavior verges, at times, on juvenile delinquency, and Marcel immediately assumes that they are not "virtuous." They must have many love affairs, he speculates, in which they always play the commanding role; they are never the ones who get hurt. He also supposes they must be of a sharply satirical mind, and he is afraid they would make fun of him if they noticed his existence, something he both terribly fears and desires.

At one point, one of the girls climbs on the bandstand in the shade of which an old banker is sitting and she jumps over him, frightening her senile victim who is made more impotent still by the brief absence of his wife: she has left him to make him believe he can still manage by himself. Marcel, too, has been temporarily freed from the surveillance and protection of his grandmother, and he visibly identifies with the old man. Fear is an indispensable ingredient in his desire, which is greatly inflamed by such a mixture of youthful arrogance and innocent cruelty. He imagines the adolescents as the very antithesis of what he, himself, is, invulnerable to the vicissitudes of existence, just as invincible in everything they undertake as he feels vulnerable and ungainly, unsuccessful and sickly.

Throughout the description the accent lies on the youthful inhumanity of the tightly knit little group. Just as in the case of Freud, the beloved narcissist is compared to animals that are not only graceful and cruel but above all completely indifferent to human beings. In Freud the animals are "cats and large birds of prey." In Proust they are sea gulls, as befits an episode that takes place on a beach. The metaphor is more elaborate but the significance remains exactly the same.

The similarities between Proust and Freud are striking. And yet, a careful observer will note a difference which a little reflection will reveal to be crucial. Freud clearly implies that the people who have renounced part of their narcissism did so as a matter of choice, not because it is pleasurable to be sure but out of a sense of obligation. They have decided to become "mature" and "virile." They are the good people, in other words, they choose the path of duty.

With Proust, there is no such thing as a voluntary renunciation. "Blissful autonomy" and "self-sufficiency" are things the narrator never freely renounced because they were not his to renounce in the first place. As far as he can remember, his lot has always been an "impoverishment" so extreme as to amount to complete destitution, too painful certainly to be freely assumed.

Of what possession does the narrator feel deprived? Of the "blissful autonomy," of course, that the desired *other* seems to possess. It is quite clear in the case of *la petite bande*. The narrator does not desire any of the girls in particular but all simultaneously, at least most of the time. The very coherence of the group, its "tightly knit" character, gives it the appearance of self-sufficiency that the narrator would like to appropriate, that awakens his desire, in other words.

What Freud calls "intact narcissism" is the main, even the sole object of desire in the novel of Proust. Since "intact narcissism" is defined as perfect self-sufficiency and since self-sufficiency is what the subject of desire does not have and would like to have, there is nothing "incongruous" in the choice of "intact narcissism" as an object of desire.

With Proust, in other words, desire can be both self-oriented and other-oriented at the same time, because the main "business" of the impoverished or even nonexistent self is to acquire the richer self that it lacks, or, if you prefer, to become "self-sufficient" at the expense or after the pattern of the self it desires, a self that already is, or appears, "self-sufficient."

Nothing is more logical, therefore, than the superficially paradoxical conjuction of self-centeredness and other-centeredness. Freud does not perceive that logic, or he refuses it because he insists on viewing what he calls "object-desire" as a selfless gesture, a deliberate and virtuous sacrifice of "self-sufficiency," rather than a fascination for an alien "self-sufficiency," forced upon us by a state of severe and involuntary deprivation in which human beings might generally find themselves in regard to that commodity. And yet, the possibility of that solution cannot be far from his mind since he observes "the great attraction" that "one person's narcissism has . . . for those other who have renounced, . . ." etc. The Proustian solution is almost visible, and yet Freud must not really see it because, if he saw it, he could not view the "great attraction" as an incongruity.

Could it be that Proustian desire is really "narcissistic" in Freudian terms, in other words that it focuses on objects "too similar" to the subject, too much like mirror images to deserve the badge of "true object-love." The following lines certainly do not support this narcissistic hypothesis:

The fact that we had, these girls and I, not one habit—as we had not one idea—in common, was to make it more difficult for me to make friends with them and to please them. But perhaps, also, it was thanks to those differences, to my consciousness that there did not enter into the composition of the nature and actions of these girls a single element that I knew or possessed, that there came in place of my satiety a thirst—like that with which a dry land burns—for a life which my soul, because it had never until now received one drop of it, would absorb all the more greedily in long draughts with a more perfect imbibition.[4]

This desire has nothing to do with the so-called narcissistic desire of Freud since it is not resemblance but an absolute difference that it seeks. And this absolute difference is the same thing, in the last analysis, as the self-sufficiency the other always seems to possess and the Ego never possesses. This grim vision of desire is as far from narcissism à la Freud as from the reassuring clichés of literary and philosophical individualism in the nineteenth and twentieth century, and yet, I repeat, Proust tends to revert to these clichés and to something very much like "narcissism," as a result, when he speaks about desire in the abstract.

To say that no one is a narcissist for oneself and that everyone wants to be one is to say that the self does not exist in the substantial sense that Freud gives to that term in *Narcissism*. But everybody is trying to acquire such a substantial self; everybody believes, more or less as Freud does, in the existence of the substantial self.

If the substantial self does not really exist, how can everybody believe in its existence? We already know the Proustian answer to that question. Everybody believes that someone else possesses the self he wants to acquire. That is why everybody experiences desire.

Snobbery in Proust operates exactly like erotic desire; as a matter of fact it can hardly be distinguished from it. A salon can become desirable only if it appears blissfully self-sufficient. And it will so appear only if it is sufficiently *exclusive*, if it excludes enough potential candidates whose very eagerness is interpreted as unworthiness. A salon is like a collective self at least for the outsiders, who desire to appropriate that self. It would be wrong, however, to conclude that the self is a purely subjective illusion. It is an illusion in which everybody, ultimately, collaborates and shares. Since every desire seeks self-sufficiency, no one really possesses it and an open display of desire amounts to a confession of nonbeing. Such an admission of failure places the imprudent and candid person who makes it in a position of inferiority. He finds himself unable to attract other people's desires, exposed to their contemptuous indifference, and, as a result, vulnerable to their own power of attraction.

Narcissism appears like a valid concept, in the case of *Jean Santeuil*, only because the novel is false, because it is a strategic extension of desire, a mere reflection rather than a revelation of that desire. The hero, Jean, is with the "beautiful people" inside the box; he is the center of flattering attention; an ex- but still very famous king helps him straighten his necktie; all the ladies crowd admiringly around him, just as in a television advertisement for an after-shave lotion. In *Remembrance of Things Past*, the narrator is outside the box, looking at the Duchess of Guermantes with desperate desire, feeling a thousand light years away from the divinity. The enclosure of the box symbolizes an autonomy and self-sufficiency that now belong exclusively to the object of desire, insofar as that object remains inaccessible. The difference between the novel that does and the novel that does not represent desire convincingly becomes manifest in these two perspectives. To regard it as a difference in narrative technique only as most critics would now do is to miss the point entirely. In the great novel, the novelist places his narrator, i.e., himself, in the position of the rejected outsider, he assumes humiliation and exclusion; this is what the author of *Jean Santeuil* is unable to do; the truth hurts too much to be faced.

What we have in *Jean Santeuil* is only one of the countless manners, of course, in which the mediocre writer can escape the knowledge of his own desire, the practical knowledge that Proust achieves only later and that nourishes the greatness not only of *Remembrance of Things Past* but of the few literary works that can be called its equals in regard to the description of desire.

Thus, the inferiority of *Jean Santeuil*, relative to *Remembrance of Things Past*, is revealed as an inability of its author to realize that the "blissful autonomy" exists nowhere, not even in the desired object. What prevents the first Proust from reaching its own genius is very close if not identical to the belief of Freud in something he calls "intact narcissism."

This suggests that the critique of *Jean Santeuil*, from the perspective of the last Proust, should extend to *Narcissism*. If we go back to Freud's remarks, we will see that they call for some kind of analysis. There is somehing defensive and self-righteous about them. Freud obviously counts himself among the high-minded people who have "renounced part of their narcissism" in order to "seek after object-love." This renunciation was necessary, we are given to understand, to make the invention of psychoanalysis possible. It had to be performed for the benefit of all mankind, but there was nothing pleasurable about it.

Freud must be one of these people, therefore, who feel an attraction for the "intact narcissism" of the coquette. He speaks of this attraction as an "incongruity," something a little odd, no doubt, which he is too observant to pass up but which is not important enough to deserve a full investigation. He does not say why this attraction should occur, except, perhaps, for the striking sentence: "It is as if we envied. . . ."

This envy is presented as something that cannot be real because the renunciation of Freud to the narcissistic position is deliberate. The question is: how does one go about freely renouncing the unassailable libido position of narcissism? Freud does not say. If the renunciation were not deliberate, if the lack of "blissful autonomy" were the major predicament of the psyche, the same terrible ordeal that it is in Proust, we would understand that desire must be a perpetual effort on our part to escape from that predicament, and we would not find "incongruous" at all the choice of objects that seem to enjoy that blissful state of being. We would understand with Proust that it is the universal law of desire.

The dutiful man who freely renounces narcissism is a mask. The blissfully decorous playboy of *Jean Santeuil* is also a mask. The two masks are different. The man who passionately embraces narcissism is not the man who virtuously rejects it, but the difference is not so important as it always seems since the narcissism embraced in one case and renounced in the other does not really exist. The Freud who invents narcissism as something of which he himself is deprived reaches deeper into the essential *abjection* of desire than the Proust who was still a *mondain*, but not as deep. I am afraid, as the Proust who had renounced his *mondanité*; and is not the same thing at all as renouncing a narcissism that never was ours in the first place for us to renounce. Freud, it seems, never gave up his belief in the narcissism of others, in an objective narcissism that the naughty and seductive people who do not heed the voice of duty must tremendously enjoy.

You will perhaps object that the juxtaposition of self- and other-centeredness that we find in Proust is not only possible with Freud but that it is also the rule, since no one can be one hundred percent narcissistic and addicted to self-love or altruistic and addicted to object love. Even the "normal" personality must retain a certain amount of narcissism. Thus, there will be a certain amount of infantile narcissism even in the man who successfully graduates to object love and vice versa.

This is true, indeed, but Freud nevertheless ends up with something quite different from Proust because his models remain mechanistic. The libidinal energy can be allocated in different proportions between the self and the other, but it remains a fixed quantity; as a result, you cannot increase the share of the one without diminishing the share of the other and vice versa. This conception leaves no room for the fundamental paradox of human desire, which is, I repeat, that the more morbidly self-centered an individual becomes the more morbidly other-centered he also becomes.

371

The substantial self and the quantitative conception of the libido are great obstacles to the understanding of desire. They turn it into meaningless paradoxes and therefore compel us to disregard aspects which the Proustian conception makes perfectly intelligible. The deficiencies of Freud's models are widely suspected; what is not realized, however, is that the choice of such models must be forced upon Proust by his continued belief in the reality of *self*-sufficiency, which is the same, really, as his belief in a substantial self. These various beliefs function, on the whole, like the primitive conception of *mana*, or sacred energy. The substantial self is crystallized *mana*. That is why any discharge of libidinal energy that is really "spent" outside and does not return to the self, as in the circular pattern of narcissism, constitutes, for that self, a material "impoverishment."

Behind its scientific appearances, the energetic model of Freud really means exactly the same thing as the literary metaphors. The only difference is that the novelist does not believe in his metaphors; they reveal a process of transfiguration akin to the primitive sacred and understood as such by the novelist, whereas it remains hidden in *Narcissism* behind the myth of a really self-sufficient narcissism.

Freud is obviously a greater poet and Proust a greater analyst of desire than the "specialists" in the respective fields of poetry and analysis have ever realized. The most characteristic aspect of a "poetic" talent is that it reaches farther and deeper with such devices as metaphors and other figures of speech than with conceptual thought. Proust is certainly closer than Freud, here, to the conceptual truth of his own metaphors. The metaphors are really the same in both writers, and they often murmur, in the text of Freud, the truth that Proust certainly makes explicit, at least up to a point, the truth or rather the untruth of narcissism, the impossibility of a self-conscious narcissism that would remain "blissfully autonomous."

In reality the concept of narcissism acts as an obstacle; it arrests our thinking at the point where Freud arrested his; it confirms our natural tendency, the tendency of all desire to consider "self-centeredness"—and "other-centeredness"—as separate poles that can become dominant in separate individuals. Our intuition will remain not only incomplete and partial but grossly misleading. The superiority of the great novelist, which lies in the perfect identity of self-centeredness and other-centeredness, will remain invisible or it will be perceived only as the "paradoxical" but ultimately unimportant and "rhetorical" nature of literary talent.

Freud claims somewhere, and he is right, that he was the first to attempt a systematic investigation of relationships that, before him, were the monopoly of creative writers. Thus, we cannot exclude *a priori* the possibility that some writers at least did as well or even better than Freud. To consider this a possibility has nothing to do with the mystical cult of literature per se or with a blind rejection of psychoanalysis. It does not mean that Freud was not a great man. As we said earlier, Proust tends to regress to a lower level of intuition, much lower than Freud, as soon as he tries to become his own theoretician.

Strangely enough the literary critics do not seem very interested in the possibility I am trying to explore. A little reflection will show that this lack of interest is almost inevitable. The literary critics, since Freud, have either been Freudian or against Freud. If they are Freudian, they will never place the literary text on the same level with that of Freud. Even the most sophisticated among them, the ones who now carefully refrain from practicing a *psychanalyse sauvage* of literary texts, have not yet reached the point where they could regard those texts as a possible source of theoretical insights.

If the critics are against Freud, they perceive the failure of psychoanalysis in its literary applications but they usually ascribe it to some divine or inane *littérarité* that would lie beyond the more or less "sordid truths" exhibited by their Freudian colleagues. It really means, in practical terms, that they have tacitly surrendered the theme of desire, in literary texts, to their adversaries. For years they have tried to convince themselves that the area of common interest between Proust and Freud is of little or no relevance to their pure essence of literature, and they have now succeeded. Most critics of Proust will embrace any topic and work it literally to death rather than even allude to the one subject that occupies Proust most of the time: desire. The dresses of Madame de Guermantes, the texture of Albertine's skin, the Platonic essence of the hawthorne bud, pure consciousness, the "undecidable" nature of the sign, the frequency of the imperfect subjunctive, the divorce between words and things, anything will do as long as they can get away from that implacable and rigorous mechanic of desire that remains at all times the principal affair of the novelist.

All the other topics are interesting, of course, but their real significance is subordinated to desire and can be understood only in its context.
It is not the "ineffable" or at the opposite end, the purely "rhetorical"
nature of the work of art that makes narcissism useless as a critical tool;
it is the faulty and misleading nature of the concept. The bluntness of
this onesided instrument ratifies our natural propensity to cancel out the
genius we do not possess, the paradoxical understanding that shocks our
own desire.

I personally feel that the language of both literature and the social
sciences tends to become more specific as it becomes mediocre. Weak
creative writers no less than weak researchers must resort to visible signs
of "specificity" as they become less and less sure of their own competence within their own chosen field of endeavor. The less we have to
say, in other words, the more jargon we tend to use.

This is not the case with such people as Proust and Freud. The text
of *Narcissism* shows that Freud is no less literary than Proust and Proust
is certainly no less psychoanalytical than Freud. There is a difference,
however: Proust did not coin the specialized vocabulary that would have
been out of place in a "novel" and Freud did not resort, most of the
time, to the sort of transposition that frees the novelist from the constraints of straight autobiography.

Between the intuitions and limitations of psychoanalytical theory on
the one hand, and of great literature on the other, there is a gap that we
must bridge. Literature and psychoanalysis in the best sense need *each
other*. My intention is not to build up Proust against Freud, or even less
"literature" against "psychoanalysis," but to facilitate a dialogue between
the two, a dialogue of equals that has never occurred so far, and through
the fault of literary critics, really, as much as of psychoanalysts. Most
critics do not have enough confidence even in the greatest literary texts
to hear the theoretical voice behind them and to make it explicit.

The relationship between texts, the role of active interpreters or
passive "interpretees" which they must play in regard to each other should
be decided on the basis not of some *a priori* decision that labels the one
"theoretical" and the other "literary" but of that diaglogue of equals I
have just mentioned; only a fair encounter will reveal the relative power
of each text in regard to the other.

It seems to me that a fair enough encounter between *Narcissism* and
Remembrance of Things Past must reveal that the whole theory of narcis-

sism is one of the most questionable points in psychoanalysis. We were irresistibly drawn, I believe, to adopt the vision of the last Proust, if not his theoretical views. This vision alone makes the itinerary of the writer intelligible, from the relative mediocrity of the first novel to the genius of the second. A writer's career can be an intellectual experience of major dimension, a genuine conquest of the mind to which even the most sympathetic Freudian readings remain invariably blind.

We found that this Proustian vision gives to one text of Freud at least the same privileged access that psychoanalysis promises in the case of the literary work but fails to deliver. Thus, after countless Freudian readings of Proust, we can propose, for a change, a Proustian reading of Freud. The idea at first sounds whimsical, but it can be shown, I believe, that *Remembrance of Things Past* is not the only literary work that provides the base for a critique of narcissism. Comparable results could be obtained with the work of Cervantes, of Shakespeare, of Dostoevsky, and also of Virginia Woolf, to name one other novelist among the contemporaries of both Freud and Proust.

We have no time for these works, but Proust is more than enough, I trust, to show the ease with which a great writer can see through defense mechanisms still visibly at work behind the slightly sanctimonious tone of the man who, curiously enough, discovered defense mechanisms in the first place.

Quite reminiscent of our *Narcissism* passage is the attitude of Swann toward the "cocotte" Odette de Crécy, his constant rationalization of jealousy as "mature commitment to object love." Swann is one of those people who can be surprised to see the nicest human beings fall in love with the most disreputable characters. Like Freud, he finds his own irresistible attraction to Odette an inexplicable "incongruity." And he does not investigate the matter too searchingly. He is too well-bred for such a course, too genteel, and secretly afraid, perhaps, of what he might discover.

The irony of Proust is evident in all this, as well as in the exclamation that concludes the volume on *Swann in Love*, the magnificent *cri du coeur* of the man who remains deluded to the end and still defines the love-object in terms of a narcissism quite alien, he feels, to his temperament and even his erotic inclinations: "To think that I have wasted years of my life, that I have longed for death, that the greatest love I have ever known has been for a woman I did not really like, who was not in my style!" ("une femme qui ne me plaisait pas, qui n'était pas mon genre!")[5]

As a fictional personality, Swann is quite remote from Freud, of course, and from the flavor that gives our text on *Narcissism* its charm as literature, a rather Herr-Professorish charm in a slightly *Blue Angel* sort of way. We are not dealing, therefore, with mere character similarities. What Proust derides, with gentle humor, is an extremely widespread delusion, the same, evidently to which the mythical psychic entity known as *narcissism* owes both its existence and persistent popularity.

Notes

1. Sigmund Freud, "On Narcissism: An Introduction," in *General Psychological Theory* (New York: Collier Books, 1963), pp. 56–82.

2. *Ibid.*, p. 70.

3. Marcel Proust, *Within a Budding Grove*, translated by C. K. Scott-Moncrieff (New York: Vintage Books, 1970), p. 271.

4. *Ibid.*, p. 272.

5. Marcel Proust, *Swann's Way* (New York: Vintage Books, 1970), p. 292. The theoretician of narcissism is still, like Swann but unlike Proust, in the position of the desiring subject, *because he does not know it*. In order to confirm this point, I will quote, in *Narcissism*, the lines that come immediately before and after the passage discussed above. They speak for themselves:

A different course is followed in the type most frequently met with in women, which is probably the purest and truest feminine type. With the development of puberty the maturing of the female sex organs, which up till then have been in a condition of latency, seems to bring about an intensification of the original narcissism, and this is unfavorable to the development of a true object-love with its accompanying sexual over-estimation; there arises in the woman a certain self-sufficiency (especially when there is a ripening into a beauty) which compensates her for the social restrictions upon her object-choice. Strictly speaking, such women love only themselves with an intensity comparable to that of the man's love for them. Nor does their need lie in the direction of loving, but of being loved; and that man finds favour with them who fulfills this condition. The importance of this type of woman for the erotic life of mankind must be recognized as very great. Such women have the greatest fascination for men, not only for aesthetic reasons, since as a rule they are the most beautiful, but also because of certain interesting psychological constellations. . . .

Perhaps it is not superfluous to give an assurance that, in this description of the feminine form of erotic life, no tendency to depreciate woman has any part. Apart from the fact that tendentiousness is alien to me, I also know that these different lines of development correspond to the differentiation of functions in a highly complicated biological connection; further, I am ready to admit that there are countless women who love according to the masculine type and who develop the over-estimation of the sexual object so characteristic of that type (pp. 69–71).

It is on such texts, rather than on the more exotic and harmless myth of *Penisneid*, that the critique of Freud from a woman's standpoint should focus. The position of Freud toward women is basically the same as the sadomasochistic position of the homosexual object in Proust. The only difference, once more, is that Proust knows it and Freud does not.

25.

"The Nine of Hearts": Fragment of a Psychoreading of *La Nausée*

Serge Doubrovsky

I HAVE SELECTED for our attention a rather insignificant detail in a rather famous scene: the scene at the café, the "Rendez-vous des Cheminots," where Roquentin finally experiences Nausea with a capital "N": "Things are bad! Things are very bad: I have it, the filth, the Nausea." [1] Along with the print, Nausea here assumes capital importance: it attains a status which is *clinical*, as the symptom of a malady, *ontological*, as the revelation, through this malady, of the subject's mode of being-in-the-world, and *esthetic*, as the call to salvation through art, which is offered here by the "rag-time with a vocal refrain" and which will be taken up again by the "book," the "novel" planned by Roquentin in the conclusion. Sartre produces a discourse which "totalizes," or rather, which progresses by a process of totalization until the moment when Roquentin can say "I understood that I had found the key to Existence, the key to my Nauseas, to my own life." Fictional language is equipped, is coupled with a metalanguage which is imperious, even imperialistic, and which

Translated by Carol A. Bové. From *Psychoanalysis, Creativity, and Literature*, Alan Roland, ed. (New York: Columbia University Press, 1978). Copyright © 1978 Columbia University Press. Reprinted by permission.

seems, from the beginning, to exclude commentary, or, what amounts to the same thing, to include it. For years, the critical result has been paraphrase. After the wealth of explanations offered by the narrator himself (an ironic, post-Proustian tribute?) what more or better, or simply, what else, can be said of Nausea than what is said in the text? What remains for the critical eye to see? Nothing, certainly, except this unimportant detail: the Nausea scene closes upon a card game which is fairly intricate, and the game itself, just at the moment when Roquentin gets up, closes upon an exclamation by the "dog-faced young man": "Ah! The nine of hearts." This paper is therefore entitled: " 'The Nine of Hearts': Fragment of a Psychoreading of *La Nausée*."

At the level of stylistic analysis, you might call it a purely realistic effect; verisimilitude in the narrative code demands that a card game be played, preferably *manille* or *belote*, in a French café in the provinces. From this point of view, the ace of clubs or the nine of hearts would do the trick equally well. For me, psychocriticism begins right where other forms of criticism stop: at the production, in the text, of an insignificant detail which cannot be accounted for by either the Sartrian metatext or by another metadiscourse. Sartre might certainly just as well have written: "Ah! The ace of clubs" or the "nine of hearts" with the same narrative-stylistic effect. It remains that he has written "nine of hearts," and it is precisely this *remains* which remains for the critical eye to see, all the more since, strangely enough, this card, displayed right in the middle of the table, *is not seen* by the players: "One of the players pushes a disordered pack of cards towards another man who picks them up. One card has stayed behind. Don't they see it? It's the nine of hearts." What is insignificant now begins to signify, since the invisible card which is right in front of their eyes is perceived only by Roquentin. This perception must in turn be perceived, and, one hopes, penetrated, by the psychocritic.

Don't worry, I'm not going to do or redo "The Purloined Letter" act, nor will I play or replay some "instance of the card." Abandoning for now this signifier at the end of its chain (which is, in this discussion, our own since it closes precisely the narrative sequence of the café), and hoping to find it later in its place, let's leave Lacan for Freud and direct our attention straightaway to sex. Like Roquentin, as a matter of fact: "I was coming to screw but no sooner had I opened the door when Madeleine, the waitress, called to me: 'The patronne isn't here, she's in town shopping.' I felt a sharp disappointment in the sexual parts, a long, dis-agreeable tickling." Before it makes your head "whirl," it "tickles," then, uncomfortably, in a definite erogenous zone. Like honor, Roquentin's penis is "ticklish" and of course, only what is by nature delicate, vulner-able to attack, can be ticklish in this way. Now, it strikes us immediately that there is a lack of proportion between the process which sets off Nausea (what in Sartrian terms might be called the "teleological circuit" of fornication: "I was coming *to screw*") and Antoine's usually very luke-warm ardor for the owner: "I dined at the *Rendez-vous des Cheminots*. The patronne was there and I had to screw her, but it was mainly out of politeness. She disgusts me a little, she is too white and besides, she smells like a newborn child. . . . I played distractedly with her genitals under the cover" (p. 59). Without having read Freud, we rightfully won-der why, when the *owner is not there*, he experiences such "sharp disap-pointment" in a zone which, when she *is there*, is, we must admit, hardly erogenous. Why this "long uncomfortable tickling" in a penis which is definitely more ticklish than it is capable of being tickled? Having read Freud, of course, we may wonder whether there is not an unconscious denominator common to the two complementary and antithetic se-quences (*I was coming to screw/I had to screw her*), an operating chart com-mon to the pleasure which is disappointed or received, or again, having read Mauron, we wonder whether the two texts are not superimposable.

Once the act is more or less completed, sequence 2 (*I had to screw her*) produces something which makes the analyst happy: a "dream": "I let my arm run along the woman's thigh and suddenly saw a small gar-den with low, wide trees on which immense hairy leaves were hanging. Ants were running everywhere, centipedes and ringworm. . . . Behind the cactus and the Barbary fig trees, the Valleda of the public park pointed a finger at her genitals. 'This park smells of vomit,' I shouted" (p. 59). Since we cannot go into the problematic of the written pseudo dream, which is not a dream, but can be analyzed as if it were (see Freud, *Gradiva*), and since we don't have the time to undertake a detailed anal-ysis, we will confine ourselves to two remarks: 1) The "dream" subse-quent to the consummation of the sex act shows the vagina to be an extremely anxiogenic source, precisely the *nauseating* site of a nightmare ("this park smells of vomit"); 2) if we grant the traditional Freudian de-coding, vermin-children, in dream language, we understand the nature of Roquentin's "disgust" for the owner who "smells like a newborn child."

The parturient organ of the woman anticipates the final horror of a kind of swooning fecundity (the chestnut-root scene): "My very flesh throbbed and opened, abandoned itself to the universal burgeoning. It was repugnant" (p. 133). *Throbbing, opening, abandoning itself*: Roquentin experiences his final Nausea as if his entire body had become *the female organ*, which is, moreover, "burgeoning," in gestation. It's an absolute nightmare. For whom? "I was coming *to screw* her." For a man. Recalling sequence 1, we observe that the disappointment of a kind of ticklish masculinity is accompanied by another symptom: "at the same time I felt my shirt rubbing against the tips of my breasts and I was surrounded, seized by a slow, coloured mist . . ." (p. 18). Usage demands that the word "breast" (and the Robert dictionary, I venture to add, confirms it), especially in the plural and in the expression: "the tips of my breasts," refers to a fundamental signifier of femininity, one of its essential appendages and endowments. A man usually speaks of his chest. Everything occurs, then, exactly as if this radical disgust for the female sex, projected as dream at the end of the completed sexual act, is introjected as *fantasy* in the aborted act, the failure to screw being in no way a failure to *enjoy* but a failure to *prove*: from the minute I become unable to prove that I am a man, *I am immediately transformed into a woman*. Such is the logic of Sartrian fantasy which thoroughly regulates the unfolding of Nausea. We could demonstrate in detail, in its four successive stages (stone, café, little Lucienne, and chestnut-root scenes), the inevitable progression of the fantasy, experienced in the merry-go-round of ambivalence, "whirling" from disgust to desire. That is, the fantasy is experienced as a number of stations of the cross at which the man-woman stops, obsessed by the sudden, forced substitution of a female sex for a precarious, masculine one: "How strange it is, how moving, that his hardness should be so fragile" (p. 22). This constitutes, at one and the same time, a malady and a remedy, since, in short, by assuming a femininity which makes you nauseous ("the viscous puddle at the bottom of *our* time"), it is a question of bartering actual masculinity for a kind of inexpugnable, imaginary one, inscribed in the symbolic domain: the "steel band" of music or the "beautiful," "hard as steel" story into which Roquentin dreams of transposing himself.

Those who are suspicious of this analysis can at least give credence to "Sartre through Flaubert," or, if they prefer, to "Sartre: A Self-Portrait." Thus, by reading Sartre reading Gustave, we reread precisely *La*

Nausée: "Flesh is complete inaction . . . now, according to Gustave, pleasure arises from a kind of swooning abandonment, from a passivity which is ready and willing; the woman feels pleasure because she is taken. She feels desire, too, of course, but in her own way . . . female desire is passive waiting. The text speaks for itself: if Gustave wants to be a woman, it is because his partially female sexuality demands a sex change which will allow the full development of his resources" (*L'Idiot de la famille,* 1:684).[2] In this respect, Antoine is Gustave's guilty conscience. "The text speaks for itself," said Sartre: yes, especially when it believes it is talking about the Other. Let's take a look at Sartre as he imagines Flaubert looking at himself in a mirror: "At the start, out of his natural passivity, he creates the *analagon* of a femininity which is concealed . . . it is possible for him, at the cost of creating a double illusion, to imagine that he is someone else, who is caressing an actual woman—himself— behind the mirror. . . . There are two *analoga* here: his hands, his reflection. In the latter, he apprehends only his caressed flesh, overlooking insignificant details like his penis or his youthful male chest" (*L'Idiot de la famille,* 1: 693). In this "Sartre through Flaubert," then, we surprise Jean-Paul as he rewrites precisely the progression of Nausea, that is, the progressive feminization of his flesh, which goes from his *hands* (stone scene), to his *face* in the mirror ("An entire half of my face yields . . . the eye opens on a white globe, on pink, bleeding flesh" [p. 17]), preceding the entrance into the café where the narrator suddenly "loses" the insignificant detail which is his *penis* and where his *youthful, male chest* becomes "the tips of his breasts." The discourse of fiction and the discourse of criticism display a strange kind of intertextuality/intersexuality. In fact, if Madame Bovary is a man disguised as a woman (*Critique de la Raison dialectique,* p. 90), there is no reason why Antoine Roquentin cannot be a woman disguised as a man. But if we prefer to believe "Sartre: A Self-Portrait," let's listen to him directly as he answers the formidable questions of the formidable Simone: "Now then, Sartre, I would like to question you on the subject of women . . . you've never talked about women . . . how do you explain that?" "I think it stems from my childhood . . . girls and women formed, in a way, my natural milieu, and *I have always thought that there was a kind of woman in me*" (italics mine).

But, not as "natural" as all that, as *La Nausée* demonstrates, and this reticence on the subject of women is in no way innocent, analytically speaking (I'll leave ideology to Simone). At the level of unconscious discourse, *La Nausée* fills precisely the strange gap in the writer's conscious discourse, and the trio "Antoine—Jean-Paul—Gustave" reveals more about it than Sartre would like to say or to admit to himself. We know that the notion of "bisexuality," introduced both as a major and as a poorly defined element in Freudian thought, receives a good deal of attention from psychoanalysts, at least from those of the Psychoanalytic Society of Paris, which devoted its April 1975 meeting to it. According to a recent report by Dr. Christian David, every successful cure implies the integration of the subject's psychic bisexuality; inversely, he tells us: "every serious threat concerning sexual identity or integrity is likely to lead to a variety of disturbances to psychic organization, to the point of psychosis" (*Report*, p. 52). And the French psychiatrist Kreisler formulates the same idea in a vocabulary which is of particular interest for us: "belonging to a sex constitutes one of the firmest kernels enabling the personality to cohere, and sexuality may be the most primitive and most powerful form rooting us in existence" (*Report*, p. 52). That Roquentin's final Nausea takes place in front of an eminently phallomorphous root ("the bark, black and swollen, looked like boiled leather . . . this hard and compact skin of a sea lion" [pp. 127–28, 129]) clearly indicates that the form taken by the subject's existential crisis consists in a kind of rooting in masculinity. "I am not at all inclined to call myself insane," writes Roquentin. He shouldn't feel this way, especially at a time when neurosis is terribly devalued and when only psychosis gives status to the writer.

The critic, however, is not a psychiatrist, and the diagnosis (if you wish, the "construction" element) is of interest only if it produces something equivalent to the stream of new, repressed material which Freud sees (*Construction in Analysis*, 1937) as the touchstone of a correct interpretation. Here, this equivalent would be the increasingly thorough integration of metonymically discrete elements of the text into a coherent, metaphoric sequence. At bottom, a psychoreading simply establishes what may be called a rigorous logic of details, to the extent that the logic which underlies the possibilities of the narrative is reinserted into the operation of the fantasy. If we fold erotic sequence 1 (I was coming to screw) down upon erotic sequence 2 (I had to screw her), we might say that the masculine obligation which has been fulfilled avoids the crisis of sexual identity, if it is true, according to R. R. Greenson's remark, that "the adult neurotic behaves as if the sex of his sexual object determined his own sex." But traces of the signifiers' first logic subsist in the second: no sooner does the Valleda in the public or public garden point to her genitals as the "sinful parts," in this way reassuring the male sleeper, than upon waking, the latter hears the owner say to him: "I didn't want to wake you up . . . but the sheet got folded under my backside . . ." (p. 59). The syntagmatic order is revealing: this vestige of "daytime" sets off *immediately afterward* another "dream" in the fictional text, a dream in which the "backside" signifier proliferates, having been repressed as a simple detail pertaining to the "real" in the vigil scene (the fold in the sheet). The obsession is fully manifested: "I gave Maurice Barrès a spanking. We were three soldiers and one of us had a hole in the middle of his face. Maurice Barrès came up to us and said, 'That's fine!' and he gave each of us a small bouquet of violets. 'I don't know where to put them,' said the soldier with the hole in his head. Then Maurice Barrès said, 'Put them in the hole you have in your head.' The soldier answered, 'I'm going to stick them up your ass' " (p. 59). Once again, a detailed analysis is impossible here. Let us mention only the triple associative constellation: head with hole—put up your ass—bouquet of violets, and, with a movement reversing the first, let's fold it back upon erotic sequence 1.

In the café where we left him, we find Roquentin in the throes of Nausea, flopping on the bench: "The bottom of my seat is broken. . . . I have a broken spring. . . . My head is all pliable and elastic, as though it had been simply set on my neck; if I turn it, it will fall off" (p. 19). Having become the "little, detachable object," the "broken spring," the head of which turns to the point where it risks falling off, reveals severe castration anguish at the source of Nausea: in vertigo, Roquentin actually *experiences* his head *as a penis*, facing the castration threat which takes aim at his narcissistic identification. "I dropped to a seat, I no longer knew where I was": the text, however, *knows* exactly where he is; when he (his head) drops, Antoine is in the spot where the "seat is broken." Now, in the crude slang which is dear to Sartre, "se faire défoncer" (to get buggered) designates the greatly feared act which transforms the masculine subject into a "queer." The anguish of castration, which feminizes, causes a return to a vulnerability which is fundamental to him: the anus is the male's vagina. Disgust (desire) for the female sex becomes interiorized in the phantasmatic register as the obsession to possess a potential feminine sex, which is actualized in Nausea. The fear of castration is accompanied by a severe complementary fear of sodomization. Let's not forget the answer to Maurice Barrès who tells the soldier to put the bouquet "in the hole you have in your head" (the soldier's head with a hole in it, Roquentin's head which has been cut off): "I'm going to stick them up your ass." Now what is stuck up this ass, if I may inquire? A bouquet of *violets*. The obsession with sodomization, experienced as feminization (fantasy being, along with common sense, the most widely shared thing in the world, Roquentin finds himself here in the excellent company of Freud's President Schreber who is "God's wife") is, moreover, designated, in the Sartrian text, by a special signifier, *violet*, since, let's not forget, Roquentin's Nausea is also a *colored* vertigo: "I saw the colors spin slowly around me." A thematic analysis of the signified would easily show that, in the Sartrian text, this color is the emblem for a sexuality which is feminine and lethal (a case in point, the cashier with whom Roquentin spontaneously identifies: "she's red haired, as I am; she suffers from a stomach disorder. She is rotting quietly under her skirts with a melancholy smile, like the odour of violets given off by a decomposing body" [p. 55]). We are, then, less surprised than Anny at this aesthetic repugnance on Antoine's part: "You swore indignantly for a year that you wouldn't see *Violettes Impériales*" (p. 140). But, still more important, violet is the Sartrian color for a formidable female sexuality even at the level of meaning: as *viol* (rape), as *violated*. This is affirmed in the next stage of Nausea when the narrator identifies with "little Lucienne" after he has done so with the putrescent cashier: "Little Lucienne was raped [*violée*]. Strangled. Her body still exists. . . . *She* no longer exists. Her hands . . . I . . . there, I. . . . Raped [*Violée*]. A soft, bloody desire for rape takes me from behind . . ." (p. 101). The very ambiguity of the expression: "bloody desire for rape" (to rape, to be raped?), which is none other than the ambivalence of active/passive desire, is momentarily resolved for the benefit of a transsexualization which is phantasmatically assumed by way of the *place* where desire takes hold of the subject: *from behind*. There is in this an exact symbolic equivalence between the way that he experiences his flesh as feminine ("My body of living flesh which murmurs and turns gently, liquors which turn to cream . . . the sweet sugary water of my flesh" [pp. 101–2]) and his universal Schreberian sodomization: "existence takes my thoughts from behind and gently expands them *from behind;* someone takes me from behind, they force me to think from behind . . . he runs, he runs like a ferret, 'from behind' from behind *from behind*, little Lucienne assaulted from behind, violated by existence from behind . . ." (p. 102). Little Lucienne, having reappeared just in time as the last link in the chain of verbal delirium, is necessarily "assaulted from behind," if Roquentin is to be able to "become" her. Here, according to the law which Freud assigned to the development of the dream sequences of a single night, which progress from what is most hidden to what is most manifest, all elements of the Sartroquentinian phantasma appear unrepressed in the delirious writing (desyntaxization, degrammaticalization, decodification in the narrative indicating that "textual work" is fulfilling sexual impulse). We have not yet arrived at that point, and in the café scene, the elements mentioned only show through something else, are a little obscured, hesitant: like cousin Adolph's *suspenders* (the traditional emblem, if ever there was one, of proletarian machismo, the Gabin-suspenders of the Prévert-Carné films), which "hesitate" between blue and mauve ("You feel like saying, 'All right, *become* violet and let's hear no more about it' " [p. 19]). But, at this stage, and it is for this reason that they are discussed, that is, written about, the suspenders cannot, *do not want to* become violet; and where Robbe-Grillet formerly saw naive anthropomorphism in Sartrian description, we see the very clear, precise inscription of fantasy, which already articulates "the time of violet suspenders and broken chair seats" (p. 21) in a strangely condensed form. The drive which is yearning and delirious is controlled by the call already mentioned to a kind of imaginary masculinity, to this "band of steel, the narrow duration of the music which traverses our time through and through" (p. 21), whose effect is indicated as specifically as is its cause: "When the voice was heard in the silence, I felt my body *harden* and the Nausea *vanish*" (p. 22 [italics mine]). A contained drive, we might say, but also one in which a dangerous and latent feminization is retrieved not only in the *female* vocalist's song, but in the very reaction of the veterinarian's little girl listening to the music: "Barely seated, the girl has been seized by it: she holds herself stiffly, her eyes wide open . . ." (p. 22). A phallic, female child, we might say, in whom what holds itself stiffly is a woman's penis. We are hardly surprised that the book's final solution constitutes a kind of fetishism of art.

Yet the café scene doesn't end with the disappearance of Nausea under the spell of the music; it closes upon that innocuous card game which demanded our attention in the beginning, less innocuous, perhaps, for being *manille*, if we consider that Nausea originally attacks the *main* (hand), which is punished later on ("I . . . stab the knife into the palm" [p. 100]). Having averted obsession with sodomization, Roquentin has yet to confront the threat of castration, in order that the well-known "masculine protest" be complete. It is this second phase of the phantasmatic operation that is carried out vicariously in the card players scene. When the "great, red-faced man" throws down his diamond *manille*, the "dog-faced young man" immediately trumps him (this head, like that of a domesticated, male animal, is an improvement over Roquentin's "pliable," "elastic" one): "Hell. He's trumped" (p. 23). You *coupe* (trump) in cards; you also *coupe* (castrate) on the analyst's couch; and there, when it comes to the father, there's no cutting out. It's precisely he who appears, only to disappear in his most classic form: The outline of the *king of hearts* appears between his curled fingers, then it is turned on its face and the game goes on. Mighty king, come from so far, prepared by so many combinations, by so many vanished gestures. He disappears in turn so that other combinations *can be born*, other gestures . . ." (p. 23). The unexpected lyricism in this passage has no meaning in terms of the "realistic" code of a narrative in which Roquentin is not known to be a great "cardomaniac" or "manillephile." On an Other Stage and in another code, the reading is perfectly logical: the "son" castrates (*coupe*) the "father," liquidates the Oedipal complex by reversing the threat; in order that the son *be born*, the "king of hearts" disappears, as Mr. de Rollebon does later on (another imaginary murder of the father). Dubbed male, consecrated truly virile, he is struck by an otherwise unexplainable "emotion" which we can well understand: "I am touched, I feel my body at rest like a precision machine" (p. 23), a rest which is well deserved after such transsexual terrors. We understand equally well the stream of memories which suddenly overwhelms Roquentin precisely at this point in the phantasmatic chain: "I have . . . plunged into forests, always making my way towards other cities. I have had women. I have fought with men . . ." (p. 23). In keeping with a masculinity which is from now on homologized, reassured concerning his two essential attributes, the screwer-fighter is at peace with his "human machine": it is normal that he *should see* what others *do not see*, since this is the site of his fantasy: the *"neuf de coeur."* [3] "New of heart," he can set out once again ("That's it, I'm going to leave") and best foot forward, except, alas, for putting his foot in it. It's the card which "has stayed behind": "someone takes it at last, gives it to the dog-faced young man. . . . Ah! The nine of hearts" (p. 23). There is certainly reason for this surprise. As far as the fantasy's resolution is concerned, you are not "given" masculinity, you have to "take" it yourself, that is, undertake it, unless you have "stayed behind," or as we say, "are left back." Not knowing what to do with it and not having yet decided to transmute or to "transmalize" it into writing, "the young man turns and turns the nine of hearts between his fingers" (p. 34). But, along with this failure, there may already be the promise of a (re)solution to come, since, next to the young man, "the violet-faced man bends over a sheet of paper and sucks his pencil."

Notes

1. Quotations are from Lloyd Alexander's translation of *La Nausée* (New York: New Directions Paperback, 1964). I have altered a few passages, especially some of Mr. Alexander's sexual terminology, which often lacks the "thrust" of the original.
2. My translation.
3. *Neuf*, of course, means both "nine" and "new" here.

26.

The Father, Love,
and Banishment

Julia Kristeva

That one who on earth
usurps my place, my place which is vacant
in the sight of the Son of God,
has made of my cemetery a sewer
  —Dante, *Paradiso*, XXVII. 22–25. (Trans. H. R. Huse, 1965)

What goes by the name of love is banishment.
  —Beckett. *First Love*

STRANGELY ENOUGH, I needed a Venetian ambience—the complete opposite of Beckett's universe—to have a sense of grasping, within the parenthesis of *First Love* and *Not I*, both the strength and the limitations of a writing that comes across less as "esthetic effect" than as something one used to situate close to the "sacred." No name exists today for such an "unnamable" interplay of meaning and *jouissance*.

From Julia Kristeva, "Le père, l'amour, l'exil," in *Cahiers de l'Herne* (1976); reprinted in *Polylogue* (Paris: Seuil, 1977); appears in translation in Kristeva, *Desire in Language*, Leon S. Roudiez, ed., Thomas Gora, Alice Jardine, and Leon S. Roudiez, trs. (New York: Columbia University Press, 1980). Copyright © 1980 Columbia University Press. Reprinted with permission.

This parenthesis, in my opinion quite adequately circumscribing that writer's known novels and plays, conveys back to me, in microcosmic fashion, the now carnivalized destiny of a once flourishing Christianity. It includes everything: a father's death and the arrival of a child (*First Love*), and at the other end, a theme of orality stripped of its ostentation—the mouth of a lonely woman, face to face with God, face to face with nothing (*Not I*). Beckett's *pietà* maintains a sublime appearance, even on her way to the toilet. Even though the mother is a prostitute, it doesn't matter who the actual father is since the child belongs solely to its mother (*First Love*). And the babblings of a seventy-year-old woman (*Not I*), the antonym of a hymn or of Molly's monologue, are no less haloed, in all their nonsense, with a paternal aura, ironically but obstinately raising her toward that third person—God—and filling her with a strange joy in the face of nothingness. Raised, demystified, and for that very reason more tenacious than ever, the pillars of our imagination are still there. Some of them, at least . . . And so:

1. A man experiences love and simultaneously puts it to the test on the death of his father. The "thing" he had heard of "at home, in school, in brothel and at church" finally appears in reality under the guise of a paternal corpse. Through it, he catches a glimpse of "some form of esthetics relevant to man" (the only one!) and discovers a "great disembodied wisdom" (the unrivaled one!). *Father* and *Death* are united, but still split and separate. *On the one hand*, Death—the ideal that provides meaning but where the word is silent; *on the other*, the paternal corpse, hence a possible though trivial communication, waste, decay, and excrement mobilizing pleasure and leisure. A verbal find seals this junction of opposites: *chamber pot*, a term that, for the son-writer, evokes Racine, Baudelaire, and Dante all at once,[1] summarizing the sublimated obscenity that portrays him as consubstantial with his father, but only the *decayed* cadaver of his father, never leaving the black mourning of an inaccessible paternal function, which itself has found refuge on the side of *Death*. From afar, and constantly threatened with being obscured, it thus provides a meaning for the existence of living corpses.

Racked between the *father* (cadaverous *body*, arousing to the point of defecation) and *Death* (empty *axis*, stirring to the point of transcendence), a man has a hard time finding something else to love. He could hardly venture in that direction unless he were confronted with an undifferentiated woman, tenacious and silent, a prostitute to be sure, her singing voice out of tune in any case, whose name remains equally undifferentiated, just like the archaic breast (Lulu? or Lully? or Lolly?), exchangeable for another (Anna), with only one right: to be inscribed "in time's forgotten cowplats," and thus to blend into "history's ancient faeces." This will then be the only love—one that is possible, one that is true: neither satyric, nor Platonic, nor intellectual. But *banishment-love*.

2. Banishment: an attempt at separating oneself from the august and placid expanses where the father's sublime Death, and thus *Meaning*, merges with the son's "self" (but where a daughter can very easily become trapped), mummified, petrified, exhausted, "more dead than alive"; a banishment robbing this sensible but always already dead, filial self of its silence on the threshold of a rimy minerality, where the only opportunity is to become anyone at all, and moreover, without the means for fading away. So flee this permanence of meaning. Live somewhere else, but in the company of paternal Death.

Banishment: above/beyond a life of love. A life always off to one side, at an impassable distance, mourning a love. A fragile, uncertain life, where, without spending the saved-up, paternal capital in one's pockets, he discovers the price of warmth (of a hothouse, of a room, of a turd) and the boredom of those humans who provide it—but who waste it, too. It is a life apart from the paternal country where nonetheless lies the obsessed self's unshakable quiet, frozen forever, bored but solid.

To love is to survive paternal meaning. It demands that one travel far to discover the futile but exciting presence of a waste-object: a man or woman, fallen off the father, taking the place of his protection, and yet, the always trivial ersatz of this disincarnate wisdom that no object (of love, necessarily) could ever totalize. Against the modifying *whole* of the father's Death, one chooses banishment toward the *part* constituting a fallen object or an object *of* love (*of* being possessive and genitive partitive). How trivial, this object of love—transposition of love for the Other. And yet, without banishment, there is no possible release from the grip of paternal Death. This act of loving and its incumbent writing spring from the Death of the Father—from the Death of the third person (as *Not I* shows).

3. In other words, the primary, obsessed man never sees his father as dead. The corpse under his eyes is the waste-object, the fallen and thus the finally possible object, endlessly expected from the first cries on, from the first feces on, from the first words on; and so firmly con-

demned, pushed aside by paternal strength. This cadaverous object finally allows its son to have a "real" relationship with the world, a relationship in the image of this very object, this miserable downfall, this disappointed mercy, this disabused realism, this sullen irony, this low-spirited action. Through this opening, he might look for woman. But the Other, the third-person father, is not that particular dead body. It is Death; it always was. It is the meaning of the narrative of the son, who never enunciated himself as anything else, save for and by virtue of this stretched out void of paternal Death, as ideal and inaccessible to any living being as it might seem. As long as a son pursues meaning in a story or through narratives, even if it eludes him, as long as he persists in his search he narrates in the name of Death for the father's corpses, that is, for you, his readers.

4. Now, how can one fail to see that if Death gives meaning to the sublime story of this first love, it is only because it has come to conceal barred incest, to take up all the space where otherwise we would imagine an unspoken woman; the (father's) wife, the (son's) mother? It is because he deduces this absence that the banished son, by analyzing his banishment, might not remain forever a bachelor—neither monk nor narcissistic lover of his peers, but a father in flight.

5. Indeed, with Beckett, the myth of the bachelor writer leaves behind the fascinated terror of Proust or Kafka and comes closer to Marcel Duchamp's dry humor. This banished lover, with all his calculations ("I thought of Anna then, long, long sessions, twenty minutes, twenty-five minutes and even as long as half an hour daily. I obtain these figures by the addition of other, lesser figures.") and his nighttime "stewpan," keeping him bedtime company better than a bride, truly evokes the auto-erotic mechanism and "Malic Molds" of the "Large Glass" Bachelor. Moreover, Lulu-Anna has all the qualities of *The Bride Stripped Bare by Her Bachelors, Even*—half robot, half fourth dimensional, a kind of "automobilism," automatically activating its "internal combustion engine" and setting forth again by "stripping-bare" movements. And even if Lulu isn't a virgin, even if she proves to be a woman with an unruly clientele, the "cooling cycle" that adjusts her amorous mechanism to that of the banished narrator places the two coital protagonists forever, as with Duchamp, into icy communication. In the manner of Duchamp, Beckett says, after and against the militant bachelors of the early twentieth century, that rather than avoid the sexual act, they should assume it but

only as an impossible relationship, whose participants are condemned to a perpetual banishment that confines them within autoeroticism. But Beckett writes against Joyce, too, ascetically rejecting the latter's joyous and insane, incestuous plunge summed up in Molly's *jouissance* or the paternal baby talk in *Finnegans Wake*.

Assumption of self through the dead father turns the banished writer into a father in spite of himself, a father under protest, a false father who doesn't want to be a father, but nonetheless believes in being one—tense in the elegance of permanent mourning. There remains for him to relish his grief, and even more so, the emptiness holding him up between Death and waste, between sublimity and pleasure, a balance of nothingness— on condition that it be written: "those instants when, neither drugged nor drunk, nor in ecstasy, one feels nothing." Living close to a woman who helps him survive in this banishment from the father's Death, he does not allow himself to be concerned about her own experience; forti- fied with this assumption of Death, he quickly gets away from her so as to devote himself entirely to his own "slow descents again, the long sub- mersion," which expressly allows him to sketch out a new meaning, to write a narrative. Assuming the stance of his father's son inoculates him forever against any incestuous, that is, "poetic" endeavor.

In corresponding fashion, for his wife—the "married" spinster—the autoerotic autonomy of her universe is ensured by childbirth. This also accomplishes the impossible coexistence of two incommunicable entities, one male and one female.

First Love suggests that, for a woman, the counterpart of what the dead father is for the obsessed man is the child, substituting for the father; that, however, is a different matter. Because in a more immediate and direct sense, what the banished man needs most from a woman is simply someone to accompany him into Death's void, into the third per- son's void. He needs the gentle touch of a mute partner, renunciation of the body, waste, sublimation, and—in order to be faithful to his dead father to the end—a double suicide.

6. The banished young man has aged. Faithful to his paternal love, he has become an old lady (*Not I*). Yet, there are no ambiguities to sug- gest the slightest measure of perversion. The body is stiff, there is no pleasure, except, in the field, the soft, solitary illumination of a head suffused by light and a mouth, grasping at the same void, and contin- ually asking questions. The father's Death, which enabled the son to

experience love, is still with us, at the end of the act, in these light beams, this void, but now it does not even lead to a pseudofictional narrative. The father's presence that caused the son to narrate *First Love* has become for the old woman of *Not I* a rhetorical device: a questioning. Corpse and waste have been replaced by a syntactic occurrence: *elision*.

Questioning is the supreme judicial act, for the *I* who asks the questions, through the very act of asking these questions (apart from the meaning of the request) postulates the existence of the other. Here, since it is "not I," not *you* either, there must be a *He beyond communication*.

The *elision* of the object is the syntactic recognition of an impossible object, the disappearance not only of the addressee (*you*), but of all topic of discourse. In *First Love*, already, the object conceals itself, slipping out of the sentence, probably remaining in that unnamable domain of the father:

> It had something to do with lemon trees, or orange trees. I forget, that is all I remember, and for me that is no mean feat, to remember it had something to do with lemon trees, or orange trees, I forgot, for of all the other songs I have ever heard in my life, and I have heard plenty, it being apparently impossible, physically impossible short of being deaf, to get through this world, even my way, without hearing singing, I have retained nothing, not a word, not a note, or so few words, so few notes, that, that what, that nothing, this sentence has gone on long enough.

What in this text still appears as a surplus of meaning, an overflow caused by an excess of internal subordination, often becomes, in *Not I*, a deletion of direct objects, and always a deletion of the object of discourse. A missing (grammatical or discursive) object implies an impossible subject: not I. And yet, it exists, she speaks; this de-oralized and frustrated mouth is nevertheless held to its trivial search: "not knowing what . . . what she was— . . . what? . . . who? . . . no! . . . she! . . . SHE! . . ." "*Mouth* recovers from vehement refusal to relinquish third person."

Here, this means that the act of writing, without me or you, is in fact an obstinate refusal to let go of the third person: the element beyond discourse, the third, the "it exists," the anonymous and unnamable "God," the "Other"—the pen's axis, the father's Death, beyond dialogue, beyond subjectivism, beyond psychologism. A disappointed Mouth, seized by the desire to pour itself out as into a wash basin. And yet there is nobody in mind, no "you"—neither father, mother, man, nor child; alone with the flow of words that have lost their meaning, that are suspended, like pleasureless vowels, "askew," "tacky"; useless, dying Mouth, dying but persistent, tenacious, obstinate voice, sustained by the same first love, looking for, awaiting, pursuing, who? what? . . . The prerequisites of writing.

Yet, beyond this amorous association of the *banished writer* with the *mad,* seventy-year-old woman, pursuing a paternal shadow binding her to the body and to language, the gap between *writing* and *psychosis* bursts open. He, writing, fled his father so that the introjected superego, adhering to its meaning, might perpetuate itself as trace through a symbolic ascesis renouncing sexual *jouissance.* She, devastated by (paternal) love, which she incorporates into her impossibility to such a degree that she sacrifices her "self" to it, replaces a forbidden, permanently mourning vagina with a mouth, through which, madly but certainly, *jouissance* seeps—oral, tactile, visible, audible, and yet unnamable disgust, without link or syntax, permanently setting her off from socialized humans, either before or beyond their "works." He writes in a state of ascesis. She experiences *jouissance* in nonsense through repression. Two boundaries of paternal love, one for each sex. They are a fascinating and impossible couple, also sustained, on both sides, by censorship of the maternal body.

Beckett's tragic irony thus achieves its maximal resonance when the son's tenacious love of Death is uttered through the mouth of a woman. Impossible subjectivity ("If I have no object of love, I do not exist"), but an equally impossible femininity, an impossible genitality for both sexes, no escape from death for either. *Not I:* a heartrending statement of the loss of identity but also, discreet and resigned jubilation, a sweet relief produced by the most minute corruption of meaning in a world unfailingly saturated with it. In contrast with the overflowing Molly and Finnegan's negative awakening stands a *jouissance* provoked by meaning's deception, which nevertheless inevitably perseveres through and beyond this unavoidable third person.

At the (phantasmatic?) dawn of religion, the sons of the primitive horde commemorated their share in the Death of the father by partaking of a totemic meal. In fact, the father's Death was a murder denied. Swallowing the totemic animal, the substitute for the father, reconciled them to his body as if it were a maternal breast; that was sexual ambiguity or travesty, and it exonerated them from any guilt in replacing the father and exercising the power they took from him. They thus incorporated into their reality what they had symbolically introjected.

But Beckett represents the other end of the process. Only refuse, "stewpans," and the "convenience" have replaced the totemic meal. Left with only failed or frustrated orality, the sons have given up any hope of either annexing, incorporating, or introjecting the father's power and/or Death. They will remain forever separated from him; but, forever subject to his hold, they will experience its fascination and terror, which continues to infuse meaning, dispersed as it might be, into their absurd existence as wastrels. The only possible community is then centered in a ritual of decay, of ruin, of the corpse-universe of Molloy, Watt, and the rest of their company, who nonetheless continue their most "Beckettian" of activities: questioning and waiting. Will he come? Of course not! But just the same, let us ask for Godot, this Father, this God, as omnipresent as he is incredible.

There probably has never been a keener eye directed at paternal Death in that it determines the son, our monotheistic civilization, and maybe even all granting of meaning: saying, writing, and doing. Carnivalesque excavations on the brink of a toppling over toward something else, which, nonetheless, remains impossible in Beckett. X ray of the most fundamental myth of the Christian world: the love for the father's Death (a love for meaning beyond communication, for the incommunicable) and for the universe as waste (absurd communication).

In this way, *one of the components* of Christianity reaches its apex and the threshold leading to its reversal: its Judaic substratum and its Protestant branch, which, lucid and rigorous, have founded speech's meaning in the Death of the inaccessible father.

The fact remains that there is another component.

Christianity, according to Freud, seems to be on the verge of admitting that this Death was a Murder. But what is more, such an admission could surface or become bearable only if the communal *meaning*, thus linked to the murder, were compensated by jouissance. Both in its pagan beginnings or its Renaissance deviation, Christianity celebrates maternal fecundity and offsets the morbid and murderous filial love of paternal reason with mother-son incest. One needs only to glance through fifteenth-century art, or better yet, to see both—*Pietà* and serene jubilation of the mother—in the work of Giovanni Bellini, for example, to understand that the fascination and enduring quality of Mediterranean and Oriental Christianity are unthinkable without this conjunction.

True, these luminously fleshed Madonnas, holding their male infants with often ambiguous caresses, remain enigmatic because of an incommensurable distance separating them from their sons—a distance especially manifest in their averted gazes, close to fainting, disgust, or nothingness. As if to say that their love is not even the baby—still an object of banishment—but perhaps now as always, an elsewhere, the same incredulous and stubborn "God is love" that in *Not I* already opens up onto *nothing*. Their child is probably there, but its presence is only *one segment* of *jouissance*, the segment destined for others. What remains, in its immensity, can be expressed by neither narrative nor image, except, perhaps, through these oblivious heads, averted from the world in a frustrated and melancholy expectation. Illuminated by absence, nothingness; and nonetheless persistent, obstinate—like *Not I*.

And yet there is a *remnant*, which cannot be found in the glance soothed by the nothingness underlying "God is love," nor in the serenely positioned, maternal body, that discretely diverted body—intermediary and passageway between an exploded and absent head and an infant to be given away. This remnant is precisely what constitutes the enigma of Christian maternity; by means of a quite *unnamable* stance, it parallels the obsessional morbidity specific to Christianity as it is to any religion, but which, in Christianity, has already been eclipsed by the God in the Madonna's eyes as well as in Mouth of *Not I*. Now, such an unnamable, unlike that of *Not I*, is not *less* but *more* than Word and Meaning. Through the recovered memory of the incestuous son—the artist—this *jouissance* imagines itself to be the same as the mother's. It bursts out in a profusion of colors, of flood of lights, and even more brutally, in the baby-angels and winged breasts sculpted into the columns of Saint Mark's Church in Venice.

An attempt was made, at the beginning of the Renaissance, to save the Religion of the Father by breathing into it, more than before, what is represses: the joyous serenity of incest with the mother. Bellini's classicism and, in another fashion, the lavishness of the baroque testify to it. Far from feminist, they can be seen as a shrewd admission of what in the feminine and maternal is repressed, and which is always necessarily kept under the same veils of sacred terror when faced with the father's Death—a Death that, nevertheless, had henceforth become nothingness in the eyes of these early Western women, looking at us from within a painting.

Too late. The Renaissance was to revive Man and his perversion beyond the mother thus dealt with and once again rejected. Leonardo and Michelangelo replaced Giovanni Bellini. Humanism and its sexual explosion, especially its homosexuality, and its bourgeois eagerness to acquire objects (products and money) removed from immediate analysis (but not from the preconscious) the cult of natality and its real and symbolic consequences. So much the better. For, through such scorn for femininity, a truly analytic solution might, albeit very exceptionally, take shape at last. It was not until the end of the nineteenth century and Joyce, even more than Freud, that this repression of motherhood and incest was affirmed as risky and unsettling in one's very flesh and sex. Not until then did it, by means of a language that "musicates through letters," resume within discourse the rhythms, intonations, and echolalias of the mother-infant symbiosis—intense, pre-Oedipal, predating the father—and this in the third person. Having had a child, could a woman, then, speak another love? Love as object banished from paternal Death, facsimile of the third person, probably; but also a shattering of the object across and through what is seen and heard within rhythm: a polymorphic, polyphonic, serene, eternal, unchangeable *jouissance* that has nothing to do with death and its object, banished from love. In *Not I, Mouth,* leaving behind an obsessional labyrinth, becomes a mirage of this possible serenity, shielded from death, that is, incarnate in the mother. Here I see the averted, disillusioned eyes of radiant Madonnas . . .

But the colors of the paintings are lacking.

Is it because Beckett's written works, after Joyce and in different fashion, seem to have their sights on some archeology other than Christianity's? Using the Latins' most analytic language, French, a language nonetheless foreign to him, a language of banishment, a language of love, Beckett doesn't oblige them to experience the explosion of a nativity whose incestuous *jouissance* they celebrated. If he had, he would have been led to write *poetry.* On the contrary, having chosen the *narrative,* frustrated but obstinate, through monologue or dialogue, he has set forth the limitations and the means—the structure—that enabled him to probe the desacralized piety of the father's Death. And he made us a present of the calm discharge that it allows.

The result is a text that forces Catholics, Latins, to assume, if not to discover, what they have borrowed from the outside (Judaism) or what they have rejected (Protestantism). Such a text necessarily attracts a certain number of admirers or even accomplices from among the "others," the "dissimilar," the strange, foreigners, and exiles. On the other hand, those who refuse consciously to acknowledge their debt to the third person will listen to *Not I* and its portrayal of senseless, radiant death in the face of a fleeing God with a feeling of terror and lack of understanding. Beckett's lesson is thus one in morality, one of rigor and ironic seriousness.

Yet, at a glance and despite *Not I*, the community that Beckett so challenges quickly notices that the writer's work *does* leave something untouched: the jubilant serenity of the unapproached, avoided mother. So beyond the debris of the desacralized sacred that Beckett calls upon us to experience, if only as lucid and enlightened observers, does there not persist an *other*—untouched and fully seductive? The true guarantee of the last myth of modern times, the myth of the feminine—hardly the third person any longer, but, both beyond and within, more and less than meaning: rhythm, tone, color, and joy, within, through, and across the Word?

Therein lie both the strength and the limitations of Beckett's fiction, at least within Christianity's closed world.

And that will have to do until someone else comes in a burst of song, color, and laughter to conquer the last refuge of the sacred, still inaccessibly hidden in Bellini's remote Madonnas. To give them back to us transformed, secular, and corporeal, more full of language and imagination. Just as Beckett restored, above and beyond his mockery and for a humanity searching for a solitary community, the trivial rigor of paternal Death—for every speaking being, a disillusioned and hardly bearable, but permanent support of Meaning.

Note

1. The references to Racine, Baudelaire, and Dante exist only in the French version of *First Love* (*Premier Amour* [Paris: Minuit, 1970]). The French equivalent of "chamber pot" is *pot de chambre*, but Beckett used the more "elegant" version, *vase de nuit*, which, if the denotation is put aside, could indeed have various poetic connotations. Quotations are from *First Love and Other Shorts* (New York: Grove Press, 1974)—Editor Roudiez.

Notes on Contributors

WILLIAM BARRETT was an editor of *Partisan Review* from 1945 to 1952. His latest book is *The Truants*.

LEO BERSANI is a professor of French at the University of California at Berkeley. He is the author of *A Future for Astyanax/Character and Desire in Literature; Baudelaire and Freud;* and *The Death of Stéphane Mallarmé*.

ELIZABETH DALTON teaches at Barnard College. She is the author of *Unconscious Structure in "The Idiot."*

GILLES DELEUZE is a professor of philosophy at the University of Paris (Vincennes) and he has published numerous works, including studies of Nietzsche, Kant, and Spinoza. He has also written on subjects ranging from sadomasochism to the logic of meaning.

SERGE DOUBROVSKY is a professor of French at New York University. His published works include *Pourquoi la nouvelle critique, Les Jours S,* and *Corneille et dialectique du héros*.

WILLIAM EMPSON, the English critic and poet, is the author of *Some Versions of Pastoral,* and *Seven Types of Ambiguity,* a classic of modern literary criticism.

RENÉ GIRARD is in the Department of French and Italian at Stanford University. His books include: *Deceit, Desire and the Novel; Violence and the Sacred; To Double Business Bound,* and *Le Bouc Emissaire*.

JAN ELLEN GOLDSTEIN is an historian at the University of Chicago.

E. H. GOMBRICH, the prominent art historian, has written *Art and Illusion: A Study in the Psychology of Pictorial Representation; Art, Perception and Reality;* and *The Heritage of Appelles: Studies in the Art of the Renaissance,* among other works.

RONALD HAYMAN is the author of *Nietzsche: A Critical Life; Leavis;* and other works. His biography of Franz Kafka was published last year.

GEOFFREY H. HARTMAN, a professor of English and Comparative Literature at Yale, recently published *Criticism in the Wilderness: The Study of Literature Today,* and *Saving the Text: Literature-Derrida-Philosophy.*

ERICH HELLER is Avalon Professor of Humanities at Northwestern University. His publications include: *Thomas Mann: The Ironic German; Essays über Goethe;* and *Introduction to the Basic Kafka.*

JULIA KRISTEVA, a leading French critic, has published most recently *Desire in Language: A Semiotic Approach to Literature and Art,* and *Powers of Horror: An Essay on Abjection.*

STANLEY A. LEAVY, M.D., is Clinical Professor of Psychiatry at Yale University School of Medicine, and Training and Supervising Psychoanalyst at the Western New England Institute for Psychoanalysis. His most recent book is *Psychoanalytic Dialog.*

HENRY LOWENFELD, M.D., is on the faculty of the New York Psychoanalytic Institute.

STEVEN MARCUS, George Delacorte Professor in the Humanities at Columbia University, is an associate editor of *Partisan Review.* Among his books are: *Dickens: From Pickwick to Dombey; The Other Victorians; Engels, Manchester and the Working Class;* and *Representations: Essays on Literature and Society.*

MARGARETE MITSCHERLICH-NIELSEN is a psychoanalyst, attached to the Sigmund-Freud-Institut in Frankfurt. She has written widely on female sexuality.

GAIL S. REED is a practicing psychoanalyst. Arthur of a number of articles on psychoanalysis and literature, she is a member of the Interdisciplinary Colloquiums on Psychoanalysis and Literature, the New York Psychoanalytic Institute, and the American Psychoanalytic Association.

CUSHING STROUT is the author of several books on American intellectual history, the most recent being *The Veracious Imagination: Essays on American History, Literature and Biography*. He is Ernest J. White Professor of American Studies and Humane Letters at Cornell University.